Experimental Conversations

Experimental Conversations

Perspectives on Randomized Trials in Development Economics

Timothy N. Ogden, editor

The MIT Press
Cambridge, Massachusetts
London, England

This book was set in Stone Sans and Stone Serif by Toppan Best-set Premedia Limited.

Library of Congress Cataloging-in-Publication Data

Names: Ogden, Timothy N., editor.
Title: Experimental conversations : perspectives on randomized trials in
    development economics / edited by Timothy N. Ogden.
Description: Cambridge, MA : MIT Press, 2017. | Includes bibliographical references
    and index.
Identifiers: LCCN 2016020048 | ISBN 9780262035101 (hardcover : alk. paper)
ISBN 9780262551540 (paperback)
Subjects: LCSH: Economic development--Evaluation--Methodology.
Classification: LCC HD75 .E95 2017 | DDC 338.9--dc23 LC record available at
    https://lccn.loc.gov/2016020048

Dedicated to Peter Hess, my first economics professor, who pushed me to work harder, ask more questions, and seek better answers

Contents

Introduction

It's difficult to say what this book is without explaining why it is. Certainly it is a book about the use of randomized control trials (RCTs) in development economics, which some have characterized as a revolution in the field. But the book is not a history or explanation of RCTs, though there is plenty of each in these pages. The aim is more than that.

Through the course of the book it should become clear that while I spend a lot of time talking to economists and have read a lot of economics papers, I am not an expert or specialist. The idea and desire to put this book together was born of that nonspecialist status—specifically my aim to better understand, to think clearer, truer thoughts about the world, and how it might be changed for the better.

In those aims I believe I am far from unique. And that's why this book is. I am grateful that my life arc put me in a place where I could have regular one-on-one conversations with Dean Karlan, Jonathan Morduch, David McKenzie, and other engaged and thoughtful economists whose aims overlapped with mine.

These economists that I found myself in conversation with were part of a significant change in the practice of development economics, a change based in using new methods, particularly randomized control trials or RCTs to answer age-old questions about the impact of antipoverty programs. As is often the case with newcomers, I was fascinated with the novelty of what this group of economists was doing and enthusiastic about what they seemed to be accomplishing.

I found that the private conversations I was able to have with these economists about their work did not match the perceptions I saw and read among policy makers, practitioners, and commenters on development and poverty programs (at the time I was blissfully unaware of most of the debates happening within the economics profession about the value of randomized control trials). It seemed to me that a much larger group of people who cared about making the world a better place were ignorant of the work these economists were doing, or misunderstood it and its motivations. I wanted to give more people a sense of how these economists thought about their own research, that of others, and how to change the world—both their personal theories of change and in the advice they would give to others based on their research. I wanted to give the economists the opportunity to speak to a broader audience outside of the heavily mediated forms of the academic economics paper or the mass media story, both of which contribute meaningfully to the misunderstandings and distortions I wanted to combat. I wanted to give other nonspecialists a chance to hear from the economists in their own words, to give a sense of what it is like to have a conversation with them and to explore their thinking beyond the narrow confines of a particular study or the difficult-to-penetrate esoterica of econometrics.

So this book is a collection of interviews with economists who conduct randomized control trials, usually field experiments, in development. But it also contains a series of shorter interviews with economists and others who are observers, critics, sponsors, consumers, or supporters of the movement to conduct more field experiments in the search for programs and policies that alleviate poverty. The list of interviewees is idiosyncratic—it is made up of the group of people that I thought were doing interesting research or had a useful perspective but also who I believed might respond to my requests.

Being a nonspecialist does not mean I am neutral. When a colleague and I launched our own business, Innovations for Poverty Action (IPA), one of the two original hubs for the promotion of RCTs in development economics, was among our first clients. I consider Dean Karlan a friend and advised him on his book *More Than Good Intentions*. I have worked closely for years with another friend and interviewee, Jonathan Morduch.

My re-entry (after majoring in International Political Economy but spending a decade in the technology industry) into the world of economic development coincided with the rapid growth in the use of and attention to RCTs. As I mentioned, I was particularly captured by the new tools and new answers RCTs were generating. In other words I was something of a fan of randomized control trials in development. As I began the formal interviews for the book, I wrote a good bit advocating for and defending RCTs in development. Those defenses, and what I heard from some of the interviewees, forced me to engage more with the thoughtful critiques of the RCT movement. That in turn led to the only significant change to the book (other than it taking several years longer than I had hoped) since its conception:

the inclusion of the shorter interviews to give voice to some of the critiques as well as to provide a better sense of the context in which these conversations about RCTs in development take place.

My aim was not to set up these interviews as debates or to directly address the specific points made by advocates and critics. Instead, I wanted readers to be able to "hear" for themselves how the parties involved think and apply research. While I ask many of interviewees about external validity[1] in the abstract, for instance, I think the most interesting and useful parts of the interviews are not the direct answer to those abstract questions but the specific answers to how they apply, or don't apply, specific research findings in the way they think about the world. I learn more from answers that reveal what someone accepts as established fact and where they still have doubts than I do from answers about how someone approaches questions of evidence and proof in general. That's why many of the interviews include descriptions of experiments and their results. What questions an economist chooses to take on, how they try to answer them in the design of a particular study, and how they interpret the results tells us not just about the preferences of individuals but also, I believe, valuable things about how that economist thinks about the power of theory, gaps in knowledge, what issues matter, and the nature of human beings and political and economic systems—even about their beliefs about free will. And, I believe, understanding those inputs into someone's thinking can help us interpret and integrate (or reject) that economist's findings into our own thinking.

The result, I hope, is a book that will serve as a valuable primary source document that helps illuminate the ideas of significant participants in the current conversation about not only the use of RCTs in development economics but how we learn about the world, what evidence is and means, and how policy should be and shouldn't be formed. Those are very broad conversations, and I have no illusions of being able to comprehensively address them in this book, though I will return to them in the Conclusion.

The longer interviews comprise several conversations over the course of up to four years that have been edited together for clarity and readability. The order of the questions and responses is not necessarily related to when the questions were asked. The shorter interviews reflect a single conversation that took place in in the latter part of 2014 or early 2015. Because the

---

1. Whether a finding in one context applies in another. See later in the introduction for a discussion of critiques of RCTs including external validity questions.

goal of the book is to provide clarity and insight, after each interview was transcribed, I lightly edited them and sent them to the interviewee for further editing and approval. For better or worse, these are not spontaneous, but at least somewhat considered, responses to the questions.

I have used footnotes extensively in the interviews to provide background and explanation of key ideas and studies referenced in the conversations. The goal is to allow nonspecialist readers to familiarize themselves enough to understand the discussion without having to leave the flow of the conversation. Endnotes provide citations to source material and further reading for those who do want to dive into specific studies or issues.

Because I hope the book will be of interest to an audience with very different levels of knowledge about the issues at hand, I have broken up the rest of the introduction into sections that can be easily skipped by those who either have no interest or are already familiar with certain matters. First is a brief biographical sketch of my path that led to writing this book that provides more information on my own biases and thinking about the issues. Next is a general overview of randomized control trials and their history in development economics, then a brief discussion of the main critiques of the RCT movement, with a final note on how to approach reading the interviews.

Origins

I'm a sucker for surprises. I have something of a disconfirmation bias (not on everything, of course). I try to be a good Bayesian,[2] but in practice, I have a tendency to most strongly believe whatever I've recently read, especially if it contradicts conventional wisdom or what I read last week.

Perhaps that's why I quickly latched onto randomized control trials in development when I learned about them. Michael Kremer, in his interview here, has characterized the ability to surprise as one of the benefits of RCTs (but also note Tyler Cowen's comment about never being surprised by an RCT). But my journey into this realm actually began with a different sort of

2. An approach to integrating new evidence into one's beliefs by considering the new evidence alongside all existing evidence. In practice this approach usually, though not necessarily, leads to small changes in what one believes (termed "updating your priors") or the certainty of one's beliefs, rather than replacing or overturning old beliefs or rejecting old evidence. The name comes from the pioneering statistician Thomas Bayes.

surprise. In 2006 I was working for Geneva Global, an organization whose mission was to help large donors allocate their international giving toward more effective charities and programs. At the time it was recommending investments in microcredit (among many other areas) with a focus on finding the "best" microcredit organizations. During that time, I attended a conference where Dean Karlan spoke about the lack of, as he termed it, "rigorous evidence" for microcredit's impact on poverty. Since I had thought that microcredit was a "proven" success at fighting poverty, he caught my attention. I invited Dean to speak at a Geneva Global event and began learning more about the fledging Innovations for Poverty Action and about RCTs and their use in identifying "what worked" in poverty interventions. What I heard was deeply appealing.

Shortly thereafter I was laid off from Geneva Global. A colleague and I decided to launch our own firm specializing in developing business books, but we didn't want to leave the world of philanthropy and development entirely. We launched a blog—*Philanthropy Action*—in the days (circa 2008) when that was both a cool and useful thing to do. There we wrote about the need for better evidence and better ideas in poverty alleviation and development. Dean and IPA hired us to help them develop a website (and we went on to help with conference planning, annual reports, and other communications for several years). It was at the inaugural IPA microfinance research conference in the fall of 2008 that I first interviewed Esther Duflo and Abhijit Banerjee in what became the template for this book. It was there also that I first met Jonathan Morduch and began many years of conversations that have profoundly shaped my thinking, but also culminating in my joining the Financial Access Initiative at NYU-Wagner, which Jonathan had co-founded (with Dean Karlan and Sendhil Mullainathan) and where I currently work. No doubt it was my association with Dean and Jonathan and their organizations that opened most of the doors I needed to make this book a reality.

All of this to say that my learning and thinking on these issues has been guided both personally and professionally through a group of people who would generally fall into the "pro-RCT" camp if not part of the explicit movement for the use of RCTs to evaluate poverty programs. And so, I was skeptical of critiques of RCTs and will confess that I generally assumed that these critiques were the result not of honest, principled thinking about the benefits, value, and limitations of RCTs but of some darker motive. Some version of the thought, "These people must have reason to hide the truth!" nestled in my mind.

Thankfully, I was nudged away from this thinking by a number of my interlocutors, particularly Jonathan Morduch and David Roodman, but also Bill Easterly, Michael Clemens, and Sendhil Mullainathan. They helped me push through my preconceptions and engage with the critics and their critiques, much to my benefit, and hopefully reflected in this book.

Trials, Controls, Randomization and Experiments

While I expect that if you have picked up this book, you are generally familiar with randomized control trials and field experiments, it behooves me to make sure no one is left behind.[3] I will strive to be brief and point to other resources with more complete explanations. In that spirit, for a more complete explanation of the econometrics of assessing causal impact and the various approaches, see Angrist and Pischke's *Mostly Harmless Econometrics* and *Mastering 'Metrics*. For a guide to how randomized control trials and field experiments are set up and run, see Glennerster and Takavarasha's *Running Randomized Evaluations*.

For those wanting a quick and simple introduction, let me begin by delineating some differences between some terms that are often casually used as synonyms or analogues: control trials, randomized control trials, and field experiments.

A control trial is part of the fabric of the scientific method. You assemble a sample and apply a treatment to one part of the sample and do nothing to the other part, the control group. The difference between the treatment group and the control group allows an assessment of the effect of the treatment. If we want to know the effect of the sun shining on a rock, we have to compare rocks that have been exposed to the sun and rocks that haven't. It is simply impossible to reliably assess the effect of a treatment without a control group. Unfortunately, a lot of research in the social sciences and humanities claims causal effects without a control group. To be clear, there is great value in descriptive research that helps us learn about the world without a control group; the problem is when such research makes a causal claim about the impact of a program or some other change.

There are multiple ways to put together a control group. Historically (and unfortunately, still today, evident if you spend any time reading business books or articles) in social science, economics, and otherwise, this was

3. If nothing less, my explanations of RCTs, their origin, history, and modern application will further illuminate my own biases and blind spots for close readers.

often done by comparing people who had received a treatment—say, participating in an agricultural extension program—and people who didn't. When dealing with inert objects like rocks, such an approach may work. When it comes to assessing living things who have varying environments, histories, motivations, personalities, and innumerable other characteristics, particularly self-determination, that approach doesn't work. People who participate in an agricultural extension program may be quite different from people who don't—in age, experience, resources, knowledge, and so forth—and those differences may be responsible for different outcomes rather than the agricultural extension program. Thus the oft-repeated dictum, "Correlation does not equal causation."

This presents a major problem for people who want to understand the effect of a program. Social scientists have over the years devised a number of ways, primarily statistical techniques, to try to get around this problem.

One approach is to try to measure the factors that might affect an outcome and match up participants and nonparticipants who are most alike (often done through a technique called propensity score matching). This can even be done after the treatment is conducted. So, for instance, you could try to match up participants in the agricultural extension program with nonparticipants based on their characteristics (age, school grade completed, size of farm, crops grown, prior harvests, etc.). Then you can compare these very similar farmers to each other rather than comparing all participants to all nonparticipants.

Another popular approach is the use of what is known as regression discontinuity. Regression discontinuities occur when there is some external factor that changes for one part of an otherwise similar group, but doesn't plausibly influence the outcomes of interest except through participation. Again, a simple example is an agricultural extension program that becomes

This image is licensed under a Creative Commons Attribution-NonCommercial 2.5 License from xkcd.com. Some rights reserved. Originally published on xkcd.com.

available to farmers in Iowa. While it wouldn't make much sense to compare those Iowan participants to farmers in Saskatchewan (because the reason the program exists in Iowa and not in Saskatchewan has many causes and effects that are likely to be more important than the content of any education program), it is more plausible to compare Iowan farmers who now have access to an agricultural training program to a set of farmers just across the Missouri River in Nebraska. The approach depends on believing that the differences between a farm and a farmer on each side of a state line are negligible. A researcher might argue that these farms are at the same latitude, grow similar crops, share access to the river, and none of the potential participants had any influence on where exactly the river lies or the political process that led to the river being a state boundary. A researcher can then use the introduction of a new program available only to people on one side of the river to figuratively construct a treatment group and a control group in order to make comparisons.

A related statistical approach is the use of instrumental variables (IV). An instrument is, again, a factor that allows a researcher to distinguish a population but does not affect the outcome of the program in question. Distance is sometimes used as an instrument—in the example case, perhaps distance from the farm to the location of the extension course. For an IV approach to be useful, the instrument must only affect the outcome in one way. In the example case this would mean that distance from the location of the extension course does not affect anything about farmers' outcomes other than their participation in the course.

In each of these instances, statistical techniques are used to create a group for comparison in order to understand the impact of a program. But none of them fully solve the initial problem of ensuring that the only difference between the treated group and the comparison group is the program or change you are trying to study.

Matching depends entirely on whether you are able to determine and measure all of the characteristics that may have an effect on the outcome: a dubious proposition at best because so many likely factors are what is termed "unobservable." Unobservable characteristics,[4] in this context, might include motivation, relationships with agricultural suppliers or buyers, actual cultivation practices (unless you are going to follow the farmers around for the entirety of the study), or microclimatic differences. Regression discontinuity and IV approaches similarly depend on important, and

---

4. Note that "unobservable" does not mean impossible to observe in theory, but unobserved within the confines and budget of a study.

difficult to prove, assumptions. In the example, suppose that on the Iowa side of the river, the farms were on a bluff, whereas on the Nebraska side, farms were in lowlands subject to flooding. For someone standing in one of the fields, this may be obvious. For an economist[5] (or a later reader of an economics paper) who has never set foot in Iowa, it is completely unknown—which makes it difficult to assess the validity of the finding. Instrumental variables are, if anything, more problematic. For instance, the distance instrument essentially assumes that the location of the course was determined independently of any variables that affect farmers' outcomes. But it is likely that in the real world, courses are held in towns that grew up as hubs for the best-performing farms in the area. That land is therefore likely more productive and more valuable. As a result the farmers who own that land and are closest to the course are already better off than those further away. Of course, it's also possible that the farms closer to towns have been farmed more intensively for more years and the soil is of poorer quality, so the closer farmers are worse off. In just that way the validity of most any matching, regression discontinuity, or instrumental variable approach can be, and is, endlessly debated (at least among economists).

A randomized control trial is an experiment in which the treatment group and control group are determined using a random draw or lottery (or some similar process). Randomization, when done properly, can much more effectively isolate the effect of the treatment from other factors that may influence outcomes. Randomization avoids having to exhaustively measure and categorize every feature of the objects of study while usually ensuring that the treatment group and control group are similar enough for reasonable comparisons to be made.[6] While randomization has major

5. Many of the papers that use regression discontinuity or IV designs are done retrospectively—the person doing the analysis is separated by time and distance from the data. It would therefore not be surprising at all to find an economist working with data about agricultural extension programs in Iowa while never having visited the state.

6. Randomization does not guarantee that the treatment and control groups are similar, in the same way that flipping a coin twice does not guarantee that you will get one heads results and one tails result. It is always possible that the treatment and control group, even though randomized, are different from each other in important ways. In most RCT papers you will see an attempt to show that this is not the case by comparing the treatment and control group along observable characteristics gathered as part of a baseline survey and showing that the two groups are "balanced." While helpful, this still does not entirely do away with the possibility that unobserved factors are not balanced and will affect outcomes. This is one aspect of the "Nothing Magic" critique of RCTs discussed in detail later.

benefits in assessing impact, it isn't easy to do. Figuring out how to assemble the sample of interest and exactly how to randomize (e.g., by individual, by groups of individuals, by towns) can be quite complicated. For instance, continuing the agricultural extension example, you would want your sample of interest either to include all farmers and compel participation in the extension program for those who were randomly assigned to participate or to make your sample all farmers who wanted to participate but randomize which ones were allowed to do so. For these and other reasons, some of the statistical techniques described above are often used in conjunction with randomized control trials. There are many, many more considerations in setting up samples, assigning treatment status, and related factors that I won't go into here but, again, point you to *Mastering 'Metrics* and *Running Randomized Evaluations*.

In summary, it is difficult to convincingly assess causal impact because it requires comparison of groups that are identical in all important ways other than what you are trying to assess. Social scientists (and indeed other disciplines) have developed a variety of approaches to create reasonable comparison groups. None are perfect, but randomization is usually the most likely to yield the necessary conditions for comparison (though even this is not universally accepted). And this brings us to field experiments.

A field experiment is a trial conducted in a real world environment rather than a controlled environment like a laboratory. For instance, the majority of psychology experiments are conducted in labs. There are good reasons for this. Labs let you more closely control what a subject is exposed to. But such close control also has a downside. A person may behave differently in a lab environment than they would in the outside world. So the laboratory setting, rather than preventing an outside influence from unduly affecting the outcomes, can become the influence affecting the outcomes (keep this in mind; it will come up again later when we discuss critiques of RCTs). Running an experiment in the field is much more complicated and expensive, however. The possible differences between the behavior of people in lab experiments and real world situations have been a major area of contention in the development and acceptance of behavioral economics. When laboratory experiments showed people allowing irrelevant factors to influence their spending or investing choices, many traditional economists objected that such behavior in a lab experiment was not a reliable signal to how people would behave in the real world when they had to really live with the consequences of their decisions. See Richard Thaler's book *Misbehaving* for a terrific overview of how such issues have been debated.

In case it is not apparent, RCT is not a synonym of field experiment. That being said, when the phrase "field experiment" is used in this book, it means a field experiment using an RCT unless otherwise noted. Most of the studies discussed in the book are field experiments using RCTs in development economics, though lab experiments and natural experiments are also discussed.

Based on the description above, it's easy to think that randomized control field experiments are the gold standard for assessing the impact of any program and guiding decisions about what policies and programs to implement or expand and which to cancel. Whether that is the case is the heart of the contention over the explosive growth of RCTs in development economics. Before we take a look at the critiques of RCTs, I'll take a brief foray into the history of RCTs in development economics.

A Greatly Condensed History of RCTs in Development

Randomized control trials themselves have a long and somewhat disputed history. There was no breakthrough moment, or particular innovator who happened upon the concept of randomized control trials in a eureka moment. There were elements of RCTs in Louis Pasteur's public tests of his anthrax vaccine. Indeed there were elements of an RCT in one of the stories in the Old Testament book of Daniel. While there are various examples like these, often but not exclusively in the medical field, stretching back hundreds of years, most agree that the major steps in using RCTs to evaluate policies and programs took place in the 1920s. Particular praise is given to Roland Fisher, who studied agricultural practices, for making major advancements.[1] Julian Jamison documents that the use of randomized assignment to treatment or control was appearing in many disciplines through many channels around the same time.[2]

When it comes to the modern use of RCTs in assessing the impact of social programs, there are two main streams—one dealing with the evaluation of large-scale, mostly government programs in the United States and Western Europe, and the other with their use in developing countries by economists.

In the United States, the first RCT to evaluate a social program was an evaluation of a welfare program. That experiment carried a lot of controversy, but a group of social scientists at organizations like RAND, Mathematica and MDRC championed the use of large-scale randomized trials to assess impact. The story of how these social scientists convinced the federal government in particular to fund such trials and to use the evidence that emerged from them is told by Judy Gueron (one of the interviewees) and Howard Rolston in their book *Fighting for Reliable Evidence*.

As the title of Gueron's book indicates, the motivation for the RCT movement in the United States and RCT movement in development economics 20 years later was the same: is it possible to accurately and reliably measure the impact of a program in order to determine whether it is worth the money spent on it? The proponents of RCTs were not the only ones proposing methodologies to provide more reliable estimates of program impact. Indeed there were raging battles from the 1970s into the present day of the relative value of different approaches to measuring impact. While few were arguing that RCTs didn't provide reliable measures of impact, the core question was the cost of arriving at the answer. Many economists argued that statistical techniques—like matching, regression discontinuities, and instrumental variables—provided reliable enough evidence without the expense and other complexities of setting up randomized trials.

It was the cost and complexity that caused many to assume that RCTs were not feasible outside of the world's wealthiest countries, where governments typically didn't have the capability, experience, or budget to fund and manage the kind of trials that RAND and MDRC were conducting in the United States. That changed in the early 1990s through two widely influential studies. The Mexican government ran a very sophisticated and large scale RCT to evaluate a new conditional cash transfer program called PROGRESA (now Opportunidades). Around the same time, Michael Kremer convinced a friend at a small Dutch NGO to conduct a randomized trial of the value of textbooks in Kenyan schools.

Roughly 25 years later, when thousands of RCTs have been conducted in developing countries, it's easy to underestimate what a huge shift this was, particularly the work by Kremer. Kremer's innovation was not just in bringing a method into a new environment but seeing that while it was true that running large-scale experiments with government funding was usually impossible in developing contexts (Mexico may not be Sweden but it is a relatively wealthy country with a highly capable civil service by global standards), there was another path to conducting such trials: working with NGOs. NGOs had several advantages over local governments: (1) they were running a wider variety of programs, (2) they were typically more flexible and nimble in their ability to change operational procedures, and (3) they did not have to pretend to serve everyone—in fact their limited budgets meant that, in most cases, they knew they could not serve everyone they believed would benefit from their programs. The latter point is key to enabling randomization and overcoming ethical concerns: if you strongly believe that the program you are running will benefit people, it would argu-ably be unethical to deny that program to some people in order to create a control group. But if you cannot serve everyone anyway, it is, again, argu-ably fairer to determine who is served via randomization than by some other method.

Running an RCT, however, is not just a question of convincing an NGO to randomize who it serves. A great deal of infrastructure is necessary to gather baseline information, implement the randomization, ensure the implementation follows the randomization plan (i.e., that the randomly selected treatment group gets the treatment and the control group does not), and follow-up with both the treatment and control group to see what happened. That infrastructure then makes it easier to conduct additional RCTs. So it was that Kremer's first RCT on textbooks soon led to what may be the most famous RCT in development economics: Michael Kremer and Ted Miguel's evaluation of the effect of deworming children, conducted in Kenya with the same NGO that had worked with Kremer on the textbook evaluation. Ultimately, an RCT nexus emerged in Kenya. Many of the econ-omists interviewed here spent time in Busia, Kenya, learning to conduct RCTs and a number of the most well-known RCTs in development econom-ics were conducted in and around Busia. Kremer later worked with Abhijit Banerjee and an NGO in India, Seva Mandir, which led to another RCT nexus in India. Kremer and Banerjee went on to work with Esther Duflo and Sedhil Mullainathan to create the Jameel-Poverty Action Lab (J-PAL) at MIT—a different type of nexus for RCTs—one focused on applying the find-ings of RCTs to policy and program design. Dean Karlan worked with Esther Duflo and Abhijit Banerjee on some early RCTs in India and Kenya and founded Innovations for Poverty Action, which now has developed an impressive infrastructure for conducting RCTs in many different countries. Ted Miguel, Kremer's partner in the deworming evaluation, went on to co-found the Center for Effective Global Action at UC-Berkeley, another center that enables RCTs and using their results to inform practice and policy.

While the earliest RCTs in development were focused on education and health, the use of RCTs to evaluate financial services, particularly microfi-nance, exploded. Just as RCTs were being proved feasible and useful in development economics, microfinance was emerging as a new and exciting approach to attacking poverty. RCTs and microfinance were well matched. Economists, of course, have a particular interest in finance and financial contracts. The contracts that govern microlending were particularly suited to being adjusted for the purposes of experiments. And microfinance insti-tutions had the information, systems, and infrastructure to make many aspects of setting up an RCT easier than in other types of interventions.

While microfinance was providing a fertile ground for the growing use of RCTs, the situation in economics PhD programs was also helping make economists-in-training particularly receptive to the benefits of RCTs. A long-term evolution (and associated intellectual battle) of how to prove causal effects in economic research had come to a head in the late 1980s and early 1990s. The use of complex statistical techniques, such as instrumental variables, had become very popular in response to criticism of general use of regressions and comparisons without plausible controls. However, as noted, the credibility of conclusions based on such techniques is wholly dependent on whether someone believes the inherent assumptions (e.g., in an IV approach that the instrument is independent of the outcome)—assumptions that are nearly impossible to prove empirically. That meant that researchers had to withstand withering criticism from reviewers not just about the conclusions that they reached but about whether the statistical approach used was valid and reliable. Meanwhile econometricians, particularly Joshua Angrist and Guido Imbens, were pointing out that most analyses using these techniques were reporting average treatment effects across a sample, assuming that the average was a useful measure when there was good reason to be suspicious that averages were themselves biased. As a result there were even more challenges for those graduate students to overcome in getting papers published and dissertations approved. In that environment the appeal of a method that seemed to provide surer ground in identifying causal effects is obvious.

Several other factors also seem to have played a role in the rapid growth of the RCT movement in development economics, particularly among younger economists. One was the seeming exhaustion of existing data sets. In the early 1990s there were very few reliable long-term data sets available for development economists to use. So many, many economists were using the same data sets over and over again. Those data sets were not only limited but confined to a few countries, mostly in Asia and Latin America (Morten Jerven has a recent book about the paucity of reliable data for African countries, even today). Young economists, to make their mark, had to do something novel—and there was little novel data to be had. Creating your own data, as a field experiment does, was one of the few paths to doing something new.[7]

7. It wasn't just young economists conducting field experiments taking this path though. For example, Robert Townsend, an economist at the University of Chicago at the time and now at MIT, began visiting a group of villages in northern Thailand regularly over more than a decade and created a novel data set. See http://cier .uchicago.edu/ for more details on what is known as the Townsend Thai Project.

The path to creating your own data was made more palatable with the decreasing costs of travel to and communications with developing countries. Of course, many things were still difficult, expensive, and unreliable, but it was much easier to do field work in the 1990s that it had been in the 1960s, and even easier today. Rapid advancement in technology also made it easier to collect, enter, and analyze data. Whereas earlier eras of development economics had been biased toward macroeconomics—because macro-level data was all that could be reasonably collected—these technological advancements made it much easier to study microeconomics and the development of regions, towns, even individual households.

The infrastructure (via organizations like J-PAL and IPA) that the pioneers of the movement set up first in Kenya, then India, and then in other countries has continued to make conducting field experiments easier. Thus we moved from a novel way of evaluating the causal impact of textbooks in Kenya to thousands of RCTs in dozens of countries in 20 years.

Still, many weren't and aren't convinced.

An Overview of Critiques of the RCT Movement

Here I want to provide a brief overview of what I perceive as the main critiques[8] of the RCT movement in development economics:

1. The "Nothing Magic" critique
2. The External Validity critique
3. The Policy Sausage critique
4. The Trivial Significance critique

There are obviously other critiques—and nuances of the critiques I do cover—than it is possible to cover here. For another perspective of the critiques, and in-depth essays from proponents and resisters of the RCT movement, see *Thinking Big and Thinking Small: What Works in Development*, edited by Cohen and Easterly.

These are not critiques of randomized control trials at their essence—few, even among the staunchest critics of the RCT movement, would argue that the method does not help us learn something about the world. For instance, James Heckman who was one of the main critics of the very large RCTs in the United States, arguing that other statistical methods allowed

---

8. I don't address the critique of randomization or experimentation on the ethical grounds because I believe that critique to have been soundly answered. The critiques presented below are ongoing debates where many thoughtful and well-informed people disagree.

reaching conclusions as reliable as RCTs at much lower cost, has participated in an RCT of early childhood interventions.[3] The question is about
what exactly RCTs teach us about the world and the value of that knowledge for making future choices. The critiques are about the claims made for
the knowledge RCTs produce and how that knowledge is applied.

The Nothing Magic Critique

This critique is so named because you often will hear something like, "There
is nothing magic about RCTs." This critique is a response to the oft-repeated
assertion among RCT advocates (and you will see this in many of the interviews) that RCTs are the most reliable measure of causal impact because
they offer the most understandable and certain way to compare treatment
to controls. In addition, advocates of RCTs often argue that the RCT method
limits the degrees of freedom of researchers to cherry-pick samples or finesse
results to find evidence for their preferred theory, and therefore provide
more reliable answers to impact questions than any other method.

One version of the Nothing Magic critique is simply stating that other
methods can be as, or even more, reliable than RCTs. This critique often
points back to or builds off of the debates around RCTs in the 1970s that
were never definitively resolved. Glenn Harrison and Angus Deaton, in particular, have consistently expressed this version of the Nothing Magic
critique.[9][4]

Another version of the Nothing Magic critique is that field experiments
in economics do not conform to the double-blind standard of RCTs in
medical practice. Ideally, neither the participants in the experiment nor
the researchers themselves know whether an individual is receiving the
treatment or is in the control group. This is why drug trials often feature a
placebo—so that both the control group and the treatment group are taking something. This is particularly important because it is well established
that taking placebos does have a positive impact on many health conditions. It is not unreasonable to believe that people who know they are in a
field experiment and know they are receiving a treatment—improved
seeds, an infusion of cash into their business, a textbook—behave differently than the otherwise similar people who know they didn't receive the
treatment.

9. Harrison's perspective is notable because he does not dismiss the value of RCTs
but strongly disputes their primacy. Deaton typically takes what might be called a
more pessimistic view, emphasizing that there are substantial problems that come
with any methodology, including RCTs.

Some critics argue that the inability to run double-blind trials, or even blind trials, means that field experiments don't provide the better answers that RCT proponents claim.

THE LIMITATIONS OF BLIND TRIALS

Another version of the critique says that even if RCTs do limit degrees of freedom, nothing is eliminated. Therefore RCTs have to be as carefully scrutinized as other methods. Recent work examining the results of medical trials using RCTs bolsters this critique; it found that the number of "no-effect" results increased markedly when researchers had to file a pre-analysis plan documenting exactly how they would assess the data gathered before the experiment was conducted.[5] Furthermore RCTs are as vulnerable to inadvertent false positives and false negatives as any research method.

As a result there is a limit to how much is gained from RCTs, particularly as running RCTs is generally more expensive than alternative evaluation approaches. While proponents advocate for increasing the use of RCTs, the Nothing Magic" critique says that there may already be little value for money in the number of RCTs being conducted.

The External Validity Critique

Clearly the goal of the RCT movement is to shape policy and programs around the world so that they are more effective. This involves not only the specific program studied in a particular trial, but applying what is learned from that trial to other situations. The External Validity critique points out that each RCT is anchored in a highly specific context. This includes such things as the implementer carrying out an intervention, often an NGO, the personnel hired by that NGO, local and regional culture and customs, the survey technique, the specific way questions are asked, even the weather. Thus the critique points out, while the results from a particular RCT may tell you a lot about the impact of a particular program in a particular place during a particular point in time, it doesn't tell you much about the result of a similar program carried out in a different context. In other words, an RCT of microcredit in urban India does not necessarily tell you anything about the impact of microcredit in rural Kenya. An in-depth treatment of the External Validity critique can be found in Nancy Cartwright and Jeremy Hardie's book *Evidence-Based Policy*. Lant Pritchett and Justin Sandefur take it in on with specific reference to the RCTs of microcredit and whether the results of one help predict the results of another, finding that a non-RCT from a local context does a better job predicting outcomes than an RCT from a different context.[6] Conversely, Hunt Allcott does something similar comparing the ability of an RCT of reminders to reduce energy consumption in one city to predict the effect of the same campaign in another city finding that RCTs don't do a great job, but a better one than other methods in common use.[7]

It's important to note that the External Validity critique doesn't just apply to RCTs. It applies to studies or experiments using any methodology. Every study is conducted in a specific context and is not necessarily valid in other contexts—at least until it is replicated in multiple contexts with similar results. David McKenzie has pointed out that there seems to be a double standard in the application of the External Validity critique to field experiments using RCTs.[8]

That being said, many published RCTs don't do enough to explain the context in which the study takes place to allow a reader to form a judgment about external validity. As Jonathan Morduch points out in his interview, the journal publishing process is biased toward broader claims of validity, which gives teeth to the external validity critique.

The Policy Sausage Critique

The Policy Sausage critique is primarily associated with Lant Pritchett— and we discuss it in his interview. The simplified version is that policies (whether policies of government or of NGOs) are created through complex and opaque actions influenced by politics, capability, capacity, resource constraints, history and many other factors. In other words, policy making is like sausage making. Impact evaluation, and independent academic research in general, plays only a small role in the policy sausage, especially if it is impact evaluation that comes from outside the organization. That may seem irrelevant to the use of RCTs in development economics, but the RCT movement is far from just an academic exercise. Many of the lead practitioners advocate RCTs not just as a better way of estimating causal impact but as an essential guide to program design and policy making.

Pritchett and others argue that the process of policy change or organizational change is completely separate from the process of knowledge creation. The bridge between the two is not built on policy briefs but on painstaking work inside bureaucracies, political machines, and organizations. External evaluation when imposed from above or outside, according to this critique, usually hampers that work rather than accelerates it. Where RCTs have influenced policy significantly, it is in areas like PROGRESA's conditional cash transfers that were conducted within the policy-making realm and because they support the existing political goals of policy makers, not because those policy makers change their minds as the result of evidence. The Policy Sausage critique argues that the RCT movement, while trying to influence program and policy, does not have a reasonable path to actually affecting policies and programs.

The Trivial Significance Critique

I term this the Trivial Significance critique to differentiate it from the common use of the term "significance" in statistical discussions, which refers to the likelihood of a measured effect arising from chance but also confusingly about the total size of the effect (in this second sense, it is a synonym of "material" in business and accounting vocabulary). The Trivial Significance critique is not about statistics or relative effect size but about absolute effect size: whether the programs and policies the RCT movement is focused on matter.

The critique can take several different guises, but all share the basic point that the programs and projects measured and measurable by RCTs yield changes, even when "successful," that are not big enough to make a difference between poverty and prosperity, even for a single family. One version might be phrased, "Yes, the program you evaluated increased the average time spent in school by a full year, but there are still no jobs available for those kids."[10] Another version is that the things that "really matter" are macroeconomic-level choices like trade policy—and those macroeconomic choices cannot be randomized. A third version is that what "really matters" is the allocation of funds (or effort) across a variety of policies or goals: Should a government spend on roads or sanitation or trade promotion?[11] While RCTs may be able to say something about what approaches are most effective in encouraging hand-washing, it is hard to imagine an experiment that could compare the impact on economic growth of spending on infrastructure to the effect on employment of providing tax credits for exporters to the effect on health of increasing pay for community health workers.

The Argument Behind the Arguments

The RCT movement has voluminous responses to each of the critiques I've just laid out in simplified form. I do not think much is to be gained by providing grossly simplified versions of the responses to the grossly simplified critiques. The critiques and the responses can put too much emphasis on the particularities of methodology, and distract from the more important disagreement behind them. That more important argument (most apparent in the Trivial Significance critique) is about theories of change; it only occasionally bursts into view, most often in books authored by development economists and reviews of those books by other development economists.[12]

Argument over theories of change—ideas about how the world changes—are hardly unique to the present moment in development economics. Indeed, it is the foundation of development economics (and much of other social sciences): how is it that poor countries become richer (or, why is that poor countries stay poor)? Obviously, this is not a mechanical process or an outcome of natural law. Poor countries become richer or stay poor because of human action. But which human actions? And what is the process for changing those actions? That is what theories of change are all about.

10. See Lant Pritchett's post "Is Your Impact Evaluation Asking Questions That Matter?" at the Center for Global Development's blog for a particularly pointed exemplar of this version of the critique: http://www.cgdev.org/blog/your-impact -evaluation-asking-questions-matter-four-part-smell-test
11. An example of this version of the critique can be found in a post on the World Bank's Future Development blog by Jeffrey Hammer, titled "The Chief Minister Posed Questions We Couldn't Answer": http://blogs.worldbank.org/futuredevelopment/ chief-minister-posed-questions-we-couldn-t-answer
12. The book *What Works in Development*, mentioned earlier, also helps illuminate differences in the theories of change among the various contributors.

There has always been wide disagreement within the economics profession about theories of change. The disagreement over the effectiveness of efforts to intervene in markets, or the benefits of reducing intervention in markets is a good example; to put a more personal face on it, think Keynes versus Hayek. Development economics has its own versions of theory of change conflicts. To outsiders, the most visible disagreement on theories of change among development economists in recent years has been between Jeff Sachs and Bill Easterly. While Sachs has promoted large-scale, precisely planned technocratic interventions (emphasizing the need to intervene), Easterly advocates for political and economic rights of individuals and the value of local knowledge, contrasting "Searchers" (enabled by free markets and effective) from "Planners" (interveners in markets who are ineffective and often harmful). Abhijit Banerjee and Esther Duflo explicitly couch their book, *Poor Economics*, as a contrasting vision between the Sachs and Easterly poles. They make a case for the value of technocratic knowledge and planned interventions, but not of the size and scale advocated by Sachs. Meanwhile, more of today's prominent development economists have staked out their own theories of change in their own books: Daron Acemoglu and James Robinson argue, most simply, that "institutions matter"; Angus Deaton that development aid does more harm than good by undermining political rights and accountability.[9]

While wary of reducing theories of change to short summaries or points on a chart, nevertheless I find it helpful in the context of the RCT movement in development economics, to think about the competing theories of change along three main axes:

- the value of small versus big changes;
- the value of local knowledge versus technocratic expertise;
- the role of individuals versus institutions.

I have not created a three-dimensional chart (I tried, but failed to produce something comprehensible) to capture these axes because they are not completely independent of each other. Someone who believes strongly in the value of big changes is obviously also very likely to place more value on technocratic expertise and the role of institutions.

There is significant variation in the theories of change of RCT advocates and critics of the movement on these axes. The general view is that the randomistas have a theory of change that, with apologies to Margaret Mead, could be stated as, "Never doubt that a committed group of small tweaks can change the world." In practice, there is significant variation within the RCT movement and between the critics, such that in some cases there is more in common between a particular RCT advocate and a particular critic than there is between two different critics. A good example is the Targeting the Ultra-Poor (TUP, sometimes also referred to as the Graduation Model) programs evaluated by teams including Banerjee, Duflo and Karlan.[10] The program is a package of interventions designed to lift people out of extreme poverty (defined as living on under $1.25 per day). The TUP program shares with Sachs' Millennium Villages Project the concept that a package of interventions is necessary to make a difference for the extreme poor. The TUP program, though, was created by BRAC, a Bangladeshi NGO, based on their long experience serving ultra-poor populations in Bangladesh in a process that bears more resemblance to Easterly's Searchers. The impact evaluations found that the TUP program was quite effective and so the *randomistas* are now encouraging the scale-up and adoption of TUP programs in more countries. Indeed, that was the plan all along (discussed in the interviews with Dean Karlan and Frank DeGiovanni), which again bears more resemblance to Sachs' model.

Underneath each of the critiques of RCTs noted above is a theory of change that differs from that of RCT advocates along at least one of the three axes. After the many conversations collected in this book, my impression is that those in the RCT movement tend to believe that small changes can matter a great deal,[13] that technocratic expertise is highly valuable, and that individuals within institutions matter as much as the institutions themselves. Those critics who invoke the Trivial Significance critique, in contrast, usually agree on the value of technocratic expertise, but disagree about the value of small changes and the role of institutions. Because differing theories of change are so foundational in RCT debates, I explicitly ask each interviewee about their theory of change.

How to Read This Book

Rather than delving further into the metaphysics of the arguments over RCTs and perhaps confusing the issues more than illuminating them, let me suggest an approach to reading this book and then get out of the way. The intent, after all, is to let you hear directly from the advocates, critics and others.

13. Rachel Glennerster, one of the interviewees, has a post that illustrates this point well by looking at how the "small" change of free bed net distribution based on RCTs can be traced to averting 450 million cases of malaria and 4 million deaths—as she puts it, "that's anything but small." See http://runningres.com/blog/2016/5/27/not-so-small

The approach I'd suggest is to keep the critiques and the axes of theories of change in mind[14] as you read the interviews:

1. Look for examples of the proponents of RCTs treating the results of RCTs as "magic" or universally better than alternative methods.
2. Look for examples of claims to external validity, and caution about external validity. More important, look for examples of RCTs causing someone to think differently about an issue, to alter her or his beliefs about how the world works.
3. Pay special attention to the discussions with each of the interviewees about their theory of change.
4. Think how the work of participants in the RCT movement is likely to materially change the lives of individuals, communities, and countries for the better. Think about alternative ways the resources—money and brain power—going into that work could be deployed to greater effect.
5. And finally, think about your own theory of change—the role of programs like those being evaluated, be they large or small, the role of individuals and institutions, the role of technocrats in setting policies and creating programs, and the role of evidence in policy and program development and evolution.

With that, I'll let what I intended to happen all along begin: letting you hear directly from the people in this book.

Acknowledgments

Well, one last thing before that. There are a variety of people who deserve specific recognition in the long, slow process of getting this book done. Among the interviewees I specifically want to thank Abhijit Banerjee and Esther Duflo for consenting to an interview back in 2008 (which doesn't appear in the book) but which kicked off this whole process; David McKenzie who spent more time with me than anyone else, tolerating my endless questions about the Sri Lanka experiments; and Jonathan Morduch, who helped tremendously on the introduction and conclusion as well as constantly nudging me to finish. Others who have my deep gratitude: Erin Graham for originally signing the book for UPenn Press;

14. A helpful mnemonic: PENS; Policy sausage, External validity, Nothing magic, trivial Significance.

Jane Macdonald for signing the book at MIT Press when the original deal fell apart; Dana Andrus, Elise Breda, Erin Jaeger, Elise Corwin, and Ann-Louise Jeffrey for helping with cleaning up the manuscript at various points; and Justin Sandefur, Alexander Berger, Rajeev Dehejia, Julie Siwicki, and JoAnne Williams for helpful conversations about the introduction and conclusion.

1 Michael Kremer

Michael is the Gates Professor of Developing Societies in the Economics Department at Harvard, a Senior Fellow of the Brookings Institution, and the recipient of a MacArthur Fellowship. Michael is the founder or co-founder of numerous organizations including the Bureau for Research and Economic Analysis of Development, Deworm the World, Development Innovation Ventures, the Global Innovation Fund, and WorldTeach among them as well as creating the idea of Advanced Market Commitments for treatments for neglected diseases. He is generally given credit for launching the RCT movement in development economics with two experiments he led in Kenya in the early 1990s.

TO: What was on your mind when you started doing randomized evaluations in Kenya? Why were you thinking about randomization and what impact did you think it would have at the time?

MK: In the early 1990s, academic economists were paying increased attention to the issue of how to get reliable econometric identification. In other words, how to separate out the causal impact of a specific policy or factor from potential confounding factors. For example, researchers were using instrumental variables techniques.

I had gone on vacation to the rural community in Kenya where I had lived and taught high school after college and was speaking to Paul Lipeyah, a Kenyan friend of mine. He had gotten a job with an NGO and told me he needed to pick seven schools for a new child sponsorship program. It occurred to me that maybe it would be possible to choose 14 schools and randomize across them to evaluate the causal impact of the program. My friend took the idea to his boss [Chip Bury of International Child Support Africa] and they decided to go for it.[1][1]

1. While this work was seminal in launching the RCT movement, the paper was not officially published until 2009, well after many other influential RCT papers were published.

Based on this initial work, it became clear to me that randomization could be made a practical tool for development economists, and that collaborations between researchers and NGOs could make it possible to test a variety of different approaches. Randomization was not just for very large scale, multimillion dollar evaluations of government programs with research questions determined by the government, but could be implemented through collaborations between academics and NGOs. It could shed light not just on child sponsorship programs but on broader questions. Within education, for example, it could shed light on drivers of human capital acquisition. How much of the poor learning outcomes in developing countries was the result of low levels of resources in schools, for example? What if we could use the fact that NGOs were putting large amounts of funding into some schools and not others, to try to understand whether low learning levels were due to lack of inputs, or whether it was due to teacher training, or poor child health or any number of other possible causes? It soon became clear that many important questions in development economics could be answered this way.

Getting involved in programs on the ground and tying one's hands by using randomized evaluations forces researchers to confront realities of human behavior, even if they don't correspond to our models. This can lead to the development of better models over time. When Ted Miguel and I did an evaluation of the deworming program of ICS, we found that deworming provided very substantial benefits—eventually leading to increased productivity in the labor force.[2] But despite these benefits, demand for deworming pills fell away sharply when the NGO imposed even a small cost-sharing requirement. A series of RCTs later confirmed a high sensitivity of demand for non-acute health technologies with price.[2][3] This accumulation of evidence helped us to refine our theories of health demand, showing that the human capital theory of investment in health needed to be adjusted. There's been a very productive interaction between RCTs in development and behavioral economics. These series of results have also had an important impact on policy. The World Bank had been an important advocate of user fees for health, but the most recent World Development Report on behavioral economics signaled an important reversal, making the point that fees can deter usage more than might be expected under a rational model.[4]

2. Pascaline Dupas has been involved in much of this work, and some of it is discussed in her interview. J-PAL has an overview of the topic with links to several papers here: http://www.povertyactionlab.org/publication/the-price-is-wrong.

TO: I'm interested in the ideas that were circulating around you when you started working on field experiments. Was that the critiques of IV and looking for better identification? Were you thinking about lab experiments from Kahnemann and others? Or the large-scale experiments in the US?

MK: In 1994 when I started the work in Kenya, I was very much influenced by the movement for the better identification in labor economics and public finance, but not by lab experiments. I see these traditions as independent, although there is now some convergence of the lab experiment and field experiment traditions. For instance, Nava Ashraf's work combines elements of each in interesting ways.

I also was not reacting to the critics of instrumental variables. Indeed, I think those working on instrumental variables and those of us working on RCTs were motivated by the same impulse, the concern that a lot of empirical work in economics at the time was potentially subject to confounders and required a lot of fairly strong assumptions. That being said, it's not like IV makes all the problems disappear, and neither does an RCT. I don't think anybody thinks that RCTs are magical, but they are a really useful tool for getting at causal impact. So I would say I was trying to get at causal impact in a way that was part of a broader movement in the economics profession to get better identification.

My main impulse was practical—to get more believable answers to real world questions. I have always been mainly interested in the underlying questions of what policies can address poverty and I realized that RCTs were a tool that could be adapted to help answer this question. I was motivated to make RCTs a more flexible and useful tool.

TO: What, of the very many efforts you've been involved in—helping begin the RCT movement, Advanced Market Commitments, Deworm the World, Development Innovation Ventures, the Global Innovation Fund— are you most proud of? What do you think will have had the largest impact looking back 20 years from now?

MK: I see all these initiatives as very closely related. Advance Market Commitments are about finding new ways to promote innovation for development. The others are also about innovation for development. Demonstrating that RCTs could be done, working out the practicalities for how to do this work, training others in the technique, raising funding for others to do it, and helping governments and others use the results in developing their policies are all part of a package. Of course, DIV and GIF support not just RCTs but innovations in development more broadly.

People often underestimate the huge amount of practical R&D that went into finding ways to make it feasible to run randomized evaluations that answer both practical and important theoretical questions in developing countries. The field experiments in the US[3] were being done with budgets of $40 million dollars or more. Such evaluations can clearly be very important, as the example of PROGRESA,[4] demonstrates.[5] And by the way, as far as I know, PROGRESA even though it was going on around the same time I was working on those first randomized evaluations, was also something that was separate. I don't think they knew what I was doing and I don't think I knew what they were doing. The initial randomized evaluations with ICS in Kenya were done on very small budgets, and we had to work things out from scratch. Working on small budgets in developing countries led to a lot of innovation about how to maximize power from limited samples, how to measure outcomes, and how to randomize. Another difference is that we were working with NGOs, as opposed to the large scale government evaluations done in the US. This was true both in Kenya where I started, and then with Abhijit [Banerjee] in India a few years later.

Working with NGOs, as opposed to big government evaluations opened up the ability to answer a much wider range of questions, because NGOs are more nimble than governments and they're used to trying different things. They're used to not being able to serve everyone, so it's more natural for them to be willing to try randomizing the order of phase-in. I helped set up a long-term partnership with ICS in Kenya, and the work Abhijit and I did with Seva Mandir[5] also turned into a long-term partnership. Within those

3. These US field experiments of federal programs are discussed in the interview with Judy Gueron.
4. PROGRESA is arguably the progenitor of modern conditional cash transfer programs, which provide social welfare payments conditional on recipients taking specific actions like keeping their children in school or getting vaccinations. PROGRESA was evaluated using a randomized trial which exploited the need to roll the program out over the course of several years and found significant impact on many measures of interest. The success of PROGRESA inspired the adoption of CCT programs in many countries around the world.
5. Seva Mandir is an NGO based in Rajasthan, India. It was involved in a number of the early education RCTs as well as the immunization promotion experiment (discussed in the interview with Esther Duflo and Abhijit Banerjee).

partnerships we were able to test all sorts of different ideas from education, to health, to women's empowerment, to agriculture. Graduate students were able to come and join those partnerships and explore new ideas, and those graduate students became junior faculty and then senior faculty, transforming the field.

I'm also happy that I have been able to work with policy makers to use these results to inform policy. Sometimes this involves scaling of particular innovations—such as deworming or chlorine dispensers—and sometimes it involves developing more general lessons, such as the impact of price on use of preventative health products or the importance of matching teaching to children's current learning level.

It takes a ton of effort to scale. That became very clear in the experience of deworming. We presented our results to policy makers and I think they were very genuinely excited about them. But a Permanent Secretary in a Ministry of Education will have many things to deal with, so sustained engagement and support are needed. In the case of deworming, for instance, we co-founded an NGO, Deworm the World, to provide technical assistance to governments to introduce mass school-based deworming programs. It took a lot of work to get the NGO started and to get some large scale programs going in Kenya and Bihar. But now Evidence Action, which took over the work of Deworm the World, is successfully supporting national programs in Kenya, Ethiopia, and India. They have already reached 140 million children in the first half of 2015 alone.

From my experience working on scaling up deworming, it became clear that there was a need for more institutional support to scale up the lessons coming out of RCTs. When Raj Shah became USAID Administrator and asked me to get involved, this is what I told him I wanted to work on. He was excited by the idea and suggested that I work with Maura O'Neill, who has a background in entrepreneurship. Together we co-founded Development Innovation Ventures within USAID to finance early stage piloting of new ideas in development, rigorous testing of those ideas, and scaling of those that proved most successful. DIV has funded a lot of RCTs around the world and has helped organizations scale those that work. This is really quite a different model to much of development aid. Instead of aid agencies making top-down decisions about what to invest in and then issuing calls for proposals to implement the vision, this approach involves an open call for innovative ideas, provides resources to support rigorous testing, and then makes further support conditional on results. The DIV approach has influenced the creation of related funds in Peru and Tamil

Nadu. DFID was interested in what we were doing, and so over the past few years I have been involved in setting up a new international venture, the Global Innovation Fund, which is supported by the US, the UK, Sweden, Australia, and the Omidyar Network. We just launched it this year, and I am very excited about it.

The modern movement for RCTs in development economics often gets put in the evaluation category, but in fact the movement is about innovation, as well as evaluation. It's a dynamic process of learning about a context through painstaking on-the-ground work, trying out different approaches, collecting good data with good causal identification, finding out that results do not fit pre-conceived theoretical ideas, working on a better theoretical understanding that fits the facts on the ground, and developing new ideas and approaches based on theory and then testing the new approaches. The idea for DIV and GIF is very much about innovation, so if you need support to pilot your idea before you're ready to rigorously evaluate impact, DIV and GIF will both pay for that. Then they'll pay for a rigorous impact evaluation, and if it works, they also go onto the next stage, which is trying to help transition innovations to scale.

So I see getting the modern movement of randomized evaluations started, showing they were possible, working with NGOs, working to try to scale successful development approaches like deworming, drawing out lessons like the sensitivity of preventive healthcare to fees, and then trying to build institutions to keep doing these things as a package that I hope will have lots of impact.

TO: There's an implicit theory of change there about the problem being the lack of institutions to generate and use evidence.

MK: I think that's right. You can see a lot of what I have worked on as creating an institutional framework to allow ideas in development to be rigorously tested and scaled. Even my early work in Kenya was building the local infrastructure to allow people to run high quality field experiments—from trained enumerators to systems people could run grants through. Many others have helped set up that infrastructure too and the world has come a long way in the last 20 years. There's J-PAL, there's IPA, there's 3ie, there's the SIEF program at the World Bank, there's DIME, so tremendous progress has been made.

TO: There's a bit of irony in the "institutions matter" critique that RCTs are paying attention to things that are too small, but the movement *has* created institutions.

MK: RCTs can't be used to answer every issue, but they can shed light on many issues.

Deworming may seem like a small question but evaluations of deworming shed light on the interrelation of health and education, peoples' sensitivity to small copays for non-acute health, responsiveness of behavior to health information, and information flow through social networks. It also helped shed light on methodological issues about measuring externalities.

There are now many good RCTs on political economy questions. Ben Olken has done a lot of good work on corruption using RCTs[6][6] and there is a lot of work on making bureaucracies more responsive.[7]

Some of my work on education that initially started as an evaluation of a textbook program wound up being about institutions. As I mentioned earlier, one of the great things about randomized evaluations is that it forces researchers to get very in touch with the reality of what's on the ground. Academics are not just sitting around theorizing about the challenges of development; they are getting their hands dirty. Very often in that process they realize their theories are wrong, and they come up with new theories. And then when you test those theories with an RCT, you are often surprised by the result. There is no room to tweak your result to fit your preconceived ideas, it is what it is. RCTs force you to confront reality.

I had taught in a school in Kenya, and seeing how few resources the schools had, made me think it must be good to have more resources, including more textbooks. But we found that textbooks only improved test scores for those who were already performing well. That made me think about the issues of fit between the curriculum and where the students currently were. Textbooks were written at a level far from the level of many students. One of the big lessons from RCTs in education is the mismatch between where curricula are and where teaching is oriented and where the typical student is. There are institutional reasons for that. There are political economy reasons for that. I think we understand a lot more about one of the key institutional problems in education because of randomized evaluations. In that case it didn't start out with an analysis of the institutional reasons for the mismatch, but the data brought us to it.

---

6. This includes work in Indonesia on extortion of truck drivers and on corruption in road building and the gap between perceptions of corruption and actual corruption. For an overview, see Olken and Pande, "Corruption in Developing Countries" *Annual Review of Economics* (2012).

7. See, for instance, Banerjee et al.'s work with the Rajasthan police, and Olken's work on performance pay for tax collectors in India.

We've identified a number of very useful interventions, such as remedial education, to address that problem, but it remains a big political economy problem to get those interventions implemented. Those are useful policies to help address this problem, but we probably also need curricular reform, and that's a harder task. But there's no reason why if we do have curricular reform, we can't understand the impact of that with randomized evaluations.

Some other critiques of RCTs, for example, about whether results from one context will generalize to others, are general points about empirical work, not about randomized evaluations.

TO: I want to go back to the issue of AMCs that we set aside at the beginning of this discussion. There's a reasonable argument that AMCs increase the number of vaccines and combined with GAVI gets a lot more kids vaccinated—and that one of the most important things to happen in development is keeping a bunch of kids from dying or being permanently handicapped physically or cognitively. How would you compare the potential impact of building institutions to generate evidence, versus "we saved a bunch of kids"?

MK: Institutions to encourage R&D on health products for the developed world include both public biomedical research funding and intellectual property rights to encourage private sector R&D. The idea of AMCs was to expand the set of tools we had available for encouraging R&D. Intellectual property rights systems create R&D incentives but also involve some static distortions, and those can be quite costly. There can also be some dynamic distortions. I had written a paper on the idea of buying out patents—firms could voluntarily sell their patents to governments, which could put them in the public domain.[7] That preserves the dynamic R&D incentives created by intellectual property rights but avoids some of the static distortions associated with intellectual property rights, as well as some of the dynamic distortions, like the incentive to develop "me-too" drugs just to get around the patent, and the disincentives to develop follow-on drugs.

AMCs for vaccines have a lot of the same properties as buying out a patent, but it seemed like they were institutionally and politically easier to do.[8] There was a huge amount of work to move from an academic idea to something that could be implemented in policy.[8][9] It was great that was done for the pneumococcus vaccine, and then that vaccine was developed.

8. This included not only the original economics papers, but a book (*Strong Medicine*) and a working group at the Center for Global Development before an organization was created and funded to manage AMCs.

I think the biggest potential benefit of AMCs would be to encourage R&D for diseases that are little more distant. In the case of pneumococcus, there was already a vaccine for the strains that were common in the rich world, but there wasn't one that covered all of the strains that are relevant to a lot of poorer countries. It was a technological challenge that I don't want to minimize, but it was less of a technological challenge than developing a completely new vaccine. I haven't spent time on this for a while, though I am writing an academic paper on vaccines and drugs right now. But, in general, I think there's scope for institutional innovation to come up with new mechanisms to encourage R&D and to make the products accessible. I hope I'll go back to doing some work on that at some point.

TO: Do you think about your role in training either directly or indirectly so many of the people involved in doing randomized evaluations? At the risk of goading you into saying some not very humble things, what's the counterfactual of a world without Michael Kremer?

MK: It's been great to work with some amazing graduate students and co-authors over the years, many of whom are now doing incredible things. One of the great things about setting up the operation at ICS in Busia has been seeing these incredibly talented people who are getting training in top-notch institutions and bringing that training face to face with life in Kenya and generating fantastic ideas.

I think that was very valuable for the students, but it's also valuable for the world insofar as a lot of those students went on to do great things. I'm very happy about that.

TO: One version of the impact of the field experiment movement is we've transitioned from a situation that, in general, serious economists didn't go to the field to one where they do. Does that resonate with you?

MK: The world needs all sorts of research.

We need field researchers, theorists, macroeconomists. There's fantastic work going on in economic history. I think the idea of spending time in the field and being involved in randomized trials and other fieldwork is great, and that is one very important set of techniques and tools. I'm also open to other approaches. I do think that, in general, it is good for development economists to have spent time living and working in developing countries, but that does not mean that every project should be based on fieldwork.

2 Abhijit Banerjee and Esther Duflo

Esther and Abhijit probably need the least introduction of any of the economists featured in this volume. They are founders of the Jameel Poverty Action Lab at MIT, arguably the most prominent center promoting the use of randomized control trials in development research—and the application of findings from that research to policy. Their book *Poor Economics* is a bestseller and winner of the 2011 Financial Times Business book of the year prize. Esther is a winner of the John Bates Clark Medal (2010) and a MacArthur Foundation Fellowship (popularly known as the "genius award") (2009). Abhijit has been both a Guggenheim and Sloan Fellow, and has served as president of BREAD, a consortium of researchers focused on development. Currently, she is the Jameel Professor of Poverty Alleviation and Economic Development, and he is the Ford Foundation International Professor of Economics, both at MIT.

Born in France, Esther attended some of the country's most selective educational institutions before moving to MIT for her PhD in Economics. In a highly unusual move, she was appointed Assistant Professor in Economics at MIT after completing her degree.

Her thesis exploited a natural experiment in the expansion of public schools in Indonesia to assess the returns to investment in schools and education in that country and was published in the *American Economic Review*, one of the profession's most prestigious journals. She has gone on to publish dozens of papers in top journals as well as be recognized as one of the leading thinkers in experimental economics in development.

Abhijit, meanwhile was born in Calcutta—his parents were both academic economists. His early work was primarily in microeconomic theory, a background that continues to heavily influence his work in more applied economics. He describes his shift from theory to applied economics as a result of "a sense that I know all this economics, so why isn't it helping me understand stuff that I see next to me?"

TO: What was the first experiment you were involved in?

AB: An experiment in a rural Udaipur district in 1996 I think. It was on changing the teacher-to-student ratio and seeing if that changed test scores. It was the first experiment of many that found the same thing, which is that you can add a lot more teachers per student,[1] you double the teacher to student ratio in this way and there's a precise zero effect on test scores. I think that we've found many times and eventually provoked us to understand a little more about the need for different curricula.

ED: My first RCT was the Balsakhi experiment.[2][1]

TO: It seems to me there's been a missing conversation between people looking at poverty and entrepreneurship in the developing world and people looking at poverty and entrepreneurship in the developed world. I find it particularly striking in terms of what we know about small-scale entrepreneurs—the local small business owner, the pizza shop, the strip mall gift store—in the US: they are low growth, low profitability, and high-failure-rate enterprises. It seems little of that knowledge or research was applied when it came to microenterprises fueled by microcredit.

AB: I think there is an important commonality and a very important difference. The biggest difference is that in places like the US where labor markets are strong, the incentive to go into entrepreneurship is very different from a setting where the low-end jobs are missing. The reason why there are so many more people in the low-end entrepreneurial sector in developing countries has a lot to do with the labor markets in those countries. The people who become entrepreneurs in the US actually do it more often out of a desire either to be an entrepreneur or that for some particular reason they don't want to be in the conventional labor market.

That's the difference.

The commonality comes in exactly in the sector you described. The area of US entrepreneurship that has that flavor of a developing country is in these recent-immigrant-run industries, undifferentiated and relatively low-tech businesses.

1. Note as discussed later in the interview, there is a difference between adding more teachers using the standard certification and hiring processes versus adding tutors who offer remedial education.
2. An evaluation of the value of adding non-union teachers to classrooms for remedial education, discussed later in the interview.

To use an example I know, imagine you come to the US because you are sponsored by your brother who is an engineer but you are 45 by the time your brother becomes a citizen and he sponsors you to come over. What are you going to do? You are not going to enter the labor market very easily. You probably also have teenage children who will have an equally hard time entering the labor market. That generates a classic labor availability-driven entry into business.

That particular end of the entrepreneurship market is very similar to that in developing countries, which is very family labor-driven. But I think the key in the conversation is the difference in the labor market. These are the people who are excluded from the traditional labor market.

ED: I don't think it's true that there's not much conversation. I think there is a lot of conversation and I think it's a lot of the same people doing the research like Sendhil Mullainathan, Dean Karlan; I work in France. We work in Chile, which is more like the US than India in many respects. There are a number of people who work in both types of environments with the same kind of method and the same type of approach to the problems.

I think there are two reasons why they have not talked about US entrepreneurship much. One is a good reason; the other is a bad reason. The good reason is what Abhijit said: at the end of the day the people who run a business here are not really poor.

When we are interested in the poor, which in France doesn't mean running a business, it means having no job whatsoever, it means dropping out of school at 16 with no skills. The research is focused on things like payday loans, not on entrepreneurship.

The bad reason is more what you are talking about. I think a lot of the discourse on entrepreneurship in the US is not centered on these guys. It's centered on Facebook and Bill Gates who are extremely interesting people but aren't representative.

I think this is changing. I see more graduate students who are interested in this idea of whether people are running businesses as a result of losing a job and those sort of questions. I don't know whether it's a real phenomenon or just looks like it, but it does seem to be something that people are starting to get interested in. Seeing graduate students taking note of these questions is a good sign for research to come.

TO: One of the things that got me thinking in this direction is the Field and Pande[3] experiment delaying the first repayment in a standard microcredit contract.[2] In the US no one thinks that banks are a good source of entrepreneurial capital. Why did people buy into the idea that a banking model was a good model for entrepreneurial capital?

AB: Let me disagree with you. I think that banks have always been a decent source for paying salaries. Essentially the only funds you get from a bank are very short term loans that you use to deal with your cash flow, like a line of credit. If you think of what a developing country entrepreneur is, she often doesn't have a lot of fixed capital.

For a lot of these microbusinesses, cash flow really is the core issue, so in that sense it's less implausible that banks are good sources of capital for microenterprises. Once you've bought the weights for your fruit stand, and you might already have that, all you have to do is replace one form of cash flow financing for the day with another form. In that sense microcredit is much more like paying salaries or wages than like setting up a business.

TO: But the capital that small businesses get from banks in the US isn't growth capital. No one really expects it to finance growth. Lines of credit have always been conceived as cash management devices, not as a solution to launch growing businesses.

AB: Even in the US, your credit line expands if you do well. And if you think that 90 percent of the capital needs of these businesses is cash flow, the fit isn't that bad. There are lots of reasons why microcredit doesn't work as well as it should, but I do feel that there's some similarity—the bank model is not entirely wrong.

ED: Two points. To some extent the fact that the businesses are like that is endogenous to the source of the money that is being offered. That is the point that the Field paper makes. That's the point that you were making. I am going part of the way to what you said.

I think the Field/Pande experiment—giving people a little bit more time before repayment is such a small thing that allows people to consider

3. In traditional microfinance, the first payment on a loan is due a week after the loan is made. Field and Pande randomly offered some borrowers a two-month grace period before repayments began. They found that those who did not have to repay the first week invested more in equipment and ultimately had higher profits, though also a higher rate of default on the loan. See video interview with Rohini Pande here: https://www.youtube.com/watch?v=rcySSYf3laM.

something like buying a sewing machine—really shows that the reasons the businesses are like that is a product of the financing. Maybe something else would be better.

However, the question you have to ask is: what's the alternative?

Maybe some form of equity is better. This is what people believe to be the right way to give capital to entrepreneurs here. But how do you do equity easily in a system where very small enterprises makes it extremely costly. So my point is slightly different, which is maybe it is not the best way to finance entrepreneurship in the best of all possible worlds, but we are not in the best of all worlds.

Maybe not. Maybe someone could still come up with a way of providing equity in an intelligent and cost-effective way. Abhijit has been talking for a while about that the fact there are many chartered accountants in India. You could use them to provide a little bit of verification. Maybe it is possible to do equity to microenterprises, but we are yet to find someone to bite, who would be willing to give their own equity.

AB: I think there is a lack of alternatives. Even in the US, most small businesses' fixed capital is financed by second mortgages on a house, borrowing from relatives, something like that.

ED: In the US, when you are big enough, you start getting access to formal finance.

AB: That's where in the US there is a huge difference. Once you've gotten to a certain size there are lots of people who give you lots of money, take equity in your business, but also even debt capital. But I think that, at the beginning, it is the case that essentially even in the US, people go to the bank to pay salaries, and then they go to suppliers who give them some trade credit and then they use their second mortgage to buy a machine. So in some ways it's not that different in developing countries. It's just that the levels of income are so low, so that you can't buy a machine with your second mortgage.

TO: But I think it is an example of something you wrote about in your book[3]: an oversimplistic understanding yields a solution addressing the wrong problem, which yields inertia to keep doing the same thing. I think a huge part of the overindebtedness crises in microfinance is that people really believed that they were providing growth capital. If you really believe that you're financing growing businesses, why would you stop? Why would you rein that in?

ED: It's been obvious for a long time that these business are not growing. The Grameen Bank has been around for many many years and their loans are still very very small. Just forget about subtle impact evaluation or whatever; it's been staring us in the face that these businesses are not growing, and the vast majority of people are not growing out of poverty or anything like that. If we had not been obsessed by the romantic idea of microcredit, then maybe there would have been an earlier realizing of what microcredit does and what it doesn't do. I think people are coming to that, to a small extent maybe because of our work stirring the pot. To be honest, it maybe would have happened anyway. But there's been a lot of delay given that the facts were pretty obvious.

AB: The crisis in microfinance in India[4] was a result of the 3 C's: credulity, cupidity, and corruption. The politicians were corrupt, we were all credulous, and the microfinance people were greedy. Put them together and you get the crisis. Our credulity was significant. Somehow we believed that all repayment happens in microfinance due to some magic, which made no economic sense. We knew it didn't make economic sense. And then suddenly one day we wake up to the fact that the actual loan officers would come to a borrower's house; maybe they don't beat the borrower up, but they do harass them.

You don't need to do an evaluation to start asking questions. You just need to think about it for 10 minutes. These are desperate people with lots of financial demands. People in the family are sick, people lose jobs, the daughter needs to get married.

ED: But they repay anyway. Someone must be very convincing.

AB: But 90 percent repay. What is going on? How could we believe this was because of some tweaking of economic incentives? As economists, I think we were basically inept in thinking about it or we would not have believed it. The core fact was staring us in the face. And we didn't look at this, we evaded the gaze of these facts that were looking back at us.

TO: Speaking of facts staring us in the face, there are some facts that I feel like are staring me in the face, but I don't know what to make of them. Where do you feel the balance of evidence is on giving people money and letting them choose, or knowing that there are some things they are under-investing in and so we should give them, say, a bed net?

4. The reference is to 2010 when microfinance institutions in Andhra Pradesh were required to stop collecting repayments by the government as a result of accusations of abusive collection practices and people being forced into debt traps.

ED: The problem is that no one has done that comparison. We know they are not buying bed nets with their GiveDirectly[5] money.[4] I guess I don't know that for a fact, but it's knowable. I think it's the type of question that will be frankly difficult to address because you're required to value benefits across sectors. So it depends what your objective is. If your objective is to control malaria, you can do an experiment where you give money and you give people bed nets or you do something else and you can see how many people sleep under a bed net at the end of the day, and what's the number of malaria infections you've averted. So that's a question that's well defined. Whether it's better to give cash or to give bed nets would require you to make a judgment about what is the importance of making people healthy versus having them buy a roof. And that's one I'm not prepared to make.

TO: Shifting to another topic, let me ask about women and girls. In almost all advertisements for aid and charity these days you see some version of the idea that the focus of aid should be on women and girls. There's indication in your book of some disagreement between the two of you on the evidence for that claim and of the need to focus on women and girls.

ED: That's mostly in jest

AB: We both agree that the idea of focusing on women and girls is very intriguing but slightly overblown. We don't actually know. Men versus women seems to make a huge difference in some places and not in others.

ED: It's not overblown necessarily. Women do spend money differently than men. The issue is whether women are inherently better people or the differences are the outcome of the social structure.

TO: You write about your fathers. Your fathers weren't drunkards who cared nothing about their children. I think about the generations of my family and we're not so far removed from rural farmers or the lower rungs of the working class. My grandparents and parents didn't go to school only because their mothers invested in them. I'm troubled about the implicit idea that mostly black and brown men in poor countries don't care about their families and white men in rich countries do.

5. GiveDirectly is an NGO that makes direct, unconditional cash transfers to poor households in Kenya. A randomized evaluation of the program was conducted finding that households increase food consumption and investment in durable goods do not increase consumption of alcohol or tobacco, and large gains in psychological well-being.

AB: That's the sense in which I think the evidence is overblown. I think that the evidence is clear that the particular forms of social dysfunctionality that emerge when economies are not working well have very different effects on men and women. That's partly because of the social roles assigned to them. So when you are a farmer and you only have a small bit of land and you realize that everybody else is making much more money than you, somehow your assigned role as the income earner of the family means you feel that in a different way than your wife who is also feeling the pinch of not being able to afford things. But in a sense it is definitely true that it is not her assigned role, and I think it makes a difference that it's not her assigned role. She is more able to discharge her assigned role than the man is in difficult economic circumstances. And that's almost surely one of the reasons why in the US, when the urban blue-collar industries went into decline, the traditional working class and particularly African American working class family got under a lot of stress.

I'm sure this phenomenon exists everywhere in the world. When you lose your job or your job is not up to snuff, it's difficult for men in traditional societies. I think it has a lot to do with the fact that their assigned role of income earner is particularly vulnerable to the shocks that the families were subject to. I do think that it's exactly what you said, I don't disagree with that. I think there is an easy essentialization of gender that is clearly dangerous.

ED: There's a factor of what I think is called "benign sexism." For instance, there are surveys where people ask, "Do you feel that women possess an inherent quality of gentleness that men lack?," something like that. And people say "yes." That's also a form of sexism.

TO: There's some hint of this as I understand the results of the Spandana microcredit study.[5] You found that women didn't spend more in the categories like education or food where people expected that women would spend more of their income than men did. I wonder if there's a discretionary income issue. Men traditionally have the discretionary income, and when they feel they have done the work to earn the income, then they have the right to spend some of it on themselves. But in traditional societies women are earning or receiving a portion of the family income for a specific task—to buy food and take care of the children. So that's what they spend it on. When women become discretionary wage earners, they behave like the men and spend more money on themselves—as is their right.

ED: That's what Chris Udry and I found in Cote D'Ivoire and we talk a bit about it in the book.[6] It is true that when women do better than men in a particular year that they spend more on food which is their particular job, their social role, but they also spend on themselves. So it's not that women do not want to spend money on themselves. Their traditional role involved making sure that people are fed. And that's less the case for men. Why societies evolved like that makes sense.

TO: There are perennial questions about external validity of any study, what results from one study tell us about what might happen somewhere else. This speaks to your theory of change. It's always been my impression that the idea is not just to transfer a program and assume it will work but to transfer and test it in the new context.

ED: Absolutely, keep testing. But it's not just repeating the same test over and over.

We have six RCTs of the impact of microcredit.[7] Most of the energy shouldn't be spent on doing 50 more of those tests in different contexts. Although there might be because it's now easy for people to conceptualize how you would do it. So the marginal costs are diminishing at the same time as the marginal returns are diminishing.

You're also seeing these eight ultra-poor studies[6] that we've put into one paper.[8] Now that there is more money and more recognition and more partners, et cetera, now that there is a system, you are seeing more replications. I've always thought that they would come, and they are coming.

Now we're saying, for instance, that the results of the six RCTs of microfinance are broadly consistent despite the fact they are in different contexts. You have people like one of my students who are trying to think about how we go from saying they are broadly consistent to being able to pull them apart by site, or by another dimension of heterogeneity, and what that can tell us. To what extent are the results pulling together and to what extent are the pulling apart? What's making them move?

So as we have these replications, as we have more tests, it's not just that we can say, "oh, nice, it replicates," or "this one doesn't replicate." Replications

6. These are a unified evaluation of a particular program targeted at those living on less than $2 a day that provides asset transfers, livelihood training, and other supports. The programs and the evaluation are discussed in more detail later in the interview.

also generate the ability to exploit that data in a structured way to learn about the importance of the context.

When, say, a government is interested in the result of an experiment, my experience is that they are not usually interested in taking it wholesale and applying it, they are interested in doing their own experiment.

There is this sort of, "experiment begets experiment." We saw that with the conditional cash transfers [CCT].[7] After the initial experiment, countries didn't just adopt the program that Mexico had. They started doing these experiments over and over again.

TO: Then they starting doing unconditional cash transfers instead of CCTs.

ED: Exactly. For a while it was just CCTs, but after some time they were like, "OK fine, can we learn what's important in the CCT?" So unconditional cash transfers came up. Or there's stuff I have done on labeled cash transfers.[8][9] So there are two ways in which the research builds on itself. One is replication across contexts, and the other is going deeper into the mechanisms and variance between subjects or implementers and other factors that have policy implications and further research implications. So you never stop testing.

But it's also true that it's never happened that a program was just copied wholesale, except with the possible exception of deworming,[9] and with deworming the theory of change is so basic at some level maybe it's

7. A now widespread social protection program, conditional cash transfers are welfare programs that require specific actions on the part of recipients, such as getting vaccinated or attending school. Conditional cash transfers came to modern prominence in Mexico in the early 1990s.

8. In an experiment in Morocco, some families were enrolled in a CCT contingent on school attendance, others were simply given cash that was explicitly for school expenses but attendance was not monitored. The authors find similar effects of CCTs and the labeled transfer. For more discussion of the study and its interpretation, see Berk Ozler: http://blogs.worldbank.org/impactevaluations/cash-transfers -sorting-through-hype.

9. The objective was to provide medicine to rid people of worms or intestinal parasites like soil-transmitted helminths. The study that many point to as the launch of the RCT movement was a randomized evaluation of a deworming program in Kenya by Michael Kremer and Ted Miguel. Eventually the study led to massive expansion of deworming programs, but also controversy. See additional discussion in interviews with Kremer, Elie Hassenfeld, and Angus Deaton.

appropriate, that you have just one study and you try to spread it around. It's empirically not what's going on.

There's a study here and a study there, and then another thing that's related and another thing that's related, and you start forming an idea for what might be a solution to a particular problem. For example, the low learning level in schools. That seems to be the case in a lot of countries, but it's embodied slightly differently wherever you go.

So you try something out in what seems to be the right context based on what you know. And you learn about all the implementation issues that come up along the way. It takes three or four experiments just to iron out the details before you can come up with something that looks more like a turnkey approach. You don't go from the Balsakhi[10] project to "here is what you should try," without 10 years of trying things out.[10] I don't think the time frame is going to be shortened that much. It's been 15 years since the first Balsakhi experiment started in 2000, and now its 2015 and we are *maybe* ready to start saying, "you can do this."

TO: I've written about what I think your theory of change is but have never asked you directly about *your* theory of change.

AB: Most of it I just keep hoping [laughter]. There are two things that all of us do, me no more than others. One is the really concrete thing of saying "look, I went and measured." In the end people have the sense that in the policy world there's a lot of respect for actually having gone and collected the data and seeing what is happening. I've talked to lots of bureaucrats. When they realize you know a fair amount about something, you get a lot of respect. Some of that comes from understanding you did an RCT, some of it comes from the fact that you've been and seen a place that they've never been.

Part of the theory of change comes from just engaging in the conversation. Policy makers often seem to live in a void. They think, "there's really not much to know, it's on me and I have to," in the equivalent of the white man's burden, "solve this problem." But when you've gone and measured something and you talk to the bureaucrat, they begin to appreciate that there is a lot of knowhow out there. I think that's the first thing we have to do. We have to show we have credibility, that we do know something about

10. An experiment to provide "contract," that is, non-union, teacher assistants in classrooms to tutor children who have fallen behind grade level. The program has since been tested in Kenya, Ghana, and other locations.

this issue. There are a lot of externalities in credibility obviously. When I meet someone and he says, "I met Jonathan Morduch and he said this," Jonathan has already paved the way to this guy listening to me. There's a collective investment in credibility that is very useful, that's why J-PAL and IPA are important. They've created an institutional basis for credibility. A lot of change is coming from the fact that policy makers and civil servants are saying, "well, there are these people who talk about evidence and they seem to know something and other people seem to take the seriously, so let's talk to them." Part of it is just getting the conversation.

In my experience, it's not the case that the policy makers have perverse views on what they want to do. They want to do something good. That's often true of even people who might in other ways not be great human beings. They might be corrupt or all kinds of things. It's not that they don't want to do anything. They have some ambition, maybe some social mindedness, maybe some ambition that if I do something maybe I'll stick around longer. For all those reasons they're responsive to things that you if you go and say to them, "what you're doing makes no sense," for this and this reason, it's not that they don't necessarily believe that.

Part of what we have achieved I think is a bit more credibility. Now, if you are in government in India, you might have heard of J-PAL and therefore if we come and say we really don't think this is the thing to do, at least you get a hearing. Some of them might actually think about it. And then they ask, "what do you think?" You do hear a lot of "what do you suggest?"

That's not just true for us. That's what's true for organizations like Pratham[11] because they have been on the ground, they have data, that whole nexus of familiarity and some expertise. All of that together is very useful in getting past that initial hesitation of, "what, do these people know any more than me?" I think that landscape has changed and I think there are enough people who believe that there is expertise out there just as they believe when they want to issue a bond they know that there is expertise out there. Even the corrupt bureaucrat calls in the three bond market experts from Goldman and talks to them.

Sadly, that's where we haven't reached yet, but we might, that when people want to do a program, they will call in people who actually have data. To

11. The education-focused NGO in India is perhaps most famous for initiating an annual report on learning levels in schools—an approach that has been copied in several countries.

some extent it has happened. Even in the previous government you saw that people like Jean Dreze, who may be wrong but at least who had done some research, had some influence. There is some understanding that there's expertise out there and programs don't necessarily work because they sound good.

I think that idea—that programs may not work—has penetrated. Perhaps what has penetrated most is that. Not so much that we know how to make things work but we can at least tell you something useful about how things might go wrong. But that's still progress.

TO: How much have you thought about influencing specifically the people who make the small changes in policy? You do this work with, I presume, the idea that it will change the way certain people behave and they'll stop trying to make the big sweeping changes because they understand how things might go wrong and instead try smaller things and test them.

AB: People talk about how hard it is to change policy or influence policy and that the institutions in developing countries are resistant to change. I feel like a lot of what we see as the culture of government is actually in some ways a very mechanical product of the last 50 years. Most countries in the world have created a whole bunch of institutions very, very recently.

Developing countries inherited a kind of a state that was not particularly devoted to the welfare of the people. So they saw these models of the developmental state elsewhere and decided, "we're going to have this particular set of people implement this particular set of things." So the institutions are not the product of a long accretion of incremental changes that made the bureaucracy particularly well suited to a particular kind of policy. This bureaucratic culture we have in so many places is just happenstance.

Most developing countries have only been independent since the late 1960s. So we're talking about a period of 40 years. It's hard for me to imagine that what we are observing in developing countries now is a steady state result of some complicated process.

Most things are done with such amazing casualness that I feel like it can't possibly be anybody's reflective thought on how or what a process should be. People were given lots of power, lots of decision rights, little training, lots of ideology. I don't feel that the bureaucracy in most places has reached an approach where it's snugly sitting and we'll never change it. Lots of bureaucrats and especially their political masters are very sensitive to the fact that somehow they lose elections. My sense is that they're quite bewildered by that. I think, in principle, there's a lot of demand for rethinking government.

When we talk to bureaucrats in India, obviously there are some who will tell you that they know everything and don't need any help. But there are a lot who say, "yes, I think we should do that; can you help us with that?" The reaction is often "why can't I get many more people like you to come in and help us with how to redesign this whole thing?" They know things are broken, too many programs don't work, but it's just too difficult in the middle of the job to fix it.

ED: I think we are reasonably internally consistent. If we want to be internally consistent, then we can't be calling for a big revolution when one day everybody will start looking only at the evidence before making decisions. That's not going to happen, let's face it. There are a lot of reasons why things happen the way they do. So if we were trying to advocate to replace the world the way it is with some fully efficient technocracy that experiments with things before trying them out and then launches them with no error in the process, that would be inconsistent with what we are saying, and *crazy*. That makes our life easier. If a big change, a revolution, is not what you are targeting, if you are targeting improvement at the margin, there are lots of margins where you can start doing things. Maybe it's a somewhat opportunistic thing to say. We don't have a huge reason to fight people who are really resistant because we can always try with someone else. Like Abhijit was saying, there are a lot of people who are willing to try things out. In the beginning of J-PAL we worked a lot with NGOs because they were more nimble. Even there you have some who are never going to change their ways, and some who are more flexible and we worked with the ones who were flexible and eventually some who weren't initially willing came to talk to us.

With the government, and with international institutions, it's a bit like that as well. You can start having conversations and trying things out and trying to improve something somewhere. So we're really talking about: can we make your school committees work better or something "unambitious" like that. And from there you can demonstrate that it can be done and eventually it can become bigger and bigger.

So, for example, we started working with the police in Rajasthan. We describe this in the book. It happens to be that at least some people in the police in Rajasthan were interested in improving performance. They tried some things and it had some effect.[12][11] Then we could use that as an example when we went to talk to the government of Gujarat about improving their pollution inspections[13] and in the process of that got the attention of the central government who were thinking about a cap and trade scheme for carbon.[12] And so Rohini Pande and Michael Greenstone, who were working with me on the pollution issue, then began to help design a cap and trade test. But it didn't happen by us knocking on the door of the minister and asking, "can we design your cap and trade system?" It happened by taking the path of least resistance.

TO: One of the things that you say toward the end of your book that leapt off the page at me is, to quote directly, "The poor bear responsibility for too much of their lives." I can imagine a lot of people reading that sentence and being taken aback. It seems to be a stark contrast with the Sen idea that escaping poverty means having more freedom, more control of your life.[13]

AB: I think we choose our words carefully. Control is not responsibility. In a sense I think having a lot of responsibility undermines control ...

ED: ... and freedom.

AB: And freedom. When you want to exercise control, you need to have the psychological freedom to actually exercise it actively, rather than passively reacting to many many things. Control is not passively reacting to many many things. It's agency. I think responsibility, lots of responsibility for very difficult things, undermines agency. It's not that you choose to do those things. It's that you have to do those things. So it's not choice. Responsibility is not choice. It's things that are dumped on you that you have to struggle with, and in the process I think your agency is undermined because you can't reflectively decide that this is the life choice that I want

12. Banerjee et al. tested a variety of approaches to improve police performance in Rajasthan. They found that reforms that ran through middle managers were not effective, but the announcement that "secret shoppers" would be visiting stations pretending to be civilians trying to report crimes and direct on-duty training improved performance.

13. This was an experiment to change how pollution auditors were paid. Auditors were paid by the firms they audited (as with financial audits). By changing how the market for auditors worked and how they were paid, auditors reported pollution results more truthfully, and audited firms were more likely to reduce pollution levels.

and this is the life choice that I don't want. I wouldn't call that being in control or being free. I think taking responsibility off people's hands and giving them a domain of freedom that is uncluttered where they can make choices without being constantly frightened by all the things that can happen, all the risks around, just the intellectual challenge of balancing 500 things, I think it is giving them freedom. Maybe it's a disagreement about the nature of freedom. *Prima facie* I would not say that responsibility is control.

ED: I don't think that's against Sen. It's going further in the Sen path. The whole argument of Sen is that freedom means nothing unless you have the capability to exercise it. There are many examples of that, but one very striking example of that which he cites is the family in Bengal that is completely free to buy grain but they have no money, so they can't do it. The point he is making is that freedom is meaningless unless there is the possibility to exercise it, the capability to exercise it. We are not saying anything different. I mean, we are not free in the US to drink water that is contaminated with *e. coli* because it comes to us clean. Is our freedom reduced in comparison to the person in Kenya who is free to do that because, if they don't want to drink the water with *e. coli,* they have to put chlorine in it. I don't think we are less free, I think we are more free.

I'm not saying that we are not making a political statement on some level on the nature of freedom, but I think it's an argument that's pretty naturally in the Sen line.

TO: Of all the things you've worked on, if you were to predict which are likely to have the biggest policy impact, what do you think those will be?

ED: It's very hard to tell because you can count the number of people touched when things work. But I do think the RCT studies of microcredit already had an impact. I do think they have already changed the industry in ways that I don't know exactly how to quantify. I can't say what would have happened without us, but I do think the conversation is different than it was in the past. When you hear the practitioners, you can compare what they are saying now to, for instance, the IPA conference at Moody's.[14] The

14. Duflo is referring to a conference on microfinance research hosted by IPA, Moody's, and others in October 2010 that included representatives from microfinance institutions. The conference was held when many of the randomized impact studies of microcredit were just beginning, and the general stance of those in the microfinance industry seemed to be that such studies were unnecessary because the positive outcomes from microcredit were well known and proven.

statement that these same guys just put out[15][14]—they've acknowledged that they lost in some sense relative to what their claims were and now they're just changing the claim—which is totally fine by me.

TO: It's amazing how hard it is now to find anyone who ever thought microcredit was going to be transformative.

ED: Exactly. But that's fine by me. I'm not in this business to score points. Just hearing the way in which they disagree with us, it has changed in such a fundamental way. I think we've had an impact there.

I think the education work can have influence because I think it's fundamentally right and not difficult, but the politics in the education world is very different. I don't know if we'll be able to manage it, but I hope that it can work. We have to try. I think we have to have a couple of successes. We have had successes, but I think they're still seen as small projects. We have to get to state-wide adoption.

Those are two areas. It's not as important, but my smokeless cookers failure of impact work is important. That paper came a bit earlier in the cycle of how these things get rolled out compared to other areas we've worked on. Smokeless cookers were going to become the new microcredit, but that work put an end to that.

TO: It's a curious case, because the improved cook stove has been around for 40 years, and you continue to hear, "we didn't get the design quite right but now we know." And then the next one doesn't get taken up, and the cycle repeats.

ED: It's still going on, but now you have more discussions about what users want, and I think more recognition that getting it right is so difficult.

Another area is the pricing of health products, something that I have nothing to do with, but I think will continue to make a big impact.

More important, I think, is the general recognition that experiments can be a part of the learning in the organization. There's a pulling back from

15. Duflo here refers to a statement from the Microfinance CEO Working Group, a group comprised of the CEOs of six large international microfinance networks, in response to the publication of the six randomized evaluations of microcredit. See Microfinance CEO Working Group, "Measuring the Impact of Microcredit—Six New Studies," 2015. The statement, and a prior statement of the Microfinance CEO Working Group disputing the findings of one of the first randomized impact evaluations of microcredit, is discussed in chapter 7, in the interview with Alex Counts who was a member of the working group at the time of both statements.

evaluation as an accountability tool, moving it away from evaluation offices and professional evaluators back to "the doers" and getting governments to accept it, more than that, excited about using it as a tool.[16] That is probably the biggest impact. It's a change of the conversation.

TO: I find it a little ironic that the most well-known set of RCT results is the "no effect" of microcredit. It feels to me philosophically that at the heart of randomized evaluations is the belief that relatively small actions …

ED: can make a difference. I don't know if the microcredit studies are the best-known set of results. Hopefully the ultra-poor evaluations will also become famous. And the GiveDirectly evaluation got a lot of play.

I think the reason why the microcredit evaluations have gotten so much attention is because microcredit is so big. So having something to say about it is important. If it had been positive, it would have gotten a lot of play too. It's not just the counterintuitive results. Many things do work so that's good too, and those things will get attention.

TO: I'm often discouraged by the reaction to programs that show improvements but small ones. It seems that there's some threshold that's quite high that people expect programs to meet. Regardless of cost effectiveness the programs have to be "transformative" or they are a failure. One example is the CCT program that was tried in NYC,[17][15] had positive and significant results, but they were small, so the program was essentially canceled.

ED: I think that's a bit of problem that we encounter as well. We have that problem with the immunization incentive program.[18] That's

16. What Duflo describes here is remarkably similar to Lant Pritchett's (chapter 9) critique of the RCT movement—that evaluation is coming from outside and therefore likely to be resisted, rather than evaluation coming from inside as part of an organization's efforts to learn and improve.

17. The Opportunity NYC program was a privately funded CCT experiment in New York evaluated by MDRC. Several of the program components were found to have small, but statistically significant, effects and to be cost effective, but the program was largely discontinued.

18. One of the early randomized evaluations to gain attention was a program in which parents were offered free lentils and a metal plate in return for immunizing their children. It had a much larger effect than improving the availability of vaccines. The study is frequently cited in behavioral economics literature as an example of people acting "irrationally" at least in terms of economic models of fully rational actors.

something I care deeply about just from a human perspective. I want to get that expanded. But even though we've never seen anything better in terms of lives saved per dollar spent, there's a lot of resistance. There are many reasons why people are reluctant about things like giving people an incentive for immunization. Some are ideological: "you shouldn't pay people to do something that's good for them." But some people say, "oh, that's good, you increased the immunization rate from 6 percent to 38 percent but there are still 60 percent who are not immunized." My response is, "well yeah, do you have something better?" We published that work in the *British Medical Journal*.[16] One of the referee responses was, "that's not enough to guarantee herd immunity, so why do we care?" Well we care because it's still good even if it's not herd immunity. We care because the 30 percent of people aren't going to die. And even if you don't have herd immunity, you still get contagion effects. All of the evidence on vaccinations is that you get effects [of lessening epidemics] at all levels [of vaccination coverage].

Of course, if you get to 100 percent, you get the big prize of eradicating a disease, like Gates is trying with polio, which is a completely legitimate exercise. But it's not like you shouldn't do anything if you can't fully wipe out a disease. There's no reason not to improve measles immunization from 6 percent to 38 percent. But people don't get all that excited about it.

By measuring well and showing what the effects are, you get these kinds of realistic answers. When you don't measure, you can always claim something big.[19] Starting from a context where most things are at least a little bit overblown, then the sobriety of measurement puts any program at a bit of a disadvantage. But I think that's a culture that could change, that people could get used to using a different lens. The honest but modest number that has been established from a trial or in another rigorous way could replace the rosy description of what you wish was happening, but that change might take a little longer.

TO: Have you seen progress in the number of people willing to take on evidence or the ability of evidence to make change?

ED: It's a revolution. It's not progress. It's like a sea change really in the last few years. Just look at the number of projects. J-PAL has 600 ongoing or completed projects. And that's just J-PAL researchers. That's the tip of the iceberg. Then there's the whole of IPA, the World Bank, who are doing their own thing, and there are many people who are not affiliated with any

19. Lant Pritchett points out that this is a reason why many organizations avoid RCTs.

of these organizations who are doing their own projects. Even the fiercest critics of randomized evaluations have tried it.

So that's in terms of the supply. Of course, there wouldn't be a supply of projects if there weren't partners to do these projects. They require partners.

My experience with working with governments is now we're able to work much more closely with them. At the moment, they are more willing to experiment than to take up new things based on other experiments. That's fine by me. You can see that there is a new culture of trying things out, and acting on the results, that is spreading much faster and farther than I would have predicted a few years ago. A lot of things have accelerated in the last two or three years.

AB: I guess, yes. Now, at least in India, the media is more conscious of the quality of evidence question. There's now an online magazine called *India Spends,* which is essentially focused on presenting evidence. The public does participate in the evidence debate. Now the next step is to persuade them that some of those people who are talking about evidence are corrupt or wrong, and sometimes both but mostly wrong. I think they are just misguided, though I wouldn't say that about everybody.

I think there is a need to get back the idea that all evidence is not equal.

You often still hear someone saying, "oh, some anthropologists found something else." But you go look at those papers and they had no control group. The battle for evidence is not a trivial one. It's easy to get confused about the fact that there are different ways of collecting data, and then there's the fact of whether there's a control group. With no control group, you have no idea what you're comparing to, but that's a totally separate issue from the ways you collect data. I think people often get confused that somehow through anthropological methods you can avoid the need for a control group. That's just a logical fallacy. You could collect better data maybe or different data, but the fact that you are interviewing people who are participants and some other people you might meet who are not participants to use as a comparison is not a matter of economics or anthropology, it's a matter of logic.

There is a lot more conversation about evidence in the world now, everywhere. Therefore there are lots of legitimate and illegitimate claims going on. But I think it's better to have that conversation than to be in the world 20 years ago when there was no conversation whatsoever. People ran cross-country regressions and made claims. That particular version of analysis, I think, has been successfully pushed off the table.

People at the table are making claims at roughly the same level of evidence, but it's still difficult for nonspecialists to understand because there are so many claims. You hear things about mixed methods, or whatever, and a lot of those claims are about not understanding what the words mean. Some of them are legitimate. A lot of them are not understanding what the words mean. They're just noise. I think there's a fair amount of that.

TO: Do you feel like there's been a significant shift in the academic community about both the quality of evidence and replication issues?

AB: Absolutely. To a first approximation, with some very specific exceptions of high-quality work on specific US programs, the level at which people understood identification was weaker 25 years ago than I think the median MIT undergraduate today. People ran regressions any which way, called whatever they wanted instruments, and made any claims they wanted. The standards in the academic community are very high, perhaps too high, but certainly not static. They have improved enormously. That's a change since I was a graduate, which was a long time ago but not the last millennium, just the past century.

TO: Is the war over RCTs in economics being won? Are you having to spend less time explaining, justifying, fighting, the internecine battles within the economics profession about the limits of RCTs?

ED: Abhijit and I disagree on that. I think it's been completely won in that I think it's just happening. A lot of people are doing it without us. It's being used. I think it is now understood to be one of the tools. The argument within the economics profession had two main consequences, both good. First, it raised the profile. If something was debated, people began to believe it must be significant.

Second, it did force us to answer the challenges. There were a lot of valid points that were raised and it forced us to react. We've become more intelligent as a result. I think Abhijit somewhat disagrees. I think he sees very prominent people, like Angus Deaton who came out so strongly against RCTs, have provided cover for people who were against evaluation to have a very quick answer, "rigorous evaluation is not all it has cracked up to be." My view is that if people were not enthusiastic, they were not going to be enthusiastic one way or the other. It's just a front that argument takes.

I think, on balance, RCTs are a useful tool and people realize that, and therefore it will continue its life.

I don't think you can do something that is important and changes the world without meeting some opposition. I also think that's a good thing. We wouldn't want to replicate the microcredit arguments, but our whole view is that things should be questioned and I think that applies to us well.

AB: I am less certain that it has been won. The acid test of whether an idea has come to stay is that it becomes something that no one needs to justify using. This has happened first to game theory and then to behavioral economics during my years in the profession. RCTs aren't there yet: it is true almost everyone is doing them, but many of them are taking the trouble to explain that what they do is better than a "mere RCT." We need to get to the point where people take RCTs to be the obvious tool to use when possible to answer a particular class of empirical questions

TO: You've been involved in at least one of the studies in the few areas where there have been a bunch of RCTs, like microcredit, the ultra-poor programs, the teacher assistants.

With the microcredit evaluations there was no *ex ante* coordination, the education studies have a lot of common authors, but I don't think those were planned as replications, and then the ultra-poor program evaluations that were very explicitly planned as a multi-site replication. Should we think about the evidence that emerges from those varied approaches differently?

ED: I think the gain of coordinating is not tremendous, but it helps ensure that you are evaluating the same thing. With the ultra-poor evaluations, even though the programs are not the same from place to place, we do know that they are a conscious adaptation of a single model. It was a nice thing to be able to say that while it's not the same program, the way in which it is not the same is a completely endogenous response to the variation in the context but the same original model.

In the case of the different microcredit programs, while all those organizations are looking up to Grameen, it's not that they coordinated among themselves. So we were lucky with the microcredit evaluations—maybe not lucky, it's not strange that many different researchers were interested in the same questions when it comes to microcredit. In the ultra-poor program, the outcomes were planned to be the same. With the microcredit evaluations, it could have been more of an issue.

AB: I think the benefits of the coordinated evaluations, it's not that you have to do exactly the same thing. In the graduation projects, you have a core that is almost identical and then a periphery of different things. The Ghana project in which I've been involved is different in many of the additional treatments than the ones in other countries, and you can learn a lot from those variations. But it's also useful to have a core that's really comparable because we're not going to have 30 high-quality studies very quickly. When you have five or six, it's still useful for them to be pretty similar in one core. So I do feel that the coordination was very valuable.

ED: On the learning level it's different because the studies are building upon each other in incremental ways. They're not like a replication of each other. They couldn't have been done in parallel. There is so much learning that is going on from one to the next. The next wave of ultra-poor work is going to be building on these first eight studies. There's going to be a bunch of ultra-poor work coming up over the next few years. It's going to be merging, I think, with the unconditional cash transfer work. A lot of the questions are going to be around just giving cash to the poor, and what things around it make a difference.

TO: Should one approach to those replications be more convincing? Does the fact that while the microcredit evaluations were all so different, and done by different teams without any *ex ante* coordination, but have such similar results convince us that we've narrowed in on the truth?

AB: What you said is exactly right. Imagine that we found, which we couldn't have guessed, that the results were different, then at that point we would have had a hard time knowing what to make of it. If there was an essentially identical design and we had different results, I think we would be much more willing to attribute that to the fact that the program itself had different impacts.

In other words you can think of it as being variation in the impact of the program or you can think of it as being variation due to the fact that the programs are not the same. In principle, if you said "it sometimes works and sometimes doesn't," that's different than saying that it works in some variant and not in others. Those are different statements. I think the interpretation of the variation in the results would have been somewhat different. I think you're right that we get more confidence because the results are consistent.

But one could come back and say that, "because there were six variants, none of them has been tried more than once, how much confidence do we have?" It's true that a few outcomes were tantalizingly close to being significant in one direction or another. Some were negative and close to significant, some were positive and close to significant, some were negative and significant but small, and on and on. If I really replicated each of those, maybe the positives would blow up more, but maybe it's the negatives that would blow up more.

The optimal design of a set of experiments depends very much on how strong your priors are. I'm writing a paper about this, so I can go on and on. If your priors are pretty weak, so you want to be satisfied over a range of priors, then you want to design a bunch of different experiments. If you're priors are pretty strong, so you know what you're looking for, then in some sense, you might as well vary the treatment a lot, so you see what you get. If I know what I'm looking for and I know if I'm supposed to find something specific, and then I don't find it, I'm willing to say this whole agenda is nonsense, then I should focus right around that; I should vary right around where I think the truth is. Whereas if I don't really know where the truth is, then it might make sense to be a bit more exploratory. To suggest that even if the truth was *this*, the evidence doesn't stand up, and even if the truth were *that* the evidence doesn't stand up. Let's try a few variants so we are not too close to one view.

Depending on how tight your priors are, your experimental design could be either mostly driven by your theory or mostly driven by, "I have no idea, let me try a bunch of different things."

Now in the case of microcredit, I think our priors are much tighter, so we'll be much more interested in seeing if we can get an impact on the top group, the top 10 percentage. And we have theories on what they need, and maybe the product to try out would be quite different.

I'm not sure that's what inspired the different approaches. These are just accidental differences right now. The differences between the set of microcredit evaluations and the set of graduation evaluations are just accidental. If we had had the choice, we would have done microcredit evaluations the same way as the graduation evaluations. To a first approximation, it's easier if people didn't say "three of your studies had collateral and 3 didn't." For someone who doesn't want to believe the results, for that person the variation is useful. To convince that person, the person who has a strong prior, you want to put the studies where the prior is. If you don't, he'll say, "well 5 out of 6 of these studies don't correspond to what I think is relevant." That's the danger.

That's why it would have been better if we had been able to say, "this is your prior."

On the ultra-poor evaluations, people had the prior that poor people will just eat the assets you gave them. So the fact that all of them basically focused on that was great. But if you thought people had lots of different ideas about what might happen, then you might want to design a different set of experiments. People had very well-articulated priors, so you want to push on and test those priors.

Now we are in a very different space. Everybody has a different theory of why the ultra-poor programs work, so now we have to do much more. We're at a "let a 100 flowers bloom" stage. So the design of the next experiment has to be based on how strong and how narrow people's priors are.

TO: At the margin, where are we in terms of the value of replication or moving on to the next questions?

AB: At this point I would say replication isn't a huge priority because a bunch of replications on the things that are close to policy have been done. Important replications have happened, in education, in microcredit, in ultra-poor programs, in cash grants. And there are a bunch more in process. And now we are in a place where we know those things, but we know only small pieces on some very important ones—like what to make of microcredit—but there's a bunch of stuff where we really have no clue—like if not microcredit, what?

There's a bunch of stuff that was very tantalizing five years ago, that in three more years will be known. I feel like right now there are a lot of questions implied by the research that's happened. "If not microcredit, what?" is one of them. I think there are lots of pointers toward "what." Another is, "why is it that we haven't succeeded using computer technology to teach better?" I think computer technology in education is one where there are so many claims, so much money, so much energy, but zero effect. There is one successful RCT we did 15 years ago and that's it.[20][17] That's the extent of all successful RCTs in that space. That's a shocking fact.

Probably the biggest benefits right now would come from research on a set of things that are close to green field research. There are a bunch of things that seem to have now become very sharp questions that need to be answered.

20. This is a study on using a math practice computer program, very close to using flashcards. Large gains were found in basic math scores in the short term, with some gains persisting over the longer term. The paper is the same as cited in note 1 above, in relation to placing tutors in schools.

3   Angus Deaton

Angus is the Eisenhower Professor of Economics and International Affairs at the Wilson School of Public and International Affairs and the Economics department at Princeton University. He was awarded the Nobel Prize in Economics in the fall of 2015 for his work on understanding poverty through household surveys rather than national income statistics. Angus has received numerous other awards, including the Econometrics Society's Frisch Medal and the BBVA Foundation Frontiers of Knowledge Award. His 2013 book *The Great Escape* focuses on the huge gains in income and health the world has experienced and why some parts of the world have gained so much more than others.

TO: I want to start by understanding if there is a critique of evidence from RCTs independent of evidence from localized studies.

AD: I am not sure I understand the question. Is a localized study one that uses 20 million observations from a census? I would have thought that a randomized control trial is usually a localized one.

TO: Yes, but there is lots of work that is localized but not randomized.

AD: I think one of the big issues is that these RCTs are typically small and localized. And a lot of the observational studies use nationally representative data sets.

TO: That's what I'm trying to home in on: the difference between a critique of a method and a critique of a sample.

AD: Maybe I'll come at that indirectly. If you go back 50 or 60 years when economists started playing with regression analysis, they thought they had a magic tool that would reveal just about everything. They would run multi-variable regressions on all sorts of things and interpret that within, in a way completely unjustified by today's standards, a causal framework. Then over the years economists and other people learned that there were all sorts of problems with that. If you go to an econometrics course now, they're not teaching the magic regression machine. It's more like the regression diseases and what's wrong with regression.[1] I think economists, especially development economists, are sort of like economists in the 1950s with regressions. They have a magic tool but they don't yet have much of an idea of the problems with that magic tool.[2] And there are a lot of them. I think it's just like any other method of estimation, it has its advantages and disadvantages. I think RCTs rarely meet the hype. People turned to RCTs because they got tired of all the arguments over observational studies about exogeneity and instruments and sample selectivity and all the rest of it. But all of those problems come back in somewhat different forms in RCTs. So I don't see a difference in terms of quality of evidence or usefulness. There are bad studies of all sorts.

I think it depends a lot on the details. I also think what strikes me as very odd about a lot of the development work, is there was a huge amount of experimentation done in economics 30 to 40 years ago. There were many lessons from there, and a lot have been forgotten. There are people still around like Chuck Manski[3] and Jim Heckman[4] who understand very well

1. See the interview with Jonathan Morduch (chapter 4) for some discussion of the history of methods in causal identification from regression to instrumental variables to randomized control trials.
2. See the interview with Michael Kremer (chapter 1) for more thoughts on "magic" in RCTs.
3. Charles Manski is a professor of economics at Northwestern University specializing in econometrics and causal identification. His books include *Identification Problems in the Social Sciences* (1992) and *Public Policy in an Uncertain World* (2013).
4. James Heckman is an economist based at the University of Chicago with a specialty in econometrics, particularly selection bias, and empirical work on early childhood education. He shared the Nobel Prize in Economics in 2000. The committee cited "his development of theory and methods for analyzing selective samples." The Prize Announcement: http://www.nobelprize.org/nobel_prizes/economic-sciences/laureates/2000/announcement.html. Heckman's Nobel Lecture: http://www.nobelprize.org/nobel_prizes/economic-sciences/laureates/2000/heckman-lecture.html.
Heckman was a leading critic of the randomized evaluation movement in the US for many years, publishing many papers suggesting that randomized evaluations were likely to be biased, produced little of scientific value, and that econometric analysis could correct for biases in observational studies as well as, and much cheaper than, randomized experiments. The effect of academic skepticism about RCTs in this

what those problems are.[1] In his recent book, Manski has some terrific stuff on RCTs, particularly on how many assumptions they implicitly make.[5][2] [The *randomistas*] like to argue that RCTs don't need assumptions but they're loaded with assumptions at least if you're going to use them for anything.

People tend to split the issues into internal and external validity.[6] There are a lot of problems with that distinction but it is a way of thinking about some of the issues. For instance, if you go back to the 1970s and 80s and you read what was written then, people thought quite hard about how you take the result from one experiment and how it would apply somewhere else. I see much too little of that in the development literature today. Maybe I'm missing something, but my reading of the J-PAL webpage makes me think that when they list estimates, they seem to suggest you can use them pretty much anywhere.

Which is pretty weird when you think about it. Causality can change locally too. Even if you've uncovered a causal effect that doesn't mean that causality will work that way somewhere else. It's not just the size of the effect.

TO: Taking this out of the development context, as you mentioned, RCTs have been done for a long time outside of a development context. There are these touchstone studies—the social policy experiments in the United States—that get referred to often. What is the difference there? Is there one?

AD: First there were hundreds of them and they still go on today. But I think that many of those studies were very high quality. I think those

---

era is discussed in the interview with Judy Gueron (chapter 5). She notes in her book that Heckman has since moderated his stance, but maintains many of the concerns Deaton notes in this interview. Of note, Heckman has contributed to RCTs on the impact of early childhood education.

5. See chapter 1 of *Public Policy in an Uncertain World*. Three fundamental assumptions that Manski details are (1) treatment response is individualistic and not dependent on the treatment received by others, (2) the distribution of outcomes in the treatment group is the same as the distribution of outcomes if everyone in a population received the treatment, and (3) long-term outcomes can be successfully inferred from the short-term outcomes necessarily measured in most experiments.

6. See interviews with Lant Pritchett (chapter 9) and Jonathan Morduch (chapter 4) for more specific discussion of issues of external validity and internal validity respectively.

people thought very hard about the strengths and limitations of RCTs, and that much of that seems to have been lost today, which is a pity.

For instance, in a newspaper story about economists' experiments that I read today, a reporter wrote that an RCT allows you to establish causality for sure. But that statement is absurd. There's a standard error, for a start, and there are lots of cases where it is hard to get the standard errors right. And even if we have causality, we need an argument that causality will work in the same way somewhere else, let alone in general.

I think we are in something of a mess on this right now. There's just a lot of stuff that's not right. There is this sort of belief in magic, that RCTs are attributed with properties that they do not possess. For example, RCTs are supposed to automatically guarantee balance between treatment and controls. And there is an almost routine confusion that RCTs are somehow reliable, or that unbiasedness implies reliability.

But this is a reinvention of statistics. Reliable is something to do with precision. And RCTs in and of themselves don't do anything about precision just by being RCTs. But when you read the literature, the applied literature, there are claims about precision that are often false. There's nothing, *nothing*, in an unbiased estimator that tells you about reliability. If you know what you're doing, you get a credible standard error, and that, of course, tells you something about precision. One of the first things one learns in statistics is that unbiasedness is something you might want, but it's not as important as being close to the truth.[7] So a lexicographic preference for randomized control trials—the "gold standard" argument—is sort of like saying we'll elevate unbiasedness over all other statistical considerations. Which you're taught in your first statistics course not to do. In the literature, and it happens in medicine too, people use this gold standard argument, and say we're only going to look at estimates that are randomized control trials, or at least prioritize them. We often find a randomized control trial with only a handful of observations in each arm and with enormous standard errors. But that's preferred to a potentially biased study that uses 100 million observations. That just makes no sense. Each study has to be considered on its own. RCTs are fine, but they are just one of the techniques in the armory that one would use to try to discover things. Gold standard thinking is magical thinking.

I think that right now the literature is claiming way too much for RCTs.

7. See the interview with Lant Pritchett (chapter 9) for additional discussion of whether RCTs or more potentially biased studies yield better estimates of impact in different contexts.

TO: Would it be accurate, then, to say that you have less of an issue with the method than the claims being made with and for the method?

AD: Yes. Except that sounds like the method's OK and it's just being misapplied. I suppose to some extent that's true. But it's not just misapplied, it's a belief that this method can do something which it can't, the replacement of statistics with magical thinking.

TO: Given the history of 40 or 50 years of people thinking hard about these issues of selection, identification, bias, and validity, why do you think the movement gained such traction in development when it did?

AD: That's a good question. There are certainly lots of problems with observational data.[8] I think people got very tired of dealing with them. I don't actually think those problems are avoidable; they have to be faced in one way or another, whatever method you use. But you can see why I think some of it is a youth over old age sort of idea. Here's a new tool, we can rethink the world with it.

I think the rhetoric was very enticing, though I don't think it delivers much. All this stuff about how policy makers can understand it, it's just the difference between two means and there is no room for controversy. But that is just a hope. A very good example is what's happened with the Kremer and Miguel Worms study.[3] That study was replicated in India in a paper by Miguel and Bobonis.[4] And that is enough to put it into practice through Deworm the World followed by Evidence Action to scale up deworming. But there's a 150 page Cochrane Review, which includes the Kremer Miguel study, which says there is no consistent or obvious effect.[5] I'm not a fan of the Cochrane Collaborations or of meta-analysis, and I have no special insight into this case, but it illustrates that RCTs don't eliminate controversy.[9]

Now I have no idea who's right and that is not what I am talking about here. But when you think about it for a minute, you may realize there might not *be* any right. What works in one place may not work in another place, especially for something as complicated as deworming when there are social interactions and it depends on the environment and on sanitation

8. Many of the interviews cite frustrations with observational data and instrumental variables as a major factor in the rise of RCTs. See, in particular, the interviews with Michael Kremer (chapter 1), Jonathan Morduch (chapter 4) and Lant Pritchett (chapter 9).
9. For a discussion of the controversy specifically and how it has affected some decisions about funding deworming, see the interview with Elie Hassenfeld (chapter 15).

and on whether kids wear shoes and on prevalence and all that sort of thing. Maybe the Cochrane Collaboration review is chasing something that doesn't exist. And I know that Michael and Ted[10] are contesting the Cochrane Collaboration's analysis.

But this is exactly the situation we were in before these sort of studies started. Different studies gave different results, and no one could really resolve the discrepancies. I think it's just a really good example that suggests that as we get more results, there ain't going to be a clean resolution in all cases because the results will sometimes be all over the place, even when they are correctly and precisely done. Discrepancies between studies have to do with much more than bias!

I think [RCT advocates] thought they were going to solve a problem, which I don't think is solvable. There is no magic bullet. That's the truth of it. It would be interesting to get some of the advocates to explain why they don't talk more about the stuff that was done in the 1960s and 70s, why that has not changed the world, and why it lost momentum, at least among academics.[11]

TO: Working on the US Financial Diaries, I've experienced some of the frustration in the trade-off between doing a project that's data and time intensive and one that's nationally representative.

AD: Wait a minute. Look at the US Census data or the American Community Survey, which I was working with this morning. I've got 20 million observations in those data sets. There's hundreds and hundreds of questions. I'm not sure why you make that trade-off.

I very much like the financial diaries work and I've learned a lot from them, and to me they are more useful than a series of randomized trials on the topic because they have lots of broadly useful information. I can make my own allowance for how selected they are and I'm not blinkered by the craziness that if it's not a randomized control trial I shouldn't pay any attention to it. Which I've heard more times than I can count.

10. Michael Kremer and Ted Miguel. For the response referred to, see: http://www.poverty-action.org/blog/cochrane%E2%80%99s-incomplete-and-misleading-summary-evidence-deworming. Note that the Cochrane authors respond in the comments. Kremer and Miguel, with others, have a more thorough response that takes into account research and publications since the original Cochrane review here: http://emiguel.econ.berkeley.edu/research/does-mass-deworming-affect-child-nutrition-meta-analysis-cost-effectiveness-and-statistical-power.

11. This issue is thoroughly discussed in Gueron and Rolston (2013), *Fighting for Reliable Evidence*. See particularly, note 2 of the chapter, "Coda: Random Assignment Takes Center Stage."

TO: There's a trade-off that's about cost ultimately.

AD: I'm not sure there is such a trade-off. Governments spend a lot of money on surveys; how expensive they are depends a lot on the questions you ask and how you ask them.

TO: But you can't add anything to something like the American Social Survey. Once you have those questions, it's impossible to learn anything different because of the bureaucracy involved to make any changes.

AD: It's not just bureaucracy. There are a 1,000 people who would like to add a question and it would get totally out of hand if you opened them up to changes. These surveys in the US, especially, if they're done by phone; it's very hard to keep people on the phone for more than about 20 minutes. So there are real constraints there. Those are much less severe in a place like India or Kenya though, especially if you're spending dollars and can benefit for the discrepancy between the PPP and the exchange rate.

TO: I guess I often feel discouraged because of those constraints, about getting answers ...

AD: Oh, but that's the beginning of wisdom. It's very hard to do science. If it was easy or there was a magic machine out there, we'd all be a lot wiser. It's just very very hard. Things like the financial diaries and extended case studies are enormously important. Most of the great ideas in the social sciences over the last 100 years came out of case studies like that. Because people are open to hearing things that they didn't necessarily plan, for one thing.

TO: Another of the common critiques of the RCT movement is a lack of a theory of policy change.[12]

AD: I think that's a very complicated thing. These things are slow often, but there is a big political element and there should be. Something I read the other day that I didn't know, David Greenberg and Mark Shroder, who have a book, *The Digest of Social Experiments*, claim that 75 percent of the experiments they looked at in 1999, of which there were hundreds, are experiments done by rich people on poor people. Since then, there have been many more experiments, relatively, launched in the developing world, so that percentage can only have gotten worse.[6] I find that very troubling.

12. See the interview with Lant Pritchett (chapter 9) for an articulation of this critique.

If the implicit theory of policy change underlying RCTs is paternalism, which is what I fear, I'm very much against it.

I think policy change very much depends on the context. I don't know if you've read Judy Gueron's book.[13][7] I learned a lot from that. What do these MDRC things do? They've gone on and on and continue to this day. Many academic economists were involved in the early days but much less since. But MDRC and Abt and Mathematica, and so on, have gone on doing these experiments for the federal government, state governments, and some in Canada. So I'm kind of curious about how they function in the policy space.

I don't think the results from these experiments have had much of an impact on academic knowledge, but that may be wrong. I don't know. I think what the experiments did was to settle disputes between competing political views. There would be a new administration and they would say, "these policies should all be abolished," or, "if we make people go to work before we give them any welfare that will cause them to earn their own incomes and it will reduce costs for the government," for example. The interesting thing is that in the US such arguments have to be costed by the CBO,[14] which actually has to estimate if the financial projections that come out of those proposed policy changes make any sense. When the Reagan people came in, they were not keen on doing any experiments at all, but when the CBO didn't agree with their estimates, they became supporters of experiments because they believed it would show that they were right. And sometimes indeed they were, at least as far as RCTs can tell.

Those experiments are mostly about what policy changes did to the budgets of state and federal authorities. They have a case load, and they often care less about the well-being of poor people than they care about the state budget. An RCT is good for that because it gives you the average cost and the average in that context is exactly what you want to know. It resolves the dispute. But that average is not generally useful elsewhere, at least without understanding the mechanisms. And MDRC wrestled with that problem of finding mechanisms from the very beginning, but they never resolved it. They thought that by going into the details, they could

13. The book is *Fighting for Reliable Evidence*, a look at the use of randomized experiments to evaluate social policy in the US. See the interview with Judy Gueron (chapter 5) for further discussion of many of the points Deaton raises.
14. The Congressional Budget Office. It's mandate includes forecasting the federal budget and how policy changes will affect future federal budgets.

find mechanisms that would generalize or transport, and they never managed to do that. You *can't* do that with RCTs. You've got to combine them with theory and observational data, so you're right back where you were.

But before you need a theory of policy change, you need a theory of transportability. Meaning, it works here, what arguments do you have that it works there? And it often seems that those running RCTs simply assume that these numbers will apply with little discussion of how to move the results from one location to another.

TO: Where do you think the development economics field needs to go from here?

AD: Economics is a very open profession. Young people who come along with bright ideas get a lot of attention, in comparison to a lot of academic fields that are dominated by old people. I think [the RCT movement] will likely fade in the same way that it faded 30 years ago and for much the same reasons. There will certainly be consulting houses that do RCTs for particular purposes, such as *ex post* fiducial evaluation. I think the academic interest will fade, as the problems are better understood, though I think that RCTs will have more of a place in the economist's toolbox than was true 20 years ago. And as with other methods, we will have a well-thought-out view of when and where they are useful. More tools are always welcome, as long as we don't think one of them is a magic tool, or that it is the only tool we need. People will go on doing RCTs along with other things too. There's a lot of competition out there, a lot of people thinking about development in lots of ways. I don't think any long-term solutions are going to come out of RCTs. We're certainly not going to abolish world poverty this way.

TO: Do you think there are promising leads in abolishing world poverty?

AD: From RCTs?

TO: From anywhere.

AD: I know what I think, which is that we should be thinking much more about politics than about micro-detailed studies. So I'm basically in the same boat as Daron Acemoglu and Jim Robinson.[15][8] I think, to a first

15. Daron Acemoglu and James Robinson have done a great deal of work on the quality of institutions, the origins of institutional quality, and how those institutions may affect economic development. They are particularly known for their distinction

approximation, it really is all about politics. And as I say in my book,[16] I think aid is making it worse, not better.[9] It's fine to say we discovered this marvelous new delivery system and here's how you should deliver aid. And it might make things better locally. You might save lives, you might get people educated, but you're not going to abolish world poverty because that has to do with politics, it's not to do with money. Certainly knowledge can help, but once again, it's a question of transportable knowledge. There's got to be some theory of how you can take it from one place to another and that requires theory and generalizations and structural models of some sort. They don't have to be intertemporal dynamic programs, the sort of thing that is thought these days to be structural modeling in economics. You have to think about why things are happening and you can't get that out of an RCT in and of itself.

TO: It seems to me somewhat ironic that the best-known RCT results are about microcredit's lack of impact. I think much of the philosophical appeal of RCTs is the hope that small local actions can matter. On the politics front, it's easy to feel that there's nothing to be done.

AD: Well, I'm not sure that's right. I think there are lots of things than can be done on the politics side. Not propping up dictatorships, for example. Or not encouraging them to come into existence by supporting governments that have no need to raise taxes. And as far as individuals doing things, I do believe in that too, very much so. But it has to be local. You can't get a team of people from MIT or NYU to fly in and set up a something-or-other, or to do an experiment in one place, and then hand it over to the World Bank for implementation somewhere else. It's certainly true that teams from MIT or NYU, or anywhere else, can help provide understanding of mechanisms. I always give the example that between France and the US they figured out that HIV was a sexually transmitted disease and how it worked. That's immensely valuable information for individuals all around the world and especially in east Africa and places where the epidemic has been really bad.

---

between inclusive and extractive (controlled by a small group that emphasizes maintaining power and extracting wealth for themselves) institutions. Their book *Why Nations Fail* provides a comprehensive overview of their work. See the interviews with Michael Kremer (chapter 1) and Tyler Cowen (chapter 19) for more discussion of these views.

16. Deaton's 2013 book *The Great Escape* is primarily about the very large gains in health and welfare experienced by parts of the world over the last 250 years, but he also argues that foreign aid contributes to extending global poverty rather than relieving it.

That's doing a lot. There are a lot of things like that we could be doing. We could stop selling arms to those countries. We're doing a lot of harm. When students come to me and ask me, "how should I help the poor of the world, should I go to Bangladesh, should I go to Africa?" And I say, "no, you should go to Washington. That's where you can do the most good." Of course, I don't mean for American poor people [laughs] but for poor people around the world.

Jonathan, a Professor of Public Policy and Economics at NYU-Wagner, is most known for his work on microfinance, which started at the urging of Jeffrey Sachs while Jonathan was pursuing his PhD in Economics at Harvard University. As Jonathan says, "when Sachs wants you to do something he can be very persuasive." Jonathan's study of microcredit and its impact led to one of the longest running controversies in impact evaluation, centered on one of the first studies of the impact of microcredit conducted by Mark Pitt and Shaidur Khandker using survey data from Grameen Bank in Bangladesh. Pitt and Khandker concluded that Grameen's borrowers were substantially better off, leading to a claim by Mohammed Yunus that 5 percent of the bank's clients escaped poverty every year. Beginning in 1998 and continuing through 2012, Jonathan (eventually with David Roodman) has publically challenged Pitt and Khandker's conclusion that microcredit was the cause of the observed benefits in the survey data, culminating in a paper that shows that in addition to methodological problems that undermine causal claims, the positive effects found in the original research were due to just a handful of outliers.

Jonathan's research on microfinance led to the founding of the Financial Access Initiative, a research center at New York University's Wagner School of Public Policy, which he directs. His book *The Economics of Microfinance*, co-written with Beatriz Armendariz de Aghion, is generally considered the go-to text in the field. But his 2010 book (with Daryl Collins, Stuart Rutherford, and Orlanda Ruthven) *Portfolios of the Poor* is probably his most influential work. *Portfolios of the Poor* is based on financial diaries—frequently collected surveys of household earning and spending.

Jonathan and I have worked closely together since 2012.

TO: A lot of your work has been on understanding what's really happening with microfinance, and making the case that RCTs were needed to really understand impact. And you've worked with many of the people most famous for conducting RCTs. But how many RCTs have you been directly involved in?

JM: Technically my first RCT was a lab experiment I conducted with Dean Karlan and Xavi Giné where we were trying to understand things like how group liability affected borrowers' willingness to take risk. But while that was a lab in the field, it wasn't really in the field the way most people think about RCTs involving real people making real choices in their daily lives. So in that sense, the first RCT I was directly involved in was just a few years ago, in South India.[1] The intervention aimed to help "ultra-poor" women, mainly divorced or widowed, get a new start in life by helping them start small businesses. It was hard work. We had data problems and ended up discarding the middle round of the survey. In the end, we found little net impact of the program, in sharp contrast to similar programs elsewhere.[1][2] It turned out that in South India, participants in the ultra-poor program didn't do better than people who found jobs in the labor market. My second RCT is underway now in Bangladesh, a look at mobile banking and migration. I've been on the edges of other RCTs, but those two are the ones I've helped lead.

So, in relative terms, I'm a child on the planet of randomizers. But I'm an old child. I was an assistant professor at Harvard when Michael Kremer was starting his first experiments in Kenya in the 1990s, and I saw the early fights for randomization up close.

As you say, I helped push things along in a small way. In 2006, when Dean Karlan, Sendhil Mullainathan, and I founded the Financial Access Initiative, we channeled much of a $5 million Gates Foundation grant to support infrastructure for doing an armful of early microfinance-related RCTs.

TO: I'm interested in that perspective from being there, shall we say, "when it all began." Especially in the question of why the RCT movement

1. This evaluation was of a program using the "Graduation Model" for addressing the needs of ultra-poor (that is, less than $1.25 a day) households. Originally developed by BRAC, the programs generally provide a package of services to households including transferring an asset (such as livestock) and offering livelihood training and income support. The graduation model has been tested using RCTs in more than six countries. Most of these trials found gains in income and assets that persisted after the end of the program. See the summary article in *Science* for complete information.

caught on when it did. What was happening in development economics conversations at that point and why did RCTs get traction?

JM: The obvious context is economists' obsession with causality. We're obsessed. And we should be. Situations in development are rife with possible biases, and they can greatly distort understanding. As a graduate student and assistant professor at Harvard, you watched every empirical paper presented be picked apart based on causal claims.[2]

An example is what I think you meant in the earlier question about my helping make the case for RCTs. After I had joined the faculty, Mark Pitt presented a paper on whether microcredit raises profits for poor borrowers in Bangladesh.[3][3] At the time, Muhammad Yunus, the founder of Grameen Bank, was telling stories of remarkable profits earned by microcredit customers. Economists tend to be skeptics, and the debate hinged on whether the profits arose because those villagers who sought microcredit started out being particularly entrepreneurial (and would have succeeded no matter what), or whether in fact the profits were due to microcredit. It turns out that Pitt found big effects using the methods available at the time. He built heavy statistical machinery to estimate the effects, and his machinery changed the story from what we saw with simpler methods. That triggered a debate that dragged on for nearly 20 years, involving building even more statistical machinery, and it still isn't clearly resolved![4][4] That's an extreme case, but the bigger point is that debates often got hung up on methodology, keeping us from getting to questions about what the facts meant.

2. See interviews with Michael Kremer (chapter 1) and Lant Pritchett (chapter 9) where they similarly argue that this dynamic played a large role in launching of the RCT movement.
3. This paper was the academic foundation for many of the marketing claims about microcredit not only by Grameen but by other MFIs and microfinance support organizations. The paper suggested that there was a substantial causal impact of microcredit on income and consumption, in stark contrast to the findings of RCTs of microcredit that have been conducted since.
4. Morduch first wrote a paper questioning the Pitt Khandker results. He was later joined by David Roodman, and the result was a back-and-forth series of papers, responses and replies, that lasted, as Morduch notes, for close to 20 years. For Morduch, the culmination was a 2014 paper with Roodman that asserts that the results in Pitt and Khandker are not reliable because, among other issues, the effect found is caused by a few wealthy borrowers. Pitt continues to disagree. An accessible overview can be found on David Roodman's blog: http://www.cgdev.org/blog/bimodality -wild-latest-pitt-khandker.

For empirical economists, the obsession with causality is the major marker of the tribe. And the obsession pre-dates randomized controlled trials by a long distance.

TO: You say that the Pitt Khandker paper is an extreme case. Is that because it was different than other work, or just because you, David Roodman, and Mark Pitt were willing to devote so much time to it? Were the debates about whether any particular claim to causality was valid coming up for every paper?

JM: Complain all you want about RCTs, but the previous methods were full of difficulties. Before RCTs, our main tool for nailing down causation involved instrumental variables. When I was in graduate school in the late 1980s, nearly everything about a typical empirical study rested on the plausibility of the instrumental variables in the paper.

An instrumental variable has to meet a particular set of standards. Take the microcredit example. Let's say you want to determine the impact of microcredit on the profits of borrowers. The instrumental variable you need would be something that can explain access to microcredit but that does not directly affect profits, except through the role it plays in spurring microcredit access. You can find many determinants of microcredit access. And you can find many variables that have no plausible independent effect on profits. But it's relatively rare to find variables that unequivocally satisfy both criteria.

The second requirement is the "exclusion restriction," and it's usually the killer. Forget using borrowers' education as an instrument; it has a clear potential independent effect on borrowers' profits. Forget using the lenders' location; it's likely to be endogenous. Forget age and gender, interest rates, and so on. So we were left with important questions, but few plausible instrumental variables. Mark Pitt and Shahid Khandker had a clever solution. They noticed a rule that restricted a microcredit institution from lending to villagers owning half an acre of land or more. The rule was meant to keep a focus on the poorest, and it proved to be the basis of a plausible empirical strategy. And it would have been plausible if the lenders had strictly followed the rule. Unfortunately, it turns out the lenders didn't—which was the start of our extended period of trench warfare.

But then things turned. We realized that even "plausible" instrumental variables weren't necessarily capable of delivering clear answers. That was staggering.

TO: I think that deserves a bit more explanation …

JM: Things started changing around the early 1990s. Before then, we usually assumed that impacts were the same for everyone in a sample. If microcredit increases profits so that 5 percent of customers can exit poverty each year, as Khandker extrapolated from his results with Pitt, we simply assumed that it was a general finding for everyone. The assumption was convenient, and in Pitt and Khandker's case, their estimating framework didn't work without it.

Few doing applied research thought much about the implications of those assumptions. Sometimes we looked at variation in impacts by education or income or some other dimension, but we assumed that, otherwise, impacts were identical. It was such a basic and common assumption that it was seldom even spelled out.

But in the 1990s, discomfort set in. Researchers became willing to consider situations where people—and the impacts on them—varied in ways that economists could neither model nor assume away. We had to embrace that some people in a population might have negative returns to microcredit, say, and some might have zero returns, and others might have large returns. The average impact was a mix of all these impacts.

That turned out to have radical implications, particularly for how we interpret results when estimating using instrumental variables. Guido Imbens and Joshua Angrist, influenced by Donald Rubin, the Harvard statistician, laid out the fundamentals of what came to known as Local Average Treatment Effects [LATE].[5] James Heckman was following similar lines at the University of Chicago. Charles Manski, too. It was a particularly exciting time at Harvard, with Gary Chamberlain, Imbens, and other economists engaging with statisticians, unified around the Rubin Causal Model.[5] That would, in turn, provide the intellectual foundation for RCTs.

Imbens and Angrist considered the world in which different people in a sample might experience different impacts. In other words, they considered the real world. Imbens and Angrist showed that using instrumental variables in the real world did not necessarily yield better estimates of the parameters we sought. What we usually sought—and what we thought we were getting—were average impacts for a population. Instead, by using instrumental variables, we ended up with estimates of *different* parameters. The work on LATE spelled out that the new parameters would be weighted

5. A framework for causal inference based on observational data developed by the statistician Donald Rubin.

averages that reflect parts of the sample whose treatment status was affected by variation in the instrument.

Take the Bangladesh microcredit example again. The rule that microcredit lenders couldn't lend to borrowers with over half an acre of land was the basis for a plausible instrumental variable. And what you get when you estimate using that instrumental variable is an impact of microcredit—but not one that gives an average for the whole sample. The weighted average instead picks up the impact on the part of the sample whose participation in microcredit changes, thanks to the rule. Here, the subsample most affected by the rule includes people who happen to own an amount of land just below half an acre. Thanks to the quirk of the rule, they're now able to participate while otherwise identical people above the line are not. By definition, this subsample owns more land than average.

Maybe the impacts on that subsample will be unusually big relative to the typical customer because the subsample has other advantages in addition to having more land. Or perhaps the impacts will be smaller if marginal returns to capital are greater for the poorest. Either way, you're no longer getting an average for the whole sample. Sometimes it's not clear what you're getting.

All of a sudden we had a different set of conversations. No longer was the focus just on the plausibility of the instrumental variable. Now the question also became: do we care about this new parameter? Sure, we can estimate it cleanly, but why does this thing—this particular weighted average of diverse impacts—matter? How is it interpreted? Maybe more important: do we even know what we're estimating?

In the case of the Pitt and Khandker study of microcredit in Bangladesh, their way of estimating was more complicated than a typical instrumental variables framework. It involved pages and pages of FORTRAN code. But it had the feel of an instrumental variables framework where, in essence, the instruments were multiple, created by interacting a series of household characteristics with variables that captured the eligibility rule. It's still not clear how to think about that in "local average" terms. It's unclear which part of the sample ended up being weighted most heavily in the estimated parameters.

That's just one example. Now we can look back at the entire empirical literature using instrumental variables and ask whether we were estimating what we had imagined. I'm not sure that the enormity of the LATE insights have been absorbed, even today. So the problem wasn't just whether a researcher's instrumental variables were plausible, or whether they passed certain statistical tests. The question was whether we knew what the estimation delivered, and how much we cared about it.

TO: That must have been very discouraging. I've sat in on plenty of these seminars and they often seem to be contests over who can find the cleverest—or bluntest—way to insult the presenter's intelligence. The grad students were already having to fight these battles over the validity of their instruments. Do you think escaping from that was a factor in the rise of RCTs?

JM: You can think of RCTs as creating a new kind of instrumental variable. Not one that you stumble across. You create it. Carefully and deliberately. That's the radical break. By randomizing access to an intervention, you create a mechanism that clearly drives exposure to the intervention and, most important, also satisfies the exclusion restriction. By construction, the randomization process doesn't directly affect outcomes. Randomization provides the golden ticket, the holy grail from an IV perspective. RCTs are a machine for creating credible instrumental variables.

But they're more than that. I'll start with an advantage—there are problems too. The RCT mechanism provides a way to respond to the LATE problem. Now researchers can deliberately determine the sample affected by the treatment. They know who is in that sample and what their characteristics are. With RCTs, we have a huge step forward in transparency and interpretation. Put aside the other statistical merits of randomization, the gain in understanding and interpreting what we estimate is huge in itself.

TO: But critics like Angus Deaton invoke LATE[6] to criticize RCTs.

JM: Exactly. Thinking in terms of LATE clarifies why RCTs are so compelling, and also clarifies why RCTs hit limits.

In the pre-RCT world, there was a big premium put on being clever. Could you think up and find an instrumental variable that might apply to a problem we care about? You also had to be enterprising, finding the right data sets. Sometimes, but not often, you'd collect your own data. The skills needed were mostly traditional research skills. We were mostly a bunch of nerds hunched over computer monitors.[7]

---

6. See the interview with Deaton for more discussion of his specific critiques of RCTs from a LATE perspective.
7. The theme of RCTs leading to development economists having more direct involvement in fieldwork and needing nontraditional skills, like working with NGOs, is echoed in many of the conversations. See, particularly, Kremer, Schoar, and Yang.

That changed dramatically. In the RCT world, there's a big premium put on being entrepreneurial. Being clever helps, of course, but it's no longer sufficient. To be successful, you have to be out in the world. You have to manage data collection because running RCTs also means that you have to collect your own data. And you have to work with implementing organizations, building relationships with the NGOs or businesses that are providing goods and services. Most NGOs and businesses don't want to randomize what they do, and you can't really blame them. So you have to find some that do, and you have to ensure that they follow the experimental protocols.

Researchers end up having to be opportunistic. If you want to study microcredit, you can't simply randomize the operations of Grameen Bank in Bangladesh. So far, they haven't been interested in randomizing. So, you look around. You get to know some other microcredit organization somewhere else, a small MFI with a different model and different target population, in, let's say, urban Dhaka. They agree to randomize their operations. Fantastic. You're in business.

The question then is akin to the LATE one: do we care about the RCT from urban Dhaka? Or, more precisely, how should we care? The MFI serves a very different population than Grameen, and does so with at least somewhat different methods. They have thousands of customers, not the 8 million served by Grameen. Would the Dhaka RCT give us any insight into traditional village-based microcredit with its focus on self-employed women?

There's an even more subtle way this plays out. An organization can't randomize their existing operations. It's too late. If they do randomize something, it would most likely have to be a randomization that determines which neighborhoods they expand into next.[8] But the organization started where it did for a reason, choosing spots where they thought they would be most effective. The hypothetical RCT can then only evaluate next-best sites. So the study wouldn't end up with an RCT that delivers the average impact of microcredit on its customers. It would end up with the marginal impact of microcredit expansion into particular neighborhoods at a certain point in that particular institution's history.

8. The other method for randomizing microcredit offers, used in the first published RCTs of microcredit by Karlan and Zinman, is to randomly approve borrowers who were narrowly excluded by some eligibility rule. However, this approach suffers from the same issue of evaluating the effect on "second-best" customers if you assume that the MFIs selected the best neighborhoods or best customers first.

This is the situation with all microcredit RCTs to date.[6] They have internal validity in the sense that the researchers obtain a clean estimate of something. That's a triumph. It's hugely important. But there remains a question about whether the "something" that we're obtaining is the main parameter of interest with respect to that lender. Usually the RCTs deliver a marginal impact on marginal customers. Perhaps that's exactly the right question for policy. If policy makers want to subsidize further expansion of a program, they want to know about the margins.

But if policy makers are considering replicating the entire program someplace else, they want to know the impact of the program as a whole. They don't really care much about the margins. Impacts on infra-marginal borrowers are especially important, and the typical RCT can't deliver them. This kind of tension, I think, is part of what colors Angus's view, or at least his feeling that the tension isn't acknowledged.

The bottom line is that there's still often a "LATE-like" dilemma when interpreting RCTs. It no longer stems from the peculiarities of the weighted averages that we estimate. Now it stems from the peculiarities of the experiments that are possible to deploy in practice. That hinges on the partner organizations and circumstances that present themselves. If researchers weren't opportunistic, we wouldn't make progress nearly as quickly. The flip side is that we sometimes do end up like drunks under streetlights.

The good news—and it's very good news—is that often RCTs deliver the parameters we seek. Or, at least, we can end up finding parameters that are interesting on their own terms. Sometimes the keys turn out to be under streetlights!

TO: That provides an entry into discussing external validity. How do we generalize from one place to somewhere else? Hunt Allcott and Sendhil Mullainathan have a paper about the use of RCTs and external validity that raises questions about the ability to use RCT results, even with replications, to predict outcomes in other areas. At the end of that paper they take a look at microfinance institutions that have participated in RCTs versus the universe of institutions in the MIX Market database.[7] They found that the MFIs participating in these evaluations are systematically different than the group that's in the MIX Market. But you've done some research that shows the MIX Market is not representative of the actual range of MFIs, so we're doubly removed from the "average" MFI.

JM: Our evidence suggests that even the participating institutions in the MIX Market are themselves a special group.[8] It used to be there would be microfinance debates, and a certain group of people, often the more commercially minded, who had worked largely in Latin America, would make arguments based on financial and administrative data. Then another group, often more socially minded, often working in South Asia, would make arguments based on ethnography and social data. What's interesting now is that we have big global databases like the MIX Market that collect data from Eastern Europe, Latin America and Africa, and different parts of Asia. They serve as the benchmarks by which donors and institutions judge progress.

But one of the things we saw, and this is work with Jonathan Bauchet, was that the data in these databases are also very self-selected. Not every institution wants to subject their data to public viewing. What we saw with the MIX Market is that participating microfinance institutions tended to be more heavily from Latin America and Eastern Europe and less focused on the poorest. They're more commercial, and probably more profitable. A self-reported database is always going to be a sliver of the universe. Hunt and Sendhil show that the universe of microcredit institutions subjected to RCTs is not representative of the sample collected by the MIX Market. It's worth considering whether those institutions studied with RCTs might then be closer to the broader aggregate. I haven't looked at it, and I don't believe they have.

There are many dimensions of difference that could matter. A while ago I talked about doing an RCT with an institution in Haiti. The lender's customers live far apart, and randomization was going to impose high costs. They balked, understandably, so we focused on other places instead. Generally, the institutions most willing to run RCTs are bigger institutions that have bureaucratic capacity. Sometimes, though, the opposite is true: sometimes smaller institutions are more nimble and more amenable to research. Either way, the institutions being studied are not a random sample of relevant institutions.

Frankly, though, it's an odd idea that external validity requires studying a random sample of relevant institutions. What's needed for a thoughtful mapping is an understanding of how institutions are unique or different in important ways, not necessarily a bias toward institutions that are "typical."

TO: Continuing with external validity, it seems that the incentives for academic research don't lend themselves to asking the same questions over time in lots of different contexts. Getting to publication means having new and novel ways to ask new and novel questions.

JM: There's a disconnection between what researchers feel is important to do and what policy makers feel is important to know and what journals are ready to publish. Researchers have incentives to be the first one out of the block with a great, new study. And as Dean Karlan has said, they also have the incentive to write a paper that pulls together lots of studies. But the incentive to do the second study and the third and fourth, fifth, and sixth replication just isn't there. It's a problem, and Dean and others have been trying to focus on it. I'm not sure how successful the project is in general, but they should get credit for focusing on the need for replication.

It's harder than that, though, because even if you did 10 studies, you're in 10 contexts. The question is: can you generalize? can you say more than "context matters"?

One big problem is that there are disincentives to be specific about your context and highlight how odd or unusual it is. If you write a great paper, it's tempting to present it as being as general as possible. You may have a clever study based in Kenya, and you might not even put Kenya in the title. You might mention Kenya in the abstract. But certainly as you talk about the results, you talk about them as fairly universal findings. Different authors are more or less specific, but there are certainly incentives to play down uniqueness.

That's a problem because in fact all results are specific and conditional to the context. Or at least that would be a reasonable starting point. Perhaps worse is that most papers lack the tables, the data, the evidence that will allow other researchers to do the mapping from one specific context to another.

Here's an example from a paper that I really like: a smart paper in the journal *Science* by Dean Karlan and Jon Zinman, based on a sample in the Philippines.[9] But you really have to dig into that paper to see just how specific the context is. They frame the paper around the hypothesis that microfinance is an answer to the problem of poverty and suggest that their work can be seen as informing that conversation. But once you dig into that paper, you see that they're working in an interesting site, but it's not a site with a lot of poor people in it. In fact most of the customers are quite well educated, they have high school or even college educations. The paper is valuable, but not because it answers questions about microfinance and poverty.

I don't think that that's because Dean and Jon wanted to distort their findings. I think it's because the editors of journals are relatively uninterested in the details of populations. In the end, the journals are doing a disservice to broader knowledge. Those details—those particularities—are essential to the scientific work of theory-building. They're essential to answering the fundamental question: "yes, it worked there, but will it work here?"

TO: So where does that leave us when it comes to external validity? Is it possible to learn anything generalizable?

JM: There are ways in which the concern with external validity is too strongly put, and ways in which the concern barely grazes the surface of the problem.

The concern with external validity is too strong in the sense that empirical work is not just about nailing down particular point estimates. It's often most valuable as a contribution to theory-building—in the broadest sense of "theory." Empirical work helps us identify theoretically relevant puzzles that have deeper consequences.

Think of the series of papers by de Mel, McKenzie, and Woodruff.[10] They measure returns to capital in small businesses affected by the 2004 Tsunami that devastated coastal Sri Lanka. They focus on four hundred small businesses in three hard-hit districts. They randomize the size and type of transfers to the businesses. It turned out that the businesses did well on average. The average return to capital was about 5 percent a month, or 60 percent a year. Much higher than the prevailing cost of capital, which was about 25 percent.

The evidence, on the face of it, suggests a huge potential for microcredit in populations like that. That's striking. The fact that microcredit RCTs have *not* shown huge average returns becomes all the more puzzling—and we're pushed to think harder about why the pieces of evidence don't line up with each other. Having a clean estimate of returns to capital is key, even if it's from a time and place that are unusual.

But they also find that the average returns to capital were nearly entirely attributable to businesses run by men. Businesses run by women had returns that were close to zero on average, and half were negative. That finding flew in the face of expectations, and in the face of rhetoric about microfinance and the opportunities it creates for women.

The results already force us to think harder about basic economic mechanisms. Why do women on the southern tip of Sri Lanka start small businesses if the observed returns are so small? Are there important unobserved returns? How do men and women cooperate and compete within families?

What kinds of market failures operate alongside capital market failures? The fact that the studies arise from a tragedy in Sri Lanka is a minor part of the story. The major part is that the evidence describes puzzles that enrich the fundamental questions we ask about capital, business, and families. And those questions can travel.

TO: It seems to me that a lot of the criticisms you see about RCTs are valid but they're equally valid about any kind of approach. External validity is a question no matter what methodology you use, for instance. So what do you think are the real limitations of RCTs and the valid criticisms of the use of RCTs?

JM: This is the big question when it comes to RCTs as a guide to policy—as opposed to as a guide to thinking and theorizing.

In thinking about policy here, we move to the traditional world of public policy analysis. It's a fairly mechanical world in which costs of interventions are toted up and then compared with benefits. It's often a difficult exercise but not always a particularly interesting one. But this is where J-PAL, IPA, and related organizations have staked their claim to relevance.

In a way, it's odd, since the best studies generated by researchers affiliated with those organizations are vital and important because they highlight theoretically interesting mechanisms and puzzles. The organizations as a group have had much less success in identifying truly generalizable results in a traditional public policy mode.

TO: Why do you think that is? What are the barriers to turning evidence from field experiments into policy prescriptions that get adopted?

JM: It goes back to the conversation about LATE, and about whether we have the information to piece together the bigger picture about how policy levers affect policy outcomes. The LATE-like issues seem more germane to RCTs than other methods.

In the microcredit example we were just discussing, I talked about how the microcredit RCTs give insight into marginal impacts, not infra-marginal impacts. That's the "LATE-like" part. Maybe policy makers care most about marginal impacts. That would be the case if policy questions hinge on the value of expanding existing operations. Then we're doing well, and the new RCTs should drive conversations.

But if policy concerns infra-marginal impacts, what do we do? We need different kinds of data if the relevant question is "should we keep supporting the core activities of existing microfinance institutions around the world?"

versus "should we subsidize additional expansion of microcredit?" In the former case, finding answers requires different methods. If we had a way to map from marginal impacts to infra-marginal impacts, perhaps RCTs could inform that conversation, but that's not on the RCT agenda. Marginal impacts are not irrelevant, but they're not the same as infra-marginal impacts. Instead, the marginal versus infra-marginal distinction is glossed over, leaving policy makers in the dark, perhaps only fuzzily aware of what the numbers from RCTs really represent. It's strange to be so rigorous when estimating and so much less so when communicating.

But that's just one angle on external validity. The other questions are generic, about connecting evidence from one place to action in another place. As we discussed a few minutes ago, a helpful step would be to turn current practice upside-down, and have authors go out of their way to underscore the particular natures of their sites. I'm not optimistic about it happening, though. I'm guilty of not doing that as carefully as I should, and I'm far from alone. The incentives push toward generalization.

The other issue is embracing the full scope of external validity issues. We often assume that the problem is mainly that populations are different. Others, like Nancy Cartwright,[9] the LSE philosopher, put the finger on differences in supporting institutions and infrastructure.

TO: Wouldn't differences like that be caught in replications? The six impact studies of microcredit were done with different MFIs in very different places and contexts, and the ultra-poor programs worked with different providers in different countries.

JM: Not really. Because the studies aren't necessarily designed to uncover whether there was variation and what exactly that variation was, much less cleanly identify which factors were more or less important. Let me give you an example. Working in South India on the evaluation of the ultra-poor program in Andhra Pradesh helped me see a third issue that relates to the ability to generalize. The issue hinges on differences in access to markets that provide alternatives to interventions. In this case the results surprised us. The program had great potential. The program transferred an asset, training, and financial tools to ultra-poor women, helping them create new livelihoods. The Ford Foundation and CGAP had placed a bet on replicating the intervention in sites around the world, based on success stories from BRAC.

9. See Nancy Cartwright's book with Jeremy Hardie, *Evidence Based Policy: A Practical Guide to Doing It Better.*

The qualitative evidence from our site suggested that it was a good program. Women who were using it really liked it, and were engaged by it. And yet relative to a control group, the treatment group didn't do better. That was the big surprise. It turned out that participants in the program could be totally happy and do well with it. But they had to then reduce other things that they were doing in order to free up time to participate. Most important, they weren't doing so much agricultural labor, which was an important source of income in the region. And many dropped out of the program in order to join the labor force. So the survivors were happy, but the average impact on income was indistinguishable from zero.

That result is different, though, from a complete failure. We saw that the program worked fairly well in the sense that it provided resources and opportunities for a group of women, and they used those resources to create new livelihoods. It wasn't perfect, but it worked decently well. The zero net impact reflected that the population had other options besides the program. In another time and place—where alternative options are less appealing—the program may well have had a positive net impact. And it has seemed to, in other locations.[10]

It turns out that there's a parallel phenomenon noted by James Heckman and his collaborators in their work on the US Job Training Partnership Act,[11] but the ideas haven't really penetrated conversations on external validity.[11] My sense is that these issues come up more commonly, and more naturally, in poorer economies.

The RCT element mattered for us because it got us to a result—the zero net impact—that was sharp and clear and forced us to think harder and understand better. You're not going to get there with a method that's less credible, or that's designed to give you the answer you expected in the first place.

10. As noted earlier there are multiple evaluations of the ultra-poor program, most of which found substantial positive and sustained impact. See Banerjee et al. (2015).

11. The US Job Training Partnership was one of the largest job training programs in the US until the mid-1990s. A randomized trial, the National JTPA Study, found zero or negative effects from participation. Heckman and co-authors point out that there were very similar, sometimes identical, alternatives available to participants in the study (both in the treatment and control arms). As a result the study was measuring the effect of the particular program, not of training versus no training, and the results say little about other contexts where different, or no, alternative programs were available.

So your original question was about criticisms of RCTs. You make a good point that the kind of criticisms that RCTs are subject to are happening partly because people are now focusing on evaluation in a serious way for the first time. So general criticisms about evaluation get attached to RCTs, when in fact they're much more general criticisms. True. But RCTs don't escape the criticisms either.

TO: Let's return to what we know about microfinance. David McKenzie and Berk Ozler at the World Bank once did a survey of graduate students and assistant professors in economics asking them about what they thought was interesting and what wasn't. One of the things that came back in the survey was that microfinance was the most overstudied problem or issue in development.[12] It seems there's another aspect there of the incentives to academics about what to study that limits what we ever learn about development, at least through academics.

JM: One reason microfinance seems so overstudied is that for a very long time it was understudied. When Beatriz Armendariz and I wrote the first version of *The Economics of Microfinance*,[13] we had to look hard for good empirical studies. By the time we wrote the second edition five years later, there was so much to write about. So there's been a real explosion of research, and it's nice to see it. But much of that work is simply making up for lost time.

There's something else going on. Microfinance as an intervention is very amenable to research—and to RCTs in particular. There are contracts to fiddle with, prices to vary, rules to change. The players are fairly commercially oriented, so they're interested in understanding how to tweak their products and increase take-up. It's a really nice laboratory for looking at a whole series of economic questions that are interesting even outside the microfinance sector. Microfinance work, for example, looks at the diffusion of ideas, the roots of gender biases, and the role of human capital.

TO: So what have the various RCTs of microfinance achieved?

JM: The RCTs showed that some of the most widely made claims about microfinance were overblown. Microcredit was positioned beautifully to be attacked by academics wielding RCTs.[12] The advocates' claims for

12. See the interview with Lant Pritchett (chapter 9) where he discusses how this creates tension between researchers and practitioners, ultimately undermining the role of impact evaluation in policy and practice.

microcredit impact were measurable and bold. The microcredit intervention was simple and contained, and the decentralized nature of implementation made microcredit relatively easy to randomize.

Microcredit advocates led by Muhammad Yunus had predicted that poverty rates could be slashed simply by making small loans available to microscale entrepreneurs. The claims were both enticing and specific.

The randomized studies challenged those claims clearly and consistently. Studies in places as different as Morocco, Bosnia, the Philippines, Mexico, and urban India showed that access to microcredit had no average impact on household income and only one showed an average increase—two showed a decrease—in consumption. True, it was a marginal impact—an effect of microcredit expansion. Still, it shot down the advocates' claims with methods that were easy to explain and difficult to impeach.

But the randomized studies weren't the first to carry the message that average impacts are small or zero, and they weren't the first to use novel methods to create credible control groups. Brett Coleman's work in Thailand, for example, has been largely ignored in the rush to discuss RCTs.[14] Without using an RCT, he showed how treatment and control groups mattered—and how the right comparisons eliminated positive estimated impacts. But the RCTs have a special power—a rhetorical power as much as anything else—that previous studies lacked. And it doesn't hurt that many of the authors have academic star power.

Where does that get us? Not as far as I hoped. Yunus had made claims that most development economists had never really taken very seriously. His claims about poverty reduction were too bold, and we knew enough about selection bias to discount the wild microcredit success stories and the raft of studies with dicey control groups. We already had studies like Brett Coleman's. In that sense the randomized studies very helpfully cleared away claims that weren't very credible to start with—or at least that weren't very credible among academic economists. That's no small feat, but neither is it a huge leap forward.

The real risk is that it's too easy for the conversation to stop there. It shouldn't. Yes, advocates made overly bold claims. And, yes, RCTs effectively shot them down. But it's a mistake—of logic and of economics—to then conclude that microcredit should be dismissed outright. The researchers involved are careful not to do that, and they deserve credit for writing thoughtfully. Not everyone has been so thoughtful though.

What the randomized studies didn't do was to give much insight into the remaining puzzle: why do people nonetheless keep borrowing from microcredit institutions, year after year? They didn't give a sense of alternative motivations for borrowers. If the central goal of borrowing isn't to increase business profits as Yunus claimed, what is it? Here, other methods—including ethnography and financial diaries—have been fruitful. Observational studies show how households often use microcredit to manage liquidity rather than to fund businesses directly. Households are using microcredit as a basic household financial management tool.[15] Is that likely to be life-changing for borrowers? No. Is it likely to be highly valued? Evidence suggests that it might be.

We remain ignorant about the broad impact of microcredit because we still have little handle on the true impact of household financial management and of consumption smoothing. The impacts may be psychological (reduced stress, a greater feeling of control) as much as material.

One reason that they haven't been a focus of the first RCTs is that these questions won't be as easy to evaluate as the clear, bold claims of escape from poverty. Facilitating household financial management may be a huge help, but it won't necessarily reduce stress. And it won't necessarily lead to smoother consumption streams if households respond to improved financial access by taking on more risk and volatility or by buying more durables. This set of dynamics is testable with an RCT, but it hasn't been, and interpretation of results needs to be careful.

TO: Should I interpret that to mean that we don't know what's going on with microcredit?

JM: We certainly don't know yet. But we are learning more, especially from studies that focus on understanding contracts and processes, not just net impacts. Erica Field and Rohini Pande, for example, have done imaginative work on loan structures.[16] And a few years ago, Dean Karlan and I reviewed a broad range of studies of prices and contracts, many of them randomized.[17]

The rhetoric around improving people's livelihoods is very powerful. Microfinance builds on this idea, and it still excites many people. The idea that small amounts of money can make huge differences in people's lives remains compelling. It's even more compelling when it links to the notion of helping people to take care of themselves.

But when we look back at it, we'll see that we were too enamored with a chain of logic that made a lot of sense to us but that wasn't deeply rooted in understandings of poor families and their needs. There are many reasons people look for financial access. Improving livelihoods is only one of them.

TO: In that regard there's still a lot of debate and dissent about how people are using credit when they get it. Not just the question about a general household benefit, but what are they using credit for? The idea that microcredit would be—and must be—used for microenterprise arose from concern that people would use loans for consumption and end up in a debt trap. Isn't that a very important piece for us to understand—what the borrowers are doing with credit if we want to understand what the right product mix is and how to have a positive impact?

JM: It is an important question, but the way to answer it is not through impact studies. Even without impact studies we've made some progress on that particular question: what are people doing with credit? What we found is very much at variance with what the pioneers had suggested.

What we're seeing is that much of the time, people are taking credit only partly to fund businesses. They're often using credit for consumption needs: they're using it to pay for school fees, to pay for healthcare, to pay off other debts that are more expensive. This doesn't come from impact studies but from traditional surveys.[18] The evidence highlights that we're intellectually trapped by the idea that consumption loans are necessarily a problem. We're trapped by the idea that the only good loan is one to support business.

We need to be more nuanced. Heaping more credit on households that are effectively insolvent just makes things worse. We've seen overlending become a problem in a wide range of places—in India, Bolivia, Bosnia, and, of course, here in the US.

But providing consumer finance to households facing liquidity crises can be powerful. Consumption loans can be helpful in the same way that having an ATM or having a credit card is very helpful—and sometimes even critical—for you and me. The question when it comes to debt traps is: is there a line at which consumption loans become a problem? And can we adequately distinguish between who's insolvent and who's illiquid?

This matters because it is essential to pushing the frontiers of financial markets. The largest underserved population on the planet is workers who seek basic financial tools, including consumption credit. This is the biggest part of the 2.5 billion adults who lack basic financial services.[19] Most don't want or need business loans.

TO: My sense is that, in general, one of the reasons economists haven't focused so much on well-being is that it's hard to objectively measure. People's feelings about their lives can vary pretty dramatically. How do you objectively measure it over time? When you start to think about financial access and well-being, what are the measures that we can use to understand whether we're having an impact? Will those be randomized trials?

JM: To give credit where it's due: economists are doing much better at collecting qualitative measures of well-being. It's no longer unusual to ask in a survey: "how do you feel today? on a scale of one to ten, how happy are you? how would you rate your emotional and mental health?"

Where we fall down is that we're still often asking these questions in big, one-time surveys. We don't usually get to know households well. That means we have a hard time making sense of the qualitative data we collect. We can note that the average level of happiness was X, but we don't have much of a story around that.

By the same argument, we're limited in the kinds of *quantitative* data we collect, and that may be an even bigger constraint for economists. Because so little of our data is high frequency (where researchers re-visit households monthly or more), we can't say much about volatility and the month-to-month ups and downs in people's lives. How exposed are people to big shocks? how well are they equipped to cope with downturns? what triggered a crisis? or an escape from crisis?

What we need is more data from more than one point in time, and we may need to focus on smaller samples to be able to do justice to the data. We need data from many years, or many months, or many harvests, rather than a one-time question on "how big is your income today?" or "how happy are you right now?"

TO: When you're thinking about your research and the methods you use, how do you think about it? Is it opportunistic? How do you think about the various forms of evidence and how do you choose what approach, say financial diaries,[13] you take to gathering evidence?

13. This is an approach pioneered by Daryl Collins and Stuart Rutherford to gather high-frequency data on household finances by conducting frequent interviews over a series of weeks or months, and asking very detailed questions about income, expenses and use of formal and informal tools. See *Portfolios of the Poor* for more discussion of the process and use of financial diaries.

JM: As I go through projects, it's a mix. I'm as opportunistic as the next researcher. But typically, I'm driven by a set of questions I want to answer. You mentioned financial diaries. I wasn't involved in the on-the-ground work done by Stuart Rutherford, Daryl Collins and Orlanda Ruthven which appears in *Portfolios of the Poor*,[20] but we're now interpreting data gathered from the US Financial Diaries. And I do think those kinds of methods, which can provide rich descriptions of household choices, can shape conversations and change assumptions in ways that RCTs can't. They're complementary.

It's also helpful to remember that one of the great papers by Esther Duflo and Abhijit Banerjee, "The Economic Lives of the Poor,"[21] was not an RCT. Instead, they look at household surveys to see what people spend their money on and how they use their time. It couldn't be more straightforward, but it was something people hadn't seen together in one place before. That was a very powerful piece. I like to think of *Portfolios of the Poor* in that same vein. We need more basic facts that are put into conversation with theory—with an eye to anomalies and gaps in knowledge.

RCTs sometimes play that role. But there are other empirical approaches that can play that role even better.

TO: What does it take to change your mind? What does it take to revise your priors?

JM: I tend to think like a Bayesian. I expect most economists do. I have some sense of how the world works, whether it's right or wrong, and with every paper I read, I think, "maybe I got that wrong. I should shift a bit."

TO: How do you think about changing other people's minds? What's your theory of change? When you think about the work that you do and why you do it, how do you think about changing the world?

JM: There are many ways. I tend to come back to two modes. One is by clarifying trade-offs, and laying out what's at stake in a decision. I've spent years counting up microcredit subsidies toward that end. The second thing is clarifying puzzles, or more specifically by clarifying that there is a puzzle. Often the problem is not that people can't agree on how to solve a puzzle but that they don't define the puzzle in the same way.

As researchers, the most precious thing that we have is our credibility. We need to be rigorous and call the shots as we see them. That's important because in the policy world, in the social investment world, in the microfinance world, so many of the voices are coming from advocates of one position or another. Even the donors who are ostensibly technocratic often turn out to be advocates for their investments. It's not that academics are apolitical, but they have a greater chance of calling things as they are. As academics enter the policy world through their promotion of RCT-based findings, it's even more important to be careful not to lose that.

The tension is that when you say critical things about popular ideas or smart people who are doing hard things, it's tough. But I'd like to think that even the work I do that's critical is in the end opening up conversations about how to do things in a better way. Or helping people reassess assumptions that then make space for more creative ideas. And I think about *Portfolios of the Poor* very much in that way. It was meant to be a constructive book. But in the course of writing that book, we had to be critical of fundamental assumptions about how microcredit works, taking apart the core idea that credit is mainly used for small businesses and enterprises.

5   Judy Gueron

Judy is the president emerita of MDRC, a nonprofit research organization that specializes in conducting RCTs in the United States. In her time as research director and then president of the organization for nearly 20 years, she directed many of the largest federal and state program evaluations, using randomized designs. She is also past president of the Association for Public Policy Analysis and Management and is currently a board member of the National Bureau of Economic Research. Judy is co-author of *From Welfare to Work* and *Fighting for Reliable Evidence*.

TO: You write in your book, "This does not mean the findings determined policy. They did not, nor should they."[1] Why should RCTs not determine policy? And if they don't determine policy, what is the role for randomized evaluations in policy formation?

JG: They should not determine policy because ultimately policy decisions are based on values and politics. Experiments get answers to specific cause and effect questions. But policy makers may have very different goals. They can look at the experiment and say, for example, "The program helped children, but I'm interested in saving money and reducing welfare spending. Did it achieve that?" They will decide what initiative they want to take based on their weighing of the goals. And that goes way beyond the research. I don't think experiments themselves chart the policy decision. As a matter of fact they, if well designed, should inform the multitude of goals that policy makers might have and then let them weigh which of those they want to give primacy to. Different policy makers, and in the US case, different states, will give different primacy to different goals and therefore reach different conclusions from the same study. Let's hope a study informs that decision. But it won't determine it.

TO: Does that process qualify for the term "evidence-based policy"? Is all that's required that there be some evidence used in making those trade-offs?

JG: Absolutely. In the cases I write about in the book the evidence played an unusually large role in shaping attitudes, shaping legislation, and shaping practice. It did play an important role, but what I argue is no one says research is going to determine policy. I can't imagine it would or should. I want to make clear that for evidence to matter, it has to be a certain kind of evidence. To pay attention to evidence, you have to at the very beginning of the study make sure it meets certain conditions.

For evidence to make a difference, you have to start off by addressing an important issue and testing a policy choice that the relevant actors will find both realistic—they can implement it, and it has reasonable cost—and compelling politically.[1] If you haven't done that, then just getting evidence won't necessarily have any effect because it's just not relevant to the current debate.

A second thing is, and this where experiments come in, it has to be reliable. If it's a cause and effect study, RCTs are unusually reliable. But it's not just one RCT. I say it over and over again: it's multiple studies in varied conditions, including real world conditions, that make experiments and evidence particularly persuasive. One RCT done here and another one done there doesn't compel action.

A third condition is timeliness. That means that up front you've got to have a good judgment about the policy context. Finally I think communication, and how you communicate results, is very important. Researchers have a much better chance of having their results taken seriously the farther they step away from becoming advocates of policy and become, rather, informers of policy. In the whole 40-year welfare research saga, people were busy actively communicating the findings but not advocating for a particular policy outcome. And that goes back to your initial question. The research itself doesn't suggest one policy option. You could look at the same results and say, "that's not a big enough change, I'm not going to implement that," or, "gee, this is cost effective. I'll do it." And that's a political judgment, not a research judgment.

1. This is a key component of Pritchett's critique of the current RCT movement internationally: the process does not generate realistic policy options because it is not built on a theory or model of policy change. See the interview with Pritchett (chapter 9) for more discussion.

TO: There's something of a difference there in the nature of what has happened in development economics and what happened in the US. The experiments in the US seem to have been bound up with a government agency implementing a policy, whereas many of the experiments on the development side tend to be an experiment on particular interventions like the impact of microcredit. The point that you make about communication is one I really want to delve into. Where exactly is that line of, for example, saying the negative income tax structure[2] doesn't move people toward work without saying, "we shouldn't structure policies this way."

JG: Researchers play the most useful role if they are not advocates of a policy but informers. Tell people about the trade-offs. What you get for this, what you get for that. If you go down this policy route, you can get this kind of, or size of, effect. The ideal role of the researcher is elucidating the trade-offs but not advocating for a particular goal, and therefore not for a particular strategy.

Let me be a little clearer. In the welfare reform area there's a choice between whether you care most about reducing poverty or reducing dependency. Those are two very different goals and different policies are more or less successful at accomplishing those goals. Different people care about each of those goals. That's not a research question. That's a political preference, and the research definitely can inform it, but which of those goals you give primacy to depends on your values, not on the research.

I think it's very important in communicating research not to come across as an advocate of a particular policy because, if you do, you risk being treated as just another advocate. And then you risk getting tuned out. There's lots of advocates out there, and you're just more noise rather than bringing science to the debate.

TO: On the development side there is a critique that the advocates of RCTs have no theory of policy change.[3] Further there are statements that RCTs, or evidence in general, doesn't affect policy makers other than the ones who thought they wanted to do something anyway. In your book, I didn't see much of a contest between methodologies or even between this evidence and that evidence. It was more a case of, "this is the evidence

---

2. The negative income tax was a policy proposed in the 1960s that would blend traditional welfare payments with the tax system by guaranteeing a basic income and smoothly phasing out assistance as earned income increased. Gueron discusses the history of the NIT in chapter 1 of her book.
3. See Pritchett (chapter 9) interview for a thorough discussion.

we have," and therefore it seemed to have a great deal of influence. Am I reading that right?

JG: The RCTs really beat the competitors. There was no debate among experts about whether to believe the results. They were believed. The question was, "what is the policy implication?" There just was not a debate over whether these were the right numbers. It was very clear that the experiments were well designed; they were well implemented, they were large enough, and they were in diverse enough conditions to be rendered credible. So there wasn't that kind of conflict.

But the research certainly *did* change people's minds, and not only the RCT evidence but some of the ancillary or complementary evidence from the process or other research implemented with the RCTs. For example, I talk in the book about the controversy about workfare, making people work for their benefits. When Reagan proposed it, some people called it "slavefare." There were people very opposed to that. But the research that showed welfare recipients didn't mind working and didn't object to the policy themselves really changed minds among Democrats who had been against this policy. The research made work requirements a much more palatable part of welfare reform. That's not an RCT result, but it was a complementary piece of research implemented with the RCT.

Another piece of evidence that really changed people's minds were the cost–benefit results. When you found out that certain policy choices actually saved money, some of that input came from the RCT but the cost data put together with it is what had such a powerful influence. From looking at the research, you both found out that people didn't object and found out the policy was cost effective.

TO: What's your perception of the impact of academic battles about econometric and experimental methodologies in the use of and believability of the RCTs? In the 1970s, for instance, you had James Heckman essentially saying you don't need to do this. There are econometric approaches that are just as good and much cheaper. Was the academic opposition bleeding into the policy debates or were those separate realms?

JG: The academic opposition was brutal. It made things very difficult. The saving grace was that in the political environment in which we functioned, people never read that academic literature. We pretended there was an academic consensus when there really was none. We just overrode it and charged forward because it was paralyzing otherwise. We believed that the econometricians wouldn't solve the selection problem and that RCTs did. So we just kept going and eventually that's the conclusion the academic community reached. But during those intermediate years it was tough going. That's why I give such credit to the National Academy study in 1985.[4][2] We clung to that. It by no means represented a consensus but it had an imprimatur from the National Academy. And at that same time the Department of Labor also looked back at a $50 million study of the CETA program[5] and concluded that there wasn't a number they could give to Congress unless it came from an RCT. We clung to that to help the states that we could convince to go in this direction understand that they weren't doing something foolish, and there wasn't a cheaper way to get a reliable answer to their questions. Certainly, had they turned elsewhere, they would have heard contrary advice.

TO: Education policy is a place where there's still considerable debate. You still hear lots of people complaining about "experimenting on my child" when it comes to randomized evaluations of education. What is your sense of why education as a policy domain is so different? There were some similar concerns early on in the welfare experiments, but they went away fairly quickly.

JG: Part of that is the power of middle class parents versus poor people. When you're deciding how to structure welfare programs, there's more of a legitimacy in asking for results, whereas education feels more like an entitlement. I think the greater challenge in education is to find a body of consistent evidence of what works. We're young in doing these experiments in education, and the treatments are more complicated. They last longer, you have to wait longer for results, and the control group is in school and being served. It's harder to isolate them from the treatment. It's harder to get reliable evidence. The objections of parents don't strike me as all that different from what we faced in other fields and ultimately overcame by explaining that we don't know whether this thing you think is so great actually works. Let's give it a chance, since we don't have enough money to serve everyone anyway. That's the same argument, but in education we need 20 years of evidence that the method provides important answers to important questions.

4. This was a study published by the National Academy of the Sciences that reviewed youth employment and training programs.
5. The specifics are described in chapter 7 of Gueron's book.

TO: That is certainly something we see on the development side. There's a set of work on how to keep kids in school[6] and then a separate literature that shows the children aren't learning as much as they should while they are in school,[7] which throws another element into the mix. A big reason we care about education is the long-term life outcomes for these students, not even what they do on test scores or if they get into college. It's "do they get good jobs?" that is a 15 or 20 years later question.

JG: I think that's why the career academy[8] study that MDRC did had such resonance.[3] It didn't show the children graduated at higher rates, but it showed that they earned more in the future and those gains went on for years. That kind of result is very impressive. We need more results like that, studies that show long-term effects. I also think the research on welfare policy that I'm describing had such an impact because there was a 30-year consistent agenda of building blocks that answered the range of policy questions that people had about welfare. They weren't one-off studies, something here, something there, or in one site. I don't think that is, and it shouldn't be, very powerful. You need a body of evidence from multiple sites and multiple studies to provide convincing answers to questions.

TO: Another part of the academic debate is about external validity: how much of what you find in one place can be applied to another. Was that a factor or were there enough studies going on essentially simultaneously because of federal government sponsorship for that not to be an issue?

JG: There wasn't just federal government sponsorship. The federal government sponsored some of this, but a lot of it was initiated by foundations or MDRC without a federal role. But there was replication of similar results across different contexts, different scale, different populations. I think that's essential. There was not rigid external validity but on the other hand the variety of conditions and implementing tests in real world contexts is what ultimately convinced Congress that they could rely on the findings. So there was a sense that it was externally valid at face value.

6. See J-PAL's overview at: http://www.povertyactionlab.org/policy-lessons/education/student-participation.
7. See Lant Pritchett's book *Education: Schooling Ain't Learning* for an overview of this research.
8. Beginning in 1993, MDRC began randomizing placement in career academy programs in nine cities. Career academies are programs that blend technical education and work experience.

TO: At the end of your book you have a coda that focuses a bit more on some of the arguments about RCTs, and in particular, you have a section titled, "Has the War Been Won?" You have the quote from Heckman there, where he says essentially, I give. I'd be interested in your answer to the question of whether the war is won. What's your feeling about how solid of a foundation randomized evaluations have as a policy tool in the US?

JG: I think it's not going to go backward in the economics profession and possibly in public policy schools. But in government, if money disappears, the work disappears. I think it's a fragile moment. Unfortunately, the evidence-based policy movement is being identified with the Obama administration. I hope it survives the next administration. Because it's not about what your policies are but it's about efficiency and effectiveness regardless of what your policy preferences are. You shouldn't be doing things that don't work. RCTs are the way to figure that out. But I think you could get the wrong leadership in IES,[9] and you could kill the whole revolution in evidence building.

9. The Institute for Education Sciences, part of the federal Department of Education, collects and disseminates data on education in the US, and sponsors research and program evaluation.

6 Dean Karlan

Dean's role as a co-founder of Innovations for Poverty Action, stickK, a company that helps people keep commitments using the principles of behavioral economics, and ImpactMatters, a consultancy for nonprofits on using evidence, signals his unusual academic path. After completing his BA in International Studies at the University of Virginia, he worked at what was then NationsBank for two years. His turn to experimental economics was in part influenced by spending the next several years working for FINCA, an international microfinance institution, in Latin America. While working on bank operations software, he also reviewed some of the organization's attempts at evaluating the impact of its programs. Finding these unconvincing, he began thinking about how to get better answers to questions about antipoverty programs.

Returning to the US he earned an MBA and MPP at the University of Chicago before going on to complete his PhD in economics at MIT. He founded IPA, frustrated with the logistical complexities of administering grants and hiring and managing the field staff necessary to conduct rigorous field experiments. Now a Professor of Economics at Yale University, Dean is a prolific experimenter who spends a great deal of time traveling the globe visiting various projects. He often takes his three children along on these travels, even homeschooling them for a year while the family circled the globe several times over.

Dean's 2011 book *More than Good Intentions* provides a wide-ranging summary of his and others' work.

TO: What was the first experiment you were involved in?

DK: I had a bit of a rocky start. The first one I designed and got into the field was around 1999. I wanted to test the effects of group versus individual liability on loan repayment and had contacts with FINCA in Central America. There was enough enthusiasm that I flew down there and made proposals, but in the end they just didn't go for it. Then in November 2000 I helped Esther and Abhijit get the Balsakhi evaluation of remedial tutoring going,[1][1] which would later turn out to be an important study. When the evaluation was just getting off the ground, I spent two weeks in India to help work out logistics with the NGO partner, to understand better what they do, where problems may arise, and so on.

From there I flew to South Africa where I started my first experiment, or so I thought.

The goal was to set up an experiment to measure the impact of micro-credit. I found people who wanted loans, did a baseline, ran them through a scoring model to make sure they were likely eligible to get a loan, did the randomization, and then handed half the names to FINCA. But then a bunch of things happened. First,FINCA took a really long time to follow up on the leads I had given them. Then they raised the interest rate from what we had agreed upon originally. So a lot of people now didn't want loans, because either too much time had passed or the interest rate was now higher. The local ex-pat manager had thought that demand would not go down or risk go up as the price went up. He said that was "academic babble." And then FINCA pulled the rug out from under me by hiring away my best employee. That was the straw that broke the camel's back.

It was a classic case where the powers at HQ said "OK, go do this," but they didn't provide any incentive to the local manager to cooperate, and he just didn't care. I put probably 9 months or a year into the program before I finally killed it.

The one good thing that came out of that experience was being able to see whether the local ex-pat manager was right, that interest rates don't matter. Since then we've learned the opposite is true. Turns out the poor care about prices of loans, just like the rest of the world.

TO: Was it FINCA that you had worked for in Central America before going into the PhD program?

DK: Yeah. That's why they were the first people I called when I finished my coursework to get my fieldwork going. The first experiment I started

1. This is a program that placed aides in classrooms to tutor students lagging behind on basic literacy and math skills. The trial found it increased average test scores (both for the tutored students and not tutored students). A similar intervention was trialed in Kenya and has been scaled up in Kenya and India, and has been implemented in Ghana.

that actually got completed was teaching entrepreneurship with FINCA in Peru.[2][2] That one started when I was in graduate school, but it was a long enough study that a later one, *Tying Odysseus to the Mast*,[3] looking at commitment savings accounts in the Philippines, started later but actually finished before the Peru one finished.

TO: Over the last few years you've been involved in a lot of studies of savings for poor households. I wonder, isn't there an upper bound to the number of people or the amount of impact you can have with savings? On the one hand, while take-up rates might be remarkably high for some of the products, given what they are, they still aren't all that high. Usually less than 50 percent of people offered an account save any significant amount. And while the idea that poor people can't save at all has been knocked down, there is still a limit to how much they can save.

DK: Some of the experiments and products have pretty high take-up—certainly above 50 percent—so I don't think we should be operating with an assumption that take-up rates for savings products will be low, or significantly lower than credit. Keep in mind that not everyone takes up credit when it's available either.

More important, we're not necessarily pushing for higher take-up *per se*. The challenge is getting people to use savings products more.

In some cases take-up is going to be limited because savings simply doesn't work in all situations. If you're looking at people who are truly in a poverty trap, they wouldn't be able to find any money to save. Figuring out when and where savings programs work is obviously key.

But there's an empirical question about how far down the ladder you have to go before you get to someone who is truly in a poverty trap and literally has no ability to save. Esther and Abhijit have shown in their research[3] that you still see expenditures on funerals and holiday festivities a long way down the income ladder—even down to the very poorest.[4] We are fooling ourselves to say that they physically couldn't save if they wanted to.

So the main situation where savings can fall short is in the case of an investment opportunity that has a huge return and needs external capital, where

2. The trial did not find significant impacts on the main outcomes of interest but did produce suggestive evidence that the training provided benefits for those borrowers least interested in the training *ex ante*.
3. The reference is to a paper that brings together household expenditure surveys from a variety of countries, "The Economic Lives of the Poor."

timing really matters and waiting to accumulate savings will mean missing out on a great opportunity. You can't proceed incrementally, and you would need to save for another year to make the investment versus using credit to get going right away.

That's a place where savings is theoretically inferior to credit, but the bulk of credit isn't used to make these large investments. Instead, what we see is that a lot of the time credit is used for consumption purposes. I have no problem with that and as long as it isn't putting someone in a debt trap they can't escape, consumption smoothing is a good thing.

But the minute I see credit being used for durable consumption goods I start asking: "OK, that's good. I'm glad they're able to do that when they weren't before, but now how do we think about helping them save up for that rather than borrowing down?" That's an example of a situation where we might see a really low take-up rate on savings or low savings deposits because credit is easier.

But that doesn't mean that savings aren't as important as credit. It means we just need to think harder about how people make choices between credit and savings.

TO: That seems like an issue of financial literacy. But financial literacy training has a terrible track record. Why is financial literacy so hard? It doesn't seem like it should be so difficult to help people improve their financial choices.

DK: First of all, it's hard because financial literacy *per se* is not necessarily useful. It only becomes useful once you are in a position to choose between good and bad products. You can teach someone until you're blue, but it doesn't really matter if they don't have materially different options to choose from.

TO: Your work with Sendhil on financial literacy and reducing debt for fruit sellers[4] is an example where there was something for them to do: plow a small part of their profits back into the business so they can stay out of debt.[5] And yet they end up back in debt fairly soon.

---

4. The experiment was with market fruit sellers who borrowed daily at very high rates to purchase fruit from wholesalers to sell during the day. All received a sufficient cash grant with which they could buy the necessary fruit to sell without borrowing; the treatment group also received financial literacy training. The work is described in detail in Mullainathan's book, *Scarcity*.

DK: I think that's the wrong way to look at that. The group that had financial literacy training and had their debt paid off took a lot longer to go back into debt than the other groups.

TO: And so the finding there was that things completely beyond their control led them back into debt? As I recall, you doubled the amount of time it took them to get back into debt, but it was still just two years, right?

DK: We only did surveys for about a year after. They did eventually go back into debt, but it dragged it out longer. That's a good thing. There was a very specific lesson. It was very, very simple.

I think the main problem I have with financial literacy as it's generally carried out is that it tends to be a never-ending list of principles rather than just very simple action steps. Teaching someone financial literacy like they are in school and are about to take an exam isn't a good way to do it. These are not people who are interested in taking exams and reading textbooks. Financial decisions are complicated, and I think we need to look more at putting in place certain products and processes that help the poor improve their decision-making.

But really, I'm just speculating here. The evidence we have on financial literacy is very thin and most of it honestly isn't very good. The fieldwork has been looking at little things, like helping people open a bank account. I think that's good—it's better than not opening a bank account—but we need to explore more.

I think, in general, we can teach things in this world. It is possible. We have schools that successfully teach complicated things. But that doesn't mean all schools are good; it does mean there is probably some way of having an impact. We just have to figure out what teaching will have the most impact.

I'm struck by two things that show up when these types of financial education interventions are done in the US. First, even though these interventions might have an impact, they may not be scalable because of the cost. Second, they're really hard to evaluate because the take-up rate is so small. When you go offer 100 people an in-depth sit-down session on financial counseling only a handful say yes.

We want to do financial counseling evaluations in the US. In order to make it happen though, we have two options. One is to set up a massive program that's going to do a lot of marketing and outreach so when we take that one person out of 100 we have sufficient power to draw conclusions. The problem is that massive of a program requires lots of cash to get the needed sample size, and administrative data such as credit reports to track outcomes. Or we find a program that is limited as to how many people they can provide services for, and then hold a lottery to randomize who does and doesn't get counseling.

There are two problems with the second option. First, there are a lot of financial counseling programs out there, so it's hard to evaluate the basic question of whether financial counseling has an effect versus no counseling at all. We have to be concerned about what the person who loses the lottery and doesn't get any counseling does. If that person goes to get counseling from some other source, we're not going to be able to tell very much about the impact of counseling. I doubt that would happen to everyone in the control group, but we don't know what the differential take-up rate would be. Second, many of the programs aren't budget constrained, they are demand constrained. Not many people actually want to use the service. The financial counseling providers have a government contract that pays them for everyone they provide counseling to, so they want to serve as many people as possible. But that doesn't leave a control group.

It's not easy to set up the evaluations. We're looking at the possibility of doing things with a treatment/placebo type setup, so everyone gets something, but the variation then is more intense versus less intense counseling. In the end we will be able to help people figure out how to save and how to make it work. But the question is, how can you actually do it in a scalable way? That's a very different question.

TO: The lack of evidence you see now of things that work or are useful in financial literacy, is that primarily an issue that we haven't evaluated the right things in the right way or is it we haven't developed programs that are sufficiently sound curricula-wise based on what we know about how people learn things like math?

DK: I think it's more on the evaluation side. But my instinct is that it's also about making sure people have access to the right products so that they can act on decisions. When we teach about savings and compound interest, there has to be a savings account available that actually earns interest over and above the fees that they can open. Beyond that we have to have products that are designed around the psychology and cognitive biases and behavioral issues that we know people have when it comes to money and decision-making. Until we have good evaluations of well-designed training in a context of good available products, I don't think we can really say that financial literacy doesn't improve outcomes—and that's ultimately the goal.

TO: I'll use that as a bridge to ask, what leads you to change your priors? You've worked on a program called "Borrow Less Tomorrow,"[5] which could have been a scalable way of doing exactly what you're talking about: improving outcomes in a targeted way by focusing on moving people to saving up from borrowing down. But the program didn't show much impact.[6] At what point do you try enough approaches to say, "This isn't a problem we can solve efficiently or at scale. Let's do something else." What is the point that changes your prior from "we haven't found the right nudge yet" to "we're looking at the wrong stuff?"

DK: There are different answers based on the situation that we find ourselves in. Usually we're doing an evaluation of an existing project that some organization has been running with all of the constraints that go along with that. In a few cases we're able to design something from the very beginning.

Even when we can propose something, we don't really get to design the project. Instead what happens is we have a general set of principles like what we had with "Borrow Less Tomorrow." What actually gets implemented is a result of negotiation over all the things we'd like to try and what the partner is willing to and capable of doing. We don't often have the luxury of, from the very beginning, setting up what we consider to be the decisive test.

So when the evaluation of one program that comes out of this process doesn't show great results, am I going to say, "these concepts don't work?" No. It doesn't shift my priors in some sort of grand way and move me away from the idea completely. It shifts me a bit, and with enough failure, yes, I'd probably decide the idea was bad from the get-go. But in any one study, it could be one of a variety of reasons why we didn't get the results we were looking for. It could be that the program wasn't implemented well. So the question is to figure out why, and use that to help figure out how to make it work, or eventually whether to drop the overall idea.

In the case of program in Tulsa, called BoLT, there were some things I wish we could have done differently but it just wasn't on the cards to do it. Even before the program launched I was thinking about ways we could try some

---

5. The program was modeled on the very successful "Save More Tomorrow" idea developed by Benartzi and Thaler. It used behavioral nudges to encourage participants to set and keep goals for reducing their debt.

of the things we weren't able to do with BoLT. So we can't simply take the results of one intervention with some known problems and declare BoLT ineffective as a savings product.

But at what point are we able to say for certain that something doesn't work? Before saying so conclusively, we'd have to have taken our best shot in at least a couple of different ways and in each case feel confident that the implementation happened in the way we envisioned. That way, you know for sure that either no one wanted the damn thing or people wanted the product, and we delivered it but their behavior still didn't meaningfully change after getting it.

TO: That's one of Chris Dunford's[6] critiques of the evaluation movement. As I'd state it, how many times do you need to test something to figure out that it's the implementation rather than the idea that has a problem?

DK: I agree with a lot that Chris has to say on this topic—though we do deviate on some points.

I think he was making a point about theory-less evaluations that end up being like a black box. Without theory, these evaluations claim to tell you that something worked or didn't but can't tell you why or anything about the context or mechanisms. In those sorts of evaluations you can't, or at least you shouldn't, take those "lessons" and go elsewhere. But a good evaluation isn't a black box. It has to use theory and ideally data and sometimes even experimental design to open that box up, so you can understand the context and conditions under which a programs works best. That's part of the role of theory in evaluations.

TO: That doesn't answer the quality-of-implementation question unless you're actually explicitly designing it in, though. Most studies aren't designed to figure out whether the idea is sound but the implementation is poor.

DK: I think there's two ways to address that question. One is data driven. The other is a bit more practical.

The data-driven way of dealing with that is to recognize that—and this works better in some situations, like passing out bed nets, than others—there could be different organizations that are better than others at

6. Dunford is the former CEO of Freedom from Hunger, an NGO that sponsors microfinance and related interventions and is well known for working closely with academic researchers.

implementing programs. So you measure institutional capacity. You can get data on, "Did the bed nets get to the houses? Were they there or not?" These questions measure the process change. Then we can ask the deeper question that we might care about by looking at what's the impact of getting bed nets on health outcomes and income, and all this other stuff.

That's only possible when the intervention is something that is very concrete and measurable, like passing out bed nets or giving kids deworming treatments.

On the more practical side, let's look at some sort of training program. Let's say you have 10 different training evaluations and you find a variety of impacts. You want to know what's driving the variety. Well, the first thing you're going to want to know is how many hours of training did people actually get. That could be your answer right there.

That doesn't tell us, though, that more hours are necessarily better than less. We want to know something about what was going on across these 10 programs that some people ended up with three more hours of training than people in the other programs did. Maybe people like good training and people don't like bad training. When there's good training, they go more. When there's bad training, they go less. There are a lot of potential factors that might account for the variety, and if you leave theory out of the evaluation, you've got nothing to unlock the black box.

But, let's say we see 10 null results. Well, I'm confident in concluding one of two things. Either don't bother doing this anymore or really think hard about doing it radically differently than you're currently doing it. If these are your 10 best shots at seeing an impact, and these NGOs had no impact, something has to change. Now whether they implemented it badly or it was a bad idea, I don't care. Unless you have some solid reason to believe that these 10 NGOs were exceptionally terrible, don't spend any more money on this.

TO: Ten failures would make you question whether it's possible to do that program well, period.

DK: Realistically, that's not the way the world usually works. If you do 10, you're going to find 3 of them work and 7 didn't, or something like that.

TO: Or one with 90 percent confidence.

DK: Yeah, at least one out of 20. Now, unless our N gets really big, we're into a qualitative space in which we're comparing the implementation of the programs and trying to understand whether there's some pattern that determines when it's working and when it's not.

Is it about who they're reaching? Is it about the actual program itself? Is it about the curriculum?

These questions should be what we use as our brainstorming material so that we can figure out what types of programs need further encouragement and evaluation. If we do an evaluation of 10 of these programs, find three that work, and think there's a pattern there and we know something about what to do, we should go and test these programs a couple of more times.

If we're finding that 70 percent of the programs are failing, we shouldn't just take the three that are working and say, "do this exactly." We need to try to understand more about how these programs work. The only way to gain that understanding comes from replication and theory.

TO: Staying on that theme of the role of theory in evaluation, there has to be some value to experiment without theory, just for basic discovery purposes, right? What's the danger of experimentation without theory and what's the right mix? When does it become too much?

DK: I actually think I'd say that experiment without any theory is a waste of time. Having said that, I think I have a really low bar for what I count as theory. I'm not sure that it's much lower than other people's, but I'm going to phrase it in a really simplistic way: I have a theory that children's health matters for learning, and that children with intestinal worms will see their health and then education improve as a result of getting deworming pills. That's a bio-theory, so to speak. Then I have theory about why people aren't already taking deworming pills. Why do we need to be passing out the pills, rather than trying to sell them? Well, that theory is a combination of information and maybe habits or even attention. The pills are just too cheap for cost to be an explanation. The theory then is that people lack information about the value of the pills, or they don't believe the pills work, or maybe that the pills actually do harm.

That theory can drive a couple of different interventions. One is an information campaign. But to do that, you have to have a lot of confidence that you can effectively distribute information in a way that reaches the right people and causes them to act. Another is just passing out the pills for free because the marginal cost is so low, probably lower than running an information campaign.

That's not deep theory. Some people use deworming as an example of theory-less stuff. I don't see why. It has theory to it. It's just not complicated theory like in risk-sharing markets and areas where people can write long papers filled with theory.

In my mind, whenever I'm dealing with anything, I always try to reduce things to three questions—even in simple interventions like passing out nutritional supplements to infants and toddlers. These are theory-driven questions that you should be using whenever you're justifying any intervention whatsoever.

The first question is about market failure. What's the market failure? Why isn't the market and the invisible hand working? Something went wrong somewhere. It can be really simple like information or transaction costs, but there has to be some reason why people aren't maximizing value on their own.

The second question is, how does this intervention specifically solve the market failure?

It could be that the intervention solves it in an indirect way. Deworming is a good example of that. Let's say that everyone agrees the failure is lack of information. Even though passing out pills for free doesn't solve the information problem, it solved the failure anyhow. In this case it could be that solving the market failure is lot harder than just bypassing it by handing out pills. Let's be pragmatists about it and just recognize that that there is something more powerful than information, which is just the paternalism of saying, "Here's a pill. Take it."

The third question is very pragmatic. What's the welfare impact of solving the market failure? It can be "black boxy" in the way you think about it, which is just to say, "what's the causal effect of A [the program] on B [the group in question]?" To make that final question interesting and convincing, you really do need to have some understanding of the first two questions.

TO: Sticking with theory, what is the Dean Karlan theory of change? How does writing a book,[7] or publishing academic papers, or doing what IPA does actually change the world? Do you perceive there's movement in the direction of demanding more evidence and more careful evaluations?

DK: My hope in writing the book was to bring the work of IPA to an audience that is not familiar with it. Many people do care about the world around them but are stuck in inaction because they are skeptical about the way things work. Some people take action based only on their gut instinct or what appeals to them emotionally. In the first case, the hope is that evaluations can convince skeptics that some things don't work, but some things do; that there's a path to doing more things that work. For the other group, the goal is to get them better information about what really works and what doesn't.

My biggest hope from the book, in terms of an outcome, is that we create future readers of IPA newsletters who, thanks to the information we're collecting, will feel confident that they are sending money to charities that are doing effective things. The biggest win at the end of the day, put in really dorky terms, is more efficient allocation of extra resources.

TO: How do you interpret the results of your Freedom From Hunger experiment?[7][8] It depressed giving less than I thought it would.

DK: I was actually fairly excited by it. In some sense, I think it was a tremendous act of generosity on Freedom from Hunger's part to let me do that study. I was very grateful to them.

The study shows that there is actually real hope for providing more and better information in charitable giving. Now this is a perfect example of a study that does need replication. One of the comments on the *Freakonomics* post was exactly right.[9] Freedom From Hunger does have a reputation. Its donors know it as being a group that cares about evaluation and research. This is their reputation. The question is what happens with other charities that don't have that reputation.

We're doing a study with MissionFish where we tested about 10 different ads for charities simultaneously on the eBay checkout line. I'm hopeful that messages about effectiveness might help other charities based on the early results we are seeing there.

TO: There's been a lot of talk about pre-analysis plans where researchers document their hypotheses and what they are going to look for in the data in order to avoid data mining. There's a similar issue that doesn't seem to get talked about as much: inadvertent data mining of public data sets. If lots of researchers have access to the data sets, you're easily going to have

---

7. This was a trial to test the effect of information about effectiveness on Freedom from Hunger donors. The treatment group received a standard donation appeal supplemented with information about the results of a randomized trial on the effectiveness of one of FFH's programs. The study found no change in the overall sample, but increases from recent large donors and decreases from recent small donors.

enough regressions run to find significance, but there's no way of knowing how much of that is happening. How do we balance transparency and data mining and confidence in the results we're getting?

DK: Here's the scenario that highlights the real trouble with a pre-registration process and pre-analysis plans. Let's say that before starting a study, I register a hypothesis about the effect it will have over the entire group. Lo and behold, I do the study and we find some average effect of an increase of one standard deviation in the block. But then my RA, just because she's curious, decides to run the data based on gender. And we find that females were actually two standard deviations better and males were zero, and it just averaged out to one. That's a huge difference and could be an important finding.

But I write a paper that sticks to my guns. I'm forced to pretend the gender result didn't exist because I didn't pre-register the hypothesis up front about it working better for women than men—I only registered a hypothesis about the effect on the entire group. Then somebody else comes along, downloads my data, sees the gender effect, and then writes that up. There's something that seems really odd about that kind of outcome from pre-registration. It wouldn't be a good process in which I'm not able to find things I wasn't expecting at the beginning.

It would be better if data exploration wasn't unfairly tarred as data mining. There's nothing wrong with writing a paper that discusses something unexpected that wasn't thought of beforehand as long as it includes some explanations for maybe why, and some further tests that were done after we discovered the gender effect. That's exploratory, not data mining. My hope is that the norm will shift to detail the pre-specified in papers, but still do the data exploration, and back and forth from theory to data, that is the norm for how economists typically analyze data.

These additional discoveries should, in an ideal world, be part of brain-storm material for the replication study process that I mentioned earlier. As long as the theory is right, we should be able to do it again—either in the same place or somewhere else—and see if it's right.

My fear is that it's hard to get true replications done in academia. Some-times it is hard to find or create similar contexts. But the problem is also driven by incentives. There is less reward in doing replications than doing original research.

Instead of just pre-registering hypotheses, all data should get posted, and that should get data mined to the hilt, just like any publically available data set. This should come with the caveat that the hypotheses posed about what is happening in the data are all posed after the fact and then the regressions are run.

The only difference between those two data sets is one has really clean scientifically engineered randomization and identification of a particular variable. You still have the same exact problems you have with that data set versus another public data set with someone sitting around and just mining it to their heart's content. But this is exactly where a registry should come in, in helping the world distinguish between those two.

I think the other thing that the registry process should hopefully encourage is more meta-analysis. We don't have as much meta-analysis as we should, and good meta-analysis depends on some uniformity in the ways things are measured. It's not to say that we shouldn't have some creativity too, but we want to be able to compare more across studies. A registry process would help us get to that.

TO: Let's talk about the investment and profit question. My perception of the research is that it's a bit all over the map. It's surprising how hard it is to figure out what is happening inside these microenterprises in terms of investment and profits. David McKenzie, for instance, sees very high returns to capital.[8][10]

DK: Right. But McKenzie's results are from cash drops, which are different from loans. It's great how microcredit has gotten rates down from money lenders. But they're not low enough that the cost of capital allows for significant profits for the average microenterprise. Remember too that we're talking about averages. There is a lot of variation in the data.

TO: So why are poor households keeping these businesses going at such low rates of profitability? Abhijit and Esther note in *Poor Economics* that many of these businesses aren't just low profit, they're unprofitable. I'm really confused as to what's happening in these microenterprises and why it's so hard to figure out what's happening in these microenterprises.

DK: There's one reason why it's very hard to figure out. It requires a lot of care and attention to detail and these firms do not keep good records. But I think the hardest thing in terms of figuring out the profitability is how you value the family's time.

8. See the interview with David McKenzie (chapter 10) for a full discussion of his series of experiments providing cash grants to microenterprise owners.

People often derive the results to be positive or negative depending on the price they place on labor in the enterprise. When you put the value of labor at zero, you often do see a profitable business. It's not making lots of money, but it is generating positive cash flow.

So what's going on in the labor market if they're making so little that they can't get a job at an equivalent or higher rate? But that's a different question.

TO: So doesn't it seem likely that they could make relatively small investments that would bump up that profitability at least a little bit?

DK: I don't think it's so obvious for a lot of people what to do to expand their enterprise, or increase their profits and make more money. And even then, the returns on microcredit aren't very high. So this is easier said than done. But David's study basically shows that this is a possibility.

TO: In the Peru business coaching study,[11] the small business consulting study in Mexico,[12] and Fischer and Schoar's rules-of-thumb study,[13] it does seem that a little bit of coaching can have an impact on these businesses.

DK: In each of those there were some benefits, but none really led to large changes when the treatment was small. Some of the training or coaching studies are pretty light and some are heavy-handed. For instance, in Mexico it was more like full-on consulting than just some training, and that did lead to big effects. We also did one in Ghana that was heavy-handed, but not as heavy-handed as in Mexico, and that showed no impact. If anything we get negative point estimates in the short run.[14] We think this has to do with firms experimenting, trying, and hoping to be big, but on average not really having room for growth. Basically there the businesses did what the consultants told them to, but they stopped doing it over time. But that's generally a positive thing because following the consultant's advice wasn't increasing their profits.

TO: So is that a story that the Ghana market, in general, is functioning fairly well, so there just wasn't a lot of room for improvement? The gains from improved business operation had already been captured by somebody else?

DK: It's hard to say. It's one of two things. First of all, we focused strictly on tailors, so that says, either the tailors had no room for growth and the market for tailoring was fairly thick and competitive or that these consultants were not well suited to playing this role. The consultants were not any better than the existing entrepreneurs at helping identify ways to improve the businesses. One big thing the consultants pushed was record keeping, which just didn't matter.

TO: For the last few years you've been working on testing the BRAC "graduation model" in several places around the world, essentially running simultaneous replications. Tell me about that work.

DK: There were a couple a-ha's that we had about 8 years ago. One is that there's a huge space for microcredit claiming and arguing that they're helping the ultra-poor, but when you look at the data, it's clear that the ultra-poor are not who they are reaching. It's also clear that microcredit is not having a huge impact on household income. There's a lot of good coming out of microcredit, but mass raising of incomes is just not happening. And so, if providing access to finance is not lifting people *en masse* up and out of poverty, then it's time to try something else.

The second thing is that there's a general sentiment that one of the issues with extreme poverty is that there are likely multiple market failures at once. The problem is not as simple as doing one thing or the other. To help people who are ultra-poor, you need a big push approach that tackles the problem in a multifaceted way. This way of thinking, to be clear, has nothing to do with microcredit—it's how many tools do you have in your toolkit?

So the Ford Foundation and CGAP approached us to ask if we would be interested in doing a multi-site, multifaceted evaluation. We were excited about it. One of the things that has always been important at IPA is the idea of replication. To learn what works, we need to get beyond the one experiment, one place, one point in time problem. One way to get beyond that is to do things more than once, and do it in multiple places so that you have a broader understanding of the variation in the context under which something works or doesn't work.

There's an academic problem that it's not rewarding to do the third experiment—you'd have a hard time publishing the third experiment. So we tackled this *ex ante* by—we didn't actually have all of them lined up upfront—what we agreed upfront was to do a series of these together. It turned out that we were able to do seven: Honduras, Peru, Ghana, Ethiopia, Yemen, Pakistan, and India. [15] The programs that are being tested there are very similar but not exactly the same. They are adapted to the local context, naturally. There's also always going to be something slightly different at each site because of the funding agency, because of the local environment, because of existing cash transfer programs. So there are subtle things that are different—and we do learn something about those types of differences—but for the most part the programs are very similar.

And it's really nice to be able to pool results across all the sites to look at, in aggregate, the impacts that we're having. So not only are we able to compare contexts but with the results pooled we have really tight errors. When we have a null result on something, we have a *really* precise null result.

TO: Given the different implementers are you able to compare the possible differential impact between the organizations running the program? I'm thinking about the Sandefur paper looking at the difference between government and NGO implementers of the extra teacher program.[9][16]

DK: No, for the same reason that they can't make any generalized statement. We can learn from what they did, but not a generalized statement about "government" and "NGO." In the Sandefur paper, they only have two observations, one government and one NGO. That helps us learn something about that government and that NGO, but generalizing about governments and NGOs from that is a bad idea. The more interesting thing is getting inside the monitoring data to look at what the government is doing differently and what the NGO is doing differently.

It's the same exact thing in ours. We have different implementers, one government in Yemen, we have a government-financed program in Pakistan, and different NGOs. But we can't say anything about government or government-financed initiatives in general.

We do have some program variations that give us some insights. For instance, in Ethiopia, we have food transfers for both treatment and control, whereas in other sites, it's only in treatment. The government was already doing food transfers on the idea that people in extreme poverty might be in a nutritional poverty trap. They don't have the caloric intake to have the energy in order to produce, so it's a vicious cycle. You transfer food so that they have the energy to engage in some livelihood program. A similar logic is at work in other programs that are transferring livestock. You

9. This paper looks at the expansion of a program that had proved to be successful in earlier RCTs in India and Kenya—adding contract teachers (e.g., non-union) to classrooms. The paper finds that contract teachers hired by NGOs are effective, but contract teachers hired by the government are ineffective. See citations to the earlier work in the endnote.

transfer both goats and food; otherwise, the people will just eat the goats to get the minimum calories they require in the short term. Transferring food makes it more likely that they rear the animals and have a sustainable livelihood.

What's interesting is Ethiopia has the biggest treatment effect on food consumption yet that food transfer happened in both treatment and control. That one program design difference does suggest to us that the food transfer is not a driving force making this thing work because at the one site that had it for everybody, it didn't matter. We still can't make that much of it; there are other stories you could tell, but it seems that the most likely story is that it's not food transfers that are driving the overall results.

TO: You've been involved in two situations where we have more than three evaluations of similar programs brought together—the set of evaluations of microcredit that were published in *AEJ-Applied*, and the graduation program evaluations published in *Science*.[17] The microcredit evaluations were all independent of each other and quite different in some regard. The graduation model replications were planned from the outset. Do we learn different things from these two approaches to replications? Should we think about the results differently?

DK: There's a third—evaluations of savings programs—but let's set that aside for now. As you point out, the coordination of the microcredit studies was post hoc, the studies occurred at different times in different places, with just the analysis and write-ups done in a way to facilitate comparison. Because of the real differences, we were hesitant to pool the data. We hadn't designed the projects to be perfectly comparable: measures, treatment, and populations had important differences, which we also tried to make clear in our introduction. While our headline findings converged—that microcredit does have important positive impacts, but it doesn't do much to bring people out of poverty—we also found slight differences in different outcomes, like business assets and investment, and we'll never know for sure what was responsible.

On the plus side, that strengthens the generalizability of the overall conclusion about microcredit being of limited help as a poverty-fighting tool: the finding was remarkably similar regardless of the particular program or measures. It seems obvious that not everything would line up perfectly. The products were different, as were the institutions and market environments. So, if everything lined up, something would be wrong.

With the graduation model, we were able to design the evaluations from the ground up to be comparable, for example, making sure that how we measure consumption in one place is compatible with another. We have much more power to pool data and compare outcomes, and to look at heterogeneous effects in subgroups by level of prior poverty, for example. So in that sense building in compatibility ahead of time led to a data set where a whole different set of questions could be answered. When it comes to the question of scaling it up, we'll also have much more confidence when going to funders of governments as to what we know to expect when implementing the program in new places. The down side is that we only tested this particular program, albeit with a few variations, and whatever we can say will be limited to that.

TO: You pointed out that it would be suspicious if everything lined up exactly in the microcredit evaluations. It's funny, that was my reaction. I find it a little suspicious that they lined up as much as they do. As we talked about earlier, the work on returns to capital diverges a lot. Given the really big differences in context between those studies, isn't it reasonable to expect a lot of variation?

DK: There are some things that by their very nature are always going to produce lots of irregularity—like microcredit. And there are some things that might just be deeper fundamental principles that cut across lots of cultures.

Health pricing, for instance, is one that we've seen over and over again in different contexts. The magic of the zero price has shown up in bed nets, chlorine dispensers, deworming. I think there are 12 to 15 in a *J-PAL* review, all showing that free really does increase take-up more than charging just a little bit.[18] The difference from 0 to 1 is much bigger than from 1 to 2. I think that's great; we're really learning something there.

TO: What are you advising students that you teach now, in terms of building their careers? Is doing field experiments, doing RCTs, the best way to make a mark and get noticed?

DK: We should neither be encouraging or discouraging any particular tool just for the sake of the tool. We should be encouraging students to look for an interesting question and use the right tool to answer it. Period.

I have learned to mostly, but not always, discourage graduate students from having field projects that rely extensively on an external partner with potentially competing interests as a job market paper. The partner's goal is not to produce a job market paper in a certain time frame, so it's dangerous to put all your eggs in that basket. I had a student who did that and it worked, but I'd always recommend a backup plan. A professor's workflow isn't always the best for a graduate student to model theirs on. As a professor you have the luxury of having 10 projects that you're juggling, and if half don't work out, you can still have 5 good projects. But look at what happened to me in South Africa, where after nine months, changes the partner made meant I had to kill the project. Imagine if I'd been relying on that one for my job market paper.

To be fair—it's not the partner's job to make sure you have a neatly wrapped up project in time for the job market—they have their own interests, which don't always align with yours. As a graduate student you don't have that much bandwidth, you don't have a support team (although IPA does help with that), and you have to do more fieldwork. If you're going to do a field project, whether it's a randomized trial or not, you have to make sure it's going to work out well.

It's a common piece of advice when someone wants to do fieldwork to say, "Fine, but you need a job market paper. You need to have something that's lower risk to make sure you have data so you can write something."

TO: Beyond the needs of graduate students, there's a general issue that it takes a really long time to run an experiment and get something published. In that group of six microcredit impact studies that were finally published in 2015 most of them finished 3 or 4 years before that—at least one even longer ago than that. And it compounds the external validity problem doesn't it? That it takes so long to make things official that the context is invariably different by the time the peer review and publication process is done?

DK: No, I don't think that compounds the external validity challenge. First, the delay to publication is no different for experimental than nonexperimental work, and external validity isn't more of an issue for randomized than nonrandomized studies. External validity comes from understanding why something works, and randomization itself does no harm. This is a common misunderstanding. It isn't that randomized trials have by their nature more external validity. But rather external validity is a concern we all have about anything we do, to know how far into other contexts we can take results.

In terms of timing, often for randomized studies we have an external force pushing to get things done. For example, I just sat through a meeting with

The Hunger Project on a seven-year randomized trial, five years between baseline and follow-up. If I didn't have a donor and an organization dying to get results and emailing us nicely, though consistently, the reality is we would end up dragging out publication of this just because of the natural course of events and imposing deadlines from other things.

There's two things that cause a project to drag on once you get the data. First is the natural tendency of us all to take on a lot of things, often more than we can actually do. And two, economics does have a journal publication timing problem. I don't know if I have a better idea of how to organize our world and how to transition to that new world. But we have journals that take a really long time to get responses back, to the point where it should be unacceptable. I have a paper out now that's been under review for seven and a half months, and have had a paper sit at journals for more than a year. The *PLOS ONE* model[10] is intriguing: let the referee process be strictly on technical grounds, and let the citations influence what is important and what is not. This would get rid of a lot of rejections merely due to taste, that a piece of work was accurate but just not "interesting," a clearly highly subjective metric.

Another issue we have in economics is we don't reward reporting of facts. We don't reward "boom boom boom" style papers. I did x, I found y, done. What happens because of that is papers have a really hard time getting through the referee process because people get really nitpicky about interpretation and theory and models and for better or worse—certainly some people would argue that's a good thing—but inevitably what that means is that it's much harder to satisfy the referee because you're being judged by a whole world of things beyond whether you generated knowledge and whether the paper is a well-executed collection of data and analysis.

10. *PLOS ONE* is an open-access journal published by the Public Library of Science. Submissions are peer-reviewed, but authors pay for publication, which has been a cause of controversy.

After spending several years in Bangladesh with Mohammed Yunus working with Grameen Bank, Alex founded the Grameen Foundation to help other organizations learn from and replicate the Grameen Bank microfinance model around the world. Alex has served on the board of several other microfinance organizations and was the co-chair of the Microfinance CEO Working Group for many years. He is the author *of Small Loans, Big Dreams: How Nobel Prize Winner Muhammad Yunus and Microfinance Are Changing the World.*

TO: How did you become involved with Grameen and microfinance?

AC: When I was at Cornell in the 1980s I was pulled between the Reagan-era "Greed is good" philosophy and social justice work. My older brother, father, and stepmother worked in helping professions such as social work and psychiatry. Somehow, melding those things together, I got interested in market solutions to poverty, and someone told me about Muhammad Yunus. So I wrote him a letter my junior year, and eventually got a Fulbright Fellowship to go spend one year in Bangladesh—as the first of what became many Fulbright Fellows with one or another Grameen organization—and one year became six, and when that was all winding down, I started Grameen Foundation.

Like many start-ups we were just in the process of thinking through strategy and purpose and mandate when we started. Looking back, I wish we had thought about this a little more rigorously, but basically we were the original Grameen organization outside of Bangladesh, essentially the original international arm of the Grameen family of organizations. Basically, the idea was to take Grameen and its approaches, its methodology, its philosophy, its people, and project them on the international stage to influence the international development and humanitarian agenda.

It was very much linked in with the original Microcredit Summit,[1] which was in February of 1997. There was a buildup to that over about a year. Professor Yunus and I—I was still living in Bangladesh at the time—saw that there was so much interest in what Grameen was doing, in microfinance in general, and in particular this global campaign to grow microfinance. To meet and channel that interest, we would have to have an entity outside of Bangladesh that was focused on the global agenda and that was Grameen Foundation.

TO: In the course of the roughly 25 years you've been involved in microfinance, how have you seen the industry change in terms of maturity, sophistication, learning, innovation?

AC: Of course, in so many ways. When I got involved, the term "microfinance" didn't exist. We had a mishmash of terminology that confused people—small enterprise credit, poverty lending, terms like that.

You don't have to go back too far to a point where a large percentage of all the clients of what we would call today "microcredit" or "microfinance" were in Bangladesh. You had another intensive market in Bolivia, though it was a small market. And you had Indonesia, which was more of an SME[2] and savings play. But the rest of the world was mostly white space. In one era, it was thought of as highly controversial, even unethical, for MFIs to intermediate savings. Now, it is considered a best practice. The idea that organizations could reach profitability in a reasonable amount of time and sustain that over time just wasn't there. So there's just been a tremendous transformation. I see four basic phases of growth in microfinance. We're now in phase four. In each of those phases there have been tremendous changes and certainly if you look collectively across them there are huge changes.

Performance standards, efficiency, level of outreach, clarity of terminology, measurement, the universal standards for social performance management, client protection, developing an ecosystem of rating agencies, microfinance

1. The original Microcredit Summit spawned an organization, The Microcredit Summit Campaign, that organized global gatherings to promote microcredit around the world. In 2016, it was reabsorbed into RESULTS, the advocacy organization that had started it.
2. Small and midsize enterprises, the distinction between microenterprises and small enterprises most commonly is whether there is an employee from outside the family of the owner. There is no common definition of the distinction between small and midsize or midsize and large enterprises.

investment vehicles, and so on. All of that. It's almost incomprehensible how [microfinance] has matured and grown. Of course, that includes growth in some markets being too fast and leading to overheating and retrenchment, but that's part of any growing industry.

TO: There is this odd situation where the microfinance movement and the RCT movement are somewhat entangled with each other. When was the first time you encountered an academic economist and the idea of a randomized impact evaluation?

AC: It's a good question. I maybe should have a better answer. Grameen Foundation shares a major funder with J-PAL, and we arranged a lunch with them when they were rebranding with the Jameel name in the mid-2000s, I think. Then a couple of the studies came out. I've always thought of RCTs as one of several research methodologies, and the studies that used RCTs as just some among dozens and dozens of studies.

I remember sitting down with David Roodman, maybe our first or second conversation, and he suggested that Esther Duflo would deservedly win a Nobel Prize for her work and I thought, "really? I should learn more about this."

Then there was a fateful meeting where Beth Rhyne and David Roodman tried to host something to get the practitioners and the RCT researchers to talk in a more constructive way.[3] That meeting was pretty much a failure. The idea from the researchers, or at least some subset of them, was that the only valid research that people should pay attention to were RCTs, since they were the "gold standard." I just felt uncomfortable with that. We had, I thought, already learned a lot from research that was using other methodologies—quasi-experimental design, nonexperimental design, qualitative research, and so on. And as I talked to other people who were serious researchers, they would tell me that different methodologies had pros and cons in different contexts and we should look at the full body of research.

I always try to pay attention to the research that is coming out, at least at an educated layperson's level. When a couple of these studies came out, I skimmed them, as I'd always done. I guess it might have been as late as

3. See David Roodman's take on the meeting here: Roodman, David. 2010. "Meeting of the Minds? Researchers, Microfinance Leaders at CGD." *David Roodman's Microfinance Open Book Blog*, Center for Global Development, March 1. http://www.cgdev .org/blog/meeting-minds-researchers-microfinance-leaders-cgd.

2006 when I first heard about them, because we commissioned Nathanael Goldberg's literature review in 2005.[1] I don't think there really were many RCTs in this field published at that point, because I asked Nathanael to look at everything. One of the reasons we commissioned Kathleen O'Dell to do a follow-up to that literature review in 2010[2] was because the RCT crowd said that the couple of new studies basically refuted all the studies that went before, so you shouldn't pay any attention to them and that only the RCT-derived body of knowledge was important. Not only were they saying, "we're adding to the body knowledge," but they were saying, "this *is* the body of knowledge." So we asked Kathleen to look broadly but to include these RCT studies, and go look with a fresh pair of eyes and tell us what you see.

TO: The statement that the Microfinance CEO Working Group made after the original working paper version of the Banerjee, Duflo, Glennerster, and Kinnan study of Spandana[3] and the statement[4] that was made after the publication of that study and several others were published in *AEJ: Applied*[5] in January [2015] were pretty different. How have perceptions changed, if at all, in terms of what's been learned from randomized evaluations since some of those difficult meetings?

AC: In terms of the initial statement, well, here we were in a situation, practitioners and advocates and promoters, where we'd been relying on what we were told was the gold standard study in Bangladesh, the Pitt Khandker study[6] that we'd been beating the drum about.[4] That study was peer-reviewed, and published. And then without a lot of warning, we were getting this message seeping into various constituencies that the Pitt Khandker study was flawed despite the academic peer review process that's supposed to give real confidence.

Now for context, at that time there hadn't really been much engagement with the research community. There had been the one meeting that I referred to earlier, which, to be honest, was kind of a fiasco. We were talking past each other. And though I proposed, during that meeting, a process for having ongoing consultations and dialogue between researchers and practitioners, no one seemed interested. So when these new studies came out, and they challenged the earlier research that we had promoted, we felt it was important to make a public statement.

4. See extensive conversation about this study and how it relates to other microcredit impact studies in the interview with Jonathan Morduch (chapter 4).

That statement was driven by the communications people, not really the operations folks or leadership. It was a little bit hastily put together by the communications teams. I think one thing we didn't think through is, who is really the audience here? In retrospect, a strategic mistake was—though I think there was an overreaction to it—the statement started with an anecdote from each of the organizations that signed on, an anecdote about what microfinance can and has done. The idea was to try to put a human face on the work as a *preamble* to talking about our substantive view about the research.

I remember having a pretty vigorous argument with Jonathan Morduch about this at a Center for Financial Inclusion Advisory Board meeting. What I got from that is that basically the research community didn't read further than those stories. What they saw was that the response to this new batch of studies was to throw out more anecdotes. The research community decided, "these people are not serious." I tried to point out that there was actually much more in that statement than the opening anecdotes, which served as a kind of preamble to the substance of the statement. What people did not seem to be willing to engage in was the answer to the question, "do you agree or not with the substance of the statement, anecdotes aside?" David Roodman was an exception.[7] He had a pretty thoughtful reaction to the statement, showing that he did read past the anecdotes.

Then you fast forward a few years, more studies are out, people like me have had more time to digest them, more questions had been raised about the Pitt Khandker studies, though the World Bank and the authors still stand by them. The more recent statement you refer to was put together less by communications people and more by operations people and leaders within these organizations, and those leaders had been in contact with researchers, often through the Microfinance CEO Working Group. It was more forward-looking than backward-looking and defensive sounding.

TO: You said there's been a problem of researcher-practitioner engagement. What needs to change in order to make the evaluations more useful for improving practice?

AC: On the practitioner side, I think people feel whipsawed by the research. You have one generation of studies that say very positive things and then suddenly other researchers pull the rug out from under us and blame us in a strange way for building up these expectations where they were actually based primarily on peer-reviewed research. I think practitioners and advocates need to get over that. And practitioners need to express more curiosity about what we can learn from research to do our job better.

Among practitioners, I sometimes hear people like Milford Bateman[5] being put in the same group as David Roodman or Jonathan Morduch. I don't think that's right. You have your gadflies and critics, who are not trying to approach microfinance in a particularly balanced or evidence-based way. They've concluded what they've concluded—that microfinance, across the board, is a bad thing—and they're looking only for evidence to support that conclusion. These are people who want microfinance to crumble. And then there are serious people, like Roodman and Morduch, who we may not agree with or at least not how they interpret the data, but who are doing things in a balanced, rigorous, and constructive way. So practitioners need to see the differences and to get out of this "us against them" mentality. There are a lot serious researchers, and we should reach out to them and see how we can find common ground, to see how we can do what we do better. The lack of curiosity and the tendency to fall into an "us against them" mentality is just not helpful.

From the researcher side, I feel people seem much more interested in jumping on to the next prestigious research project than being committed to disseminating their research in a way that actually improves practice and policy. I think that's been terribly neglected. Since that original statement that we were just talking about, there are researchers that have apparently tuned out the practitioner community, which just seems absurd to me. If you're doing research to improve practice, why would you tune out one of the constituencies you're hoping your research influences and benefits?

I also don't feel the financial services providers that have been chosen to be studied are particularly representative of financial services providers to the poor generally. If a better job was done to choose more representative organizations, if that was done a little more scientifically, rather than opportunistically, we'd be having a richer and more meaningful conversation. But that goes back to the practitioner side. A lot of the practitioners have not opened the door to researchers, so that may be one of the reasons why there's this kind of a skewed research, including research on some second-rate financial service providers, which then colors the results.

5. Milford Bateman is a freelance consultant on development programs and occasional visiting professor who has written very critically of microfinance, notably in his book *Why Doesn't Microfinance Work?*

Randomization is all about getting a representative sample of the clients of an institution, but that's really not applied to the selection of financial service providers to study, among the thousands who are out there. I think, in general, what's been missing is a kind of person or people who could serve as a bridge between the two communities. Chris Dunford, Beth Rhyne, David Roodman,[6] have all tried at times. But no one took that role on, on a sustained basis. We need someone who could be trusted by and understand the psychology of both communities, and get them collaborating more constructively. That kind of elder statesman or stateswoman, someone who saw this as their responsibility, is lacking. Where there have been efforts, it feels like the whole is less than the sum of the parts and that we're lacking people who see bridging the gap as their responsibility.

I also think that we need to incentivize researchers to design their research so that it can best answer the question, "how can financial services delivery to the poor work better," rather than focus on the very basic question, "does (some/any current version of) microcredit work?" Furthermore we should incentivize researchers to put at least as much work into disseminating their findings as into the research itself. I have proposed that a prize go to the researcher whose research has most influenced policy and practice. I have also proposed that we do research on the effectiveness of research in influencing policy and practice. If it doesn't, shouldn't we consider it a failure? Incentives like these might shift how researchers, practitioners, and policy makers interact.

TO: There's a shared problem of both the funder community and the academic community being susceptible to fads. If you think about the impact of the evaluation work on funding versus the impact of a new generation of funders who want to look at something different instead, how do you assess the effect, or lack of effect, in relation to those two phenomena?

AC: Among the most serious providers, the main driver of change has been their culture of innovation, their efforts to improve service delivery or maybe being pressed by competition. A lot of them don't receive any donor funding. If they have external investors, and they are represented on the governing body, they may advocate for some particular innovation. But, in most cases, what drives organizational change in the largest MFIs is a

6. Chris Dunford is the former CEO of Freedom from Hunger; Beth Rhyne is the Managing Director of the Center for Financial Inclusion, which is sponsored by Accion. Both Freedom from Hunger and Accion are part of the Microfinance CEO Working Group.

curiosity driven by either desire to provide excellent service in a changing market or to respond to competition.

The larger funders of microfinance—Gates in recent times, MasterCard Foundation, Omidyar to some degree—have been significantly influenced by the research and that has over time influenced what they fund and that does influence what some practitioners do.

For the largest players, the development of new products is largely driven by competition and that cultural desire to provide better products even in the absence of competition.

TO: In terms of the overall funding situation, have you seen the funding environment change in the last five years?

AC: I think there was a general overreaction to the research. This was compounded by the fact that some politicians and media set out to debunk microfinance, occasionally using the research selectively to bolster their case. Donors have focused on several narrow areas: digital financial services and Africa, mainly. Grant-making outside these areas has dried up.

I think there are some real opportunities that are being missed because of that orientation. People tend to miss that we've built up a valuable infrastructure providing credit and sometimes a few other products to the poor. You've got to figure out how to use that infrastructure to deliver savings, insurance, social services. That infrastructure essentially pays for itself, but often does not generate much surplus to invest in innovation. I think there are some really exciting opportunities for smart subsidy in leveraging the infrastructure of microfinance to deliver new and better services, whether financial or nonfinancial. There are opportunities to do things that could radically reduce the cost equation, which could make some of these marginally profitable institutions more profitable. That would in turn allow them either to reduce costs to clients, which you would think would increase impact, or to put that into more self-directed innovation or ancillary services.

Between some people taking a warped version of what the research says, combining that with some negative press, combining that with the inevitability of fads coming and going in this field, and we've swung really far in one direction that neglects the enormous potential of leveraging this infrastructure. I was just in a meeting for Fonkoze. After the Catholic Church, Fonkoze has the most infrastructure in rural Haiti. Fonkoze is getting close to profitability, but it's not going to be able to invest much in innovation because the profits will be limited. And keep in mind that profits can be a political liability, especially the kind of profits necessary to fund a lot of innovation. Smart subsidy could allow optimal use of that infrastructure for client benefit.

We don't sit here and debate whether we should be working on healthcare for the poor, or water and sanitation for the poor, or education for the poor. In the same way it's kind of silly to debate whether the poor need reliable financial services that are tailored to their needs. Of course, they do. In today's society lack of access to financial services that meet your needs is as debilitating as not having access to education or healthcare. Both of those things, when done wrong, can be a negative. Expired vaccines and medications can kill people. But that's not an argument for not investing in healthcare for the poor.

We've learned a ton about how to deliver those services and how to piggy-back other services on top of them to create social value. We've got research, we've got people, we've got the infrastructure.

I think Esther Duflo said that subsidy should not go into the standard microcredit model. But who's practicing that model? Why is that even a question? Most people left the standard microcredit model behind years ago. Subsidy shouldn't go into propping up the 8-track tape. But nobody is arguing that it should.

I also don't think a purely digital approach that disintermediates the human element at the end of the transaction is the way to go. I think we're going to be sorely disappointed if we put all our eggs in that basket.

Xavi has collaborated with many of the other economists in this volume—Karlan, Morduch, McKenzie, and Yang—while building up an impressive set of research since he joined the World Bank as a Young Economist in 2002. Now a Lead Economist in the Development Research Group, his research focus has been on access to financial services and rural finance. His travels have taken him to rural areas of Thailand, Pakistan, India, Kenya, Malawi, and the Philippines as well as into the computer lab, where he collaborated with Dean Karlan and Jonathan Morduch on a series of simulations designed to answer questions about how microcredit borrowers think about risk and group liability.

Much of his research has focused on uncovering the decision making of poor households when it comes to financial services. Why do they repay loans? Why don't they buy insurance? Why do they struggle to save? To find answers to these questions, he uses a variety of methods including examining administrative records of governments and financial services providers, audit studies (also known as "secret shopper" studies), as well as RCTs.

TO: What was the first field experiment you were involved in? How did you get started in RCTs?

XG: The first RCT I was involved in must have been the evaluation of DrumNet in Kenya.[1] I came late into the project, after Dean [Karlan] and Nava [Ashraf] had worked on it for a while. They had run into some implementation issues, mostly due to someone in the partner organization that was making life impossible so they had sort of given up on it. And Dean said

---

1. This is an evaluation of a program to encourage Kenyan farmers to grow crops for export. Of note, shortly after the evaluation, the EU changed its regulations and effectively shut out the Kenyan farmers from the market so while the evaluation found the program worked and raised farmer income, it was soon discontinued.

to me, "if you want to jump in, be my guest." So I traveled to Kenya, and it turned out that there was a new guy in charge of the program that understood the value of research and who was very cooperative. So we were able to get things back on track. Although a lot of the leg work had already been done, I still learned a lot about how to design treatment arms to test certain hypothesis and about how to run an experiment in general. About the same time Dean and I were working with Green Bank in the Philippines[2] and then eventually I started the work with other colleagues at the Bank on weather insurance.[3] Looking back, I definitely learned a lot from Dean in both contexts and that allowed me to pursue other RCTs in other contexts.

TO: Is that path dependence? You had the opportunity to work with the method and then you stuck with it, or was there something specifically attractive about the method that kept you doing a lot of RCTs?

XG: It's a good question. I was interested in certain questions that are impossible to answer just by collecting observational data because there are no exogenous sources of variation to exploit. What an RCT allows you to do is to precisely create this exogenous variation so that you can answer the question. But in my work I've tried to frame the question first, from theory, and then to design the RCT to answer the question.

TO: Turning more specifically to some of your work, let's start with the factors that drive take-up of financial products. Across the board, I think a lot of people don't realize how low take-up is of not only insurance but also credit and savings products. What are the drivers of take-up or the lack of take-up? Is it price, is it trust, is it something else?

XG: In terms of reasons for take-up, it's all of the above. There's no universal explanation for why people take up products. You have to look at the specific context, competition, the characteristics of the products offered, before you can uncover why people take up products or don't.

Take this series of audit studies of retail financial products that started in Mexico, and now have been done in several other countries, to understand the quality of the information as well as the quality of the products being offered.[2] It's quite interesting because, by law, in Mexico financial services

2. This collaboration resulted in a number of experiments including work on group versus individual liability in microcredit and commitment contracts.
3. This includes work on designing rainfall insurance contracts, barriers to market adoption of formal agricultural insurance, and on the production decisions of farmers who have formal insurance.

providers have to offer a "no-frills" savings account. It's an account with no fees for opening, withdrawals, or balance inquiry, and so forth. By law, the banks have to offer these accounts even though they lose money on them.

So when you send a "secret shopper" into the banks looking for a savings product, they are never actually offered the no-frills account. Of course, the banks won't make it easy because there's a disincentive to the banks to open these accounts. They lose money.

The point that I want to make is that part of the take-up problem, especially in the case of savings, is that some of these products are pretty crappy. If we see no demand for these products, maybe that's a good thing actually. If you put money into one of these accounts, check the balance a few times, make a few withdrawals, half or all the money has been eaten up by fees. So the characteristics of the product are very important.

But, of course, there are other issues when you're thinking about brick-and-mortar type products. Transaction costs are a huge issue, not only travel distance but also the fact that these folks don't feel comfortable entering these facilities. They think banks are for the rich. They are actually treated pretty poorly, and they feel they don't belong. So there's a lot of reluctance to do so.

I think a very promising area is mobile banking, agent-based banking— depositing or withdrawing money with a shopkeeper. These accounts are virtual and are cheap to maintain, so you can actually start offering products that someone might want, that are inexpensive.

On credit, well, people do want credit. In some cases there is too much supply and reckless lending practices, like what we've seen in India.[4] But in other places there is still a problem of access to credit at all, rural Malawi for instance.

Insurance is another case altogether. If you look at data from Findex,[5] the percentage of folks who report having insurance is very very small. We have

4. This is a reference to the overindebtedness crisis in Andhra Pradesh, India, in 2010 which led to a battle over regulation between the state of Andhra Pradesh and the central government, and eventually to major downsizing of many of India's large microfinance institutions such as SKS and Basix. A useful overview of the crisis as it was happening can be found at: http://www.cgdev.org/blog/backgrounder-indias -microfinance-crisis.

5. Global Findex, or the Global Financial Inclusion Database, is a data-gathering project overseen by the World Bank and funded by the Gates Foundation, which gathers information on the use of financial services from representative samples in 148 economies.

no idea if that's because the products are being offered but people don't want them, or because people don't know about them. Or, if the issue is that banks are simply not offering them. You mentioned the trust issues, and those are certainly very important in insurance take-up, especially at the beginning. Buyers have to believe that the institution offering the insurance will in fact pay out on a claim. Many potential buyers might have been burned in the past.

The trust issue can definitely be overcome. Once you start paying claims, people realize these institutions are real. And some of the products have been designed specifically to pay out frequently. But, of course, those products don't have large payouts. So there's a trade-off between developing trust and good value: having a product that pays out when you need it and a product that pays enough when you need it.

TO: There are two narratives about what's happening in these poor households. One is that there's rampant market failure: there's lack of information, there's lack of trust, there's lack of good products, there's lack of demand measurement. The other narrative is that these households are fairly sophisticated and understand what they need and that the products on offer aren't what they need. Which of those do you subscribe to?

XG: It's a bit of both, but I'd sign up more for the market failure narrative. Poor households are hedge fund managers, you might say. They manage tons of stuff. They have to devote their limited resources and attention on choices that have huge stakes and manage all kinds of risk and uncertainty. But if you look at the quality of information that financial services providers offer on their products, it's pretty dismal. If you ask any account holder about the terms of a loan or the fees or commissions that are built into the savings accounts they have, they have absolutely no idea. They can hardly tell you the name of the bank much less the terms of the product.[6]

The same is true for most people. If you ask me the specific terms of my mortgage, I might be able to tell you the rate, but I don't know what the other terms are. I didn't look at all the fine print in the contract. But we're protected because of some policies and regulations. But more important, if I miss a payment it's not a crisis, and if I realize I'm stretched for cash flow, I have a variety of options to make sure I don't go into default.

6. Refer to the 2016 Client Voice Project for in-depth surveys of clients' understanding of the terms and conditions of the financial products they are using. http://smartcampaign.org/tools-a-resources/1075

But poor households don't have options, so mistakes are very costly for these folks.

But I wouldn't say they know exactly what they want and they are able to assess and evaluate all the different offers and they end up choosing the right one; absolutely not. There's a huge diversity in terms of financial products and a lot of them are terrible.

TO: If that's the case, shouldn't we see better results from financial literacy and education campaigns? It's a pretty dismal record.[7] Your work on educating people about insurance[8] didn't show much impact and that's generally what happens with literacy campaigns—they don't have much impact.[3] So if it's a problem of information and understanding shouldn't we see larger effects?

XG: Several things come to mind. When you're talking about financial literacy and education,[9] there's something called a teachable moment. Education will generally have larger effects when people are actually facing a decision. So people learn, and they can act on the education at the same time. Whenever you offer financial education, you've got several factors going. First, there are the subset of people who are interested and have the time in the moment. And then, it's a subset of those people who will have the opportunity to use what they learn in a meaningful way. They may not have the chance to choose between products or make a financial decision with consequences. That's why studying financial literacy is tough—you lose power very quickly.

You can look at whether you've improved knowledge, and second you can look at whether you've changed behavior. Measuring improved knowledge

7. In general, rigorous studies of financial literacy programs have found very little impact. A recent meta-analysis of 201 studies of financial literacy intervention found that 0.1 percent of the change in financial behaviors measured is due to financial literacy interventions. See Fernandes, D., Lynch Jr, J., and Netemeyer, R. (2014), "Financial Literacy, Financial Education and Downstream Financial Behaviors," *Management Science* 60 (8). See additional discussion of financial literacy and training in general in interviews with Xavi Giné, Dean Karlan, and David McKenzie.

8. Giné and colleagues tested a variety of interventions to better understand the low take-up rates of microinsurance in rural India, including price, trust, and product understanding. While there was evidence that decreasing prices and increasing trust would stimulate demand, there was no effect from attempting to educate potential customers about crop insurance.

9. See interviews with Dean Karlan and Antoinette Schoar for additional discussion of financial literacy programs.

is fairly straightforward. And many financial literacy programs do show improved knowledge at least in the short term. But what you typically don't see in these studies is changes in behavior. So, for instance, you may not see people switch to a different and cheaper provider of remittances or save more or choose a better loan.

But even there it's hard to say whether you're seeing a "failure" in terms of behavior change. A lot of these studies are very partial in terms of the behavior outcomes they are looking for. So, for a particular household, it's not clear that saving more is a good path to better overall welfare at a particular time. The fact that you don't see people save more isn't necessarily an indication of the failure of financial literacy.

Now, the best time to provide financial literacy education is in the moment the consumer is choosing. But, of course, no financial services provider is going to offer that education. There's a reason these products are shrouded in vague information. The financial services providers are not altruistic with a goal of maximizing welfare of the consumer. So now you have the problem of figuring out, if you're not the financial services provider, who to offer the education to, who are the people that really need it because they are making choices in the short term. The education that is being offered may not be what the people need.

Think about the Rules of Thumb study[10]—people going through the typical class weren't learning much or changing behavior.[4] People who got the very general rules of thumb did seem to grasp them and use them. But then again those general rules may not help drive the changes you're looking for. Will rules of thumb let people choose the best savings account? I don't know.

TO: Let's talk about another kind of financial decision making: deciding to repay a loan. There's been this long-standing assumption that repayment of microcredit is driven by group liability or at least social pressure. You've done work in this area in several different countries. What do you think is really driving repayment behavior?

XG: Group liability, understood as making each borrower liable for other group members' loans, might be a factor. But there's also a separate factor.

---

10. Drexler, Fischer, and Schoar compare formal accounting training (e.g., double-entry bookkeeping) with much more simplistic "rules of thumb" training (e.g., keep business cash in a separate drawer from personal cash) for small shopkeepers in the Dominican Republic. They find no effect of the formal training but some positive effects of the "rules of thumb," particularly in bad sales months.

Many groups have public repayment. Everyone pays at the same time in front of everyone else. So there may be individual liability but still some of these group dynamics and shame may apply.

Given that, loan officers can be pretty harsh in terms of eliciting repayment. There's a lot of unpleasant things that can be done short of breaking someone's legs. And you saw some of that in India.[11]

In many cases the explanation is that people want to maintain access to credit from the institution. So they repay. In cases where there's competition, it's less clear what is happening. Someone could default on one institution and just go to another institution, especially if there's not a credit bureau. Though it's important to note that in places where there are multiple lenders, there may not be a credit bureau but loan officers from different institutions who talk to each other.

In terms of group versus individual liability, we've seen everything in sort of an equilibrium that there are enough folks that do repay that you have high repayment rates. In Kolar, a town in Maharashtra in India, there was an incident when the committee of Muslim religious leaders said that repaying microfinance loans was unlawful.[12] And all of the sudden you see massive defaults as people hear the announcement of the fatwa. Clearly, these are strategic defaults—people weren't suddenly unable to pay, they made a decision not to pay. What we were able to do there was to compare groups that were composed of Hindus and Muslims, and especially looking at people who were in multiple groups with different religious mixes.[5] We were able to start testing the effect of social pressure. The idea is that if there are a lot of people in my group who are not repaying, there is no point in me repaying. The whole point of group liability is that if the whole group repays there is a loan in the future. But if I know there is not going to be a loan in the future, why should I repay my portion? Even if I could or would under individual liability, I won't repay.

11. Again, this is a reference to the microfinance crisis in Andhra Pradesh in 2010. While there were many unproved allegations of borrowers being driven to suicide, there was ultimately some credible evidence that some SKS loan officers, in particular, were engaging in strongly coercive tactics when borrowers fell behind on repayment. See, for instance, this article from the Associated Press based on internal SKS documents: http://goo.gl/yZ3mlM.

12. This situation occurred in 2009, and was unconnected to the 2010 Andhra Pradesh crisis. An overview can be found at: http://online.wsj.com/public/resources/documents/AKMIReport2010.pdf.

So think about one guy who has loans with two groups. One is majority Muslim and the other is Hindu-dominated. What we see after the fatwa, compared to before, we found that this typical person will default on the Muslim-dominated group and not on the Hindu-dominated group. You don't have to work very hard with the data to see that. So there is a social pressure or social conformity factor going on.

I think, by the way, that's it's a bit unhealthy to put so much focus on repayment. The banks have to worry about correlated defaults, but there are two things banks should care about: repayment and customer base. Banks should be making a trade-off between absolute repayment and expanding the customer base.

I've been doing some work on government institutions and the repayment rates for government loans is abysmal.[13][6] That has all sorts of moral hazard and expectations involved. If you ask people to rank the priority of repayment, they always put the government lender last.

That's partly because the borrowers know they can put political pressure on the government institutions. They have an expectation that the government will bail them out if they don't repay or at least adjust the terms of the loan.

TO: It seems to me that you're saying that people really value the option of future access. You put the government institution last in line because you have reasonable faith that even if you don't repay, you'll still be able to access credit from the government in the future.

XG: What I was saying was actually something more basic. Suppose that you're farmer who has gotten credit from the government institution. There was a poor monsoon, but at harvest you do actually have the money to repay. If you go ahead and repay, then you'll have to do so on the original terms. But if you don't repay and wait for the government to announce a relief program, then you can take advantage of that. So you wait and don't repay even though you can. But everyone is waiting, not just you. That forces the government's hand—and reinforces the moral hazard. It's very common.

So what we've done is to collect proprietary data from banks, publicly available administrative data, and survey data on wages, productivity, and

13. This work is discussed in more detail later in the interview.
14. This was approximately 1.7 percent of India's GDP at the time.

consumption to assess one of the largest borrower bailout programs in history, enacted by the government of India. This loan waiver program consisted of unconditional debt relief for more than 60 million rural households across India, amounting to a volume of more than US$16 billion.[14]

There are two contrasting views about what to expect from such program. One is the "debt overhang" view. The other is the "moral hazard" view. The debt overhang story suggests that farmers that took a loan and were unable to repay will not invest in the future because the return to their efforts would be appropriated by the bank. According to this view, this lack of incentives is responsible for ongoing low agricultural productivity, so the loan waiver could actually spur economic activity by providing defaulters with a fresh start. The moral hazard view suggests that the loan waiver may undermine the culture of repayment and exacerbate defaults as borrowers in good standing perceive that defaulting on their loan obligations carries no serious consequences. If that view is right, banks would shift lending away from areas with many defaulters.

The Indian loan waiver was a good way to test these competing views. We were able to use plausibly exogenous variation in bailout exposure. And we found that when banks get the waiver funds, they completely shift lending away from districts with high default to districts where there was little default. Overall, there is no new lending. Not to prior defaulters or to borrowers in good standing. But borrowers who had dutifully repaid prior to the bailout program now started to default, especially in districts with higher default. So after seeing people they know being bailed out, it looks like they thought "what the heck, I may as well default too." And there is absolutely no effect on the real economy. It does seem that our data does not support the "debt overhang" view at all.

It speaks somewhat to the recent debate after the 2008 US financial crisis. In one camp folks like Larry Summers or Tim Geithner were saying the crisis was caused by a bank run and not by fundamentals, so you had to stabilize the economy before anything else. They designed a plan to recapitalize all the banks, starting with the stress tests, and so forth, to try to shore up the banks and to shore up confidence in the banks.

But several months after, unemployment was still high, and consumption and consumer confidence was still down. So folks like Sufi and Mian[15]

---

15. Atif Mian and Amir Sufi make this argument in their book, *House of Debt* (University of Chicago Press, 2015) with a great deal of supporting argument and additional data on their blog, houseofdebt.org.

suggested that the crisis was caused by a version of the "balance sheet" view. They said average Americans were highly leveraged through their home mortgages, as they had been buying ever more expensive houses that they couldn't really afford. But once home prices stabilized or started falling, they realized they couldn't meet the mortgage payments, so they cut back on consumption, especially durables. And since demand for durables declined, so did labor demand and people stated to be laid off, reinforcing a downward spiral. The policy prescription according to this view is debt restructuring, which looks a lot like what the government of India did. I don't want to draw too much of a close analogy here because the contexts are so different, but India tried the policy and instead of banks lending again and spurring activity, they just shifted resources with no effect on the real economy.

TO: There's another story though right? Clearly, there was moral hazard. And you could assume that the banks knew, in general, what the farmers would do, but they have imperfect information. They don't have an in-depth knowledge of the psychology of each of these farmers. They use an imperfect screen but a rational one, nonetheless, when deciding how to implement the policy.

XG: Perhaps banks were overreacting, but they knew their clients well, both those that had defaulted and those in good standing, and yet, by and large the banks decided against new lending especially in places with high numbers of defaulters.

TO: That's the story we had all along about microcredit and credit constraints right? Banks had imperfect information. They couldn't tell who was creditworthy, and they were excluding whole classes of customers because they couldn't distinguish the creditworthy from the uncreditworthy.

XG: Well in the standard microcredit model there is a joint liability clause to encourage borrowers to self-select into groups of safe borrowers. So the bank solves the informational problem by incentivizing prospective borrowers to self-select. And in the Indian case, the banks already had knowledge of these customers. They weren't new customers, but existing customers that the banks had information on whether they were repaying or not.

TO: That the "good" borrowers were defaulting when they saw what was going on suggests that these farmers are fairly sophisticated—they're making strategic defaults. They may not be able to tell you the terms of a particular loan but they understand what really matters in these contracts.

XG: I think you're absolutely right on that.

Let me give you another example: the work I did with Dean Yang in Malawi[16] with fingerprinting.[7] There's no unique ID system in Malawi and there's high turnover over among loan officers. What that means is that all institutional memory about borrowers is lost when a loan officer leaves. What's happening in this situation is that a lot of folks go take a loan and default. They know they can get a loan in the future even though they default because they can change their name or somehow convince the next loan officer that they've never borrowed before. What that does is create a situation where, on the one hand, there is limited supply of credit. The banks are playing a one-shot game, every period, every season there is a *tabula rasa*. You can't offer dynamic contracts because there is no way of rewarding the good borrowers or penalizing the defaulters.

Enter fingerprinting. What the institutions can do now is require finger-printing as part of the loan application so that they can create credit histories for their borrowers. They in effect tell applicants, "you can default, but there is no way you'll be able to fool us into giving you another loan in the future." All of sudden that creates the possibility for the bank to use the dynamic incentives, provide better terms for faithful repayers and shut out the defaulters.

What actually happened there—going back to your sophistication story—is that the individuals that were more likely to default *ex ante* are actually increasing repayment dramatically. In fact, it's quite interesting. First off, they are borrowing less, making sure that they can repay whatever they took out and they repay more. There's less diversion of the loan into other spending. These are agricultural loans to buy inputs for a crop. The loans are funded by an institution that is buying the harvest. So what these people did is put more of the loan and more effort into farming, and they get better yields and they repay at a higher rate.

TO: Presumably the people in the community knew who the defaulters were. Wouldn't the people in the community have incentive to reveal the defaulters, just in terms of keeping the bank in the community? If there's a serial default problem in my community and the bank leaves town, that cuts off my access to future loans doesn't it? What I would think would happen is that either everyone realizes after a few seasons that repayment

16. See the interview with Dean Yang (chapter 12) for additional discussion of this study, particularly the finding that some of the people induced to repay because they had now identifiable higher earnings as a result.

doesn't matter and no one repays and the bank leaves, or the community starts self-policing so that the good borrowers can maintain access to credit.

XG: What's going on is that repayment is not zero. You have three types of folks. Folks that are very honest and diligent about repaying even in a one-shot game. And then you have people who are either not very good farmers and can't repay, and then the strategic defaulters who are good farmers and can repay but choose not to. That group is going to max out their loans and then not repay.

In that scenario you can have an equilibrium where interest rates are high to account for the strategic defaulters but the bank is still operating. If the default rate is such that it can be managed by interest rates, then the system still works.

But sometimes you also have government coming in and altering the equilibrium. Say there was a drought and the government decides that farmers don't have to repay their loans. But even still there is money to be made. So the system doesn't completely unravel. Not everyone will default.

TO: That situation seems to bear out the original thinking behind group liability.[17][8] In the absence of good knowledge of the borrowers, you outsource your information gathering and policing to the community. But you brought up the alternative story that it's the group meeting not the group liability that matters.

XG: In theory, there is a big distinction between group liability and individual liability. In practice, the line is very blurry. You clearly have institutions like the one in Malawi where you have group liability on paper but, when you start talking to loan officers and borrowers, you see that group liability is not really enforced. What happens is that in a group where you have a few defaulters, the repayers are still getting loans the next season. The loan officer just moves the good borrowers to a different group. And the loan officer may directly or indirectly encourage seizing the defaulter's movable assets. There are institutions that enforce group liability more than others, but it's a blurry line.

In that kind of context, there is no incentive to tell on those who have defaulted. If you are a repayer you are going to get a loan the next season. If it was true group liability, then you would see that the group members

17. This framing of why microcredit worked—outsourcing monitoring of borrowers from the lender to group members—can be traced to Joseph Stiglitz who proposed it and built a model suggesting that it enhanced welfare.

were working harder to kick out the bad guys. But in practice, there are multiple lenders, multiple groups, and different ways of gaming the system, so both the repayers and the defaulters likely can get credit in the future.

Let me nuance that a little bit. First off, in this case of fingerprinting you would actually perhaps see the effect be the largest when the bank is dealing with completely individual clients who don't know each other. That's not the situation that we had. What we had were actually groups of farmers getting together—to get a loan, you had to be part of a group. You're absolutely right that the group of farmers could have served as a first pass of screening to keep out the strategic defaulters. But the groups didn't have enough of a commitment to do that. These groups had, on average, default rates of about 30 percent. So there was scope for fingerprinting to change behavior.

Now, going all the way back to the insurance take-up question. One of the reasons that take-up is so low is that you have to think about what the government is doing in terms of stabilizing incomes and stabilizing consumption after the fact. So the farmer can buy insurance, but if the government is going to *ex post* provide a safety net when things truly go bad, then I'm already insured. Why buy insurance? Lots of people have some form of insurance, formal or informal.[18] They already have some type of insurance if you think about it. For instance, India has this guaranteed workfare program[19]—everyone is entitled to a minimum number of days of paid work with the government.[9] So that's an example of a government insurance mechanism. When the monsoon is bad, people work more days in the workfare program. In that situation, should they buy private weather insurance? Maybe not. In Malawi, it's not so formal. But the government has a history of intervening if the rains are bad. The effect is the same. If the rains are bad, the government will step in and cancel the loans. So why buy insurance for poor rainfall? And why not take a risk on defaulting on your loan? The government may just bail you out.

18. See interview with Jonathan Robinson (chapter 18) for a discussion of informal insurance mechanisms and their inadequacy.
19. The National Rural Employment Guarantee Scheme, NREGS, nominally provides employment income as a safety net for rural Indians. In practice, the program has many issues that limit accessibility and effectiveness. It has also been the subject of what may be the largest RCT ever, involving 19 million people, conducted by Karthik Muralidharan and Paul Niehaus. A randomized evaluation found the issuing of biometric IDs improves the efficiency and effectiveness of NREGS.

TO: So the ideal, at least in the short term, for borrowers and private lenders is for the government to pay for the insurance.

XG: Right. That's where I see index insurance going. Like the case of Mexico. Index insurance can be used as a way of stabilizing budgets. If there are bad rains, there are huge government outflows for agriculture. Why doesn't the government buy insurance against bad rains? That's basically what Mexico is doing with the CADENA program.[20]

TO: I want to talk more about the reality of microcredit contracts and how they are being enforced. How big of a problem for research is the assumption that what headquarters says is the product is what's actually being offered in the field? You indicated that there are lots of times where the loan officers are selectively enforcing or selectively altering the terms of the contract. Or even accidentally misrepresenting the product to the customer.

XG: That's a good question. Researchers will usually, or at least should, go and spend a lot of time talking to loan officers and trying to make sure that the product offer is standardized. There are certain features of a product that are hard to manipulate, especially at institutions that are using technology intensively, because a lot of the features—interest rates, repayment schedule—are built into the software. The loan officer can't arbitrarily change those things. But you're right that when it comes to enforcement and other softer aspects of the product, those can definitely vary by loan officer. You should conduct focus groups to try to understand to what extent these things do change. I've not seen a systematic analysis of whether there are institutions that are more uniform than others in delivering and enforcing their contracts.

Now, that's not going to be a big problem for internal validity. If you've got your power calculations right and you are randomly selecting loan officers into the treatment and control groups, then, while you're going to have variability from officer to officer, that should balance out. If you're especially worried about that, you can also run experiments where each loan officer has a treatment and control group. Dean Karlan and I did that in the

---

20. For an overview of the CADENA program, under which the Mexican national government provides climatic catastrophe insurance to small farmers, see: http://goo.gl/Cz6jw0.

group versus individual liability study in the Philippines, so we were able to look at loan officer fixed effects.[10] That's an approach if you're worried about some of these issues.

In more general terms, though, yes it's something that needs to be thought about. These are products that are offered by people, so there is going to be some variability. I think this is an area that can be researched. Microfinance products are thought to be these cookie-cutter products where the loan officer has little or no flexibility to change the terms, but there is some discretion for sure: whether or not they accept certain borrowers, how they form groups, and so forth. They can and do manipulate those things. Whether or not that is systematic probably depends on the institution. It's still a black box. There's not a lot of research being done there. We don't really even know whether the knowledge of loan officers is the same. I would submit that sometimes the loan officers don't know much about the terms of the products they are offering.

Going back to Mexico, one of the requirements is that banks publish the *costo anual total* [CAT], or total annual cost for a bank account. That provides a summary measure of the cost of a savings product, similar to what an APR is for credit. It's the rate, net of all fees and commissions. So, when we were mystery shopping, we had some of our "high-literacy" shoppers ask the bank officer to explain what the CAT was; not the figure, but to explain what it meant. It was amazing. Only in 2 of our 120 visits were the bank personnel able to explain what the CAT was. They had no idea. If they have no idea what it is, how can they explain properly what the products are?

These loan officers are typically fresh out of college or inexperienced. They get some training but typically not a lot. They have rules and incentives and targets, and they follow them. When you do an RCT, that's fine in terms of the internal validity if you're randomizing the loan officers, but for external validity it's still something of a black box.

TO: It's interesting to me that loan officer behavior comes up often when we talk about "Credit Plus" products[21] but is hardly ever discussed in the context of basic savings or credit programs.

XG: Well, for instance, in a savings intervention, the research team will often play a very hands-on role in terms of designing the offer, the rules,

---

21. Credit Plus are products offered by microfinance institutions that include additional services such as training, agricultural extension, and health services.

the forms. So there may be less variability. But you also see research that is varying the loan applications, or the acceptance rate, or something like that. So in those cases you are likely to have handled variability. But after the loan is made or the savings account is opened, that's where you get more variability in terms of enforcement or follow-up.

TO: I'd like to delve into the series of Malawi experiments. I'm very interested in your take in what's happening in the Commitments to Save work—where at first glance at least the results don't seem to make any sense.[11]

XG: Noooo … well actually you're right. (Laughter)

I think the value of that paper is that at least we're able to knock down an explanation that is probably the first that comes to mind when thinking about commitment products. That's the so-called self-control problem. There's no way that the commitment group showed larger impacts because of the commitment accounts' ability to tie the hands of the farmer. We know that simply because there was no money in the commitment accounts. So, by definition, it's not about tying their hands.

Folks in the commitment account group and folks in the ordinary account group basically proceeded to withdraw all the money in the account and keep it at home. As soon as word comes that there is money in the account, they all rush to the bank, withdraw it all, and take it home. The people with access to commitment accounts couldn't withdraw the money in those accounts obviously, so they didn't fund them. They only funded the ordinary accounts, and then withdrew all the money just like the people who didn't have the commitment account.

So that indicates that it's not a self-control problem. But if it's not self-control, what is it? That's where we, unfortunately, fall short. In hindsight, I wish we'd designed things a little differently so that we got a few other measures.

There are two alternative stories. One is that it doesn't solve self-control problems but solves "other-control" problems. Another story is that it's about mental accounting factors. But we can't say anything about that. We've got a little bit of anecdotal evidence but not enough to say anything about whether those stories are right. So more research is needed.

There are some big picture things that do make sense though. Sales from tobacco are 40 to 50 percent of overall agricultural income. What we found was that about 80 percent of the funds saved by the commitment account group goes into tobacco-related investments. So they seem to have made a decision to use the money for investments in the future. In some other studies you see that for every dollar saved, you see a 10 cent increase in investment. That's definitely not what we're finding. What we're finding is that you're saving 20,000 kwacha and investing 17,000 kwacha. What that means is that the account holders were somehow able to save that 17,000 kwacha and avoid the temptation to spend it until the next planting season.

The bad news is that we don't find decreases in transfers out, which is another popular explanation: you're using the commitment account as an excuse to be able to turn down requests from other family members or others in the community. But there's a huge problem in measuring the transfers. Every time we think about it, we want to kill ourselves. We didn't do a good job of eliciting when the transfers were made. Ideally, you want to trace out when the transfers happened between planting, harvest, and the next planting. So you can imagine a situation where the transfers went down between harvest and planting, but then actually went up after the next harvest when people realized they had more disposable income because they'd invested more and produced a bigger crop. But unfortunately, we didn't gather the data to look at that.

There's even another explanation that does involve the commitment accounts. It's possible that the people in the control group take their earnings from the harvest and rush out and spend a lot right away, overspending on current consumption, you might say, so that they can avoid requests for transfers. They know the requests are going to come and they won't be able to say no, so they just go ahead and spend the money now. Meanwhile the people with the commitment accounts bring the money home but use the commitment account as an excuse to turn down transfer requests. So both groups are turning down requests—and you don't see a difference in the totals—but there is something different happening in the background related to the commitment account. One group is consuming, the other group is saving. But again, unfortunately, we don't have any way of teasing that out.

We do have some anecdotal evidence that people were more selective about who they made transfers to. So people we interviewed said something like, "my sister always comes and asks for money for clothes, and I was able to say, 'sorry, the money is in the commitment account,' but my neighbor's child was sick so I gave him some money." So there may have been more flexibility in what requests to accept, but we can't really say much about the other-control problem. I wish we'd done a better job on that.

Another explanation is mental accounting. The only difference between the commitment account and ordinary account—everyone was given some financial literacy education, a speech about the wonders of saving—but it was the commitment account group that had to sit down and think about how much money they wanted from their harvest to go into their commitment account or the ordinary account. So it's possible that just having to think about how you are going to spend the money creates the nudge that they needed to avoid temptation to current consumption. We try to look at whether people remembered *ex post* the balances, but at the end of the day, because we weren't thinking about this possibility when we were designing the questionnaires, we just didn't ask the right questions.

That's where that research stands. Clearly, the commitment accounts helped. Clearly, commitment accounts do not solve a self-control problem, at least in our sample. But as to the underlying mechanism, we're less clear. Now, there's also this issue of one versus two accounts. Whether it's physically having two accounts or allocating money into different buckets that matters, we don't know. So what we're doing now is trying to delve into that. In the next round, one group is offered one account. The other group is offered two accounts and a subgroup has commitment features on one of the two accounts. The other subgroup doesn't have the commitment features but can "label" the accounts. And they all have the opportunity to sit down and allocate the future income to different uses.

TO: The results do align with the Dupas Robinson Health Savings Accounts results.[22][12] What's happening there is not classic self-control, it seems to be some combination of mental accounting and goal setting.

Another thing that comes up in the Commitment to Save study is the declining return on investment that the farmers get from these investments that they made. It seems that they were pretty savvy in plowing their resources into the best land. How concerned are you about that?

XG: One thing that's important to remember is that these guys did have access to loans prior to the savings intervention. Because there is a unique buyer of tobacco, repayment could be guaranteed. However, even though they were getting loans, the loans were fixed. So these farmers were still constrained. So that's why we see increases in investment, to begin with. So, while you're right that the returns were lower on the margin, those

---

22. Discussed in detail in the interviews with Pascaline Dupas (chapter 14) and Jonathan Robinson (chapter 18).

investments were probably the best uses of the funds that the farmers have. Had the loans been larger, we might not have seen increases in investment. But we knew that the farmers were constrained, so it makes sense that they would increase investment.

TO: That brings us back to the questions around take-up. In this case it's investing more, but it's the same issue around adopting technology or investing in better inputs or managing risk. So we're back to the opening question: why is it so hard to get people to adopt these products or technologies that do pay off?

XG: As I said, it's not an easy answer. Well there are several answers. Information might be one. Liquidity constraints might be another. Risk might be another. Then there's trust, and what not.

Then there's the context. For any individual subsistence farmer the returns to any of these investments might not be that high. They might not have access to markets or infrastructure or the labor to harvest a larger crop. Where crop markets and labor markets are functioning well, that's where you do see these investments. In some of these villages in Africa where there is poor infrastructure and thin markets and no access to irrigation, then maybe the returns are not that high. And by that I mean the absolute value of the gains may not be that big. The ROI may be high, but it may not, produce very much actual money. That's Rosenzweig's argument in his review[13] of *Poor Economics*.[14] If that's the case, then the farmer may not truly think it's worthwhile to invest.

In the end, I think it's a combination of these stories. We're still struggling to uncover what's going on in different contexts. Think about the programs in Malawi and in Tanzania, which is only about subsidizing the cost of the inputs. There's a food security concern, farmers are not using fertilizer. Let's subsidize fertilizer and see what that does. Fine. But of this plethora of barriers, you're only affecting one: liquidity constraints. What about risk? What about complementary inputs? What about information? What about markets?

So I think it's a combination of all these things. And depending on the context, some are going to be more relevant than others. But there are examples of overcoming these barriers. In India, you have the Green Revolution. People did adopt technologies and did invest, and it had a tremendous impact on hunger and well-being.

TO: What is the emerging theory of change on how to deal with these barriers? Is the underlying argument that you need a big push to address all of them at once, or do we need to make whatever small changes we can make along the way?

XG: I'm not an advocate of doing everything or that everything is needed at once to make an impact.

In the end we're researchers. What we are trying to do is help policy makers understand what are the underlying market failures or the underlying constraints so that they can do something to alleviate it. If you do everything as a pilot, there's no way to tell what is working and why. Maybe some of these interventions are redundant and the money would be best used somewhere else. However, when thinking about pilots or what not, there's only so much appetite that policy makers or the partners that you are working with will have. So you're always trying to do research under constraints. There's the budgetary constraint, there's the management constraint, there are political constraints. Sometimes the policies just can't be changed in the political environment. There's something to be said for trying things on a large scale, but that doesn't mean doing a lot of things at the same time.

Where I sit at the World Bank Research Group we're basically hired to do impact evaluations. In a way the question is given to you. Figure out whether this works and why. I don't have the luxury of designing things from scratch. Think about, say, access to financial products. We take access as the final goal. We're going to figure out how best to increase access, to knock down the various barriers to adoption.

In the larger scheme of things, I don't get to think about the issues of "should we be focused on financial access or CCTs or training?" I do think everyone would benefit if there was more microfoundations theory that would allow us to do some policy analysis *ex ante*. That would allow us to predict what the biggest payoffs likely would be. We're just not doing that at the Bank, and I think that would be really useful.

Don't get me wrong. We've been able to do a lot that is useful, creating a symbiosis in terms of marrying theory, RCTs, and policy. But we're not doing much at the big picture level.

TO: So once you've got a good answer to your question, how do you use that to change the world? From your perspective, are experiments better at driving policy change? Are they more convincing to policy makers and practitioners?

XG: It depends on the context and question. Policy makers have more and more appetite for research-based policy recommendations. But whether they design or tweak programs with these recommendations in mind is another matter.

The audit study that I mentioned earlier is a different approach than experiments and is getting a lot of traction. The initial work was in Mexico, but now it has been replicated in Ghana, Peru, and soon Colombia. And the results are very comparable across countries. Essentially that very little information about the products is provided voluntarily and that consumers are not offered the lowest cost product. That's because the bank staff have incentives too. So this work has clear implications for disclosure policy that should be easy to implement. Who's going to argue with trying to provide better information? In other contexts, translating recommendations to policy is more difficult.

TO: This does speak to one of the critiques of external validity of RCTs: that so much is dependent on the provider. Some of what the audit study shows is that it's not just dependent on the bank, it's dependent on the person who actually talks to the customer.

XG: But there are broad patterns. We presented the results to the bankers association in Peru. While some of the bank representatives were pretty defensive, some of them asked "I want to know how I rank in relation to other providers like me; we want to know where we failed." These were the individuals responsible for the recourse mechanisms, customer service, and for the training of staff, so they wanted to know how to improve the training. While this is not going to change the incentives that staff face to sell a particular product, lenders can be forced to use standardized formats, like the Schumer box in the US,[23] to make comparisons across products easier. We actually tested a version of a standardized disclosure format in Mexico. Just the way you present information changes the likelihood that a consumer will choose the cheapest product by more than the difference between a consumer who went to university and one who didn't go to university. Education and financial literacy matter but far less than how the information is presented.

However, this standardized format only helps choose between the products offered by the provider. A consumer may choose the lowest cost

23. A standard format for disclosing information about credit card terms named after Senator Charles Schumer who introduced legislation requiring it.

product at that particular bank, but the product could still be very costly compared to similar products in the market. So the next step is to encourage the consumer to shop around. To do that, I am pushing for a standardized format that includes a signal about how good the product is relative to the market. So imagine that in the format there is a green light/red light or a thermometer, or a grade that tells you how this particular loan offer compares to other possible offers. That would give you a signal about "quality" of the loan product and whether it makes sense to go to another bank to try to get a better deal. This is different from what is actually happening.

TO: So the observational study is driving some policy change in these countries, but it's not answering a larger question. RCTs can do that, but they are an expensive way to answer questions. When you're choosing what questions to answer and how to answer those questions in an environment with fewer resources to go around, does that influence what questions you try to answer and what methods you use?

XG: I think we've not yet reached the point where there may be diminishing returns to more RCTs. While replicating similar designs in different contexts is important, perhaps a more fruitful approach is something like what Ken Wolpin and Petra Todd have done in the context of Progresa: build a structural model and estimate it using pre-program data, then simulate it to see how well it fits the post-program data.[15] Researchers could also create holdout samples—observations not used to estimate the parameters of the model but to assess the out-of-sample goodness of fit. If the holdout sample comes from a very different context and the model is able to rationalize the data, then one gains confidence in the model. Once you have a model that fits the data within the sample well, and is able to replicate choices also outside the model, then you can better see the likely effects of whatever policy you're interested in. That's the point of the lack of external validity criticism of RCTs. This is what I try to do with Hanan Jacoby in the context of groundwater markets in India.[16] We have data for six districts, two of which are very drought prone, but very different in many dimensions. But we believe that the decision to sell water and under what contract is fundamentally the same in all districts. So we use the four districts to estimate the model and then we feed in the data from the two different districts to predict the contracts that would arise if the model were correct. We find that the model does well predicting the groundwater market dynamics in these two very different districts. So we have a lot of confidence then that this model will be useful in a lot of different contexts, thereby addressing the point of external validity.

TO: What does it take to change your priors? Do you think in Bayesian terms? What does it take to change your mind about whether something works or not?

XG: Very little.[24] A lot of times I've been surprised by the results in the work that I've done and that forces you to rethink things. Once I understand the mechanisms, I'm happy to update. I'm actually notorious for not knowing *ex ante* what will be the driver of impact. Typically, when I think about what the likely gains or the mechanisms operating in an intervention are I'm way off. A lot of times the models of behavior I have in mind don't encompass the features that really matter. So I have to change my mind all the time.

24. See Tyler Cowen's interview (chapter 19) for a similar perspective on RCTs ability to change one's mind.

9 Lant Pritchett

Lant is professor of the Practice of International Development at the Kennedy School of Government at Harvard, and a senior fellow at the Center for Global Development and Bureau for Research and Economic Analysis of Development. Lant spent more than a decade in various research roles at the World Bank. He is author of *Let Their People Come* and *The Rebirth of Education: Schooling Ain't Learning*.

TO: As I read what you've written on RCTs, I see two streams of critique. One is, "we're focusing on things that are too small." The second is the overhyping of certainty as a result of the methodology.

LP: I would say there are three critiques.

One critique is you're tackling only small problems because you're tackling problems almost by construction that are individuated. Meaning, the level I'm intervening at is the person,[1] whereas what we economists know and specialize in is how systems work.

The only insight that economists bring to the world is that it's not at the individual level that success and failure happens. The interaction between individuals is what matters. That's the insight of Adam Smith right? The market as a system mediates the actions of self-interested individuals to produce teleologically unintended but normatively rankable outcomes. Meaning, to rephrase Adam Smith, the butcher doesn't give you meat because he likes you, he does it for money but that produces actually really good outcomes that nobody intended.

1. See interview with Frank DeGiovanni (chapter 13), where he comments on only funding RCTs for programs that operate on an individual level because community-level interventions are too hard or too expensive to evaluate with RCTs.

So in RCTs you've reduced the system to the individual. Nothing super-important about development happens at the individual level.[2]

The second critique is the RCT folks have the fundamental political economy of policy change wrong.[3][1] Think of any development activity as being a mapping from inputs to activities to outputs to outcomes. The claim the randomistas make is we're going to take cash, we're going to turn it into the activity of doing RCTs, and that's going to lead to better outcomes. But they just don't have a coherent, much less evidence-based, causal model of how the outputs they produce are going to yield the outcomes they intend.[4] That requires some positive theory of policy: how do policies actually get made, adopted, and implemented? They have this just unbelievably Cro-Magnon simple model of policy adoption that essentially asserts that once there is better knowledge in the world about policies, that will lead to better policies being adopted and implemented.

You could make an argument like that, but it's just wrong. So they're wrong about the fact that the outputs of RCTs are going to change policy.[5] What's amazing is that precisely their critique of all other development endeavors is that they were wrong about their causal model of outputs to outcomes. Their attack on microcredit is that while it's true you can turn inputs into loans and those loans produce activities that are outputs, you were wrong about the causal model by which the availability of microcredit would transform outcomes for individuals.

2. For more on Pritchett's thinking on "small" interventions in the history of development, see his post on the Center for Global Development blog, "Is Your Impact Evaluation Asking Questions That Matter?," http://www.cgdev.org/blog/your-impact-evaluation-asking-questions-matter-four-part-smell-test, where he argues that few, if any, of the interventions studied most via RCTs played any significant role in the development of wealthy countries.

3. For additional background to Pritchett's point here, see "The Policy Irrelevance of the Economics of Education," a paper prepared as part of a Brookings conference titled, "What Works in Development? Thinking Big and Thinking Small." The collected papers from the conference have been published in a volume with the same name.

4. Most of the interviews include a question about the individual's theory of change and their experience in their work driving policy or product changes.

5. See interview with Frank DeGiovanni (chapter 13), where he argues that RCTs have been necessary to influence policy makers to consider "graduation model" packages of interventions for ultra-poor households.

It's their most powerful critique of what everyone else is doing, and yet they don't have a coherent answer about what they are doing. What is their coherent model that moves from the outputs of the research papers to the outcome of better lives for poor people? That has to be a political economy model. A political model if it's public policy you think is changing, or an organizational model if you think you're going to change the behaviors of organizations. It's just so frustrating because you can't even have this debate with them. They don't even pretend to have a coherent model of this. And yet it's precisely the criticism they levy against everyone else.

The third critique is they are just deeply wrong about the science and what science means and how science works. Meaning they're wrong about the relative importance of internal versus external validity.[6] There are multiple levels to that critique. But they're just obsessed with internal validity and their basic response to the external validity problem, since they started, was, "well we'll deal with that later, since we have no internally valid estimates of program effects. Why are you worried about whether the ones we have are externally valid?" A bunch of us were saying there's not going to be any external validity. This is not going to add up to anything because there's huge heterogeneity in program impacts based on nonrigorous methodological studies.[7][2] Now the future came and they've just replicated exactly the same variance we already knew was there. If you're a policy maker and want to know if I undertake a program of this type, what will its impact be in my context, they have contributed exactly zero to answering that question. People are no better off in terms of knowledge than they were before.

Everyone who was a practitioner of any type knew external validity was a huge problem, and part of the reason the RCT skeptics pooh-poohed the internal validity obsession was because they knew it wasn't that big of a deal. Now with the randomistas own data we can show that we were right and they were wrong.

6. See interview with Jonathan Morduch (chapter 4) for more discussion of the history and importance of internally valid estimates of impact.
7. An example can be found in Pritchett's paper "What Education Production Functions Really Show." While the paper is focused on a model explaining the allocation of education spending and ways to improve the effectiveness of education spending, it illustrates how broad the range of program impact estimates was in studies of marginal products of education investment.

We now have six estimates of the impact of microcredit. If we were going to predict microcredit's impact in some context, would we be better off with the nonexperimental internally invalid estimate from our own context or an RCT from another context? The answer is you would increase your prediction error by using the RCT over your own context's bad estimate.[8][3]

I don't see how the debate can be won any more conclusively than that. What they are proposing as a scientific approach leads to significantly *worse* prediction errors than the stupidest possible alternative of just relying on the existing OLS[9] estimates in context.

TO: Isn't there an aspect of the external validity question that comes down to whether we are learning things about contexts or about human beings and behavior? Haven't we learned something about human behavior?[10] Something similar to the systematic biases from Kahneman's research?[11][4]

LP: I disagree there. An economist might say that all human beings seek to maximize utility right? That's true but it's also contentless. Because what maximizes utility in two different contexts might be completely different. Proving that human beings maximize utility in lots of different contexts doesn't answer any questions about the absolute magnitude of program impacts unless you also argue that what is in fact in the utility function is the same and roughly to the same degree in all contexts. There's no evidence for that. Economists have never asserted that.

8. In two papers co-authored with Justin Sandefur of the Center for Global Development, Pritchett argues that the differences in effect size from one context to another dwarf the differences been randomized evaluations and nonrandomized evaluations of impact in the same context. Therefore a more accurate estimate of effectiveness can be found by relying on a nonrandomized evaluation in the same context than a randomized evaluation from a different context. Specifically here, he refers to an analysis of the papers in the January 2015 issue of the *American Economics Journal: Applied Economics*.
9. Ordinary least squares is an econometric approach to assessing how one variable influences another where treatments have not been randomized.
10. A version of this same question is posed to many of the interviewees, most of whom believe that RCTs have been particularly effective at uncovering common human behaviors and that these insights are particularly useful.
11. Daniel Kahneman, who shared the 2002 Nobel Prize in economics despite being a social psychologist, pioneered the exploration of cognitive biases and their effect on decision making, with important implications for economics.

Our whole point is that people have different utility functions. That's why trade exists. The point of EC101, the first model you learn, is that people trade because they have different preferences and that leads to higher welfare for both people.

When anthropologists run the same experiment in different contexts, they get very different results. So as far as I know, one of the few things we know scientifically across lots of cultures is playing the ultimatum game. And if you play the ultimatum game across a lot of different cultures, you get extraordinarily different results.[12] The idea that there is external validity in program impacts but not in something simple like the ultimatum game just seems loopy to me.

Speaking of having it both ways, the argument that there will be external validity because there are universal features of human beings kind of runs up against the issue of working on "big" versus "small problems." If these heuristic biases are universal or nearly so, then it is hard to make them the explanation of huge variations across countries in development outcomes—either across countries or over time. If these Kahneman-like systematic flaws in rationality are a barrier to development, then why are the USA and Japan and Europe developed?

Now let's go back to basic science. Physics 101. If we write down a Newtonian law of motion, we do it because we know that there is invariance. If we translate an experiment to some other space, we're going to get exactly the same result. That's a classic example of an invariance law. There are certain aspects of medicine where we have invariance. We kind of know how cells behave. An invariance law can also specify ways in which the outcome will vary—because of temperature, for example. So we can do experiments on cells from all over the world and expect the results to be the same.

But that's precisely what we don't have in economics. What we do have says that people and systems are not invariant. So, for instance, no one ever expected that the impact on a person of having the offer of microcredit at a given interest rate would be constant in some way. That's just absurd. The fundamentals of how to do science somehow got lost in the enthusiasm for RCTs.

TO: Why has the RCT movement captured so much attention and energy?

12. See interview with Dean Yang (chapter 12) where the use of the ultimatum game, sometimes referred to as the dictator game, is discussed.

LP: I think there were three separate trends. The success of any social movement usually takes a confluence of things. It's often the case that many of the elements existed for a long time. There had been a civil rights movement since the end of the Civil War at least, so why did it suddenly have success in the 1960s and not before?

First, the RCT movement was in some sense the logical extension of debates about identification[13] that had been going on since the Cowles Commission.[14] In the logic of many disciplines you could make a name for yourself by being skeptical about the previous findings, which gave you an excuse to re-estimate what people had already estimated with your new technique. So there was this intellectual trend to be more and more skeptical of anybody else's claim to identification. Randomized trials became the gold standard for identification.

The point should be made very clearly that there was already a massive and sophisticated randomized control trial effort about social policy in the United States[15] that had existed since the 1970s.[5] I would make the assertion, and then maybe walk it back a bit, that nothing the current randomistas have done approaches the RAND health insurance experiment[16] of

13. See interviews with Michael Kremer (chapter 1) and Jonathan Morduch (chapter 4) for more discussion about these debates and their impact on the movement.

14. The Cowles Commission for Research in Economics, now known as the Cowles Foundation, is a research center focused on using statistical and mathematical models to explain the economy, with a special emphasis on better identification of causality.

15. See interview with Judy Gueron (chapter 5) on this topic, specifically about the lessons learned from using RCTs in social policy in the United States. Also note Gueron's and Howard Rolston's book *Fighting for Reliable Evidence*, which is a thorough history of the use of randomized evaluations in the US, and a discussion along similar lines with Tyler Cowen (chapter 19).

16. The RAND Health Insurance Experiment was one of the first large-scale social policy experiments in the US. The study randomized cost sharing for medical insurance (what we now generally refer to as co-pays and co-insurance). The study found that paying some amount for health services reduced use of those services, but that the reduction was equal across highly effective and less effective services. While free healthcare improved some health measures among the poorest and sickest patients, overall there was negligible impact on health from consuming less healthcare. Cost sharing also did not change people's risky health behaviors such as smoking. http://www.rand.org/pubs/research_briefs/RB9174.html.

the 1970s in terms of sophistication, in terms of importance, in terms of methodological rigor.

So there was this trend that I can sit in a seminar in Cambridge and whatever instrument you propose, I can concoct a story in which your instrument is wrong. The end game of that is that grad students increasingly despaired of getting their dissertations approved because their professors could think of some crazy way in which it might be the case that their instrument didn't produce completely clean identification. The logical consequence of that trend is people resorting to RCTs so they could take the debate about identification off the table. So that was one reason, and it was entirely internal to some subcomponents of the economics discipline.

The second thing[17] is that in aftermath of the cold war, aid was increasingly under attack and increasingly defensive.[6] The World Bank, DFID, USAID, and so forth, had a problem because they had lost a huge part of their political coalition. All of the critiques that programs weren't having the impact they were supposed to have become existentially critical. So all of the sudden, people like Abhijit Banerjee saying things about the World Bank and its lack of impact evaluation had to be responded to in a way that made enormous amounts of money available—because the aid community was politically vulnerable.

And the third element is the rise of large-scale philanthropy. Within the development community there have always been development people and charity people. I've always been a development guy. By development, I usually mean national development, large-scale social policies. If you come to me and say I can make that guy better off by putting in place a charitable program to give him food, I'd say, "Of course, you can. Go ahead, but don't call it development." The rise of the MDGs, which were part of the defensive reaction of the post–cold war weakened aid industry, and the rise of places like Gates[18] created a philanthropic interest in precisely the small questions. After all, you come to people in the World Bank with one of these charity programs and they would say, "You realize this is trivial in terms of what we're trying to do in the national development process, right?" But what's the philanthropist's problem? The philanthropist's problem is that I don't want to bother with national policy, I don't necessarily

17. This point is expounded on in Pritchett's paper "Can Rich Countries Be Reliable Partners for National Development?"
18. Here specifically meaning the Bill and Melinda Gates Foundation, launched in 2000, and the largest private foundation in the world.

want to work with governments at all. I want to take some cocooned channel of inputs into activities into outputs into outcomes and be sure that's actually going to be effective in a way that I can combine some warm glow of giving with some hardheaded analysis.

The only people for which the RCT movement is in fact a tool for the job is philanthropists. These are guys who are interested in the charity question, not the development question, for the most part. From the charity perspective, there's a nice confluence between the methodological demand for statistical power and of being able to tweak at the individual level. I can give this person food but not that person, I can give this person a bed net but not that person. Because after all, I'm giving something individuated, because I'm not trying to affect policy, I'm not trying to affect the government,[19] I'm not trying to affect national development processes. The rise of philanthropic concerns in terms of the overall action in developing countries is an important piece.

So you have the confluence of those three things. The methodological stance that there was no clean identification outside of RCTs, the defensive stance of the aid people who had to be seen as responding to these critiques (and the best way to respond was to give money to the people making the critiques), and the rise of philanthropy created this powerful nexus that accounts for the money and effort devoted to RCTs.

TO: Your PDIA[20] paper, in some ways is a theory of change involving small changes over time driven by individuals.[7] The people in the ministries or institutions are running programs and learning things and some number of them are deciding to make changes, some number are trying to tweak things to make them better. There's another critique of the RCT movement that says we should really just be studying institutions. You've made points about the "smallness" of RCTs, but you've also made the point that change doesn't happen by remaking the Ministry of Education, it happens from a bunch of people within the Ministry making changes over time.

LP: First of all, PDIA is a theory of change of organizations, not individuals. Its ontological unit is the organization. The whole distinction is separating from the capabilities of organizations that arise from the combination

19. See interview with Frank DeGiovanni (chapter 13) for a discussion of the Ford Foundation's efforts to affect government policy.
20. Problem Driven Iterative Adaptation.

of the capacities of individuals and the structures of organizations, not the capacities of individuals alone. We have a role for individuals in the organizational process, but it's a theory of organizational change.

I have a paper called "It Pays to Be Ignorant," which is a positive theory model as to why organizations don't do an RCT.[8] Imagine that your inputs are coming from an external source. To the extent that the RCT is a tool of the external authorizer, it *has* to be resisted by the organization. Let's say I'm an NGO and I'm getting grants from somebody and I'm competing for grants with lots of other people. And someone comes along and says, "We can do an RCT, and with the RCT you'll discover your true effectiveness." But once you discover your true effectiveness, you're pinned down. You can't game people that it's higher. And you are competing to get grants for, say, microcredit from an organization that might also finance girls' schooling and transparency. But your competitors for those grants aren't pinned down. So the only organization that would take that bet is one that's truly desperate. Part of my ability to persuade the grant maker is by making over-inflated claims of my effectiveness, just like everybody else is doing. As long as that's working, why would I ever agree to be pinned down about my true effectiveness with an RCT? If I'm doing transparency interventions, then I want there to be RCTs of microcredit. Then I can make outrageously huge claims about how effective my transparency initiative is going to be without being pinned down, while the microcredit people are hampered in their persuasion by evidence. The funder might be dubious about my claims and revise them down, but not as much as I'd be risking by doing an RCT. So it pays to be ignorant.

Now in our MeE model, the little "e" is experiential learning.[9] Our point is that you can do internal RCTs, meaning in the process of implementing your project you can try it multiple ways and judge the relative effectiveness of those ways, but without ever pinning down the outcome effectiveness. Our proposal for PDIA is a little bit hedging that bet, but it's much more like the feedback that organizations need. What they need feedback on is really about how activities translate into outputs. A lot of organization dysfunction isn't coming from the fact that they have the wrong causal models from outputs to outcomes; it's that they're not effective as an organization in going from inputs to outputs. In that space you can do lots of RCTs to see what techniques get you more outputs, say, higher loan repayment, without ever putting the core organizational link of outputs to outcomes at risk.

Nobody is against the methodological argument that RCTs produce clean identification of impacts. Everybody understands that. But if you want organizations to do more RCTs, they have to be more aligned with a positive model. If you want to do an RCT to change organizational behavior and you want organizations to do more RCTs, you have to align with the true purposes of the organizations.[21] Any external use of RCTs by donors, funders, ministries of finance, ministries of planning, whoever, is by its very nature a conflictual thing that is not going to build organizational capability or organizational interest in the learning coming from the RCT.

TO: It's obvious that you think many of the people involved in the RCT movement are very, very smart—and that's why you lament that these folks are spending so much time on RCTs. What's your theory of why these very smart people are "wasting their time"?

LP: If the papers they were writing were being written by public health PhD students at Kansas State, I would think it was an enormously productive use of their resources. But that's not who these people are. The main founders of the movement are all geniuses.

For example, Michael Kremer is an unbelievable genius. If you look at the O-rings paper,[22] that could have, and should have, been fundamentally transformational in the way we thought about policy and economic growth and everything else.[10] But have you heard of it? It disappeared without a trace. I think I have four papers with more citations than the O-ring paper and that's just wrong because that paper is way better. And Esther too. She's

---

21. See the interview with Rachel Glennerster (chapter 17) on why organizations choose to be better consumers of randomized evaluations, and the interview with Dean Yang where he talks about the skill of designing evaluations that will provide useful operational information to implementing organizations.

22. Based on the space shuttle *Challenger* disaster, caused by a single component, O-rings, failing, this is a theory of how production evolves in firms, and in countries, when the value of an output can be destroyed by a single mistake in the production process. The model can explain large differences between incomes in nations and why firms in less developed countries are primarily small. Marginal Revolution University has a useful explanation of the O-ring theory here: http://mruniversity.com/courses/development-economics/o-ring-model.

According to Google Scholar, as of August 2016 Kremer's O-ring paper is his most cited (1549), followed by his deworming RCT paper (1497) and a paper on population growth and technological change (1359)

unbelievably smart. The others I don't know as well but seem equally intellectually endowed and capable.

So the answer is, one, I don't know and, two, it should be obvious that after some time we should have stopped talking about these things because you can't keep talking about them.

They're not bad decisions from a disciplinary point of view. The disciplinary logic was inevitable. And these people took the disciplinary logic toward a big shift in disciplinary approaches. It was a necessary next step. Where they were willfully ignorant in my opinion was on the other two fronts. On the positive theory of policy adoption and on the importance thing.

One reason I often sound very frustrated about this is that it is not as if all of the things I am saying are "lessons learned." I, and many others, were stressing all three points from the very beginning. I was, curiously, the task manager of record at the World Bank of Kremer's textbook experiments in Kenya.[23][11] So it isn't like "well, we did experiments for a while and we learned they weren't the panacea (or even very useful medication) like we had hoped." It is more like "we ignored the wise advice of every practitioner about why we were wrong and turns out, they were right and we were wrong after all and we are kind of at square one where we were 10 or 20 years ago on all the big issues."

TO: I'd like to ask about a specific application of RCTs—unconditional cash transfers. This is a case where the question wasn't "what's the exact impact of a cash transfer" but "will people misuse and abuse unconditional cash?" Now we have a bunch of different tests in different contexts with different programs and implementers,[24] and they all seem to line up to say that, "no, unconditional cash transfers to poor people aren't 'wasted.'"[12] I find it hard to believe that you could produce convincing evidence of that

23. In this study, Glewwe, Kremer, and Moulin find, in a randomized trial, that providing textbooks to schoolchildren does not raise average test scores, while raising the scores of the best students. See the interview with Michael Kremer where he comments on this study informing his understanding of the issues with inappropriate curricula in developing world educational contexts.

24. For a useful overview see Blattman and Niehaus's review in Foreign Affairs. Notable individual studies include Blattman et al. in Uganda (a comparison of a training program with an unconditional cash grant), Baird et al. in Malawi (comparing a CCT to a UCT), and Haushofer and Shapiro in Kenya (measuring the impact of an unconditional cash grant).

without RCTs. Is that a useful application of the methodology? Are there better, faster, cheaper ways that question could have been answered?

LP: This is a great example as it illustrates all the points.

First, this question was answered and had been answered dozens if not hundreds of times with nonexperimental methods. After all, a pretty fundamental part of economic theory says "money is fungible" and "people maximize welfare" so the incremental impact of "in-kind" and "cash" assistance should be exactly the same. Unless the "in-kind" assistance is a "corner solution"—and even there with resale, it should be like cash with a discount for the transaction to get it into cash. Anyone who could be persuaded by evidence was already persuaded. If people had not been "persuaded" it was due to either organizational interests—NGOs want to deliver in-kind for a variety of reasons, farmers want in-kind delivery of food because it gives them a good price selling to governments—or political interests—they didn't want to make transfers anyway.

And it is hardly like "unconditional cash transfers" are an innovation. After all, that was the widespread design for many social programs before the RCT-driven fad of "conditional cash transfers."

Second, you're saying that people are now convinced whereas they weren't before. Who are you talking about? What is the evidence that RCTs have been widely more persuasive? Now that people are looking at this, my impression is that being told evidence is "rigorous" doesn't actually have any additional persuasive power.

Sure, there is a mini-fad in this direction among a few philanthropists, but I have yet to see mainstream NGOs or governments engaged in a wholesale revision of their policies.[25] And where this is a debate at scale, in India, for instance, this is a debate that has been ongoing for decades and all the proponents of cash were proponents of cash before any RCTs. That's because they are mostly economists and hence understood that cash is always superior in any nonpaternalistic approach. What is shifting is the politics of the debate and the evidence of waste and corruption in in-kind delivery is more "persuasive" than evidence that it is not "wasted."

Third, this illustrates the "small" and "charity" related element of the debate. Evidence shows that if you want large-scale poverty reduction at the national level from high levels of extreme or even "2-dollar-a-day"

25. See the interview with Chris Blattman (chapter 20) where he generally agrees that there has not been much policy change as a result of the studies of unconditional cash transfers.

poverty, you need broad-based economic growth. The East Asian countries[26] that eliminated mass poverty in rapid fashion—Korea, Taiwan, Malaysia, Indonesia, China, Vietnam, et cetera—did so through growth. In fact in many, if not most, inequality was stable or rising during the period of rapid poverty reduction. They didn't do it through unconditional cash versus less effective in-kind transfers. So while some countries like Brazil have made some progress with more effective transfer programs, this was from already being a middle income country with almost no extreme poverty. If I am a philanthropist and want to do charity work, yes, give cash. But again, don't pretend *that* is "development."

26. See interview with Tyler Cowen (chapter 19) where he notes that further study of these examples is likely to be one of the most influential fields over the next 30 years.

David is a Lead Economist in the Development Research Group at the World Bank. In his profile for DevEx's "40 Under 40 in DC," David makes the jolting claim that he decided to study econometrics to "answer interesting questions about the world." Some would certainly raise an eyebrow at the notion that econometricians ever even see the world, but David spends plenty of time in the field. His wide-ranging and globe-spanning research takes on migration, microenterprises, gender roles, firm management, regulation, and informal economies as well as more esoteric econometric and methods questions.

David's research on the causes and impact of migration—a topic he became interested in during his undergraduate studies in Auckland, New Zealand, as he encountered Pacific Islander immigrants—covers the effect on incomes both for those who migrate and those left behind, as well as the impact on education attainment, mental health, and nutrition.

In the field experiment world, David is most known for his work with microenterprises. He has extensively studied microenterprises's profits, returns to capital, employment behavior, management and investment choices—and whether anything can be done to improve them. More recently he has also been studing larger firms and the effect of management on productivity and profits.

TO: What was the first field experiment that you were involved in?

DM: It was the returns to capital work that I did in Sri Lanka,[1][1] followed closely by the same type of project in Mexico.[2] I was still at Stanford at the time but in the process of moving to the World Bank. The way it came about is that I'd done some nonexperimental work with Chris Woodruff where we had been trying to look at what the return to capital was for microenterprises.[3] We had used Mexican data and estimated that the

---

1. Discussed in detail later in the interview.

return to capital there was very high but people were not convinced by the nonexperimental results. We were not ourselves completely convinced, so we thought it would be great to test in an RCT context. We applied for funding to try to do it, but it was hard. Nobody had done anything with firms really. The way we ended getting funding was that the tsunami happened. We had put in an application to the National Science Foundation [NSF] to do the work in Mexico. We didn't get it, though they told us we were close. Shortly after that, they said, "We now have this funding to do research in tsunami-affected countries. Would you be interested in doing this experiment in one of those countries?" We ended up scrambling to see if we could make something work in Sri Lanka.

TO: Did you already have a design and you were trying to implement what you already had, or did you have to start from scratch and design something?

DM: We had a design that we had proposed. It was a pretty simple experiment: give cash to small businesses and see what happens, see if you can measure the returns. So we had designed things in terms of how much cash to give and whether we should give it to them as untied cash or have it be in-kind, something that they chose for their business. There were some elements that echo some subsequent experiments that people have been doing on cash and conditions, like the GiveDirectly evaluation.[4] Being our first experiment, we were very underpowered for those elements though.

At about the same time we got a little bit of money from the World Bank to try this in Mexico, so we launched something similar there as well. It turned out not to be as successful as Sri Lanka. It was a tough place to collect data on informal firms. There was a lot of suspicion and a lot of mobility of firms, so there was a lot of attrition. It worked out well that we did it in Sri Lanka in the end.

TO: I'm interested in your path into the method. Was it really trying to be more convincing? Was it that RCTs were "in the air" and you were looking for new and interesting things to do?

DM: It was one of those things where we had presented our nonexperimental work, and you have conversations with people over lunch afterward. The conversations were always about this question of whether small businesses are able to get returns on small amounts of money or if they were stuck in a poverty trap where they would have to have a relatively massive amount of capital to make a lumpy investment, and otherwise, they're stuck earning subsistence returns and a little bit of capital is not going to help. People were saying, "Ideally you'd just give people a bunch of capital and see what happens, see if they can get returns." Then, as you say, RCTs were in the air. There was a sense that this was actually something that may be feasible to do rather than just wishful thinking. We started thinking about it and applying for funding. It was difficult to make the case, and it's still difficult for people today, that you can do a field experiment and it's going to turn out well when you haven't done it before.[2] It's always a struggle to get funding. I think it's also perhaps a little bit harder to do it when you're dealing with small firms than when it's health or education, and people are less concerned that funding the intervention is somehow going to be politically sensitive. If you're giving people vaccines or malaria nets it's seen as a good thing. Whereas if you're using NSF money to help firms in another country, then it's a threat to America's competitiveness somehow. There are some issues there that we had to deal with as well.

TO: Those Sri Lankan subsistence entrepreneurs are gunning for Silicon Valley, I'm sure. Tell me about how that original returns to capital experiment worked in practice and what you found.

DM: The starting point is why, when there are so many microenterprises, so few of them grow, and so few of their owners seem to climb into the middle class.

So we gathered a sample of microenterprises and randomly assigned some of them to receive a cash grant larger than the lump sum they could typically accumulate on their own, either $100 or $200, and some to not receive a grant. Then we compared them and looked at their performance over the next two and a half years. In Sri Lanka we got these very surprising findings. We had very high increases in profits for male-owned businesses when we gave them grants. Their profits showed a real return on capital of about 11 percent per month which is incredibly high. But there were 0 percent returns to giving these grants to women.

TO: But returns by gender wasn't what you started the project to look at it, was it? It came out of data to try to measure returns for microenterprises in general?

2. See conversations with Antoinette Schoar (chapter 16) and Tyler Cowen (chapter 19) about how similar issues may be affecting career development and the future use of RCTs.

DM: Right. In Sri Lanka, we had a sample of men and women, but gender wasn't the principal focus of it. When we went into Ghana, we wanted to see if this finding would hold up in another setting and, in particular, in a different context.[5] In South Asia, we know that women have very low labor participation rates, but in Ghana, women are actually the majority of small business owners. We purposely chose Ghana because it's a country with this long history of women running businesses and is more gender equal than most countries in terms of labor force participation. In Ghana, there's this feeling that women can work and can do things. So that's why we chose Ghana.

We replicated the experiment there and we gave these grants of about $120. We gave half of the randomly assigned grant recipients the grant in cash and half of them got the grant in-kind. With the in-kind grants we said to the owners, "We'll go with you and buy you something for your business, you tell us what to buy." The basic result in Ghana was, again, big returns on capital. On average, for both men and women we find big increases in profits when we give the in-kind grants. Their profits went up about 30 Cedi a month, about a 20 percent return per month on the grant.

When we gave the women cash though, there was no increase in business profits. And when we look more closely at the data, even for the in-kind grants, the increase is really only happening for the top 40 percent of women. So women who were starting off in these subsistence businesses earning a $1 a day had no benefit in terms of business outcomes from getting more capital. The grants all seemed to get spent on household needs. For men across the board, with the in-kind grants we see these large effects on profits, and while noisier, there also seem to be some benefits to the men of cash grants. For the top 40 percent of women we also get big increases in profits if we push them to invest in their businesses via the in-kind grant, but not if we just give them cash without any restrictions.

TO: The result that these grants only matter for the top 40 percent, looking at it in hindsight, was that predictable? Were those 40 percent in industries that one would have expected to see higher returns?

DM: They seemed to not have been differentiated much in terms of the industry they were in from the women in the bottom 60 percent. The difference was in baseline profit levels.

The bottom 60 percent averaged about a $1 day in profits but the top 40 percent were earning about $5 a day in terms of profits. So it's quite a difference in terms of size of profits. These women were better educated;

they were wealthier to start with. They were more likely to have gone into business for business reasons rather than other reasons.

So there's something different about the types of women who are running those businesses and were able to generate high returns from the grant, but it's not that they are choosing different industries.

TO: In Sri Lanka there appears to have been significant industry-related differences. The women were primarily concentrated in industries with low returns to capital like lacemaking.

DM: In Sri Lanka we found there to be two main reasons for the gender difference. The first seemed to be this industry difference, women who were in traditional female industries had the lowest returns. But even when we looked at retail trade where both men and women worked, men were doing better. The second thing, though we could only look at this suggestively because we hadn't set out to look at this in the first place and our sample sizes became smaller, but it seems there was something to do with intra-household cooperation. Women who said their husbands were more supportive of their businesses seemed to be doing better. The data seem to suggest women perhaps were not investing optimally in their business for fear that the proceeds would just get captured by others. It's very hard to distinguish how that happens—who is capturing that profit: people inside the household, people outside the household, or even whether it was captured from themselves. Maybe they were thinking, "I don't trust myself not to spend loose cash," so they overinvest in equipment and don't buy enough working capital.

TO: You've followed up that original work in Sri Lanka with an attempt to help women shift industries.[6] How did you randomize that? Did you try to explore the issue of intra-household cooperation?

DM: What we've done there is we've taken a group of 600 women who currently have low-profit businesses clustered in the types of industries that are mostly female dominated. We've used our three years of survey data to find out what type of industries women seem to be earning more in and have more prospects for growth. Then we've given them a five-day business training course, based on the International Labour Organization [ILO] Improve Your Business curriculum,[3] and as part of that training

---

3. This is a materials-based (as opposed to hands-on) modular training program for entrepreneurs that is widely used in microenterprise training programs: http://goo .gl/wyWQiW.

we've also provided them with this information about what the opportunities are in different industries in terms of how much money women like them earn. Those tend to be industries where both men and women work, but we also tell them about some more female-dominated industries that seem to have higher prospects. So, for example, bakeries seem to do pretty well in comparison to making lunch packets for neighbors. Baking cakes is something not as many people do—you need a little more capital to be able to do it—but the returns seem to be pretty high. So we give them that information and see whether that pushes them into higher potential return industries. Some of the sample also received training with additional capital grants to see if they need additional capital in addition to the information and the training to switch industries and start achieving higher levels of profit.

Bottom line is that we found business training was quite helpful in getting people to start new businesses and sort of speed them along that trajectory. But the amount of training that we had and just telling people about what the relative returns were in different industries wasn't enough to shift them from one industry to another. But that part of the intervention wasn't super strong. It was one day added on to the end of five days of standard business training.

TO: This is particularly interesting because it's a vexing problem in developed economies too that most people starting small businesses go into industries with low barriers to entry, low capital requirements, and low returns.

DM: Exactly. What we've been doing in Sri Lanka, in a separate project, is trying to understand what it really takes to make this jump to hiring employees. That's the big distinction between being self-employed and starting to grow a business: when they start hiring workers outside of the family.

I think a lot of us who have been working on microenterprises think these are the key critical questions. What are the constraints to getting some microenterprises to grow, to have a level increase in profits? With grants and microfinance it seems like you can lift people a little out of poverty; you can raise their incomes a little bit, but then they level off. We've done these grants, and we've found they lift profits at least in male businesses and they stay higher for three years at least, so this one-off grant does at least semi-permanently raise their incomes but it's just a level increase. It doesn't shift their growth patterns. They don't get better and better over time, they just move up a level and reach a new equilibrium almost.

Can we put them on a growth trajectory? I think it's still valuable on a mass scale if we can lift people's income for a long period of time with these one-off interactions, but we'd like to know whether we can alter the growth pattern at least for some of them.

TO: Lots of people in aid would love to find a one-off interaction that has three-year effects, but it still doesn't get us where we actually want to be.

DM: Exactly.

So we have a sample of just over 1,500 men, where we're trying to—well, if you think about in terms of a production function, we're trying to hit A, K, and L^4 together and separately. But basically what we're trying to do is look at what the constraint to growth is and do we need combinations of things to overcome those constraints.[7]

We did three separate interventions. One was a matched commitment savings program, essentially with the goal of building a pool of capital, $150 to $200, that they could only access at the end of nine months. The second was the ILO's Improve Your Business training, which is a five-day classroom-based business training course. It's the most used business training curriculum around the world. It covers marketing, planning, cost control, record keeping, a bit of financing. It's been adapted for Sri Lanka and taught there for eight years. And then something we think is really innovative, that we haven't seen anyone do, we used a wage subsidy program. We subsidized, by giving them a grant of about half the market wage, these sole proprietors to hire their first worker for six months and then we phased the subsidy out. The idea is that this gives you time to learn whether your business has what it takes to support an additional worker and whether you have what it takes to manage a worker. It also sort of subsidizes that training period for both the owner and the employee. So, for instance, we talked to a guy who runs an aquarium for tropical fish. He says it takes him a month of having someone work with him before he can be trusted to be left alone with the fish and six months to get him up to a level of skill that he can produce at an export standard. So we're subsidizing that training process, but he's likely to keep the worker on once the worker is trained—at least that's the theory.

4. The standard simplified Cobb–Douglas production function—a way to understand production capacity of a firm under various conditions—is $Y = A \times L \times K$, where Y is total possible production, A is total factor productivity, L is labor inputs, and K is capital inputs.

TO: The other really interesting thing about this study is that there are lots of waves of follow-up. It's been about six years since the program started and you've had lots of rounds of follow-up, right?

DM: We did surveys every six months for the first four years, and then annual surveys for the next two.

In the initial waves we saw an increase in employment with the wage subsidy and that some of this employment sticks. The wage subsidy program, about 22 percent of the people who we offered this to—it was a random sample of microenterprises mostly with zero employees—were willing to take our subsidies and hire a new worker. They were usually businesses that were more established, with better business practices or more capital at the outset. It seems like those on the cusp of growing were more likely to take the subsidy. The ones who did take the subsidy retained workers after the subsidies were removed. The difference between treatment and control was 8 to 10 percent higher employment rate even after the subsidy is removed. So it looked like we were getting almost one in ten small businesses to make this jump to be an employer as a result of this wage subsidy.

Now, in the next follow-up, the picture changed. It was surprising to us. The savings program didn't have any impact in the short run on employment, but over time it built up the capital stock of the businesses. By the round of surveys two years after the program ended, we saw employment effects from the savings treatment that were not much smaller than the wage subsidy program. Building up capital in these businesses seemed to lead to employment.

TO: So the subsidy was sort of this peak effect where employment goes up and then settles back down to this level of about one in ten? But the savings was a steady rise?

DM: Between the rounds there's a lot of noise, but certainly it seemed to pick up. Some after the first year, but after the second year it picked up a bit more.

And then we looked for complementarities between the various treatments. Some groups got the capital and the training and some groups got the capital and the subsidy. But there really didn't seem to be anything going on. Our point estimates were all negative and nothing was significant. So it didn't seem like you needed capital and the subsidy. You don't need the training to make the worker or the capital productive; getting the capital doesn't make the training work.

TO: Back to the original motivating question. Is there any indication that this is changing the growth trajectory or is it just another leveling up of the profits?

DM: So the savings program seemed to have increased profits, while the employment program seemed to have increased revenue just enough to cover the extra expenses of the worker. So the subsidy creates a job that's pretty much paying its marginal product.

The next question is whether they become more productive over time staying in the business and the firm is able to gain more profit or whether we've just pushed these subsistence firms to a slightly higher level but they can't really continue growing. Obviously there are going to be firms in both categories, so now it's finding out which is more common.

We still have been doing surveys the last couple of years trying to track that long-term impact. The story we're seeing is that we managed to get people to hire workers and have positive effects on employment in the short run with the wage subsidies. When the subsidies ended, some of those workers were then fired or let go; some of them stayed on. But then Sri Lanka's economy really boomed after the end of the civil war, and the control group started growing pretty rapidly as well. So we have this situation where the treatment effect erodes because of control group catch-up rather than the gains for the treatment group going away. What we still need to analyze is whether there's any five- or six-year impacts in the data we've collected more recently. So it's still in process, but it seems like there are not the same level of constraints on the labor market as there are on the capital market side. The idea that they're constrained from moving from 0 to 1 workers because of labor market constraints doesn't seem to be borne out by what our experiments are saying.

TO: It seems to me the business training results are muddled but generally not very good. You've done a review of the business training literature[8] finding not particularly strong effects. Sometimes where we see effects, the effect is teaching people that they shouldn't be in business and they shut down.[5] For the Sri Lankan women, you're accelerating their process with some training but not causing big shifts in their long-term prospects. Blattman et al in northern Uganda find there's some benefit to

5. This is found in a working paper by Calderon et al. looking at a business training program in rural Mexico and discussed in McKenzie and Woodruff's 2012 review cited above.

training but not enough to justify the cost.[6][9] Where are you now on the value of training?

DM: We did this review piece, and I think you've misinterpreted seeing lack of evidence as evidence of no impact. One of the things we point out in that article is that most studies are incredibly underpowered, so they can't rule out 50 percent increases or 40 percent decreases in profits or sales. Out of 14 or 15 studies, two had enough power to detect a 25 percent increase. I think part of what we're learning is that it's just really tough to actually see effects from these programs with the sample sizes that people have been running.

Let me make two other comments on that. One is that I think the things that these programs are trying to do, the types of practices that these programs are trying to teach, are important. I have some new work[10] that's trying to do for small business practices what Bloom and Van Reenen have done for large enterprises in terms of identifying what practices make a difference in performance.[7] We have a list of about 26 different practices that firms should be doing. It seems there are very strong associations both in the cross section and over time that these practices matter. But the problem is that most of the business training programs are just not that successful at driving dramatic changes in those practices. And the typical program might cover one or one and a half practices. A five-day training program might lead people to do one and a half or two more practices. It's not that surprising when you're not changing these practices much that it's hard to measure those effects.

So what's the realistic expectation that we should have for these types of programs? I did some work on vocational training in Turkey.[11] It was a three-month-long program and we find a 2 percent increase in employment and incomes. We had a large sample, 5,000 people, so we could get significance. Several people noted that typically, for a whole year of schooling, you see about an 8 percent gain, so why should we think that a three-month program is going to give you more than a quarter of that. Most business training programs that are being studied are five-day, forty-hour

6. See the interview with Chris Blattman (chapter 20) for more discussion of this study in particular and the cost effectiveness versus cash in general.

7. Bloom, Sadun, and Van Reenen lead the World Management Survey project, which is a long-term effort to identify management practices and their impact in 40 countries and multiple industries. The project has identified a set of general management best practices that are highly correlated with firm performance. See www.worldmanagementsurvey.org

programs. And if we were to scale that and think about what the returns to schooling work would say should be the effects of business training, there's just no way on earth we'd be able to detect effects of those sizes.

So we might think schooling does a whole lot of things. Business training or vocational training is more focused and concentrated than general schooling, so we should see more. But I think it's a gut check in thinking about what we can hope to get from training. It's really hard for a whole year of schooling to have that much effect on people. There may be some cases where people are coming out of conflict, or they're in very remote, isolated rural areas where there's supernormal returns to be had, and you can shift the needle a little more. But in the average place, if we think a year of schooling has an 8 to 10 percent return, at most we should be expecting a 2 to 3 percent return from doing a three- month course. Then you bring that down to five days, what should you expect then? I don't know. I go back and forth. Because, on the other hand, you have these information interventions in some domains where one-hour interventions have surprisingly large effects. I guess everybody would like there to be easy fixes that you can do pretty quickly. But it's also incredibly hard to get people to come away from their business for any amount of time. So I'm just not that optimistic that if you have to spend three or six months in training, that you can get people to do it. Bottom line answer is I think we need a lot more work on what the content of business training is instead of just generic business training. There may be some things where the returns are very high from small interventions, but a lot of it is just like schooling. It's good, but it takes time to get effects.

TO: The liberal arts folks will be very pleased to see that three months of vocational education doesn't do anything more than three months of general schooling. Let's talk about microenterprise profits. You've written a paper on how to measure profits of microenterprises.[12] You found a lot of these small operations are profitable, but there's a lot of questions about that. Why is it so hard to measure profits?

DM: There are a couple of things going on there. The first is how you value the time of the people participating in these enterprises. Our measure of profits includes any return to the labor of these enterprises. If you worked on this business and your business earned 3,000 rupees this month, that includes a return to your own hours of work. If you start trying to value the opportunity cost of that labor and you calculate it at some sort of market wage rate, quickly you'll find that many of these businesses look unprofitable.

I think this is one of the key questions about how to think about microenterprises and what we should do to help them, especially when you are looking at women in these businesses. For these women, there usually is no outside option to generate cash.

TO: How do you asses the opportunity cost when the labor markets are so thin? Is that it?

DM: That's one part of it. The second part of it is something that comes up in the profits paper. If you ask people detailed questions on revenues and detailed questions on expenses, there's a lot of noise in each of those numbers. A small shopkeeper is buying stuff in one period and selling it in another period, and you're trying to match all those things together. When you do that, you're going to find that revenue minus expenses is really, really, really noisy, and a bunch of studies have found negative values on that measure.

Now what we do in the profits paper is to try to better match expenses and revenue. Rob Townsend has done some work with his Thailand data to better understand whether you should you use accrual or cash methods for measuring these enterprises.[13] Especially when you're looking at a short time horizon like how the business has done in the last month, or last three months, the mismatch between when things are bought and sold can make a lot of firms look unprofitable. But under a longer run view they would be profitable.

But when you start to ask people to recall lots of small transactions over six months or a year, that's pretty hard to do. So in these studies of microenterprise profits we usually ask for recall over just a month span. But that's where you get the mismatch between revenues and expenses. I think that's why when you directly ask people about profits most of them say they are profitable.

TO: As long as you don't factor in the cost of labor.

DM: Right. There's this really nice paper by Shahe Emran and Joseph Stiglitz on why it is that microfinance can get women to run somewhat profitable businesses with chickens and things but they never get those businesses to grow into something greater.[14] And the whole thing is that the women in these Asian countries have no other options. When their time value is 0, they can do this, but as soon as they have to hire somebody at market wage, it becomes unprofitable to expand.

Certainly one of the things that comes through in *Poor Economics* is that almost everyone wants a wage job, but that's not often an option. There's an open question whether casual labor or running a microenterprise is closer to a wage job. That's going to depend on country, local market, skills, et cetera.

TO: In the profits study you asked people to use ledgers to record their costs and revenues, presumably to aid recall. But that seems like that would be a very helpful tool to the average small enterprise—it's certainly part of the standard advice to new business owners: keep careful records. But you found that people didn't typically use the ledger for very long, and its use didn't seem to have much impact. The Drexler, Fischer, Schoar, work in the Dominican Republic found not much impact from formal accounting training but some notable positive effects from teaching simple "rules of thumb."[15] How do you match up those findings?

DM: There's a couple of themes there. One is that our study is from a general pool of microenterprise owners and not those who have already self-selected themselves or been selected by MFIs. So, when we found that 50 percent of people will only keep up these ledgers, if all those people happen to also be microfinance clients, then maybe the MFIs are doing a good job selecting for clients more inclined to do that. Second, we weren't giving them any training, we were just giving them these sheets of paper with five columns and asking them to write things down each day. Some people did and kept doing it, and others said there's no real value to me, so they quit doing it.

With the rules of thumb, Greg and Antoinette are not finding it has much impact on ultimate business outcomes. They tell a nice story but if you look closely they have a bunch of sales measures. One of the four sales measures is significant at the 10 percent level—sales in a bad week. So it's not clear that it's really having a huge impact, even that training. What they're pointing out is that it has more impact than formal training.

As we talked about, I think this is an issue with a lot of these experiments. The power these studies have to answer some questions is really low. And these profit measurement issues sort of feed into that. So, if you look at the Banerjee and Duflo Spandana paper, for instance, there's a huge amount of noise in their profits data.[16] I did some calculations and I think it came out that they would need 2 million people to find an increase of 10 percent in profits given the take-up of microfinance and the noise in profit measurements. Measuring these profits is crucial for our understanding for figuring out what makes sense, but it's incredibly hard to measure.

I've got a paper called "Beyond Baseline and Follow-Up" on measuring profits based on the work we're doing in Ghana.[17] There we used PDAs to do our measurements. Each wave after the first wave, we put in the previous wave's data, and we checked the business's profits relative to last month. If the change was too large, we would ask the owner again. So we would see that a business's profits were 100 Cedi last month, but this month the owner is reporting it's 1,000 Cedi. So we ask them, "Did we get things wrong?" Not implying that they're lying to us, but that we made a data entry error. The remarkable thing to us is that in 85 percent of the cases, they did confirm that their profits did change that much from one month to the next.

Part of it is just seasonality, but part of it is one of the things that comes up in *Portfolios of the Poor*[8] There's a huge variation of incomes on a day-to-day and a month-to-month basis. You have good months and bad months. Some months you get sick and you don't earn much; other months something else happens. It's a huge challenge for trying to look at some of the impacts of our programs on profits if profits are jumping around this much. It's not just all measurement error, some of it is the general challenges that are facing the business.

So our solution to that is we can try to measure things more times. The work in Sri Lanka has 11 waves of data on these firms. So, if we get one or two bad months, we can average that out. In Ghana we had 6 waves. The point is, more people should be doing this. The standard approach to doing these experiments is to measure the baseline, run the program, and then come back and do one more survey a year later or two years later. That works really nicely for things like health and education where the outcomes are highly correlated, but it doesn't work so well for things like business profits or consumption. The standard methodology needs to change.

TO: Outside of development economics, there is this broad agreement that picking winners is simply not possible. No one can predict the market. But in this vein of research there is an element of picking

---

8. *Portfolios of the Poor* is a book based on collecting financial data from households weekly, termed financial diaries, to better understand how households living on under $2 a day manage their finances. See more discussion in the interview with Jonathan Morduch (chapter 4), a co-author of the book.

winners. I'm a little surprised at how seriously both researchers and funders seem to be treating the possibility that you can pick winners. We know that you can't systematically pick winners in a developed country where you typically have much better information. Why would people think you can pick winners in an environment with less information available?

DM: I think there are two answers to that. First, we're not talking about picking the guy who is going to be Google or Microsoft, or anything like that. The question is can we pick the guy who's going to have 5 workers rather than 0 workers and the guy who's going to go from 5 workers to 20 workers. At that scale, can we better target who has what it takes to grow? We think there are a lot more market failures in developing countries. We think the education markets fail particularly. And so people who have high ability are not necessarily going to be the ones getting the schooling and training they need. If we think social connections are important, then high-ability people may not be getting the financing they need. So I think it's not unreasonable to think there are a lot of people with untapped ability that are out there and that relatively simple screening devices could at least help us do a little bit better on it. Asim Khwaja at the Kennedy School has worked on this with a bank where they're doing psychometric screening like employers use and personality tests and cognitive ability tests to evaluate borrowers.[18] Whatever we do, it's not going to be perfect. We're not going to identify only winners, but if we can get 20 percent of the people that we lend to, to do better, rather than 5 percent, that's really something. It's not something I'd want to put a lot of money into as an investor, but as a lender who's thinking about screening out the people who are not going to do anything in their businesses and making my lending more tailored to people who have potential to grow, it has a lot of potential.

TO: Ultimately, picking clients who are going to be more profitable over the long term.

DM: Exactly.

There's this untapped market of urban males. We now have these studies in a three countries in three different regions of the world, Sri Lanka, Mexico, and Ghana. And all of them have found that it's these urban males that have really higher returns to infusions of $100 to $200 of capital. So one of the things we were discussing is what we can do by tapping those gains and giving them the capital so that they can move up to the next level. That seems like an untapped opportunity.

TO: Returning to the issue of business training, rather than picking high ability business owners, have you thought about what possible interventions there are that aren't so intensive to speed the spread of management technology?[9]

DM: It's something we're doing right now in Colombia. We pitched ideas to a few governments in Latin America about doing experiments on varying the level of intensity. The most basic level of intensity would be to just show firm managers the results of the Indian experiment.[10][19] We'd go to a textile firm manager in Latin America and show them the study we did in India, the results from implementing these practices, and suggest that they should consider doing them. If it's that these practices are fairly easy for them to implement but there's an information problem— they don't know whether these practices work—than that should solve the problem. The second level of intensity would be to set up something like agricultural extension agents, where you have a few model factories that get free intensive consulting on the condition that you let managers from other factories come in and see how your processes have changed. That might be problematic in some very competitive industries. The more expensive way would be to set up a factory like you set up model agricultural plots. For some industries that would be more practical than others to have this sort of inflatable factory that you can come into. You see these things at trade shows where manufactures demonstrate new machines. You could have a model factory line and have people come and see that. The third level of intensity is more like the India program of intensive consulting. That was a demonstration project, so we gave the consulting to the firms for free, but the proposal was something like a matching grant program. There are programs like this all over the world where the government encourages firms to get some certification with some incentive. Today we don't really know a lot about the effects of

9. Management technology refers to the knowledge and practices necessary to run a business well. It's a central theme of the work McKenzie has done with Bloom and Van Reenen, referred to earlier.

10. This is a study of providing management consulting to mid-size textile factories in India. The authors, including McKenzie, find large gains in productivity when factories managers learn better business management practices such as planning work flow and inventory management. The study is discussed more later in this interview and in the interviews with Antoinette Schoar, Xavi Giné, and Dean Yang.

those but that's what we are trying to do, to learn more about those types of projects.

In the end, we were able to design something with the government of Colombia that lets us compare the one-on-one consulting work with a group-based intervention. [20] We're working with the auto parts sector with 160 firms to test these different interventions.

One branch is one-on-one consulting in different aspects of management practices. That treatment group has four to six months of a consultant coming in and working with them in different operational areas. The group-based treatment is working on those same areas but doing it in groups of five or six firms. There are some group-based classroom activities where they cover best practices, and then they visit each other's firms so that, if someone is doing some practice well, the other group members can go into their factory and see how it's being done in practice. The hope is that this will be both a cheaper way to implement it and will allow for some peer learning. Ideally, it's something that may last beyond the scope of the intervention if these networks we've created where firms can learn from each other survive. Of course, the concern that everybody has is whether people are reluctant to share with possible competitors. So the groups are made up of firms in the same broad industry but not competing directly with each other. In this case all the firms are making parts for cars, but in a group some people are making rubber mats and some are making windows and some are making bumper parts, so they're not competing on the same products.

TO: Showing Colombian factory managers the results from India raises the issue of external validity. Let's turn the conversation to methodological issues.

One of the standard defenses of the RCT methodology is to appeal to the fact that this is how you conduct medical trials. But there is this growing recognition that the track record of medical trials isn't great—a suggestion that a majority of peer-reviewed papers in medical journals can't be replicated. What should that tell us, if anything, about field experiments in economics?

DM: I think it's naïve to believe that incentives aren't influencing results in our field. But I think there is a little bit of a difference in that we are not trying to get drug approvals—some fraction of the problems in medical research are driven by that. The other thing that we grapple with more than medicine is we acknowledge every time that we aren't just giving a pill that is going to be taken with 100 percent adherence. This has come up a lot in AIDS trials where initial results weren't replicating, and it turns out that different populations had different adherence. Medical trials often have big questions about selection, adherence, attrition, and things like that. I think in our work we pay a lot of attention to these behavioral chains, who is coming in, who is dropping out, what are all the behaviors that influence the outcomes. If we're thinking about external validity, then it's important that we recognize, and are explicit, that process matters a lot and context matters a lot.

There's this interesting paper by Sendhil Mullainathan and Hunt Allcott looking at a behavioral intervention by an electricity company where they compare your usage to your neighbors'.[21] This study was done in 19 different markets, so they have 19 randomized trials, and the results vary a lot. You can't predict very well what will happen in one market based on what happened in another—but they do much better than they would with nonexperimental approaches. There are a lot of things about context that we don't measure and we need to measure better, but I think we're getting better.

TO: What does it take to get you to change your mind? You've done these studies on the differential returns to male-owned and female-owned businesses and you suggested earlier that urban males are an untapped group that we should be targeting more. How many studies would it take that contradicted your results before you would agree that your results were the outliers?

DM: That would be interesting. Here's where context would matter a lot. First, I would need to see studies in the same context and in the same location that were finding different results. It has to be the same type of population; otherwise, you start to worry that there is something strange about the population. Now, for me to conclude that my population is a strange one and that the results that are true in my context are not true elsewhere, that's a much smaller leap. I would need to see two or three other studies that apply the same methods with different populations with different results from mine and that would make me wonder about the generalizability of my results.

The other thing I think we're facing, to be honest, is a lot of our studies are underpowered as we talked about earlier. Not just our studies but studies in general. Researchers just don't have enough money. But even if we had enough money, there may not be a large enough sample available at all.

Especially when we start looking at SMEs. It becomes more and more of a problem because there just aren't enough SMEs out there in a lot of countries especially that want to participate in particular projects.

We've done all these studies and they're underpowered to detect average effects. And the interesting effects often happen in the subgroups, so we're playing at the margins of what we can say with a lot of power. Especially, when the outcomes we are looking at are things like profits, consumption, or income. It's very noisy data. It's genuine noise too not just measurement error. When we look at our Indian firms, they had 200 workers. If one gets sick, it doesn't make that much of a difference; if one machine breaks down, it doesn't make that much of a difference. In a microenterprise, if your guy gets sick for a week, that's making a huge difference to your income flows.

TO: Volatility and uncertainty is one of the things used to explain why it's so hard to, say, get farmers to adopt improved seeds or use fertilizer. The farmer knows how much risk there is that something will go wrong, that he's not willing to take on one more variable or expose himself to bigger losses. You've done some work on insurance for retail shops in Egypt who should find insurance useful if their profits are as variable and uncertain as farmers' profits are.

DM: There has been so much attention to insurance for farmers—weather, crop failures, and the like—but not attention to how you design insurance for urban firms. One of the areas where I think we need to do more is urban poverty or urban enterprise. The question is what sort of shocks can you insure people against. There hasn't been great success in health insurance programs. The jury is still out. Those programs haven't really been able to effectively replace the alternatives, or they are only insuring against extreme shocks and in a sample of a couple of hundred people you don't see that happen very often.

Egypt was one application where it seemed particularly salient. Egypt had this big revolution. Microfinance institutions were worried about whether people would be willing to borrow or make investments given all the upset in the economy. So our thought was let's design an insurance product that can help protect against risks if the economy implodes or things get worse. The idea was if the firms are holding back from productive investments because of uncertainty, if we provide some insurance, maybe they'll go ahead and make those investments. So we had insurance that would pay out if the stock market was suspended or curfews were imposed or if fuel subsidies were removed—which would probably lead to riots—things that would reflect the economy getting pretty dire. We offered this to people who were at the cusp of deciding whether to renew their microfinance loans for another year or not, in the hope that this would lead them to be more likely to renew and to invest in long-term, productive activities. We surprisingly found that despite very high rates of take-up, which is always a concern with new insurance products,[11] it really led to no changes in behavior. The firms weren't more likely to take a loan. They didn't spend their loan any differently. It didn't change their production decisions. What we found is that these microbusinesses really typically use loans for working capital needs. Those were not irreversible investments. So, even if the economy was to go south quickly, you could quickly reverse those investments— either sell them off or wait before restocking inventory. It wasn't like buying a big machine that you were stuck with.

So then we wanted to move up the firm size distribution, figuring it might work better for larger firms. But we weren't able to offer it in a second year because of the coup that took us pretty close to our payout thresholds but didn't quite get there. That led to clients complaining and that meant that the MFI was unwilling to sell the product again. There were some design lessons from the experiment both in terms of who to target and how to write those contracts. So I think the underlying idea is worth more testing to see how you insure these firms against political and macroeconomy risks. It's something that a lot of firms say is a constraint. It just doesn't seem to be a constraint for these very micro firms.

TO: Piecing together evidence about how microenterprises are using money: infrequently it's in durables. Frequently it's in working capital, but those investments are relatively liquid. That aligns with what you've seen in a lots of other contexts.

DM: Yeah, lots of pretty liquid investments. But the lesson from our earlier work is that the return from those investments can be pretty high. When firms are reasonably credit constrained, just having more stuff and more variety to sell can be pretty beneficial for them.[12] We know a lot less

11. The barriers to insurance take up are discussed in more detail in the interview with Xavi Giné (chapter 8).
12. See interview with Jonathan Robinson (chapter 18) for a discussion of research on the benefits of investing in inventory, and the interviews with Robinson and Karlan for additional general discussions of why microenterprises do not make profitable investments.

about them fundamentally changing their production processes or moving into different industries, or the capital it would take to do that. But certainly just a little bit more capital at the margin invested in more stuff to sell seems to have big returns in these types of firms.

TO: You mentioned at the very beginning that one of the reasons to do your first RCT was people not being convinced by the nonexperimental evidence. Have you found that the experiments you've done have been more effective convincing people, changing people's mind, or shifting their priors?

DM: Certainly they are more useful for changing academics' minds and academics' priors. On a policy front it's never as clear what actually does manage to change people's minds. The couple of things that I've done that have had the most policy impact, one has been experimental and one has been nonexperimental. Often just very good descriptive data that focuses people's attention on something they haven't focused attention on before has changed people's minds in policy as much as any experiment. We did a study where we carefully mapped out what the costs of sending money from New Zealand to the Pacific Islands were, and what the constraints to doing that were in terms of regulations and banking laws.[22] That really focused attention in the region on this issue that migrants were spending 20 to 25 percent of the remittance to send money and that was much more than it was in other parts of the world. So those simple descriptive stats ended up leading to changes in banking laws in New Zealand and to new commercial products. There was no RCT, just basic descriptive work. On the other hand, some of the experimental work has also been useful in having something where it's very easy to explain to policy makers: we did this here, we gave this group something and this other group didn't get it, and you can see the difference it made. The work I did in India on improving management has started to have some traction in different countries. The follow-up work in Colombia is a direct result of that. The Colombian government was very taken by the experiment, and it's very clear that there is a causal impact of improving management practices on productivity. They said, "We'd like to see if we can get that in our country too." It was a lot more convincing to them than any nonexperimental approach would have been.

11   Nancy Birdsall

Nancy is the founding president of the Center for Global Development, a think tank devoted to improving the policies of wealthy countries toward developing countries, from aid to trade and often beyond. It is distinctive for not just generating ideas but for getting those ideas implemented. Before founding CGD, Nancy held senior positions at the Inter-American Development Bank and the World Bank and was director of the Economic Reform Project at the Carnegie Endowment for International Peace. She is the co-author of *Cash on Delivery: A New Approach to Foreign Aid.*

TO: Within the "walls" of CGD[1] you have both Dean Karlan and Lant Pritchett—perhaps polar opposites in terms of their perspectives on RCT's usefulness in development. Given that CGD's explicit goal is to influence the world, how do you fit together people who have such strongly held but differing opinions on how to do that?

NB: As background, CGD is decentralized in the extreme. Each fellow sets his or her own agenda. We have incentives for people to address questions that are important and that have policy relevance, and even incentives for people to push through engagement with the policy world if they have a particular viewpoint and they can document it with evidence or concepts. But people can take different views. So that's the background of why we can have both Lant and Dean coexist here.

I think the foreground is, that like many people who are not a major participant in one or the other side of that debate, I see lots of benefits in both approaches. We had a working group that did a report—I was a co-author, but really the two people who did most of the work were Bill Savedoff and

---

1. Both Pritchett and Karlan are nonresident fellows.

Ruth Levine—called *When Will We Ever Learn*.[1] Esther Duflo was part of the group. Bill and Ruth and I struggled a little bit because Esther was insistent that the only valid approach was the RCT. My own view is that is not true. And we pushed hard and in the end the report also refers to evaluation using statistical methods—good econometrics. Maybe you don't get as foolproof a result but you can address larger questions as Lant and others indicate.

At the same time what is most interesting about RCTs for me is that even when they are narrow, they address a problem that has been clearly defined. A lot of development programs come with a solution before the nature of the problem is set out. The obvious example is the push to get every child in primary school. But the fundamental problem that those in school weren't learning very much hadn't been defined.[2]

And it's still the case. I was in Tanzania, for instance, but you can pick any country. We were there discussing Cash on Delivery aid.[2][3] There was a conference sponsored by Swedish Aid and DFID that had a bunch of people from the education ministry. At the conference the results of the UWEZO study[3] of educational achievement were presented. They showed that children, particularly at the lower levels, weren't learning very much. It was quite shocking. They also did some assessment of whether teachers were present and found things like in urban schools teachers were only there something like two hours a day. But the education ministry staff was still just totally focused on inputs: more money for schools, more teachers, more books. So even when the information is there, it takes a long time to get people to change their priors on what is the problem they face. Maybe you have to hear it over and over. It has to capture people's imagination. So the UWEZO tests eventually made their way into the press, and after several years the poor results are more widely understood in Tanzania—the fact that they need to deal with not only enrollment but whether children are learning. It's happening slowly in India as well. It takes a long time and it needs to be compelling. That's the value of RCTs. They create these very compelling stories.

2. An idea, championed by CGD, that rather than having international aid flows be directed to specific projects, outcome goals should be set and aid delivered conditional on meeting those goals.
3. UWEZO is an assessment of learning levels among children in Tanzania. It is modeled on the ASER evaluation pioneered by Pratham in India.

TO: So do you find that RCTs are more compelling to policy makers, to ministers of education, to ministers of health?

NB: I can't answer that well. I think in the short run they're more compelling to readers of academic work. At the same time my crude theory about the impact of research is not that research feeds into policy directly. Research kind of goes up in into the air, into the clouds. If it's good, if it's interesting, and perhaps especially if there is some compelling behavioral story behind it, as is often the case with an RCT, it gets circulated and cited. Eventually it filters down to World Bank operational people and donor staff and people in the ministries.

I was the head of the policy research department at the World Bank, and there were always complaints about how the people on the project teams weren't reading the reports. And I was constantly trying to explain that the people in operations are not going to read and digest the results of what you show with your survey of expenditures in Malawi or Thailand. But it's going to eventually filter through to them, especially if it gets into academic journals. RCTs have that advantage. By being rigorous and being duplicated and becoming an input in lots of dissertations, they filter through.

TO: I've heard it said that policy makers just need a professor at an Ivy League who says "it is so" and it doesn't matter what the methodology is.

NB: I think that's true only if the minister already wanted to go in that direction. Maybe in a few cases and at a few times you have that magic combination. My story about Tanzania suggests it's a much longer, tougher path, and the probability of it sinking in eventually is much higher if it's been duplicated in other countries and there's a pattern, and somebody writes a book.

Lant's book on education—in the beginning when it was in draft and I'd read it, it seemed just so repetitive. And eventually it sinks in how bad the situation is. Even so, I think there's real political resistance in many low-income countries to doing testing that's equivalent from year to year because it puts the politicians in a tough spot in the short run, and politicians have short-run horizons. That's what happened with UWEZO. It's interesting because there has been testing in many countries in Africa, but the tests are not necessarily equivalent from year to year. They're set so the right number of kids get into secondary school or into university. But that's a whole other story.

TO: A number of big ideas have incubated within CGD. In addition to supporting some of the *randomistas*, you have advanced market commitments [AMCs],[4] cash on delivery [CoD] aid, migration. So if you're looking at those things and project looking back from twenty years in the future, which of these ideas that have gotten some support here will have made the biggest difference?

NB: I think it's migration. It's going to take longer, but it's as though the world is catching up to the points that Lant and then Michael [Clemens] have been making. Lant has been making that point that this is an irresistible force. It's not going to stop. Then Michael's done great work, including some with Lant, looking at migration as the way people escape poverty, historically and now.[4] It's the simplest and most effective antipoverty program. Pretty much everyone wins.

It also just turns out that it's something that's global. It's a development issue but it's so big, so universal. People move and they move for economic reasons. It's just bound to stick as an issue. Michael and others are coming up with string of good ideas on how to make it work, even given the legal constraints that most rich countries have put in place.

CoD Aid, which is kind of my baby, is another idea that I think will matter. I think aid matters less, but there are ideas that are embedded in CoD Aid that can be implemented by federal governments, not just aid agencies. People have conflated it too much with incentives at the individual, household, or even NGO level. It's about getting the funder out of the way so that the recipient of some largesse from outside, whether it's a state in India or a country in Africa, is responsible and accountable to their people. So for me, it's about building democracy and accountability and good government. In that way it's a lot like our Oil-to-Cash idea.[5][5] Give people not only transparency about what's going on but a reason to care. So I think that set of ideas that is around outcomes-based transfers will ultimately matter a lot.

4. Advanced Market Commitments are a device to allow governments to commit to purchasing a certain amount of, for instance, vaccines for tropical diseases in order to provide incentives for private sector research. See the interview with Michael Kremer in chapter 1 for more discussion on AMCs.

5. The proposal is to direct resource-rich countries income from the exploitation of natural resources into direct payments to citizens, similar to the dividend received by citizens of Alaska.

TO: What's your personal theory of change when it comes to policy? Is it an evidence channel: policy and practice change because of quality of evidence. Is it a channel of quality of ideas on some measure other than having lots of statistical backing? Is it a charisma channel? Having a person who can advocate well for an idea and be persuasive. You've seen people trying to push policy through each of those channels.

NB: It's a very nice framing: evidence, quality of ideas, and charisma. I think charisma only works at the local political level. Local could be a country or a province or a town. And it usually only works in the short run. There's the risk that when that charismatic leader is gone, the idea doesn't stick. Charisma can also lead to bad policies.

TO: James Scott[6] would say evidence can lead to very bad policies too.[6]

NB: My theory of change is that you need it all. You need to bang your head against a wall. You need a lot of activity. You need movements. We're not going to get change on climate policy with evidence. If there's a public good where collective action is hard to get going, you need pressure from civil society organizations and intellectuals. You need that combination. And then sometimes there are ideas.

My mini-philosophy on CGD is actually very much about ideas. It's a bit how Esther Duflo writes in a different context: pick some small things and sometimes they have butterfly effects. Take AMCs. AMCs are not a big distraction from everything else that matters for health in the world. You can do it while still doing those other things. But if it works, it could make a big difference.

For a think tank like CGD it's not so much about finding the new Keynes—that one person who can influence policy for decades afterward—but about lots of ideas. Why don't we have Development Impact Bonds? Why don't we push biometric IDs for people in the developing world because we'll then have the possibility for more leakage-free cash transfers? Why not make cash transfers a benchmark for aid? Why not have better schemes for managing global public goods? These are small ideas in a way, but they can accumulate.

That's a problem with everyone doing RCT-type work. There's not enough youthful energy focused on finding ways to get going on fixing some big

6. See Scott's book *Seeing Like a State*, which delves into how governments have used what they perceived as evidence to drive policies that force people to conform to the evidence.

problems. We had a talk last week on zoonotic diseases. There's not enough attention on those issues where there are huge risks but they're in the long tail.

It seems that RCTs are not very interesting for a lot of economists. It's almost too easy for a dissertation to do a RCT. To hook into one of Michael Kremer's or Dean Karlan's arrangements, go to the field, collect data. The economic questions are pretty simple. In that sense, I think it's unfortunate if 70 percent of PhD students are doing RCTs.

Now I think RCTs have gotten more interesting over time. The questions and the approach are getting more interesting, particularly in terms of more attention to behavioral studies. But not in terms of greater attention to the big questions of economics of scarcity and allocation. Even some of the big microeconomics questions, say labor economics, is grossly under-studied now.

TO: That's one of the critiques of the RCT work. That no matter how many chlorine dispensers you install, it won't have as much of an effect as getting one institution, say the Ministry of Education in India, to work better.

NB: I do wish that we could fix policies and fix institutions with a stroke of the pen the way exchange rate policy can be fixed. If you're talking about opening markets and taking away really bad rent-based import tariffs, then maybe the charismatic professor working with the new minister of trade can make a difference because, once a change like that is implemented, people start to benefit early on. But unfortunately, there's only a small set of policies in the economic sphere that are like that. Most have trade-offs, even trade policy, in the short run. So they have to backed by more, not just evidence, but the quality of the ideas and the charisma of the person making the argument.

I think behavioral economics, Sendhil Mullainathan's work, for example, is important.[7] It in part came out of RCT-land, and I think that's good. Is it transformative like, to use your example, fixing education in India? No, but I think it's a big idea because it clarifies for non-poor people that poor people have the same values and interests. They are not stupid. They are handicapped in making decisions in their own long-term interests by being poor. It's actually better evidence for a poverty trap than anything that Jeff Sachs or the poverty trap adherents have come up with.

When thinking about how policies and institutions change I think you also have to look at Lant and Matt Andrews' work on PDIA—problem driven iterative adaptation.[8] Basically it's their theory on how policy changes in ways that really make them better: work with the locals, discover a problem, let them figure it out, keep the space open, don't come with solutions.[7]

But to me that's all complimentary. You need the big ideas, you need the compelling stories, particularly about people's behavior. You need people who can represent and explain those ideas. And you need to let people figure out how to apply those ideas to whatever context they're in.

TO: You mentioned earlier that some of the *randomistas* were too insistent that only one kind of evidence is believable. But there's also a theory of change that says that the way you move sectors is by having someone stake out an extreme position. You have to go beyond what is radical so that today's radical looks middle ground. One could make an argument that there wouldn't have been as much progress in pushing on quality of evidence in policy if someone hadn't drawn a line in the sand and forced others to grapple with the limitations of other methodologies.

NB: I think that's true for quality of evidence. But you're associating that change, I think, too closely with the RCT movement. There are different approaches that are also, for some problems and in some cases, equally compelling in terms of providing evidence. And those evidence-based studies that come from careful use of econometrics and statistics, sometimes they only clarify questions, it's true. They redefine or reframe an important question, but that's sometimes true of an RCT as well. It depends on the issue at hand. You can't do an RCT on whether industrial policy will work in some settings. But you can learn from cross-country comparisons.

I'm a big believer in rigor in evidence. But there are limits. There's this false analogy to medicine. But the human body is the human body. The differences in every single country in every single political and institutional arrangement are more like the variation in people's personalities, not the differences in their physical makeup.

7. Discussed in the interview with Lant Pritchett (chapter 9), but it's also notable that this recipe is quite similar to how Michael Kremer (chapter 1) and Dean Karlan (chapter 6) discuss the value of RCTs in their interviews.

There's a reason that people like Lant and Angus Deaton are out there resisting. They're resisting because they are truly worried that the RCT movement is soaking up a lot of space in terms of limited amounts of money, limited numbers of graduate students. Are the kids in PhD programs who are doing RCTs learning about Keynes and John Locke and Adam Smith? Are they learning economic history? I'm not sure they are. Economic history is so fundamental for learning about economic development, more than the math and statistics that it seems they're spending so much time on in PhD programs.

Dean is a Professor in the Department of Economics and the Ford School of Public Policy at the University of Michigan. Dean's doctoral research was based on a natural experiment: variation in rainfall amounts across Indonesia. The fact that the country maintained both detailed records of weather and census-type data allowed him to show how Indonesian families prioritized the needs of male children during hard times.

While continuing to exploit natural experiments, Dean's research now includes many randomized controlled trials. That research looks at microfinance, risk and insurance in poor households, and corruption. He also has done extensive research on migration and remittances, in particular looking at interventions that might increase the positive impact of remittances.

TO: Why don't we start with natural experiments versus field experiments. Tell me about how the Indonesia rainfall paper came about.[1]

DY: I had actually worked on exploiting rainfall variation and weather variation for a couple of years before I got the idea for that paper. I am far from the first person to use weather variations to achieve exogenous variation. At Harvard it was an idea that was floating around. Michael Kremer was my advisor and Ted Miguel[1] was wrapping up his graduate

---

1. See chapter 1 for an interview with and background on Michael Kremer. Ted Miguel co-authored one of the original development RCT papers, "Worms: Identifying Impacts on Education and Health in the Presence of Treatment Externalities." His work also includes use of rainfall variation to estimate the economic conditions on conflict, and innovative work on corruption with Ray Fisman (e.g., how corrupt political cultures affect things as varied traffic tickets and stock valuations). Miguel is a co-founder of CEGA, a network of researchers with similarities to J-PAL and IPA, and of Berkeley Initiative for Transparency in the Social Sciences, which encourages preregistration of studies, pre-analysis plans, open data, and replication of experiments.

work and they were thinking about things like this. Weather was one category of exogenous variation that people tried to exploit in their dissertation work.[2]

One of my dissertation chapters was looking at weather variation and how it affected international migration from the Philippines and how households responded by sending migrants overseas. Weather variations were very much on my mind at that time. But how the Indonesia paper emerged was kind of idiosyncratic. I was preparing a lecture for my master's level course in development economics here at Michigan. And I read an article by Bob Fogel whose work was about how early life conditions, nutrition investments in early life in particular, influenced people's outcomes over a lifetime.[2] I discussed the paper with my wife who is a health economist, she's my co-author on that paper, and somehow we both had the brainstorm that it would be great to bring a strong causal identification to these claims Fogel was making about how early life conditions are important for people's long-run outcomes. Over the course of his career, Fogel accumulated a lot of compelling material, but we both felt that a strong causal identification was missing. So we decided to work together on trying to find a context in which we would be able to link weather events around the time of one's birth to later life outcomes.

It was an unusual way for a research project to emerge because we had this idea about how to achieve causal identification, but we didn't know where we were going to do it or what data set we might be able to use. I tell my students this all the time—you really need to have a lot of pots on the fire because you never know when all the pieces are going to come together for you to write a good paper.[3] You not only need to have a good idea of how to achieve causal identification, but you also have to find a context and a data set with which to work, if you're not running your own experiments that is.

So we basically set out and scoured all the data that we could find that had the specific set of elements that we needed to have. It turned out that Indonesia was just about the only place that we found where we could do this

2. See interviews with Michael Kremer (chapter 1) and Lant Pritchett (chapter 9) who discuss the overall trend of economists seeking methods to better identify causal impact, and as Pritchett puts it, to withstand criticism in graduate seminars.
3. A theme echoed by Dean Karlan (chapter 6) and Chris Blattman (chapter 20).

because the Indonesian Family Life Survey[4] (IFLS) turned out to have all of the data items that we needed. We then just needed to buy some supplemental weather data from the Indonesian government.

It was actually a surprise to us, in retrospect, that there was only one country and one data set that we could have used to write this paper. If the IFLS didn't exist, or if they hadn't collected very detailed data on birth year and place, we wouldn't have been able to write this paper. There was one other candidate data set, a Russian living standards survey from the 1990s, I think.[5] It had a similar structure with data on date and location of birth. But we didn't think it was as promising a context as Indonesia, mostly because we didn't have a strong prior that weather shocks around the time of birth would have a strong effect on people's later life outcomes. We thought if there was, we'd be more likely to see it in Indonesia.

TO: There have been a lot of studies and natural experiment papers using Indonesian data, presumably because it has these very good data sets. There are a few other data sets that crop up over and over. People tend to use them because they are accessible and a lot cheaper than running an experiment or collecting new data. Do you worry about external validity issues because of that? That there is something systematically different about Indonesia reflected in the fact that they do collect good data? Or, alternatively, that so many people are running so many tests against that data that there are going to be false positives?

DY: You could frame your question about development research as a whole. What percentage of results that are published are spurious or can't be replicated? That's a broader concern about the production of knowledge, and what we can learn from articles that are published in journals. I don't think it's anything but a good thing that in Indonesia there is high-quality socioeconomic data collection by the government and by independent researchers like IFLS.

But to address one of the things that you mentioned, yes, Indonesia is a very specific context. But it is a large and important country. So, even if one made the argument, which I'm not making, that findings from Indonesian

4. The Indonesian Family Life Survey is an ongoing project of the RAND Institute. Begun in 1993/1994, it has a sample representative of more than 80 percent of the Indonesian Population. The fifth wave of the survey is scheduled for release in 2016. http://www.rand.org/labor/FLS/IFLS.html.

5. A summary of the living standards survey can be found here: http://goo.gl/NRxKCY.

data only applied to Indonesia, they can have very important human consequences. The point is right that you have to worry about external validity with any research project. Lots of folks ask me about whether my Indonesia findings are likely to apply in sub-Saharan Africa, and I can't do anything but speculate. I certainly wouldn't want to make any strong statements about how it would apply there.

The other question was about specification searching, or not necessarily specification searching but related to publication bias.

TO: It's not any particular individual running tests until they find something, but the fact is that with the public data sets you get a lot of tests being run, and no one knows how many tests are being run.

DY: I wouldn't necessarily frame the issue as being related to any particular data set, but you're absolutely right, there's a limited set of publicly available data sets out there. And researchers are behind the scenes, unobserved by the larger research community, running tests and looking to see what statistical relationships exist in the data. Then the articles that end up being published are these subsets that end up with statistically significant and publishable results. I think it's widely appreciated that there is publication bias. Some fraction of these results is going to emerge by chance.

TO: What was the first RCT you were involved in and what attracted you about the method?

DY: I'd been exposed to a number of RCTs in graduate school. My adviser was Michael Kremer who really started off the whole wave of RCTs. It was something that was definitely in the air as a methodology, and I got to witness firsthand from the working paper stage all the way to successful publication how to use the methodology, what the challenges were in being convincing and answering more fundamental economic questions. I found it very appealing, and perhaps had some early insight into how these things were done even though I didn't actually work on any of them as a graduate student.

I graduated in 2003, and I was actually exclusively working on non-RCT projects but as I got out of the phase of getting my dissertation chapters published and started to think about new things to work on, I naturally gravitated toward the RCT methodology. I think I also probably felt that I had the raw skills that could make these things work, that perhaps this was something where I might have a comparative advantage.

I worked in business for three years before going to grad school so I felt like I had some ability to see things from the standpoint of practitioners and business people and to frame a research study as something that could also be of business interest to, say, a microfinance institution. And that's turned out to be the case. I feel like I've been able to find studies, and set up studies, that have been of mutual interest to the research community and to the business community, that could provide important bottom-line contributions to MFIs or remitters. I also think I had more of a taste, or less distaste, for management of fieldwork than other academics, at least on average.

TO: I'd like to ask about how you interpret and internalize evidence. You've done work in Malawi on commitment savings devices.[3] Lots of people are working on similar studies, trying to understand the underlying pathways of commitment devices. If those other experiments showed something quite different than yours, what would it take for you to conclude that the Malawi results were the outliers?

DY: What would it take to move my priors in the opposite direction on a particular finding?

TO: Right, but let me broaden it. Do you distinguish between evidence from natural experiments and randomized experiments? Are they essentially equivalent in terms of how we should interpret results from each of those methods? Or should we think of them differently? More generally, do you think in a Bayesian way? What does it take to change your mind?

DY: That's a great question. When it comes to methodology, I don't think that evidence from one type of study should necessarily be privileged over another. I don't have a strong stance on that. Most of the issues I would raise are practical and have to do with how easy it is to do a good job with a credible causal identification using one approach versus another. The broad point I would make is that both types of approaches should be in the development economist's toolkit. I don't think it's right to throw out one tool or exclusively privilege another. But the two different tools have real plusses and minuses. The beauty of randomized trials, in my mind, is that you can achieve much stronger claims to causal identification, conditional on the experiment being conducted appropriately and dealing with issues like selection and attrition. The drawback of RCTs is that it's often extremely difficult, if not impossible, to answer certain questions. I think development researchers have been pushing the boundaries on the types of questions that RCTs can answer. I expect that's going to continue because there are great returns to pushing those boundaries. But certain types of questions are probably never going to be answered using RCTs, like most major macroeconomic questions. Practically, there's a limit, a limit we haven't reached yet, to the number of real world organizations or governments that are going to cooperate in designing and implementing an RCT. As researchers, we don't have the ability to actually run a program. So, for the most part, you have to collaborate with someone.

So the ability to ask questions is only partly under the control of researchers. You have to have real world organizations that are willing to randomize. For a long time that limited the ability of researchers to ask questions like "what is the impact of microcredit on household well-being?" until Abhijit and Esther[4] and Dean and Jon Zinman[5] were able to find MFIs that were willing to randomize in some way.

Those are the downsides of RCTs in my mind. The beauty of the natural experimental approach is, in principle, that there's no limitation on what research questions you can answer. In reality, you never know whether you're going to be able to find a particular measure, but the range of questions is not limited in theory to any particular realm. The challenge is finding causal identification, finding some natural real world variation that will allow you to answer a particular question. The other key downside to the natural experimental approach is that because one is not typically able to work with explicit lottery-based randomization—in the real world there are very few programs that are lottery based—one always has to spend a great deal of time convincing people that you've found plausible exogenous variation. I would say, the typical natural experimental study—though some studies are quite convincing—is much less convincing in terms of causal identification than an RCT. Even though one can try to provide auxiliary evidence or subsidiary analyses to try to rule out alternative stories, typically it's not possible to dot all the I's and cross all the T's and to rule out with 100 percent certainty all potentially confounding stories about the causation in a particular context.

TO: Taking from your point about the cleanness of the identification, part of that is understanding the pathways. That's one of the big questions in your Malawi paper and in fact in a lot of the commitment savings experiments: why does a commitment device help? In the Malawi study, having a commitment savings account helps even though people didn't put any money in their commitment savings account. And in Jon and Pascaline's health savings[6] account study,[6] having a box helps people save even when it's not locked. So how are you thinking about what the pathways are? How is it that commitment savings matter if it's not really a commitment?

DY: You're bringing up one of the research questions that really keeps me up at night and that I'm very keen on continuing to pursue actively as a researcher in the next several years. Precisely because I think it's very much an open question, why commitment savings have the effect that we're observing in the real world. One distinction I think is very important to make is the distinction between self-control and other-control problems. The traditional thinking about commitment devices like commitment savings devices is that they help solve self-control problems. If people have a present bias, for example if they have hyperbolic preferences, then that may generate demand for commitment. There will be some demand from people who are at least partially sophisticated about their self-control problems for devices that help the future self have more control over current resource allocations than the present self. That's one explanation for why demand for commitment arises and why commitment devices might have positive effects on people's outcomes.

But there's another explanation that has to do with other-control problems. Basically the idea is that individuals are faced with demands from within their social network for sharing their resources. This is very much related to the operation of informal insurance mechanisms within village societies.[7] For example, when there isn't government-provided or privately provided insurance against the shocks that people experience, informal insurance operates within social networks. There is often a social norm that extra resources or a resource surplus should be shared with others in the social network. That social requirement to share can also generate demand for commitment devices that will help the household protect their resources from the social network.

It's actually an open question in my mind whether other-control or self-control issues are the dominant factor behind demand for and impact of commitment devices. There's some evidence that demand for commitment devices is higher among people who know they have a present bias. For

6. See interviews with Pascaline Dupas (chapter 14) and Jonathan Robinson (chapter 18) for a thorough discussion of this experiment.
7. See interview with Jonathan Robinson (chapter 18) for additional discussion of informal insurance networks, and the effect formalizing insurance mechanisms can have on them.

example, there's a very nice paper by Ashraf, Karlan, and Yin on the Philippines that shows that demand for commitment devices is higher among women, though not among men, who appear to be present biased based on the baseline survey.[7] But I think we've got a ways to go in figuring out the relationship between self-control motivations and other-control motivations within a particular context.

That motivated the design of the commitment savings project in Malawi that we conducted.[8] But as you know, the results of that study were somewhat ambiguous. It didn't do a very good job distinguishing between the self-control and other-control motivations for commitment devices.[8] I still think that's a very important open question that I'm very keen to shed light on, for instance, with some follow-up work that we're currently doing in southern Malawi. In our original Malawi work, as you raised earlier, one of the puzzling questions is we found positive results for people with commitment accounts even though they didn't save very much in that account. One possible explanation is that being offered the commitment savings account allowed people to credibly claim to their social network that they didn't have access to their resources when they actually did. But another possibility is that the offer of a commitment savings account somehow changed farmers' reference point; it had a psychological effect by affecting the farmers' goal setting, for instance. The treatment may somehow have gotten farmers oriented to higher production, and therefore they start increasing their fertilizer use, which leads to higher crop output. It wasn't via an explicit savings mechanism, it simply affected their goal setting.

That's very much speculation on our part. Because we didn't anticipate this finding, we didn't design the experiment to look at that possible channel of the effect. Implicitly, or perhaps sometimes explicitly, encouraging farmers to be more ambitious about their input use and their crop output goal for the next season may actually be introducing a confounder to what we were originally intending to investigate, which was the impact of commitment savings. That finding is going to make us more cautious in our study design in the future so that we can cleanly separate a goal setting or an encouragement effect from the actual financial products that we're offering.

8. See interview with Xavi Gine (chapter 8) for more discussion of the study design and the unanswered questions.

TO: Is your thinking about this informed by the El Salvador remittances control studies?[9] You can look at the account ownership study, in particular, in terms of other-control issues. The treatment of giving more control over bank accounts had very material effects. I guess one of the more interesting things there is how much spill-over into other accounts there seemed to have been. Giving them other-control in one account seems to have affected their self-control.

DY: I think you're absolutely right, even though it's a very different context. Some of these same issues come up in the remittances work and certainly influenced my thinking in terms of the results of the savings study. The El Salvador work is very much about other-control, giving migrants better ability to monitor what their relatives in El Salvador are doing with the resources they send home. One very important point that we make in that paper is that at least part of the result, part of the impact that we had, almost certainly is a joint effect of offering the financial product alongside the encouragement to use them, and in particular, the encouragement to exert control of the resources that are sent to El Salvador. Unfortunately, the design of our project in retrospect doesn't allow us to cleanly separate the offer of the product from the encouragement to assert control over resources in El Salvador. That's certainly going to affect design of subsequent work. The reason why we think this encouragement effect was important is exactly the results you mentioned, the treatment that we found had the greatest effect on savings in El Salvador also led migrants to save more in the US bank accounts that were not the subject of the experiment. Our experiment didn't have any influence directly on access to US bank accounts. That result, more savings in the US accounts, to us, points very strongly to some sort of financial education or empowerment effect. That's been very influential on me as well in thinking that these offers of financial services can also have an effect via financial education. If you don't want to call it financial education, you can think of it as encouragement to use certain financial strategies that the respondent might not have considered previously.

TO: This control theme and what influences people's behavior brings me to the fingerprinting experiment in Malawi.[10] The results there line up very nicely with theory in terms of affecting adverse selection and moral hazard. But there's also something very interesting happening there in terms of paternalism. Overall, the history of development is littered with a lot of programs designed to control the behavior of the poor, based on the belief, explicit or implicit, that they aren't able to control themselves. That's changed a good deal. But there are strong arguments for nudges and other mechanisms to help them follow through on their own preferences. There's even an argument that helping poor households gain more control of their own lives in the long term might require exercising some control in the short term.

DY: I think that's a first-order question when thinking about our finger-printing study in Malawi. What ended up happening, in practice, when we fingerprinted farmers for the study on a randomly assigned basis, was that the fingerprinted farmers in the highest risk category of borrowers responded to the fingerprinting by allocating more land to paprika and using more inputs on their paprika plots. And this was good news to the lender because that's what the loans expressly were for. Basically the first-order concern of the lender was that the loan be used for paprika cultivation and not something else. This was important to the lender for two reasons: one, because the whole reason why the loan was given was that paprika growing was thought to be a profitable and income-increasing activity for these farmers; second, because the paprika was sold through a controlled marketing channel. Basically the only practical option for the famers was to sell to this one paprika buyer, and the company had an agreement with the lender that it would extract repayment of the loan from the farmers' crop proceeds before turning over the remainder of the proceeds to the farmers. So growing paprika not only was thought to be income-raising for the farmers but also dramatically increased the lender's likelihood of getting repaid because the paprika buyer was garnishing the farmers' proceeds to repay the loans.

The very interesting possibility, which we unfortunately didn't get strong enough statistical results on, is the possibility that compelling farmers in this highest risk category to grow paprika could have actually raised their income. Unfortunately, our sample sizes weren't large enough, and therefore the statistical significance levels aren't what we would want them to be. But there's very suggestive evidence in the paper that income actually rose substantially for farmers in this highest risk category. So when they were compelled to grow paprika instead of using the loan for something else, they actually experienced an increase in income. I very much want to do a future study that increases the sample size so that we can test to see whether or not in fact there were increases in income due to fingerprinting.

If that result holds, it really does connect back to your question. If, by cracking the whip on borrowers, we find they actually raise their incomes, that would bring the question to the fore very, very prominently. I don't think this intervention would cross the line into an ethically questionable area. In fact I think it's still quite far from an ethnically questionable area. The context is really private lending transactions: lenders providing loans for a specific commercial purpose. I don't think it's questionable that a lender can, if it chooses to do so, seek to require that the loan be used for the purpose that the loan was intended for, particularly if empirically we find that strong control over the use of the loans ends up being beneficial for farmers, by raising their incomes.

But I think it raises other very interesting and important questions. If the results hold in a larger sample, you have to ask why the farmers weren't taking these actions on their own. Certainly that would call for more work explaining why farmers weren't taking advantage of these opportunities. Are the farmers present-biased? Is there some other factor preventing them from taking these actions without compulsion from the lender?

TO: That brings us back to your work with migrants and much softer forms of control in terms of encouraging spending by remittance receivers on education. There seems to have been large effects in both cases you've studied.

DY: The first project was in El Salvador, funded by the Inter-American Development Bank and partnered with a foundation in El Salvador. It basically allowed migrants to fund individual sponsorships for students of their choice in El Salvador. From the standpoint of the student, they are getting education expenses paid for. Since in El Salvador most students are attending public schools, and public schools are free, the funds aren't paying tuition. The treatment is framed as a support mechanism for students so that they can afford to go to school. The migrant's contributions get distributed to students on a monthly basis over a ten-month period. The students get an ATM card that's refreshed every month with an additional contribution that is 1/10th the amount the migrant put into the pot. It's intended to cover travel and daily expenses to keep the student in school.

We actually learned early on that, when offering this facility, there was very little demand for the product as we designed it. So we fairly quickly decided to add a couple of treatment conditions where we would subsidize the educational sponsorship. We found some resources to match the funds migrants were contributing. In one treatment we offered a one-to-one match; the other treatment was a three-to-one match.

It was something of a disappointment to us that migrants didn't value the control in and of itself, and there needed to be some sort of match for them to be willing to do this. While there was no demand for channeling remittances to education when it was unsubsidized, there was a significant and empirically relevant level of demand when we provided matching funds, either dollar for dollar or 3 to 1. What's more, the money, once it got channeled to the family in El Salvador, did have substantial impact on educational expenditures and educational and child labor outcomes for the beneficiary students in El Salvador. Educational expenditures went up, as you would expect. The increases were concentrated in the targeted beneficiary students, and as a side point, there wasn't a diversion of educational resources away from other children in the household. So this was really an increase in educational expenditure on the targeted students. The students were more likely to be in private school as a result and less likely to be in the labor force.

Another striking result is that it looked like once these families got these transfers, they actually topped up the resources they received with additional funds. In fact the level at which this was happening was actually quite substantial. For every dollar that the beneficiary households received, they put in an additional $3 themselves, so the total expenditure went up $4 for every dollar that these families received via remittances intended for education.

TO: That doesn't fit with an obvious story that education is a lumpy investment where it was hard to acquire the lump. If they are tripling it, it seems like they wouldn't have had that much of a problem making the investment in the first place.

DY: I agree the magnitude is strikingly large. There *are* big confidence intervals around that estimate. When you look at the 90 percent confidence intervals, there are somewhat more modest increases, but it is statistically significantly different than zero.

I think what's going on here is that private school investment, where we saw a lot of the effects, is a lumpy investment. And it's indivisible—you can't send your children to half of a private school. I don't think it's right to say that the families could have done this themselves. Once you get a transfer that is, say, 25 percent of what you need to pay for private school, you might decide at that point that it's worth it to put in the remaining 75 percent.

TO: The money is delivered month by month—is it a question of confidence that the money is going to be there so they're willing to make the investment because they know there's going to be a flow?

DY: The timing does mean that the families need to trust that this mechanism is going to work as promised and the money is going to flow into the account each month. The families, given the timing of the experiment, had to make a decision relatively quickly after receiving news of this subsidy about whether to put their kid into private school. And it seems the people who decided to respond moved very quickly. On the other hand, it wasn't universal. Certainly, it wasn't everyone. Not every migrant set up the transfer, and not every family responded by sending their kids to private school. Many did. The tuition payments can also be spaced out over time. You don't always have to pay your tuition all at once in advance. I don't think the spacing out of the transfer was a huge deterrent to moving the kid into private school.

The lesson from the experiment ended up not being so much about control over remittances, as it turned out, because there was no demand for the unsubsidized payment mechanism for education. But it did provide some evidence on an additional lever in the development policy toolkit. If you want to promote education in developing countries and you want to leverage funds from international migrants, then this is one type of program that development policy institutions might consider. It's probably not the world's most cost-effective program because it does involve providing matched funds, but it does have positive effects and does lead families to top up and invest even more money. It has something like the flavor of a CCT[9] program.

9. Conditional cash transfers (CCTs) are a welfare policy whereby recipients receive a benefit conditional on meeting certain requirements such as children being vaccinated or attending school. The first of a modern wave of CCT programs was launched in Mexico in the early 1990s under the name Progresa (now called Opportunidades). Of note, the Progresa program was evaluated using an RCT design around the same time that Michael Kremer (chapter 1) was running early experiments in Kenya, though the two efforts were not connected at all (see Kremer interview). Since the original Progresa pilot, CCTs have become popular throughout the developing world and are even being tested in the US. However, increasingly impact evaluations have found that the conditions themselves have little effect and unconditional cash transfers achieve many of the same outcomes. See interviews with Pascaline Dupas (chapter 14) and Christ Blattman (chapter 20) for further discussion of unconditional cash transfers.

TO: But a CCT program with a 4 to 1 match for the development institution.

DY: That's exactly the way we're thinking about it. There are some numbers at the end of the paper. For every dollar of donor funds provided for secondary or tertiary education, you can generate additional contributions amounting to nearly four dollars.

As it turns out, most of that comes from the beneficiary households. For every dollar provided, you can get 33 cents from the migrant and $3.62 from the households themselves. It's not necessarily the case that if you scaled this up and people really trust this mechanism that one would see exactly these same results. I would expect, or at least I would hope, that one could get away with lower match rates if this mechanism was really scaled up and people realized that it was a legitimate program, and so people's concern that their money would be stolen or misappropriated was relieved. This was very much a pilot program, and the migrants had plenty of reasons to be suspicious that we were really going to follow through on this very generous match.

TO: Let's talk about the project with the Filipino migrants in Rome. What did you learn from that in terms of migrants desire to influence the spending of remittances?

DY: I wasn't deterred by the early El Salvador results that showed very little or no interest in the unsubsidized product. I thought there might be demand for this product in a different context. In Rome it is a very different migrant population. It's largely legal contract work that these Filipinos are involved in Italy as opposed to the Salvadoran population in DC, which was a mixture of documented and undocumented immigrants. The Salvadorans, on average, had lower levels of income than the Filipinos in Rome. So we were fortunate to get a pilot grant from USAID via their Development Innovation Ventures[10] facility.

What we ended up doing in that project was, first of all, we designed a payment mechanism in collaboration with one of the Philippines' largest banks, Bank of the Philippine Islands, whereby a migrant could go to a branch in Rome and sign up to use this payment mechanism, which we called EduPay. The bank would channel the funds to a particular school in the Philippines and credit the account of a specific student chosen by the

10. See the interview with Michael Kremer where he discusses his role in founding DIV.

migrant. A large part of what we were doing was trying to see if there was nonzero demand for the product. We didn't feel we had enough funding to do a large RCT on the impact. We imagined this as a first step to a later RCT, the first step being to show that this mechanism could actually work and people would demand it in nonzero numbers.

The second thing we did was a "lab in the field"-type experiment with migrants. So basically we would intercept migrants in Rome and ask them to participate in a lottery and survey to gauge their degree of interest in channeling remittances toward education. At the very end of the interaction we offered them the new EduPay mechanism. The lab in the field experiment had a couple of purposes. The first was to tease apart a few different reasons why people might have a demand for a product like EduPay. And the second purpose was we wanted to see if the experimental behavior, the measure of how interested someone was in a product during the lab experiment, would correlate with actual demand for the product.

The primary thing I'll emphasize is that when you offer someone a direct payment mechanism for something like education, there's at least two things bundled in there. One is the signal by the migrant that the migrant wants the funds to be spent on education. The second is actual control of funds by having them directly channeled to the educational institution.

Because you have these two elements, it raises the question of what is actually driving the impact. Is it having an effect by taking control out of the hands of the recipient or is it just because of the signal to the recipient of what the migrant's intention is? You have to wonder if rather than going through all the bureaucratic processes to move money directly to an institution and to benefit a specific individual, could you just accomplish the same thing with a signal?[11]

So when we intercepted the migrants, we told them, "You've just been put in a lottery to win 1,000 euros," which is a substantial amount of money, "but we need you to tell us now, if you win, how do you want to allocate the money between yourself and one or more individuals in the Philippines." We allowed the migrants to say that they wanted to take all 1,000

11. The mechanisms described here are similar to a study discussed with Pascaline Dupas, in which the Morrocan government provided an education CCT grant but in practice the conditions were not enforced (the researchers refer to it as a "labeled" grant). The signaling mechanism of encouraging families to spend on education seems to have positive effects on school attendance and completion.

euros themselves or to take some split and distribute it in any way among individuals in the Philippines that they selected. It was very flexible. A base case for the money was distributing cash, just a standard dictator game[12] but with multiple possible recipients on the other side. Then we changed the situation a little bit, and we allowed the migrants—as an option, not as a requirement—to also send a signal that they wanted these funds to be used for education. We called it the education-labeling condition. If a migrant chose to send a certain amount of funds to person A with an education label, the funds would be delivered with a note that said "These funds are intended for the education of ...," a person the migrant identified. But it was purely an option. The person could just send cash with no note as well.

If you compared people with the labeling option with the basic dictator game condition you can see whether people were willing to remit additional money if they were able to send a signal about how they wanted the money spent, at least specifically for education. And we found that had a substantial impact. It raised remittances by about 15 percent compared to the base case. In the base condition, the migrants actually shared the majority of the funds, they shared on average 600 euros. But when they could label it they shared about 90 euros more. That's a substantial increase.

That's the first insight from the paper. Simply allowing people to label funds for education and provide a strong signal of what they would like the funds to be used for raised remittances substantially. We had an additional condition on top of the education label option. We provided another condition that allowed the migrant to send the funds directly to a school. So, in addition to sending cash, or sending with a label, the migrant could send the funds directly to a school in the name of a particular student of their choice. In that case we didn't see much more additional increase in remittances on top of the education label condition. We saw an additional,

12. One of the common lab experiments in economics and anthropology is the dictator game. While there are many variations, in the basic exercise participants are organized into pairs. One is then given cash, which that person can choose to keep or split in any ratio with the second participant. The second participant has no say in the split—hence the term "dictator." In theory, a purely self-interested person would keep all the money, offering none to a partner, since there are no consequences for not sharing. Note that Lant Pritchett (chapter 9) discusses the wide variation in results of playing the dictator game in different cultures as part of his argument that findings from field experiments are context specific and cannot be reasonably assumed to apply in other contexts.

maybe 2 percent, increase. We concluded that directing funds to the school was valuable in and of itself, but it was a minimal benefit compared to just labeling the funds.

The other thing that we were able to do with the experiment was to show the degree to which people are interested in educational labeling, which we measured at the individual level in terms of sharing with people in the Philippines. That's highly predictive of demand for the actual EduPay product when it was offered to them. As opposed to when you construct a measure of interest in the EduPay experimental condition, that doesn't have much additional predictive power vis-à-vis the interest in the educational label condition. On both fronts it's intriguing new evidence that simply giving an easy way to label funds for particular purposes can increase remittances substantially.

TO: So there seems to be a story there about enabling conversations about how money is spent as opposed to an actual wish to tightly control the behavior of people I'm sending money to. Lots of households have a really hard time having conversations about how to spend money. Husbands and wives always have differences in preferences for spending money. Those can be very high stakes conversations. So the label that allows a conversation without starting a fight could presumably be very valuable. In the El Salvador study—the El Salvador product wasn't truly constrained, and with this one the recipients could have diverted these funds. It was a strong signal but a weak control mechanism.

DY: I like the way that you're putting that. One thing that people raise legitimately when I describe these results, especially the education label results from the Philippines study, is why couldn't the migrants have sent those signals themselves.[13] It's not a particularly costly signal to send. It seems a little bit odd that migrants would respond so strongly to an ability to do something they could have done themselves. I think you're right that these are difficult conversations. You might not necessarily want to tell someone to their face how you think the funds should be spent. And maybe it's more palatable if it comes from an intermediary of some sort. Of course, these were windfall funds, not funds coming from peoples' bank accounts

---

13. There is a similar question in the results from Dupas's (chapter 14) and Robinson's (chapter 18) health savings lock box study. The strongest effect is from a mechanism—putting funds in a separate box—that the households could have put in place without the intervention. For more discussion on these points, see the interviews with Karlan, Dupas, Robinson, and Blattman.

directly. So the migrant might be able to say that this money came from this organization as a windfall and it wasn't my doing that these funds were labeled for education. So they could distance themselves potentially. Or at the very least it might have been a safer way to start a conversation about financial management in the household. I think there's definitely a lot more to be done in figuring out whether this could work in a scaled-up fashion or in what way one can get migrants to be comfortable sending these signals in a way that sort of preserves their social relationships with the recipients back home. It's definitely very intriguing and a direction I'd like to be working on.

TO: At least in the US a lot of effort goes into teaching husbands and wives how to say these things to each other, which is how I think of things like pre-marital counseling and even a lot of couples therapy. That suggests to me this is a costly signal to send.

You mentioned earlier your experience working with and partnering with institutions. What is your experience in having the output of RCTs adopted by those institutions? Have you seen them actually change products, deliver new products, change policies as a result of what studies have found?

DY: There are several examples. It hasn't been universal, of course. But in terms of successful examples, the first big RCT I did was the study of joint savings accounts between migrants and their family members in El Salvador that we conducted with Banco Agricola (BA), which we talked about earlier. BA had a great deal of enthusiasm for rolling out this product to its customer base, almost as soon as we developed it, and started offering it to migrants in the DC area. So they were chomping at the bit and couldn't wait to advertise the product and offer it on a large scale as soon as we were done with the end-line survey. We actually show among the results in the paper[11] that pretty soon after the end of the end-line, when the bank started offering the product widely, the control group started to look very much like the control treatment group. We take that as evidence that BA was marketing and promoting the accounts pretty widely and that they were being taken up by the customer base. So 24 months after the start of the study, we could no longer detect any difference between the treatment and control group in usage of these accounts. We were very happy about that result. It was clear that not only did we produce what we thought was an interesting study that was revealing about how savings works with transnational households, we also came up with a product that this private institution thought was beneficial to its bottom line as well.

So that was a very gratifying situation. Something similar happened when we worked with Opportunity Bank of Malawi on commitment savings accounts. They adopted a couple of these accounts that we developed in collaboration with them. The bank, as far as I can tell, continued to offer and has offered on a wide scale these products even after our collaboration ended.

On the other hand, there's another innovation, specifically the fingerprinting for microborrowers to improve personal identification, which was something the institution that we originally collaborated with didn't end up adopting on a wide scale. But I think that was mainly because of budgetary constraints. The institution did try to get grant resources from international donors to implement the technology itself but wasn't able to do so. I think for reasons separate from our original collaboration with them, they moved away from agricultural lending as an organization, so they've ended up being in a situation where they wouldn't profit greatly from implementing the technology.

We're still pushing ahead with new work on fingerprinting in Malawi. We're looking to see if we can make this work in other microfinance institutions. So I'm still optimistic that this will get scaled up if we see effectiveness in a larger experiment.

TO: Is the key variable there how convincing the studies were or your experience in designing studies that have operational relevance?

DY: That's a valid point. I think our results from the BA study might have had some impact on the bank deciding to really roll out the products on a wide scale and market them heavily. But it was probably mostly driven by the bank's own internal calculations of how profitable these products were, and it was already seeing them grow within its customer base. So it wasn't so much about understanding the treatment versus control impacts.

In the cases of BA and OB in Malawi, I don't think expansion of these products or the appeal of the products was due to the research results really. To be frank, it was that they found the products to be profitable and worth continuing after we had set them up.

I think the one case where I feel that there is strongest evidence that there was something likely to be scalable was in the biometric fingerprinting context. When the first fingerprinting study came out in the AER in 2012, it got news coverage, and in particular, it seemed to me in specialist industry outlets related to technology in financial services and the microlending world, so that gives me confidence that this is something that could be scalable.

We haven't seen it yet. This new work that we're doing in Malawi funded by USAID DIV is intended to show the benefits of fingerprinting across multiple MFIs in a context where the fingerprint identification is used as part of a national level credit reference bureau. So, if we can show that it can work at a large scale in Malawi, this will encourage much more large scale adoption.

TO: Are we at peak RCT? How are you advising your doctoral students now as they think about what avenues to pursue? Is doing field experiments a likely path to advancing their careers?

DY: By revealed preference, I certainly couldn't advise students not to do RCTs. I'm mostly doing RCTs today, but I'm not exclusively doing them. I always have non-RCT work underway. I have that same attitude with my students. I think RCTs are an incredibly powerful methodology. And whenever I have students who are inclined toward an RCT of some sort, I encourage that and try to work with them on that. I'll often get students involved in my own RCT projects. In rarer cases students want to set up an RCT entirely on their own, separate from anything I'm doing, and I'll certainly try to help my students take that path as well. But RCTs aren't for everyone. We discussed earlier that there are specific skills, capabilities, predilections, that make the methodology something that is more or less attractive across different researchers. So I don't push them on people but I don't discourage them if they want to work on an RCT.

I think RCTs are an incredibly important tool in the development economist's toolkit, but there are a number of other methodologies out there through which we can extract truth and knowledge from observational data, natural experimental approaches, working with real world sources of exogenous variation. I have had a number of students in recent years who haven't done RCTs at all, and have worked primarily with natural experimental approaches and observational data, and other students who work with a combination of approaches in their dissertations. I really think despite the attractiveness of RCTs from a number of different standpoints, they're not the only methodology that we should be thinking about. There are often questions that come up that we can't answer with RCTs, and I think we can find nice credible identification strategies that are not based on RCTs but are based on other sources of data. We should be considering those questions and those studies as well.

Going back to your original question, I don't think we've reached a point where we have too many RCTs. I think there are way more questions out there in development economics that remain unanswered than we have capacity to address as a research community. And I'm not sure that we should say that any methodology has been overused at this point. The big concern in my mind is I'm really struck in some sense how small the research community is in international development economics. The number of development economists is far outnumbered by the number of, say, liver scientists. I have a friend here who talks about how the American gastroenterology meetings are about the same size as the entire AEA[14] meetings. And the international meetings for liver scientists, which is a subset of gastroenterology, is about the size of the biggest conferences among development economists. In the big picture there is not an oversupply of researchers working on questions in development economics. I think the big issue in my mind is that there isn't enough development economics research going on period! It's really not something that attracts the same kind of funding as one subfield of medicine. So in that context it can't be the case that any methodology is truly overused. We need more of every type of study.

But I guess if you pose it as there's a limited number of development economists and given that limited number of researchers are we overusing one particular methodology, namely RCTs, I don't think that's the case either. It's far from the case that everyone is doing RCTs. There is still quite a diverse set of research going on out there. I would hope that people are applying the methodology that is relevant and appropriate for the question, not just trying to limit themselves to only questions that RCTs can answer or trying to answer every question with the RCT tool.[15]

14. The annual American Economic Association meeting, as it's commonly referred to, also includes the meeting of the American Social Sciences Association and various other groups. Attendance at the 2015 meeting was 12,859 in total, a more comparable estimate of attendees is roughly 8,500; at the 2014 International Liver Congress it was 10,810, and at the American College of Gastroenterology it was 4,607.
15. See interview with Nancy Birdsall (chapter 11) who voices this concern.

13   Frank DeGiovanni

Frank DeGiovanni is a senior adviser to the president of the Ford Foundation after serving for many years as the director of the Financial Assets program at the foundation, overseeing Ford's global efforts to help the poor build assets. In that role he helped fund a number of significant RCTs as well as providing funding to a variety of the organizations that provide infrastructure for field experiments.

I have been a direct beneficiary of Ford Foundation grants from the Financial Assets program.

TO: What field experiments has the Ford Foundation funded?

FD: Of things I'm responsible for, we funded one large randomized control trial of children's savings accounts, a demonstration program in Oklahoma for 4 years,[1] that gave matched savings accounts to children at birth. Then we funded a demonstration of a graduation model for ultra-poor households,[2] providing a package of assets, training, a time-limited cash stipend, and small-scale savings to ultra-poor families to demonstrate whether it was effective at helping them improve their life conditions. We did that in Peru, Honduras, Ghana, Pakistan, Ethiopia, and in two

I am a direct beneficiary of Ford Foundation grants from the Financial Assets program.
1. The SEED program in Oklahoma (not to be confused with the SEED commitment savings evaluation in the Philippines) randomly assigned children born in Oklahoma to receive a college savings account with an initial deposit of $1,000 from the state. Additional deposits were matched at varying, randomly assigned rates. For an overview of the study, see: http://csd.wustl.edu/Publications/Documents/RS14-08.pdf.
2. The Targeting the Ultra-Poor Program is a package of interventions targeted at households that are "too poor" for microcredit. It was created and tested by BRAC, with results positive enough to encourage replication and testing in other areas. The TUP evaluation is discussed in more detail later in the chapter, and also in the interviews with Dean Karlan (chapter 6) and Jonathan Morduch (chapter 4).

sites in India. Seven sites total. USAID provided most of the funding for the Ethiopia evaluation and a number of funders, including the Ford Foundation, supported the Ghana demonstration.

TO: You've been involved in trying to change products and policies for a long time. Do you think RCTs have helped that process? Is it a better tool or just another tool for accomplishing those goals?

FD: I think RCTs are particularly important when you're trying to change a paradigm, an established paradigm, models, policies where the people who believe in that paradigm are going to insist on rigorous proof, proof of causality, and where you need to marshal the strongest evidence you can to change prevailing wisdom. I think that's the major case in which I would want to fund an RCT. In the absence of data that in essence disposes of alternative explanations, you're going to have a hard time convincing policy makers that the policy or the model that you're advocating for is better than the prevailing system.

In the US, kids' savings accounts is an uphill climb because we're saying if you really want to give poor kids a chance for upward mobility, give kids a savings account at birth and let it grow for 18 years. It isn't an easy sell in the current political climate of constrained budgets where every program choice is a zero-sum situation. And the graduation model is a model that is going to move people earning less than a buck and a quarter a day up the ladder, so, if it works, it's really going to transform their lives. And what we're now suggesting is that governments should adopt graduation models as part of their social protection policy. We have the data to show that the treatment households fared better than controls, and that the model could produce important outcomes if adopted as policy. We couldn't do that otherwise.

That's the first rationale for me, but it also has to be a situation where you're working with individuals. If you're intervening in communities, it's very hard to select controls. There are some situations where it's very difficult to figure out how to do an RCT. We supported a lot of livelihood development work where I couldn't figure out how to do an RCT because I couldn't determine how to identify controls. So there, where I might have wanted to do an RCT, either I couldn't figure out how to do it or the expense was too much. I can't afford to do RCTs for all the things I'd like to do.

TO: Let me ask about value for money. Are you finding that there is good value for money in something like the ultra-poor graduation evaluations where there are so many different programs advocated by so many different people? Is it helpful, do policy makers perceive what you've done differently because you have RCT evidence from seven different sites?

FD: In general, I think that the answer is yes. But I also think that it depends on the context within which the research is conducted and the politics of a situation. With the matched children's savings accounts program in the US, the initial findings were less than overwhelming. But the more recent analyses are now identifying more promising positive results. Frankly, I think the mixed results probably occurred because we only followed the families for 4 years after the birth of the child, and I think we need to follow them for another 10 years to identify the full impact of the intervention. In that case, we didn't have good theories about how long it takes for these effects to manifest themselves. For some of the interventions that we really care about, we don't have good theories about the duration of impacts. Nonetheless, the positive findings that have emerged about the impact of children's savings accounts on the treatment families has motivated a number of state and local policy makers to adopt children's savings accounts into state and local programs.

And I think that in the graduation model we tested we also didn't have any preexisting inkling, hypothesis, or conceptual model of whether it would take two years, three years, four years. But fortunately, these people were poor enough, and the intervention was powerful enough, that after three years you could see significant differences. But it didn't work everywhere. One of the two sites in India didn't have positive impacts big enough to be greater than the controls. But I think in the case of the graduation model, in the absence of showing positive effects, we would not have policy maker interest. No way. We invited a number of governments to meetings to discuss the research results from the demonstrations. The fact that the model produced such significant results helped convince the governments to now begin to pilot it in their countries.

We undertook the graduation demonstration as freestanding NGO-driven pilots. Now some governments are willing to adapt and adopt the model into their own programs. Peru is piloting it. Colombia is piloting it. Indonesia is considering adopting elements of the model. We have interest from four other Latin American countries that all want to pilot their own versions, and they wouldn't do this in the absence of these data.

Now was it worth it? We spent somewhere between $4 and $6 million to test the model. I do not have the funds to spend that level of resources on every single program that we support or want to support. I would try to do it when I have interventions that are important enough and where we're trying to change paradigms. And where I feel comfortable enough that we can control for confounding factors. And when I can convince people to overcome the ethical concerns they have about randomized experiments.

I'm also a firm believer in mixed methods and that you need the ethnographic component. I think the RCTs tell you what happened. They don't necessarily tell you why it happened. I think you really need the insights that you obtain from the qualitative work to understand why people are doing what they're doing. The regression coefficients identify the most important relationships and that x causes y, but they don't tell you why people are behaving the way they are. So I think the ethnographic component is very important.

I part ways with some of the economists I've talked to on this. Some of them just won't consider ethnographic research as an equal partner in an RCT.[3] They fundamentally reject the idea that ethnographic research can tell you anything causal and that can make for an uneasy partnership in an evaluation—because the ethnographers obviously think their work is of high value. I do not want to debate whether it is possible to derive causal insights from ethnography. But I do think that it is possible to draw very useful insights about how community dynamics and culture affect people's lives, and to identify people's own insights about their own behavior.

TO: When you mentioned the spread of the graduation model in Latin America, I immediately thought about CCT programs, which grew in much the same way—there were some rigorous evaluations and it spread quickly. Do you see that policy makers are changing what they look for in evidence?

FD: My sense is that people are looking for something solid to base decisions on. Take the CCT work. I think the governments are struggling with the fact that while the CCTs have been very good in terms of improving food security for families and benefiting the next generation in terms of keeping them in school and improving their health, the programs have not done very much for the adults in those families. The governments are seeing that the families aren't graduating out of the CCT program. And they're

3. See interview with Antoinette Schoar (chapter 16), where she discusses the potential benefits of working with anthropologists on study design.

seeing evidence that when the children age out, because they're finishing high school, that the adults are not much better off after 12 years or so than before they entered the program. So now the governments are saying, "I need something different. I need to do something about this." So along we come with the evidence from the graduation model that if you give very poor families the gift of an asset, and you give them training in how to use the asset, and you give them a cash stipend for some period of time and you build their social skills, then in fact their income grows, their assets multiply, they seem to be more self-confident. The ministers say "Wow, can we integrate this into the CCT programs and help the adults graduate?" Peru and Colombia have integrated the graduation model into their CCT programs as a way to help the adults.

So they're casting around for something else to do and they see this evidence. I think, in the absence of the evidence, no amount of advocacy would make a difference because there's too much skepticism. We ran into the bureaucrats saying "Poor people can't save. If you ask them to save part of their stipend you're going to reduce consumption. So forget it. This runs counter to the program and we're not going to do it." So you have to provide them evidence that poor families can save without reducing consumption. And they say, "Oh, well maybe we can think about this." You need the evidence. They're looking for something, but without the evidence, you're not going to get the attention.[4]

I do think they look for highly respected researchers to bring that evidence to them. And the policy makers, I think, also want to know that the researchers are familiar with the context and with their country. You need researchers who can work well with partners, who can deal with people respectfully and take concerns seriously.[5] Researchers who show that they think of the people in the experiment as people and not just test subjects.

That's part of the tension in field experiments. At least for me, it's a question of how do you do this in a way that treats people fairly but also tests the hypothesis. I think that tension has to be managed well. In the graduation model tests we had one organization that refused to implement the pilot because it said it was unethical to not provide the services to everyone who needed them, and we couldn't convince them otherwise that the

4. For views on the process of evidence turning into policy change, see interviews with Lant Pritchett (chapter 9) and Nancy Birdsall (chapter 11).
5. See interview with Antoinette Schoar (chapter 16) for a similar point.

random assignment was a fair way to distribute the program when there were inadequate resources to serve all eligible families.

TO: You mentioned things that you'd like to test that you couldn't figure out how to do an RCT, or where an RCT would be too expensive. What's an example of something that you'd like to test but where you're can't overcome that hurdle?

FD: I'm supporting work on livelihood development. There are 4 or 5 agricultural standards systems, like Rainforest Alliance and Fair Trade, that identify standards for environmental practices and labor practices, and many companies now will only buy products that meet these standards. And there's a question about whether these standards are pro-poor, do they benefit poor farmers? So I have a major project underway to evaluate whether these standards do benefit poor farmers. The grantee, the trade association for these standards systems, is designing evaluations in Indonesia, Kenya, and a third country to be chosen. I'd love to have at least one of these three evaluated by RCTs, but it's been really challenging to do an RCT because you have to find communities where the farmers are on the verge of getting trained for certification. They're not a naturally occurring phenomenon, like randomly selecting 500 kids at birth to get the savings accounts and 500 to put in a control when you have a list of every kid born. So it has been difficult to determine how to use an RCT for these evaluations. The researchers are saying we'll probably have to do a quasi-experimental design.

TO: I'm interested in your discussion earlier of the path from CCTs to the graduation models. There's an implicit story of how change happens in the real world. You fix one thing, and then you see something that's still broken and you work on that problem. One critique of the RCT movement is that they are doing things that are just too small. What's your personal theory of change? Is it incremental? Ford talks a lot about systems change. How do you see systems changing most?

FD: The focus of most of our work is changing systems, as we want to see the work that we support achieve scale. The two most important routes to achieve scale are to influence public policies and to change market practices and behavior. The most effective strategy to promote system change will depend on the context—the specific issue, the political and economic climate, the nature of the civic infrastructure, and so on. In some cases, provision of better information about an issue derived from rigorous research to policy makers might be sufficient to promote change in policies. In other situations, policy change would be unlikely to occur without widespread advocacy and grassroots organizing.

So I do not have a single theory of change regarding what it takes to promote system change. It depends on the issue and the context. In the case of the graduation model, we believed that it was critical to test the model rigorously to determine whether it would produce the significant impacts that we hypothesized. We then developed a strategy to present the results to high-level policy makers, and supported an organization to work with governments to help them understand how adopting the model could help the governments solve the problems they were trying to address. In this case the RCT was necessary to document that the model "worked." But it also addressed a need that governments are trying to address—how to address the fact that CCTs have not adequately improved the livelihoods of the adults in the families after years of receiving CCT benefits.

There are other situations where research results alone may not be adequate to change systems. You need to support organizing and advocacy to secure the support of champions for the change and to garner political support for systems change.

I don't think that RCTs must be restricted to examining subjects that are "too small." I may be biased, but I believe that the graduation model is a "big" intervention, with the potential to make a significant difference in the lives of millions of very poor households. So if there is a critique that RCTs are not being used to evaluate important issues, then it may only reflect past studies, not the potential of the methodology.

14   Pascaline Dupas

Pascaline's original goal was to work for an NGO in Africa, not be an economist and researcher. Her initial work in the field, as a research assistant on a project in Kenya being conducted by Michael Kremer and Esther Duflo, came about only because she couldn't find a job directly with an aid organization.

After returning from Kenya, a friend's question about how to give responsibly led her (and fellow economists she had worked with there, Jessica Cohen, Elizabeth Beasley, and Carolyn Nekesa) to start an NGO—Tam Tam—distributing bed nets. Tam Tam's work won her a grant from the Mulago Foundation, which supports social entrepreneurship. At a gathering of grantees, other award winners criticized the idea of giving away bed nets because recipients wouldn't properly value them, and therefore wouldn't use them. That critique eventually led to one of Pascaline's most widely known pieces of research—an experiment to test whether charging at least a nominal fee for bed nets at a clinic in Kenya increased use (it didn't, but it did dramatically reduce the number of people who had bed nets).

While in Kenya working for Duflo and Kremer, Pascaline met Jonathan Robinson. The two have collaborated on several projects since, including one of the first field experiments on the impact of microsavings. Currently Pascaline is an Associate Professor of Economics at Stanford University.

TO: Let's start with the first Kenya savings study.[1] One of the more interesting things that came out of that research was how different the returns were between men and women. Did you go in thinking that there were going to be some fairly significant differences? How do you start thinking about why there are such large differences?

PD: If we had anticipated that the research would find such large differences, we would have had a different sample. In particular, we would have had more men. Our ability to say much is curtailed by the small sample that we have.

I don't think we've thought about it so much, in part because, if you find that something matters differently for men and women, it's hard to figure out the policy implications. You can't change people's gender.

You also have to consider whether there is some other issue that gender is just proxying for. So you have to know the constraints that people face and then understand why women face a different set of constraints or different variables in their environment. With the first study with Jon[1] on savings, we can't actually go very far answering those questions because we had very different sets of people. The men and the women were in different occupations, and the selection of occupation likely matters a great deal. So, for example, in our sample it's possible that we are looking at the savviest women versus the dumbest men. That being said, in terms of speculation, there are stories that we could tell about why you would expect women to benefit differently.

There is some evidence, though not as much as people sometimes try to make of it, that men and women have different preferences in terms of consumption. They value certain things differently. It might be the case that women value savings for consumption later in time, while men prefer to consume things right away, so they don't save. But that's mostly speculation at this point.

To be able to really understand this better, we went back to do some studies that are very similar to the first one but with a truly representative sample taking gender into account. To do that, we did a census to count everyone we could find within a specific radius of the market center. Having everyone in that radius in our sample means there is no self-selection into the study based on the different occupations, and we had both men and women. We also used the household as the core unit and randomized the households in terms of the husband, the wife, both, or neither getting the account. That would give us a much better view of whether there are differences in preferences within the household. And also it would let us see whether targeting savings products at a specific member of the household can have a different impact.

So we did these follow-ups in Uganda, Malawi, and Kenya. Unfortunately, the main result is that take-up of formal saving services was very low in all

---

1. Jonathan Robinson is a co-author of the savings studies and a frequent collaborator.

three settings because of the relatively low quality of the financial institutions. We've written up the Kenya results where 63 percent of people opened an account, but only 18 percent actively used it.[2] What people told us when we asked why they didn't use the accounts was that, one, they didn't trust the bank, two, that service was unreliable, and three, that the withdrawal fees were just too high. The Uganda and Malawi results will be in one paper where we find similarly low take-up and zero average treatment effects, since with such low take-up it's like looking for a needle in a haystack. Clearly, the 18 percent or so of people who use the accounts and keep using them must be better off from them, but some may invest their savings in health, some in education, some in a business, some in animals. It can be anywhere, so finding a treatment effect on anything is very difficult.

TO: In the savings follow-up and the health savings project, different from some of the earlier studies, you went back to the participants and did some extensive qualitative interviews to ask them to explain how they were using the products.[3] Is that an outgrowth of seeing where some of the earlier studies left you, that they didn't really get you to understand why the choices were being made? Are you designing in more qualitative work into your initial designs?

PD: Jon and I are big fans of qualitative research. Sometimes it doesn't make it into the paper because not everyone values that as much. But for us, it's always important to ask those questions. So in the first savings study we did do some qualitative interviews with people—we called them debriefings. We found them extremely helpful just to convince us that the data are not just noise. If we see something that seems to have a big impact, we want to go talk to people and see if they perceive it as a big impact as well.

In the health savings study, we did the qualitative follow-up because it was more puzzling that people would be helped by just having a simple box. A box is not very different than a pillow or a mattress or a hole in the ground. The quantitative analysis helped, but there is still the ultimate question of why it helped, and also why they didn't think of it before because it's not a particularly revolutionary idea.

So it's helpful to make sure the quantitative research is as good as it can be. But sometimes it still leaves you with question marks.

TO: As you said, one of the puzzling things about these results is why these people hadn't bought themselves a box given the high impact. How do you think about that question? Why do these reasonably intelligent people who are capable of managing their own lives not do these seemingly simple things already?

PD: That's an important question we asked ourselves. It's funny because when we started this experiment, we knew that people were going to ask us that question. At some level we were hoping it wouldn't work because, if it did, then it was going to be really puzzling.

But what seems to come out of the qualitative work we did is that people did not know beforehand that just mentally allocating money to a specific goal can help. Or that just having one place where you put all your coins can help. So some of the things that people told us afterward, were "I didn't realize that if I decided that this is what I want to spend on, then it's easier to not spend that money on something else."

My sense is that as individuals in rich countries we never had to come up with these types of devices on our own. When we were born, they were already there. It's true for me that when I have cash in my wallet I spend it faster. So I withdraw very little amounts of cash at a time. But I never had to think about things like whether I should have a savings account or whether my paycheck should be direct deposited because those were the default options that were just there.

Part of me thinks we shouldn't really ask this question of why people don't think of it for themselves because, for most innovations in the world, just one person comes up with the idea and it just spreads. And in fact you just need to experience it once. In the health savings study we find these very long-term effects, that after three years people are continuing to use the box ...

TO: and fairly quick spillover to other members of the community ...

PD: Exactly. This is the type of thing that you never forget. You'll know these tricks of how to manage finances if you just experience it once. So there's a positive spin on this finding: once the idea is there, people latch on to it. The negative spin is: why is it so hard for people to come up with the idea in the first place?

TO: As you were talking about that I was thinking about mint.com and standard financial counseling, at lot of which boils down to this same simple advice. Evidently the average American is not making a budget, not keeping track of what they spend. There aren't very many adults who keep piggy banks or do mental accounting more sophisticated than a retirement account, which they have because of tax incentives. So it's not all that different.

PD: Right. For example, at home we have a box where we keep coins. I try to avoid coins, but my husband drops them all over, and now we have a small child, so we can't have coins lying around. So I follow my husband around and put the coins in the box. And every three months he gets so excited about this windfall of $20. The fact that people do not necessarily correctly forecast how much small change they waste is not so surprising.

TO: There are two, not necessarily mutually exclusive, general explanations for some of this. There's the management technology explanation[2]—management is a technology and it disperses unevenly, so once people get these ideas, they latch onto them and they get big results from simple stuff, for instance, Nick Bloom and co-authors' work in India.[4] Then there's the cognitive load theory[3]—these things are obvious but these people are confronted with so many choices every day that they don't have the time to stop and think how they can improve this little piece of their lives. Which of those do you think makes the most sense, or is there another explanation in terms of the adoption of some of these simple ideas?

PD: More than the cognitive load, I would focus on attention burden: what are you going to pay attention to? But to answer your question about management versus load, it's probably a mixture of the two. There is evidence of both factors being at play.

And this is more speculative, but there might be a third explanation, which would be that what people can do is adopt the management mechanisms that you talk about, but the impact of that isn't much. It's not like they're suddenly going to send their kids to Stanford or have a really nice house with a bathtub. It's nice, of course, to get a bed net and lower the chance your child suffers from malaria. But maybe, in the grand scheme of things, what people really aspire to is unattainable, so people get discouraged.

2. See the interviews with David McKenzie (chapter 10) and Chris Blattman (chapter 20) for more discussion of the impact of the technology of management.
3. One of the core insights of behavioral science is that people have a limited amount of capacity to pay attention and make decisions and do not always allocate that capacity optimally, leading to irrational or poor decisions. For more on behavioral science and decision-making, see Mullainathan and Shafir, *Scarcity*; Kahneman, *Thinking Fast and Slow*; Thaler, *Misbehaving*.

Most people have television, radio, or access to an Internet café, so they have some view of how comfortable life can be in the rest of the world. Maybe they feel that even if they save, whatever they can really get is not that great. Some of the people we have talked with in Kenya, when we ask them what their savings goals are—without priming them—have very ambitious goals. They want to build a house, they want to send their child to university. But even if they save, they are never going to get there. So maybe they don't have enough information or these intermediate goods are not glamorous enough to capture their imagination. So maybe you need a combination of the management technology and the excitement. Maybe we should make bed nets pink so that all the little girls want them.

TO: That explanation is consistent with the finding of the false perception of education as a step function rather than a linear function.[4][5] Roland Fryer has done a bunch of work in the US with incentives in the classroom.[5][6] One of his findings is that one of the reasons that some of the incentives don't work is the participants just don't understand how to do better in school. It's not that they don't understand the program or value the reward, but they literally don't know what specific steps to take to do better in school. It doesn't help to incentivize them if they don't understand the technology of how to achieve the goal.

That raises the issue of the assumption that the developed and developing worlds are so very different and there's not much to learn or apply from one domain to the other. But I see more and more often that the problems are the same. For instance, budgeting problems are the same everywhere.

When you started, did you think of your research as only applying in the developing world? Do you see these as people problems, poor people problems, or poor country problems?

PD: I do think that people are the same everywhere. And that the same behavioral patterns are there for everyone. The big difference though, is if

4. An overview of research on perceptions and actual returns to education can be found in Banerjee and Duflo, *Poor Economics*, chapter 4. A summary can be found in this presentation from Banerjee: http://pooreconomics.com/sites/default/files/ Education_1473_lecture11.pdf.
5. A core theme of Fryer's research is on how to improve the quality of education in US schools. This includes paying students and/or teachers incentives for outcomes, evaluating charter schools, and understanding school management policies. See the Education Innovation Laboratory website for a complete look at his and his colleagues work: http://edlabs.harvard.edu.

you're poor, or living in a poor country, the markets are not working or the markets you have access to are terrible. So the consequences of being in distress are just way worse. There are the same personal barriers to savings for people in rich countries and poor countries, but in rich countries people have access to savings accounts and bank branches and CDs and even layaway programs at WalMart. So for me ultimately the problem in poor countries is that markets are just failing.

Whether it's trading markets or the market to save, insurance markets, loan markets, overall you've got some massive failure. That's the biggest difference. So taking behavior and preferences as given, keeping utility functions constant, the person living in poverty is going to have a lot more trouble.

Our papers may look like they are focusing on some fundamental behavioral problem, but ultimately the prime issue is that all these markets are failing.

TO: Speaking of utility functions, let's turn to the Morocco water paper.[7] Charles Kenny's book[6] takes economists to task for focusing too much on incomes and economic growth rather than noticing that people are enjoying their lives more.[8] That seems to be the case in Morocco. I thought it was very interesting that people were using the time savings for leisure. There was no investment in more production. A great deal of the advocacy for water projects is built around the idea that if we free up women from gathering water, then they can do all of these other things to improve their lives. But that's not what these women did. They decided instead to just enjoy themselves a bit more. Who are we to begrudge that?

Do you think economics research needs to take into account that people just want better lives, not just about measuring incomes, the research needs to focus more on the happiness part of the utility function?

PD: There are two answers to this question. When people do what we did in Morocco, which is offer people something and then look at the impact on their lives, you have to be careful to measure aspects of well-being that aren't picked up in income.

But that's not always easy and not necessarily the thing that most people would want to fund. In fact, when we shared the results of the evaluation

6. In *Getting Better*, Kenny lays out the evidence that while poverty remains entrenched, the lives of the poor on many other measures, including health and happiness, have improved dramatically.

with the company that was providing the credit program for people to get tap water, they were very disappointed that we didn't find any effect on health or income. They thought it was terrible. But we had to tell them it was not terrible. People are happy. They took up the program, they are paying off the loans, and they are happier. That's great. But for the funders, they initially perceived it as a failure. Eventually they came around, but their initial reaction was if there's no impact on health or income, it's a failure.

Typically the way economists deal with this issue of making sure that you pick up welfare impacts and not just income is by doing revealed preference analysis. What we mean by that is that if people buy something and continue buying it, it means they are better off with it than without. For most products on the market, you can use this metric of whether people keep buying to judge whether it makes them better off. What's tricky is when you don't have that metric. That's when you need to create special data to measure people's happiness.

So overall I don't think the research is missing that dimension so much because of this ability to look at what people do for themselves in the long run. But sometimes it takes a long time horizon to see things like that. So, for example, take the whole microfinance debate and scandal in India with accusations about people committing suicide because of the debt burden. By revealed preferences, people are obviously worse off if they are committing suicide. But of course we don't know really that it was the loans that caused the suicides. I bring this up only to say that for many issues it takes a lot of years before we can really say something because we have to have enough data to observe what people do beyond just taking a second loan after the first one. It's going to take many years to use revealed preferences to really tell us something about the impact of having access to loans.

The randomized access to microcredit experiments could have included in their surveys a module on happiness—I don't think they did—so perhaps that's unfortunate, but the next ones will.

TO: Your bed nets work and the "Keeping the Doctor Away"[7][9] work both point to the idea that too many things just cost too much for people living

---

7. This is work by Jonathan Robinson and co-authors which estimates the effects of liquidity, peers and information about health risks on demand for health products in Kenya, Guatemala, India, and Uganda. The paper finds that demand is highly sensitive to price but not to other factors, such as knowledge about risks or peer behavior.

under $2 a day. There is a growing movement making the case for "just give money to the poor." Do you think one of the things we're learning is that we are programming too much looking for specific outcomes rather than just channeling liquidity to the poor and letting them make their own choices?

PD: These are two somewhat different issues because, it's true that people don't buy bed nets because the prices are too high and that they don't buy chlorine dispensers or soap because of the price. So it could be that if you just give them more cash, they'll be able to buy those things. But there are so many things that they don't buy because they don't have the money. So, if you just give cash, you have no idea what they'll buy.

TO: But then you get to rely on revealed preferences.

PD: Yes, you can see what they do with the money. But for the revealed preferences argument to work, you have to make sure that people have the right information. And some of the work that has been done on this issue of adoption of health technologies indicates that people just don't know what the returns are on the different things they could buy. It's not irrational to believe that it's hard and expensive to educate people on the relative returns of various health investments, and it's just easier and cheaper to just give them in-kind transfers. If I think people should have bed nets, I just give them bed nets and I don't have to worry about whether they would spend cash on them.

It's kind of a paternalistic approach, but it's not obviously a bad premise. In Morocco, with Esther and Florencia Devoto, we did a cash transfer program for education.[8][10] And we found large effects on reducing the dropout rate and re-enrollment of kids who had dropped out of school. There wasn't much difference between the conditional arm and a transfer that was just labeled for education. The effects seem to be based on convincing parents that education is important, something they get from seeing the government invest in by providing the transfer. So that's an example where you can nudge people toward making a particular investment without fully tying their hands.

8. In an experiment in Morocco, a program originally designed as a conditional cash transfer to encourage girls to stay in school became a "labeled transfer," as it became obvious that conditions were not being enforced. The study finds significant positive effects on school attendance and significant positive effects on parents' beliefs about the value of education. Since schools in Morocco are free, there was no expectation that the cash transfer would be spent directly on education.

I think ultimately I don't really have evidence to back this up, but my hunch is that if people had more cash, they would most likely spend a good chunk of that money on things that have very high returns. I'm not aware of any substantial cash transfer program to the poor that was unconditional in sub-Saharan Africa. I guess there is the program that Craig Macintosh and co-authors have in Malawi, targeting young girls and their families. [9][11] They give a quite substantial amount of cash to people. But I'm not sure they collected consumption data, so I don't think they know what they spent money on. It would be nice to know that.

From the work with Esther and Florencia in Morocco we can't say very much about consumption and what people choose to spend on in total because the amount of the transfers was very very small in relation to annual consumption, something like 5 percent, so it's not like it's going to make a huge difference in people's spending.

TO: But a lot of these things that they are not buying are just not that expensive. A 5 percent boost should allow them to buy shoes or a bed net, and if the literature is right and you are halving malaria risk or lowering intestinal worm risk by 95 percent, then you shouldn't need large transfers to see these things start to show up.

PD: It would be interesting to drop some cash and see what people do. Maybe the studies by Chris Woodruff and David McKenzie[10][12] when they dropped some cash on firm owners can look at this, but I'm again not sure they have data to know what people did with the money other than checking to see if they put into the business.

TO: Interestingly in Ghana they found for women it made a difference whether it was in kind or in cash. There's some evidence that it really does matter what form the aid takes. It doesn't have to be conditional, but it can't be fully liquid.

9. Note these comments pre-date the GiveDirectly evaluation by Haushofer and Shapiro (2016). Sarah Baird, Craig McIntosh, and Berk Ozler have a series of papers on conditional and unconditional cash transfers to adolescent girls in Malawi. The studies show positive, but differential, impacts for conditional and unconditional grants.
10. Suresh de Mel, David McKenzie, and Chris Woodruff have run experiments in Sri Lanka and Ghana providing cash grants to microenterprise owners. See the interview with David McKenzie (chapter 10) for complete discussion of these studies. As Dupas notes, the studies were not designed to measure household consumption but business activities and profits.

PD: It would be interesting if they measured things like happiness to see whether women who didn't invest the cash in their businesses invested in other things that actually had higher returns in that specific moment.

TO: I think they mostly found that it just leaked away. One of the stories that David talks about is there there's this "frozenness"—there are too many choices and so they wait while they decide, and the money gets spent here and there, and by the time they choose, the money is gone. It's not a conscious decision not to invest but a case of too many choices.

PD: If that's the case, then it's an easy to solve problem. Before you give them the money, you ask people what they are going to do with it. Have them do the brainstorming before they get the cash. That would be consistent with the piggy bank having an effect that we found. Once people have set their mind on something, they can make sure the money doesn't leak out. You just need people to focus on one thing they want to do with it.

TO: In the health savings experiment, all of the treatments had a mental accounting feature right? It was just a question of whether you were directly holding yourself accountable for your mental accounting or someone else was exerting that control.

At the same time there is the Karlan Mullainathan fruit vendor study.[11][13] That was another situation where the gains leaked away. The fruit vendors all ended up back in debt. It's just sort of shocking because they experienced the difference of being out of debt firsthand but still couldn't hold on to those gains.

PD: Yeah. Maybe there are some very high return things that we can't really see. Maybe not helping a friend in need is extremely costly to people.

TO: That's a good point to turn to the issue of social protection and social networks. One of the stories about why the savings boxes work is the ability

11. This work is described in Sendhil Mullainathan's and Eldar Shafir's book *Scarcity*, chapter 6. Karlan and Mullainathan provide a one-time grant to fruit sellers who had been borrowing money each day to buy inventory. This dramatically increases the fruit vendors' profits, since they do not have to pay very high interest rates on the daily loan. They also provide a randomly selected group of them financial literacy training. They find that the literacy training increases the amount of time between the grant and a return to the status quo of daily borrowing.

to protect cash from the larger social network. I think *Portfolios of the Poor* illustrates how much more money is flowing through those networks in small amounts than it appears from the outside.[14] The "Pretending to be Poor" study[12] and the Giné, Goldberg, Yang Malawi study[13] similarly bolster this argument that it's about the ability to protect assets from community claims on them.[15] At the same time there are anthropological and socio-logical perspectives that would say, "You're giving people tools to destroy the social networks that protect their communities. Why would you think that's a good thing?" Do you think there is something of a zero-sum game there, that enabling people to build assets goes hand in hand with breaking down those traditional networks?

PD: Yes. Most likely. But the question of whether these networks are good or bad is still open. If you look at Europe and the US, they don't have these informal insurance networks. Though in the US that might be a role played by churches. But if you look in Europe, if you have a sick child, it's not like you're going to knock on the neighbors' door—in fact people never knock on the neighbors' door.

If you compare rich countries with poor countries, you'll find that rich countries are much more centered on the nuclear household. Even the uncles and aunts and the grandparents don't check in that much. There is not as much solidarity across siblings in the US or Europe as in Africa. If you're doing much better than your brother, it's unlikely you're going to foot the entire bill for your nephew's education. That's definitely something that happens a lot in poor countries. It is sometimes argued that these very strong social networks can have positive effects because they prevent anyone from hitting the bottom, but maybe they can have negative effects in that they prevent anyone from truly going to the top. If you know that, if you're successful, you're going to have to share with everyone, there are some disincentives to doing well, at least at the margin.

12. A study in Cameroon, noting that a substantial portion of microfinance borrow-ers had savings equal to or more than what they borrowed, held at the same institu-tion surveyed these borrowers to understand why. They find that one of the reasons borrowers report is to appear to be poorer than they are so as not to have other com-munity members request financial help.

13. A study of commitment savings accounts among farmers which finds that house-holds with commitment savings accounts are able to invest more and have higher crop yields. It's important to note that the savings were not held in the commitment savings accounts. This study is discussed in detail in the interviews with Xavi Giné (chapter 8) and Dean Yang (chapter 12).

Something that I've thought about and I'd like to be able to study more seriously is the possibility that in these situations where sharing is expected that you don't want to tell everyone that you are doing well. So one of the reasons people seem to have weird beliefs about the returns to education could be that they only get partial information. You send your child to school and the kid does very well. He goes to the capital city and he makes a lot of money, but he doesn't tell you how much money he makes because he doesn't want you to know. He doesn't want his siblings to know, or his nephews to know, so this information doesn't make it back to the village. So everyone believes the returns to education are lower than they are. There could be all of these other effects of too much sharing within the network that keeps people down.

You could also argue that if you are sharing risk, on the one hand, it could help people take risks because there is this insurance. But on the other hand, it might prevent people from taking crazy risks because the network might say, "No that was too crazy." All in all, if you just do this mental cross-country regression, it doesn't seem that development and strong social networks go hand in hand. But whether that means having people move toward independence from the local informal social network and toward more formal insurance is part of the path to development is unclear.

TO: There's a similar story that takes a very different form, in the US at least, about the kid from the small town being held back and having to "escape" to the city to find himself and be all that he could be. Usually that's not about economics but about self-actualization. But in some ways it's the same story: you have to break free of these small community networks if you want to be anything other than what's already there.

Let's talk about how you came upon field experiments. Presumably you didn't enter university thinking, "what I want to do with my life is to run RCTs on poverty interventions in Kenya." Tell me about how you encountered field experiments, what attracted you, when the light went on, how you ended up where you are now.

PD: I did my masters in France with a specialization in development. It was not applied at all. After that, I wanted to get some experience in the field. I wanted to know what exactly it meant to live in rural Africa. And at the time, being 20 something in France, I thought the only way to experience Africa was to work with an NGO. So I tried to get a job as a volunteer with an NGO, but I couldn't because, well, having a master's in economics is useless. No one was really interested in hiring me. So I accepted a fellowship to go spend a year at Harvard, which was actually a great honor for me to be able to do that, but at the time I didn't really realize it because what I really wanted to be doing was going to Africa. I was a visiting student, auditing classes, but I still really wanted to go to Africa, so I was grumpy about it. At some point someone heard me complaining and said, "You should tell this to Esther Duflo because she really needs people to go and work with her in Africa."

It turns out that she and Michael Kremer needed an RA, someone who could leave within a month, so I just left and went. I was very lucky because the Harvard dean allowed me to postpone the second half of my fellowship, so that I could come back to Harvard after Kenya.

When I got there, I was doing a lot of really low key stuff like labeling stool samples and entering data in Excel and fixing ID numbers in the database and all of these really basic tasks. But at the same time there were all these things going on in the field, and I would go along with the enumerators who were doing the surveys. What I really got out of it was some sense of what it means to be dirt poor. Talking to people got me even more into development economics because I saw all these basic problems firsthand. People and kids are dying. Before that I'd never really seen what it meant to have a child die—and there I had friends in Kenya whose children died. So I just wanted to work on this from then on.

I decided the best thing I could do in the short term was work for an NGO. But Esther convinced me, even though I didn't want to, to go back and do a PhD.

In terms of methods, field experiments were what I knew. But more so, there are these questions that jumped out at me when I lived there and there were no data. So I felt I needed to start gathering data to answer them. But that's very costly, and I thought, if I'm going to raise money to collect data, I might as well have exogenous variation of some sort to make it easier for me to answer the questions I was interested in.[14] All of the questions I was interested in from my time there were questions that could be answered much better if I just did it with experiments.

Having worked for Esther and Michael gave me some credentials and that was the beginning of that phase. At the time very few students were doing

14. Tyler Cowen (chapter 19) discusses the value in the economics profession of being able to create your own data. Jonathan Morduch (chapter 4) discusses the somewhat unique ability of field experiments to create variation on the factors you are interested in studying.

RCTs, so it was easier for me to find funding. By the time I finished my PhD I was like a spoiled brat because I was used to being able to collect my own data, which means you are able to answer exactly the questions you are interested in. It's such a luxury, and I just got used to it. And I have to admit I barely know the existing data sets. But I don't really know any other way of satisfying my own curiosity and answering the questions that I think are important right now to make a difference in people's lives.

TO: Is there a core set of questions that you are interested in? Your work has been very broad from an outsider's perspective—water, pricing, savings, health, education

PD: I focus on capital accumulation and the various ways people accumulate capital. There is human capital—health, education—and physical capital. So I work on health and adoption of health products, investments in education, looking at the production function of education, how do you make kids learn when they are in school. I look at savings because you need money to invest in health, or education, or to build physical capital.

TO: So how do you get from, as you were saying, the reality of being poor and having a child die from a preventable disease, to the academic question of capital accumulation?

PD: This is just a big word, capital. Human capital is health, education, it all comes down to what parents in a household invest in. The starting point for the savings work with Jon was literally this observation that one of our friends in Kenya had a child who died because they couldn't just go to the local shop and buy anti-malarials. It wasn't a huge amount of money, though not cheap, but it was just a question of, "how can they not have 200 Kenyan shillings [$2 to $3] at home that they can just use to rush to a drug shop on a Saturday afternoon when the child is running a fever?" So that very basic question was the starting point for a lot of research that Jon and I have been doing together and sometimes separately. And it's not like we've consciously talked about it with each other, but we'd been impressed by these same types of experiences when we overlapped in Kenya.

There's another story for some of the work I've been doing on pricing. It was the same starting point: health is an issue and people die when they ought not to. At the time I was very naïve. When I came back from Kenya, a friend asked, "If I gave you $5,000, what would you do with it?" I thought about it for 10 minutes and I said, "Well I would give bed nets to people."

So he said, "OK, I'll give you $5,000." I called Michael Kremer and asked, "If I was to create an NGO that would give bed nets to people, what would you think of that?" And he said, "That's a great idea, I'll give you $10,000." So now I had like $15,000 potentially—I have to do it even if I only give out $15,000 worth of bed nets. It's better than nothing. I contacted some friends, Jessica Cohen, who is now at Harvard School of Public Health, and Elizabeth Beasley, who is now at Sciences Po in Paris, and together we created TamTam, which gives free bed nets to pregnant women through prenatal clinics. And we thought we were doing something good.

Because of that, I ended up getting a fellowship from the Mulago Foundation.[15] I went to their social entrepreneurship gathering to talk about what I was doing. Everybody there came down on me and said, "This is the most horrendous program. Giving free bed nets to people, how are you sure people are going to use them?" And that's when I realized that this is actually a debate. There is an unanswered question here. I thought I had a completely rational approach to this whole thing. But I thought if people feel so strongly that this approach is wrong, maybe there is something to their objection.

So that's why we did the first bed net pricing study with Jessica Cohen—Mulago funded it—to find out if these people were right.[16] To test this idea that if you give something for free to people, then they were not going to use it, but if they paid something for it, then they'd be more invested in it and they would use it. We found that if you give people a free bed net, they do use it to the same extent than if they paid for it.

So I went back to Mulago for a meeting and I said, by the way, I tried this out and it seems it's OK. Then people complained, "They're going to get used to getting it for free. Now they'll never want to pay for it in the future." So I did another study that looks at the long-run effects of free distribution.[17] I wanted to see whether people actually benefit from free short-term distribution because it enables them to learn what the returns are.[16] But you also have to see if those learning effects are trumped by the anchoring effect

15. The Mulago Foundation funds social entrepreneurs attempting to build scalable interventions in health, education, conservation, and livelihoods. Of note, the Foundation has made grants to both J-PAL and IPA.

16. An example of some of the curious disconnection in various parts of the economics field, but particularly with management research. The question of whether giving away goods for free impairs future demand or willingness to pay has been exhaustively studied in marketing and management fields. As you can guess from the number of free samples you receive, it generally doesn't.

of a free good. I didn't find much problem with anchoring. I found learning was really what dominates.

That's how I've gone from one thing to the next. So I know it can look very disparate looking at my website and the papers floating around, but there is actually a link between most of these studies. And there's definitely a lot of crossover in terms of learning and thinking. So when I design a new study, I have in the back of my head all of this learning from these previous studies I've done. Of course, most of the learning comes from other people's studies, but it's really a discipline where you want to build up a core of knowledge.

For example, to show the link between the pricing stuff and the savings stuff: in that long-run bed net demand study, the way I was looking at it was randomizing the price people had to pay in the first year and then looking at how they invested in the second year. But when I did the randomization in the first year, I gave people a voucher, and they had three months to use the voucher. And I observed that within the three months, many more people bought a bed net at a nontrivial price than if you just give people a one-time offer. In the first study with Jessica, we gave pregnant women at a prenatal clinic a one-time option to buy a bed net. But the number of people who have cash on them to buy at a moment's notice is not that high,[17] even at a very small price. Even if you tell them they can come back next week with the cash, not many of them came back. But if you give them three months to save, then already you can see somewhat of a higher demand. It's not that high but still there was some hope that over time people manage to save a little bit. So that also contributed to thinking about ways to increase people's saving for health investments, and that, among other things, led to the health savings study with Jon.

TO: Some of people's doubts about free distribution is that the history of free distribution of health products, or what have you, is not great. One of the reasons all those people, I presume, were telling you it was a bad idea is that things like bed nets have been given out, but then you see them being used as fishing nets or something else.

PD: I don't know about that. Maybe there was one person who used a bed net as a fishing net and that person got caught on film. I don't know.

---

17. The issue of short-term illiquidity, grounded in volatile incomes, and how it drives behavior is a central theme of the book *Portfolios of the Poor* and is discussed in the interview with Jonathan Morduch (chapter 4).

But I personally have not ever seen anyone do that, even in fishing communities.[18]

TO: In general, though, take-up is a problem. Not just bed nets but any technology. It seems to be much harder to get people to start using things in the first place than a rational perspective from thousands of miles away would expect. A lot of people come to this area specifically because of the take-up problem. Why can't we get people to use these things, why won't they use fertilizer, why won't they buy bed nets, why won't they save money if they get such high returns to capital in their business?

PD: I know, but if you give people fertilizer for free, they use it. So the problem is more that these things are risky. It's not a complete slam dunk. Some of the work that Michael, Esther, and Jon have done on fertilizer[19] shows that it takes a while to figure out the optimal use of fertilizer and also there is huge variance in the returns.[18]

This issue of take-up, I think there are really two questions: If you give people something for free, are they going take it up or not? Then there's the question of why don't people invest their own money in these things? That's not obviously a puzzle from the get-go. It could just be that people are misinformed about the returns or that there is substantial risk and people don't have enough insurance to protect them.[20]

On the first question, which is why people don't take up something that is free, there is always a lot of anecdotal evidence, but I've never seen a rigorous study that found that. In fact recently there was this huge uproar within IPA Kenya because Vestergaard Frandsen was going to distribute this

18. I now know all available rigorous evidence is in Dupas's favor. Attempts at documenting anecdotes alleging misuse of bed nets have generally failed to find any systematic evidence. See: http://web.stanford.edu/~pdupas/Dupas_letter_editor _NYT_malaria_nets.pdf.
19. The best-known work is on a voucher program that allows farmers to buy fertilizer for the following season at harvest time. This "commitment" leads to a substantial increase in fertilizer use and higher crop yields in the following season. As part of this work, Duflo, Kremer, and Robinson also have a separate paper focused on the returns to fertilizer. They find that while there are high returns to using the optimal amount of fertilizer, the use of fertilizer in the specific amounts recommended by the Kenyan Ministry of Agriculture (based on experimental farm results) are not profitable for farmers in the area studied.
20. These ideas are explored further in the interviews with David McKenzie (chapter 10) and Jonathan Robinson (chapter 18).

Lifestraw product[21] to thousands of households in Kenya. Everyone was so upset with them. They thought it was the worst technology ever. In fact my good friend Kevin Starr of Mulago talked about it at PopTech, making fun of LifeStraw as the stupidest technology.[22] And I was wondering why people were so upset with these Vestergaard Frandsen guys for just trying to help get clean water. So I've been collecting data quietly just on adoption of the technology. I'm surveying a lot of people in Kenya for another project, so I added a question, "Hey, by the way, how do you treat your water?" And I'm finding that this Family Lifestraw water filter has been widely adopted and people report using it. And it's not like we're affiliated with Vestergaard Frandsen, so they have to lie to us and pretend they are using it. I don't see why they would pretend to us that they do. But so far at least 40 percent of people are really excited about their Lifestraw and are using it and it's a good thing. It's cleaner water. But for some reason it has gotten terrible press within the NGO community and the impact evaluation community and people have this idea that it's the worst thing, and I'm not sure that I understand why.

All in all I'm not convinced that there are barriers to technology adoption that are not within the standard way of thinking. Take condoms. Obviously there's a cost of using condoms, and that's why people don't immediately start using condoms. But over time you see people get over this, and now we see much higher rates of condom use. The question I think we have to answer about low take-up is trying to understand why is it that people are so risk averse that they don't want to invest small amounts of money when they are uncertain about the returns. That's a more important question than whether they pay for it or not. Why are people so averse to things that are new, and what can we do about it?

21. Vestergaard Frandsen is a Dutch company that manufactures water-filtering equipment and bed nets among other items. The LifeStraw is a water filtration product that resembles a straw.
22. The video of Starr's talk can be seen at: https://vimeo.com/17292835.

15 Elie Hassenfeld

Elie is co-founder and co-executive director of GiveWell and a managing director of the Open Philanthropy Project. GiveWell is a nonprofit that performs extensive research on charitable programs seeking the best giving opportunities possible, publishing all the details of its analysis to help people decide where to give. GiveWell's analysis relies heavily on RCTs proving the impact of interventions. Unlike most charity evaluators, GiveWell has recommended only a handful of charities since its founding in 2007.

I have served as a GiveWell board member since its founding.

TO: Tell me about GiveWell's general search for evidence and where you look for evidence as you evaluate interventions.

EH: GiveWell's mission is to find outstanding giving opportunities and publish the full details of that analysis to help donors decide where to give. Over time we've primarily focused on organizations working in international aid. When we look for organizations in international aid there are two parts of our process. The second part is looking at individual organizations and evaluating their monitoring and evaluation information, and assessing whether they seem to be a high-quality organization that would be deserving of additional funds. But the initial part of our process is searching for programs that have very strong evidence of "effectiveness." And what that means to us is programs that have—sometimes only one study but often more than one—rigorous evidence. What we mean by "rigorous" is an RCT. So we'll search for programs that have a large body of academic, not charity-specific, evidence, that the program has had a meaningful effect on the problem it's trying to solve. So a good example of this is bed nets that protect against the mosquitos that transmit malaria. There are more than 20 RCTs that show that, when you give someone a net, they tend to use it, and those nets protect against malaria and save lives.[1] So our process is one that starts by searching for interventions that have strong evidence,[2] and once we've assessed that evidence, we try to find organizations that are implementing those interventions.

TO: Isn't there a difference between an RCT that shows a bed net is effective at preventing malaria and an RCT of an organization that shows that they are effective at distributing them to people that need them? How do you assess the effectiveness of the organization at actually delivering the program?

EH: Most of the time we'll look at RCT evidence and then that evidence will raise questions about the success an organization would have when implementing the program. So when using the example of bed nets you can imagine that when a particular trial took place people used the nets consistently because it was on a small scale and the researchers were particularly focused on ensuring use. That might not be the case if the nets were distributed at larger scale. So one question would be whether use would translate between the trial and larger scale-up. Another question would be how long nets last. Another question we've faced is, since the time of the trial, have conditions changed in such a way that the effect of distributing nets today would be different. Two specific examples of that are that child mortality has fallen significantly in the 20 years[3] since many trials were conducted. That's obviously a great thing but it could reduce the cost-effectiveness, the bang for your buck, of distributing nets. If fewer people are dying from malaria then it's possible that nets today have less of an effect than they did in the past. Similarly there's some evidence of insecticide resistance, which would obviously make nets less effective. So our basic approach is to start with the trials themselves as a very important piece of evidence that this intervention at least in some cases has this causal impact. Then we try to identify the questions that remain about impact when you

1. For a complete review of these studies see GiveWell's site where they publish their full review of evidence on each intervention and charity they study. http://www .givewell.org/international/technical/programs/insecticide-treated-nets.
2. The list of interventions or "causes" that GiveWell has investigated can be found at http://www.givewell.org/international/technical/programs.
3. A useful visualization of the decline in child mortality can be found at Gap-Minder: www.bit.ly/QISGYa. For a thorough review of improvements in child mortality and other gains see Charles Kenny, *Getting Better* and Angus Deaton, *The Great Escape.*

think about an organization that is scaling up that intervention. Then we try to do research on those questions either by getting information from the organization itself or by doing additional independent research.

So in the case of the Against Malaria Foundation (AMF), it conducts follow-up surveys—6, 12, 18, 24 months later—of people to whom it has distributed nets measuring the condition and durability of the nets and also checking if people are actually using them. Then we have done additional independent research to try to learn how changes in insecticide resistance may have changed the effectiveness of nets since the studies were conducted.

TO: One of the criticisms of academic research from practitioners is that it takes so long to be published. In January of 2015 we finally saw *AEJ Applied*[4] publish six of the microcredit impact studies, most of which started at least 4 years ago, some as much as 10 years ago. Given all of the things that can change over that time scale, in general do you find issues with the academic research you're working with being old or in a context too different from where you're trying to apply it?

EH: We definitely find the RCT evidence is a major input into our process. Like I said with bed nets there are things that can change since the time of the trials but what the trials show, and I think they likely show it in a relatively long-term way, is that nets protect against mosquitoes that transmit malaria. This isn't a fact that seems likely to change until and unless there is a major change in the prevalence of malaria or a major uptick in insecticide resistance.

Another example is the deworming trial.[5] The studies that find long term effects of deworming likely show the relationship of treating children who have a parasitic infection with a pill and that having a long term effect on their development. These are things that don't seem likely to change over the three to seven year time frame that it can take research to get out.

I do think there are some downsides, obviously, to the time it can take for research to be published. One is that there can be questions that we want answers to where it may not even make sense to conduct the type of

4. *American Economic Journal: Applied Economics* published six randomized evaluations of microcredit in its January 2015 (vol. 7, issue 1).
5. This is a reference to one of the seminal studies in the RCT movement: M. Kremer and E. Miguel (2004), "Worms: Identifying Impacts on Education and Health in the Presence of Treatment Externalities," *Econometrica* 72 (1).

study we would need. A good example of that is deworming. We still have relatively little evidence that deworming has significant long-term effects. We have one, maybe two or three,[6] depending on which studies you include. So we have very limited studies showing long-term effects. With bed nets we have more than 20. But to conduct another long-term deworming trial would mean 10 years and millions of dollars and those years and that money is probably better spent on other things, in particular scaling up this program that is already so cheap.

One mitigating factor here is that we often review working papers, sometimes even before they appear publicly, as input into our process. We don't have to wait for a study to be peer-reviewed before we can consider it as evidence.

TO: The deworming example is particularly interesting because perhaps more than any other of the influential RCTs there has been debate about what the effect of deworming actually is. GiveWell has recommended deworming charities but has also recommended funding to the Cochrane Collaboration,[7] which has questioned the validity of the impact found in those deworming studies.[8][1] How do you think about the conflict there?

6. See below for a discussion and citations of these studies.
7. In 2012 GiveWell recommended that Good Ventures, a large foundation that GiveWell partners with and advises, make a $100,000 grant to the Cochrane Collaboration. The Cochrane Collaboration performs and publishes reviews and meta-analyses of randomized evaluations in health (www.cochrane.org). See a description of GiveWell's recommendation and the circumstances around it here: http://blog.givewell.org/2012/09/27/us-cochrane-center-uscc-gets-our-first-quick -grant-recommendation/. The Cochrane Collaboration has never been designated a "recommended charity" by GiveWell.
8. In 2012 the Cochrane Collaboration published a meta-analysis of deworming studies, concluding "it is probably misleading to justify contemporary deworming programmes based on evidence of consistent benefit on nutrition, haemoglobin, school attendance or school performance as there is simply insufficient reliable information to know whether this is so." See: http://www.cochrane.org/CD000371/ INFECTN_deworming-drugs-for-treating-soil-transmitted-intestinal-worms-in -children-effects-on-nutrition-and-school-performance.
   A response to the meta-analysis from Michael Kremer, Ted Miguel, and others, can be found here: http://www.poverty-action.org/blog/cochrane%E2%80%99s -incomplete-and-misleading-summary-evidence-deworming.
   Note that the Cochrane authors respond in the comments.
   Finally, GiveWell's response to the Cochrane meta-analysis can be found here: http://blog.givewell.org/2012/07/13/new-cochrane-review-of-the-effectiveness-of -deworming/

EH: I think the evidence for deworming is one of the most interesting challenges we've faced over the last few years as we've been researching it and the related charities. There definitely are significant questions—we had significant questions—about whether or not deworming has a long-term effect. Until a year ago the only evidence that demonstrated that deworming had a long-term effect was the follow up from the Kremer Miguel deworming study[2] and a retrospective study by Hoyt Bleakley on hookworm elimination in the American South in the 1920s.[3] Those were the only two studies that demonstrated a long-term effect on cognitive development and earnings. Last year [2014] Kevin Croke put out another study that seems to also show a long-term effect of deworming.[4] I won't go into the details of the study but basically there are these three pieces of evidence that show a long-term effect and that contrasts with many short-term studies that in particular the Cochrane Collaboration is including in its review that seem to show little to no effect on short-term indicators. So we're left with these questions like, "How can a program have a long-term effect on earnings and cognitive development if it doesn't have a short-term effect?"

So we find ourselves trying to work through these questions. Is it possible that in the case of Kremer and Miguel that there was something unique going on? The initial work there took place around Lake Victoria in the late 1990s during an El Nino period. There was a lot of flooding so infection rates and intensity of infection may have been significantly higher than they are today. Should we expect going forward that was a unique case that is not likely to repeat in other locations?

Another possibility, depending on how you slice the studies, is that maybe the main effects or main actor is schistosomiasis, one of the infections and not soil-transmitted helminths [STH]. The Cochrane Collaboration review focuses particularly on STH and not on schisto so it's certainly plausible that high-intensity schisto infection is the driver of the impact. In the Kevin Croke and Bleakley studies, neither of those had schisto. Overall we find ourselves looking at this and it does not offer a clear-cut definite case of impact. What it offers is a plausible case of significant long-term impact at very low cost. So we've recommended funding to deworming with these caveats in mind. I think it's a great giving opportunity because of the combination of low cost and possible high impact, not because it's a case of definite high impact.

TO: The Cochrane Collaboration specializes in meta-analyses which can present some difficulties because there are so many differences in the studies you are trying to combine. One of the things that we've seen emerge recently is more explicit replication attempts in social psychology but also in development economics, looking at graduation programs, for instance. What do you find more convincing, or what would you find more convincing, a meta-analysis of 10 studies that were conducted by different people in different contexts or an explicit replication in six locations of the same program?

EH: It's a hard question to answer in the abstract because it really depends on what you know about the studies. It's clearly better to have more evidence and more studies are likely to increase your confidence in what you know. But meta-analysis can also not have details about what exactly the intervention was, or how it was carried out or whether there were methodological issues with particular studies. We would prefer to have a smaller amount of high-quality evidence than a larger amount of questionable-quality evidence. You can see that come through in our materials. When we talk about deworming we focus heavily on the three papers that I mentioned and we don't really get into all of the other short-term RCTs beyond the Cochrane Collaboration summary or all of the other qualitative evidence around the program.

TO: What would you like to see more of? Would you like to see more funding for replications of the programs that don't have very many studies? Or more funding for high quality meta-analyses, especially given that the former costs a lot more than the latter?

EH: We would definitely like to see more funds go to studies that have had very promising effects but have only been studied once. This is actually something that we have recommended Good Ventures make some grants to. Particularly some grants to Evidence Action where they're working with Mushfiq Mobarak to start thinking about what it would take to scale up the seasonal migration intervention he studied.[5] That includes thinking about whether we need to do some replication of part of it to learn about how it might change at larger scale. That's an example of a single study and it would be great to see it replicated. Another is the incentives for immunization study.[9][6] We'd love to see more evidence of that

9. This is a reference to Duflo et al.'s study of increasing vaccine coverage by offering mothers a plate and a 1 kg bag of lentils as an incentive to have their children vaccinated. This study is also discussed in the interviews with Banerjee and Duflo (chapter 2) and Tyler Cowen (chapter 19).

program because the impact evaluation was done in one place at one time with a particular non-profit partner and there are questions about how well that would translate to a larger scale or in another context. I think that's definitely necessary.

The other type of information that we would like to see is better monitoring of global health programs. This is maybe a little off the topic but it is just shocking to me that we have so little information about how deworming programs are carried out. Whether infection rates really fall in the real world, whether children actually receive the pills. And the same is true as you look across global health programs. It's true for bed nets—the monitoring information that the Against Malaria Foundation collects and makes public is the best information that is publically available, as far as I know, on the success of specific net distributions.[10] The information available about salt iodization programs and how they have reduced iodine deficiency globally leaves something to be desired and could be significantly improved. We are surprised at the lack of high quality monitoring information that is available, or at least that we've been able to find, as we've looked at these global health interventions.

I think more meta-analyses are useful though I'm not convinced that in the areas that we work—collecting studies on global health and development— there are significant sets of studies that haven't been sufficiently aggregated into a meta-analysis except perhaps in the case of cash transfers. We haven't seen a really good Cochrane style meta-analysis of those RCTs of the various outcomes that are tracked and that's something that we would really like to see and would be helpful to us.

TO: Another of your recommendations that has generated some pushback is GiveDirectly. It's my impression that there were stronger negative reactions to that recommendation than to any other recommendation that GiveWell has made. Is that accurate? If so, why do you think that is? Have people been giving to GiveDirectly in the proportion you expect relative to other recommended charities? Would you have considered recommending GiveDirectly without seeing the Haushofer and Shapiro RCT?[11][7]

10. See interview with Jonathan Robinson (chapter 18) for discussion of an evaluation of a bed net distribution program.
11. Haushofer and Shapiro evaluate GiveDirectly's program and find that the unconditional cash grants are spent on consumption and investment, also yield declines in spending on alcohol and tobacco. They also find gains in several measurements of household psychological welfare and happiness.

EH: Our recommendation of GiveDirectly had the strongest negative reactions, but it also had some of the strongest positive reactions, so we have donors who give to all of our top charities except for GiveDirectly, and others who only give to GiveDirectly. I think the primary driver is that cash is pretty understandable as an intervention; it's something that donors can more easily relate to, so people have pretty strong intuitions about how good an intervention it is. Some people think that people receiving cash won't make good decisions about how to spend and may buy things like alcohol or tobacco. Donors on the other side really like the idea of giving recipients the opportunity to help themselves.

Another reservation people have had about cash transfers is the feeling that they are unlikely to accomplish as much good per dollar as cheap health interventions such as bed nets and deworming.[12] Our cost-effectiveness analysis does estimate that bed nets and deworming outperform cash transfers, but not overwhelmingly, and this analysis doesn't fully account for some of the strengths of cash transfers as an intervention and GiveDirectly as an organization.

We did recommend GiveDirectly before the Haushofer and Shapiro RCT was completed. The RCT came out at the end of 2013 and we recommended GiveDirectly in 2012. We based that recommendation on the body of evidence supporting smaller, conditional cash transfers around the world. We noted that GiveDirectly's significantly larger transfer was materially different than most of the other studies of cash transfers' impacts, but we still felt that the evidence from those studies was strong enough to warrant a recommendation. The fact that the Haushofer and Shapiro RCT was underway gave us additional confidence because we knew that we would gain additional information in the near future.

12. See the interviews with Banerjee and Duflo (chapter 2) and Pascaline Dupas (chapter 14) for more on the comparisons of cash transfers and bed net distribution.

Antoinette is the Koerner Professor of Entrepreneurial Finance at MIT and a co-founder of Ideas42, a behavioral science consultancy. She has a different focus than many of her colleagues studying poverty and development with field experiments—the interaction of management, finance, and firm behavior. This has led her to study entrepreneurial finance, corporate diversification, governance, and capital budgeting decisions.

But it has also led her to study how banks in developing countries make loan decisions, how banks can more effectively manage their loan portfolios, and how microenterprise owners manage their finances. She is also intensely interested in how to boost high-growth entrepreneurship in developing countries.

TO: Your work spans a pretty wide range and lots of different methods. There's theory, there are public data sets, there are lab experiments and field experiments. Let me start by asking how you think about the various kinds of evidence and the role of theory, versus regressions on public data sets, versus field experiments

AS: I feel there is a role for a diversity of methods, and each of the methods have different strengths in what they can be used for. Experiments allow you to be very precise about testing detailed channels and impacts but often confine you to setups that are quite specific. That can reduce external validity.

Work with secondary data often has the opposite problem: they might cover a large sample of subjects but might force you to compromise on methodological rigor. In addition you have to consider the cost/benefit trade-off. Field experiments are very expensive. The big trade-off between running field experiments or using administrative data is that, on the one hand, field experiments give you the soundest and most robust results. It's the closest we can come in economics to the scientific method. But the drawback of field experiments is that in economics of course we can't recreate the lab for all applications, especially macroeconomics. It's not like biology when you can manipulate bacteria any way you want. We can't test exogenously varied inflation rates across countries. It's not feasible. So that means that very often field experiments are limited to more micro-questions. But it's not just micro-questions that we want to answer in economics. So then we have to step away from field experiments to natural experiments and other data sets.

In terms of theory versus empirics, theory is a way of organizing your thinking. In the end it's setting up a hypothesis so that you have something to test. That's why I also think that theory is most useful when it gives enough structure that it can actually allow you to refute hypotheses. The most frustrating theories are the ones that are so flexible that they fit any finding. This doesn't help me to make better sense of the world. But it's important to start from a theoretical framework rather than just a story because it forces you to be more precise. I think of myself primarily as an empiricist, so theory to me is very helpful when it helps me to unearth new empirical insights.

When you think about running a field experiment, especially field experiments that engage real organizations on the ground—let's say for me that's financial institutions or firms, for others its NGOs—you always have to ask what is the specific context in which the experiment is being run. While I firmly believe randomized control trials are the soundest and most robust method that we have, it is important to understand that the implementation of the field experiment often hinges on the particular operational capability and the type of firm or the type of NGO that you work with.

Maybe that's obvious, but when we run regressions on certain sub-industries or geographic areas, we often ask, what is the external validity at a broader scale? We shouldn't be blinded that in a field experiment, the external validity is affected by the type of firms that might be willing to work with researchers. They may be the best firms that are out there. Or they may be the ones that feel they have nothing to lose in sharing data or running an experiment with me. That's something that we need to keep in mind when running experiments.

TO: What was the first randomized experiment that you worked on?

AS: The first one I worked on was with ICICI Bank in India testing credit scores. It was an interesting product: a current account for small businesses that they would keep for six months, and if the transactions in the current account looked "reasonable," then they would be given an overdraft on the account. So what we did is we randomized the amount of credit and even who got credit, in the sense of who was approved for an overdraft, and then we tested what type of transaction-based credit score predicted default behavior. It wasn't the typical credit score you have in the US, where you have a lot of past credit information on a user. We used only the past information from the ICICI account itself on how the business owners managed their money: how many transactions they made, how many checks they bounced, what kind of turnover they had, how many customers or vendors they were paying, all those type of things.

TO: When I look at your body of work, I notice a blending of organizational concerns, corporate finance, and behavioral issues. You don't see that all that often in the field experiment literature thus far. The focus tends to be on the behavior of the borrower or the person at the end of the line, but not all of the things that lead up to that. Do you think that's a gap in the field experiment literature—that it's focused too much on the individual and not on the organization as a whole or the loan officer?

AB: You're right that we normally see the intervention at the consumer level. Randomization often is easier at that level. It's very rare that we can randomize at the organization or firm or delivery level. That is much harder to do. Getting a chance to do that is, of course, great. That is why we have done studies using audit methodology,[1] so you can observe the reaction of firms to certain interventions even without having to engage the firms.

But what I really like about running field experiments is that even if you're working with one bank or one NGO because you have to engage with the organization to implement something on the ground, if you want to do a good job, you have to get involved in the details. Which means that you get constant feedback on what is feasible and what is implementable or what is

1. An audit methodology involves randomized checks to see if a protocol is being adhered to by the participants—for instance, whether a bank teller charges a customer the right fee, whether a health clinic worker dispenses the proper dosage of a malaria medicine, or whether a teacher is using computers as part of a lesson plan as expected. Audit methodology often involves a "secret shopper" who pretends to be a customer to assess the real world behavior of subjects.

practical and what is just a pipe dream. What sounds great in an ivory tower may be impossible in the real world. For me that's extremely useful and a terrific side effect of experiments. You are right that the outcomes could be shaded by the type of firm that you work with and the type of governance structure they have, it's still better than not getting that kind of feedback.

And I feel very often that, as social scientists, our research production function is somewhat remote from the actual organizations that we are studying. We normally don't get to see how the sausage is made, how the actual implementation happens. That's to some extent why I feel that if you look at engineering or biology or biotech, one of the good things that the close connection that those natural sciences have with implementation is that they actually constantly get that feedback. I think a lot of creativity comes from that.

TO: You mentioned how invigorating it is to work with people who can tell you what is realistic and plausible. In terms of the economist side of that equation, do you think those are learned skills or are they attitudes that are somewhat personality driven? Is this something that any PhD student could learn how to do well, or is there a subset of people who will be really good at doing field experiments?

AS: I do think it's learnable but also that there's heterogeneity. Some people are clearly much better at it. The thing that I don't know yet, and it is something important, how much does the skill of managing an experiment—but also being willing to engage with real world actors—how does it correlate with typical research skills that we value.[2] Let's say at the very top of the distribution you have people who can do both, they can do everything. And also they have a lot of institutional support even when they can't do it so well, to help them. Of course, at a more junior faculty level it's much tougher for someone who doesn't have those managerial skills or isn't as good on the managerial side to supplement those skills. But if this correlation is not a positive, then we should be a bit worried.

2. See further discussion of these points with Michael Kremer (chapter 1), Dean Yang (chapter 12), and Tyler Cowen (chapter 19). Cowen shares some concern about selecting for the wrong attributes in researchers while marveling at the economists who are both top researchers and excellent managers of field experiments; Kremer notes the difficulty and novelty of working with organizations in the ways required by field experiments, and the value of creating institutions that allow those interactions to happen; Yang talks about the differential skills that allow a researcher to design studies that are of both academic and organizational interest.

To be honest, I do think it takes a mindset of wanting to learn from people and respecting people who are not necessarily focused on research and science and who don't talk in abstractions but who will always give you individual examples because that's much simpler for them. Sometimes it's very easy to dismiss those types of insights because they seem so pedestrian when you're trying to say something about mechanisms or channels and they are not phrased in an abstract way. But distilling from the things that people say in very non-academic language, that's a skill that needs a lot of training and we don't get much training in it. I've often thought it would be very good if one could team up with anthropologists in the early phase of a project because anthropologists are much more trained in doing qualitative field interviews and field observation, which might be a nice complementarity.

Another factor, given that we're all not really trained to be managers, is to make sure there's no slippage in what was actually implemented on the ground. It's really not obvious how to manage projects for details like that. That's where a lot of organizational support but also a lot of care from the researchers is needed.

TO: Is it your feeling that the field experiment movement has had an effect on economics as a whole in terms of raising the bar for evidence and causing people to rethink what the standards are?

AS: Absolutely. There's a huge impact. Now we have to say in which fields. In development economics it had the first impact and the biggest impact. If you look at junior faculty nowadays, to a large extent they have to do RCTs to even be considered for tenure at a top department. Just doing observational work is usually not enough. In fact I think it has gone almost too far because there is so much operational risk in these types of experiments—not just if the result comes out interestingly but maybe the organization abandons you in the middle—there's actually a lot of risk for people's careers because you only have seven years before someone comes up for tenure.[3] It's a bit concerning because it makes efficient promotion much noisier. The other place where we see a lot of impact of RCTs is in health economics or labor economics. Even in the US, there are more and more experiments being run. People look to experiments as more or less the gold standard.

---

3. See discussion with Dean Karlan (chapter 6) and Chris Blattman (chapter 20) on this point, though both focus on the particular issues of graduate students rather than junior faculty.

Of course, there are many really important questions in development, in labor, and in public finance or whatever that can just never be answered with an experiment because they don't lend themselves to an experiment. I feel in development now it's reversing a bit. But there was a time when I feel that the method was leading the question, and not vice versa, and that's never good. So you have questions like economic policy and regulation that were going a bit by the wayside because you can't randomize and so it was almost impossible for a junior person to work on those questions. I think that's actually starting to change because of the availability of large-scale data sets—Haltiwanger with US census data[4] and similar things becoming available in Brazil, Indonesia, Thailand, India, and so forth—we see those topics coming back and I think that's a good trend.

TO: If you need to have the skills to run a successful RCT in order to be seriously considered for tenure, then that really changes what the requirements are for students. If we posit the managerial skills to run a successful experiment are heterogeneously distributed and difficult to learn, are we selecting for the wrong things?

AS: Even if they're not difficult to learn, as long as they're tougher to learn for the better researchers that's not good. On the other hand, I think it often happens in economics, and possibly in other fields as well, but definitely in economics, when a new tool becomes available it's like "we found a hammer, everything is going to be a nail." So everything had to become RCTs and now the newness is gone, which is good because people start to realize it's a good tool in certain situations but the hammer is not leading the research question. That's why I'm not so concerned anymore that there are serious distortions from running RCTs.

TO: Turning to the specifics of some of your research, you've done work on reminders and interactions with borrowers in India and Uganda. In the Uganda case you found that SMS reminders to repay were effective. But there are two underlying questions there. One, why do SMS reminders work? And if they do, why did it require an experiment to get people to think of doing this?

AS: There are two answers. I agree with you that it might not be a stunning insight that you should try and remind people. In fact there were many banks that sent people text messages before we decided to try to

4. See below for a discussion of Haltiwanger's work on entrepreneurship and job creation based on US census data.

measure the impact. But the reason there are so many studies looking at SMS is the attempt to understand the magnitude of the impact. In the context of the study in Uganda, what we were actually trying to understand is exactly what you are asking: why is something as simple as a reminder having such a large effect?

In finance one of the things we always think about is the difference between strategic default versus inadvertent or unwilling default. The way we view most of the lending market, the type of financial products being devised and how we price them, is exactly along those two dimensions. We want to discourage borrowers from willful or strategic default when they actually could pay, but for those who are economically distressed, we want to forgive some of the loan so that we can recover as much as we can but allow them to become a good customer in the future.

In that world, there would be no room for reminders. A strategic defaulter would be laughing at you for sending them an SMS, an economic defaulter would be crying because they want to pay but just don't have the money. What we wanted to test was not just if it helps but to understand if there is another kind of default—that people just forget. But why do they forget? In a rational economic model the one reason you could imagine is if the person deliberately forgets because the interest rate, even including the penalty interest rate, on the loan might still be better than your access to credit outside of that. Imagine the only form of credit I have is borrowing from you. And let's say that somehow, by paying late, I can make one more investment or take on one more project and then pay you later. As economists we would think I will do that if my return from paying late, and therefore having this credit for a little while longer, is higher than the cost of the loan. In that situation the reminder shouldn't work. But if what's happening here is that people's lives are very busy and very unorganized, then sending a reminder could have a salience effect. Then you are actually doing them a favor by reminding them that the payment is due.

That is what we were trying in the Uganda experiment, the impact of reminders versus giving them reductions in the interest rate. The other treatments were exactly designed to see if these people were rationally trading off the costs of capital between the loan and other forms of capital. We feel that the fact that reminders have a large impact seems to suggest that really what looks like "default" is truly just that at least some subset of the people are not managing their finances well enough. It also means that the credit risk of the borrower depends on the way a bank structures the loan product, not just the inherent type of the borrower.

TO: The Dominican Republic study on rules of thumb is another example of people not managing their finances well.[1] Even there, though, the effects weren't very large, although better than most financial literacy work, which has not found much impact.[5] If people are just struggling with the basics of financial management, why is that we can't find effects from financial literacy training that are as large as what we see from the small business consulting studies?

AS: I would say two things to that. You're totally right that most financial literacy training work has shown very little to no effect. But our rule of thumb implementation does show some effect. It's important to point out that in the average week the intervention has only minimal effect on sales, but it does have a big effect on weeks when people have very low sales outcomes. We can do more work to understand that better, but what the rule of thumb training seems to be doing is alerting people that, when they are hitting tough times, they need to get more proactive to undo the effects of the negative shock. That could be a very good thing for people who are relatively poor and therefore the marginal value of a dollar or marginal consumption is very high.

I do believe what our rule of thumb study shows is that being more creative about how things are taught seems to be a first-order factor. Many of the training programs I've seen on financial literacy seem to respond to low effects of the program by piling on more information. They make them more complete, but they also make them more complex. But that seems to have a detrimental effect because maybe you are burdening people who have limited attention, or low prior education, with a very complex system. So we have to be much smarter in how we improve financial capabilities of people, paying more attention to how we teach and what we teach. In the end it is not about turning people into finance professors but helping them to make good decisions. In fact let's be honest about one thing: training individual people is always very costly.

So I think from a lot of this behavioral finance evidence, we are starting to have a much more promising way to design financial products and

5. In general, rigorous studies of financial literacy programs have found very little impact. See Fernandes, D., Lynch Jr, J., and Netemeyer, R. (2014), "Financial Literacy, Financial Education and Downstream Financial Behaviors," *Management Science* 60 (8) for a thorough meta-analysis of financial literacy program evaluations. There is additional discussion of financial literacy and training in general in the interviews with Dean Karlan (chapter 6), Xavi Gine (chapter 8), and David McKenzie (chapter 10).

channels for distribution that make it easier for people to make the right choice for themselves, even if they are not super-financially sophisticated. There still is a lot of work to do, and there is a lot of political debate that has to happen around financial regulation because it is a political decision about how much regulation and disclosure we want to put on these things. We don't make everyone be an engineer to drive a car or an automotive expert to decide what car to buy, but we have standards for safety and other sources of information that give people the opportunity to make a good choice.

TO: There is a strong overlap between this problem in developing countries and in developed countries. How much information presented in what ways is useful to protect borrowers or consumers? What is your feeling about how much the research in developing and developed countries should overlap? Are the contexts so different that there is little cross-applicability or should the Consumer Financial Protection Bureau (CFPB) be paying more attention to reminders to save and rules of thumb and other studies in the developing context?

AS: I'm going to give you an economist's answer: it depends. My prior is that people are very similar across the board. In that sense there are probably a lot of things where the CFPB or whatever regulator could learn from what is done abroad, and vice versa. Where the difference comes, and where one has to be very careful, is that the context of the financial market is different from place to place. And that can create big differences in the outcome. Just to give an example, in the US you will find that I think people ultimately do have more trust in their financial institutions— believe it or not these days, but they do trust their banks more than people in Uganda. One thing we've seen in, say, Uganda, is that people have so little trust in the banks per se, that most middle class savers in Uganda have split their money across five different banks. They are insuring against the failure of any particular bank. That can have big implications, for example, on the impact of disclosures.[6] In the US we have seen that even better disclosures[7] often have a muted effect, since people do not pay much

6. See the interview with Xavi Giné (chapter 8) for additional discussion of disclosure and how to provide information that is useful to poor consumers in a way that spurs action.
7. A useful discussion of the challenges of designing effective financial product disclosures can be found at: http://www.federalreserve.gov/pubs/bulletin/2011/articles/DesigningDisclosures/default.htm.

attention. Now think about a situation like Uganda if people have to look at disclosure forms for 5 different accounts. That's only one example of where context would matter a lot.

TO: Speaking of generalizability and trying to tie these threads together, let's talk about studies of business consulting like Nick Bloom's work in India[8][2] and your work in Mexico.[3] If I understand those pieces of research correctly, a big portion of the work in Mexico seems to be around marketing practices, whereas Bloom's work was focused on operations. Why do you think the Mexican firms were more interested in marketing? Had the Mexican firms figured out the operations but not the marketing?

AS: That's a very good question. There are two reasons. One is almost mechanical. In Nick and his coauthors' study in India, from the beginning the type of consulting the firm agreed to give was operational consulting. So they didn't get a random subset of firms and see what they needed and deliver that. They offered a specific type of consulting to firms in the garment industry. Part of it was they had a prior from the beginning that what the garment industry needs is improvement on the operational side because a lot of these firms have standing contracts and commitments from their buyers.

We worked with nine lower-end consulting firms, compared to Bloom,[9] to provide services, so they were the types of consulting firm that normally serve these types of businesses; we allowed the firm and the consultants together to decide on what is the most valuable margin on which they wanted to work together. In a way that's why there is a lot of variability in what our firms chose to work on.

The other difference is that it is true that the firms in India that Bloom chose to work with were much bigger than the firms that we were working with in Mexico. I do believe that for these firms that we were working with operations are not as important because a lot of them are service sector firms rather than manufacturing firms. Even for the manufacturing firms in our sample, it's very small scale manufacturing where maybe operational issues wouldn't matter so much. Because we were working with a much

8. David McKenzie is a co-author of this work. There is much more discussion of consulting and training interventions in his interview. In brief, this study provided business operations consulting to Indian textile firms and found large gains in profits.
9. In the India study, the consulting was provided by a "large international consulting firm."

bigger sample of firms we didn't want to impose one thing on all these different types of firms.

TO: In one of your papers you try to bring all of this up a level and ask what kind of capital is missing.[4] I think that's what you are saying, that different types of firms in different contexts are missing different types of capital.

AS: Our answer in that paper is a little bit more specific than just different things are missing for different firms. We are trying to say that very often it is human capital. When human capital is missing, it might interact with other forms of capital so that it might be difficult to detect that it is human capital that is missing. As an example, if you are a bad entrepreneur who doesn't know how to manage your firm well, it might be that you are very bad at convincing a bank to give you a loan. So you also have trouble with access to financial capital. But if I just asked the firm or I looked at where obvious constraints are, it might look like they don't have enough cash. In reality it might not be the case that the banking market isn't working well in this country but that despite the banking markets being good or bad, this particular entrepreneur can't figure out how to access a loan. So it wouldn't help to infuse more capital into the banking system or into the specific firm because the real issue is the human capital of the entrepreneur. If he can't figure out how to access capital that is available, he or she is unlikely to invest that capital productively when it was made available. What is needed is to somehow improve the human capital base of the entrepreneur.

TO: There's another alternative—the market is efficient: the banking sector is operating efficiently, and denying capital to those who can't use it well. This relates to a footnote in your paper that intrigued me: people with higher managerial capital would have lower returns to marginal increases in financial capital. If I'm interpreting that correctly, the idea is that with strong managerial skills the entrepreneur would find effective ways to deploy other resources to overcome those constraints. So that entrepreneur might not have that high of a return if you give him or her more financial capital. A finding that such an entrepreneur had low returns to financial capital might actually mislead you on capital returns because the best deployers of capital had already found a way around the challenge. Is that right?

AS: Right. But that depends on this assumption that we are making in this paper that if we are in a neoclassical world where the production functions are concave, then, if you have already figured out how to be larger, your marginal return to capital is lower because of the shape of the production function. If you were in a world where the production function was convex, that could, of course, be different.

TO: Have you looked at Benjamin Olken's "There Is No Missing Middle"[10][5] paper? Does that at all, and if so how, change thinking on the state of small and medium enterprises in middle income countries?

AS: This is an interesting paper. But the title is a bit of a misnomer. Normally, when we worry about the missing middle, it means that there are few midsize firms and that small firms are not becoming midsize or large. What they're showing is that there does not seem to be a big fraction of employment in very large firms in developing countries. There's no middle because there is not this massive positive tail. Many people, when they say missing middle, seem to be loosely saying that there's tons of employment in small firms and tons of employment in very large firms, but nothing in the middle. What Olken's data show is that's not the case. It's showing there's tons of employment in small firms, there's some employment in mid-size firms, and even a bit less employment in the very very large firms in developing countries. You can interpret this as there's no missing middle, or you can interpret this as there's even less employment in very large firms than we thought, and we're back to the question of why is it that the small firms, at least some of them, aren't becoming large and creating lots of jobs as happens in Western countries.

TO: As I interpret the evidence that we have so far, there is a very clear distinction between the needs of the microenterprises and small and medium enterprises, but it's not clear where the breakpoint is. Have you thought much about where the breakpoint between microenterprises and SMEs is, and how we do effective targeting?

AS: I think this is a very important question. I have a paper that is trying to argue this broader point. There are big differences in what we call entrepreneurs—transformational versus subsistence entrepreneurs.[6] And I argue

10. There is a generally held belief that in developing countries, the distribution of firms is skewed to the very large and the very small, with few mid-size firms and very few rapidly growing new firms. This phenomenon is termed "the missing middle." Hsieh and Olken's paper uses data from India, Indonesia, and Mexico to argue that the apparent "missing middle" is an artifact of how firm data was organized in other work.

that the aspiration levels, competency levels, and growth trajectories that these two different groups of entrepreneurs would take, and therefore the kind of inputs they need, are very different.

You are totally right, though, that I don't think anyone has figured out a good way of doing *ex ante* screening of entrepreneurs to figure out who is who. That is something that investors struggle with all the time, but academics do as well. *Ex post* we can see that these people are different. There is some interesting work, not experimental, but using US census data that shows that in the US only about 7 percent of firms or small businesses that get set up create about 80 percent of the jobs that are created by small businesses.[7] But those that do start employing people do it from the very beginning. It's like from the beginning there are some that want to grow and hire people, but the majority of the small businesses seem to stay or want to stay at that small level.

You see the same thing when you look in developing countries. You see that the transition from small to medium entrepreneurs is really very very low. If you talk to venture capitalists and risk capital providers, they will tell you that they are looking at lots of soft factors, but I don't think we or they have a good handle on this. We don't even know how much of business outcomes are shaped by the environment or by some inherent qualities of the entrepreneurs. Those 93 percent of small businesses that don't create many jobs, is it something inherent in the entrepreneur's ambition that keeps them from hiring or is there some other constraint in their environment that is leading to lower their aspirations? If it's the context, then perhaps there is something we could do about that.

TO: This is another example of the overlap between developed and developing world entrepreneurship. Many of the small businesses started in the US seem to look a lot like market vendors in the developing world. They aren't offering a differentiated product, and they don't have growth plans.

AS: These are the people we call subsistence entrepreneurs. The difference between developed and developing economies is the infrastructure that allows the transition from small to medium to large. That isn't there in most developing countries. Maybe what that tells you is that you shouldn't be frustrated that small businesses don't grow because most small businesses may not want to or have the capability to grow. But what we need to make sure is that those entrepreneurs who have the ability and aspiration to grow get the access to resources that allows them to grow. That's where in many developing countries the channel really is broken. If you look at the largest firms in the developing and the developed world, there is a lot of turnover in the developed world. In the US, the Fortune 100 are often very young firms, relatively. If you look in India, the large firms are the Tata's, and the like, that are 100 years old. The fact that there is so little turnover is a problem in developing countries.

TO: Moving to some more specifics on entrepreneurs and SMEs. In your paper on French entrepreneurs you ask how people learn about entrepreneurial skill.[8] To me, that's a really big question in developing economies because we have so many people learning about whether they can run a microenterprise by trying it. Dean and Chris Udry have the "Hoping to Win, Expected to Lose" paper about why training doesn't seem to help very many people.[11][9] What's your thought on realistic policy for helping people learn about whether starting a microenterpirse is a good option for them? For a lot of people, self-employment is the only option. But presumably we should be aiming for differentially getting the people for whom it's a good option into self-employment. Where are we in terms of policy options?

AS: It's obviously different in a developing country than in France because these are people who had pretty generous unemployment insurance. Because they would lose the insurance income if they started a business, there was a huge barrier to becoming an entrepreneur. The change that we evaluate was a removal of that cost. So the policy change seems to be a positive. And now I've talked to people in the US about providing greater flexibility in how people can draw down their unemployment insurance because of that study, and that seems to me like a good idea too. But of course this is all conditional on having unemployment insurance.

In developing countries the people who are becoming entrepreneurs don't have these large personal costs of entry. So there I think what you would need is giving them the resources, the opportunity to learn. So, for

---

11. The paper proposes a model that people are unaware of their entrepreneurial skill and ability to run a successful business but are optimistic enough to invest in starting or expanding a business. If that is the case, then it is plausible that the short-term average returns to those investments will be negative, since many of the entrepreneurs will learn that they don't have the requisite skills and the investments do not pay off. The authors run an experiment offering capital and training to microenterprises in Ghana and find evidence for the model and review other similar experiments and find mixed support for the model.

example, easier access to finance, and in particular to very flexible financial arrangements, would be a huge benefit here. Or giving opportunities for people to develop the necessary skills. Often small-scale entrepreneurship is about services like plumbers and handymen and electricians, and those types of businesses, so giving people that type of training, either as an apprentice or in a form of an apprenticeship system, would go a long way in emerging market countries.

TO: Do you think we know how to do that? The training literature is pretty discouraging.[12]

AS: I agree the classroom training literature is discouraging. What we don't know so well, what we haven't seen carefully evaluated, say with an RCT, is an on-the-job training program or even apprenticeship-type of set-ups.[13] That could be a very different thing. People need to be able to start businesses, and they also need to be able to fail in a low-cost way. A benefit of the US system is that you can fail and it doesn't mean the end of your career or your successful economic existence.

TO: As you point out in the paper, that's conditional on a belief that while there is heterogeneity in entrepreneurial skill, it's not widely varied. The wedge, as you call it in the paper, is not large. Is that an accurate reflection of your beliefs? That across the world entrepreneurial skill is varied, but a lot of people have enough skill?

AS: I would believe that there are many people who are able to run small-scale businesses and they are not very different in their skill set. The people that are being encouraged by this employment reform that we're studying in France are not going from being unemployed to running a firm with 200

12. See the overview provided in "Hoping to Win, Expected to Lose" discussed above and in D. McKenzie and C. Woodruff (2014), "What Are We Learning from Business Training Evaluations Around the Developing World?," *World Bank Research Observer* 29 (1). There is extensive discussion of training and its effects in the interview with David McKenzie (chapter 10)—his views are not as pessimistic.
13. There are indeed very few such evaluations. One, which is discussed in general terms in the interview with David McKenzie, is a test of a vocational training program in Turkey. While short-term effects are positive, the gains dissipate within three years. See S. Hirschleifer et al., "The Impact of Vocational Training for the Unemployed: Experimental Evidence from Turkey," *Economic Journal*, forthcoming. (The paper is posted online at *Economic Journal* but still as an "Early View" before publication. http://dx.doi.org/10.1111/ecoj.12211.)

employees or more. But I would also think that's something that you don't know up front too well, and therefore getting this type of downside insurance that we observe in our paper allows you to experiment and to learn about your type. In contrast, I think at the very top of the entrepreneurial distribution, there is massive heterogeneity of skills, and it is very important. I think there is massive heterogeneity of luck too. So here I am not sure if the same policy predictions apply.

What I do think applies is that people often don't know *ex ante* whether they are good at it, and therefore they need to try and they need to experiment. The only problem is that at that the top end of the talent distribution, it might be more expensive to experiment, since the firms are larger.

TO: One of the other implications of the broader work that Nick Bloom[14] has done is that in the developing countries the capability of firms is much more variable than it is in developed countries. Given that idea, is it almost hopeless to try get enough data to overcome the noisiness of capability to find conclusions that we can rely on?

AS: I wouldn't be so pessimistic. I would say that one thing that seems to be the case in what Bloom is finding is that it looks like the type of practices that firms in developing countries adopt are farther away from the frontier—the frontier here defined as the US, UK, Germany, and other advanced economies. There's still a lot we need to understand around that research. If I'm in India and still operating this really old-fashioned machinery, maybe doing all this fancy operational improvement—just-in-time management, and the like—might not even be possible and might not be something that is viable. So, yes, they are away from the frontier, but it may not be that they are adopting the objectively wrong type of management practices but that they are adopting the best practices given their constraints. When this market develops, maybe they will start adjusting their management practices as well. The second big question, of course, is what is the right way to teach improved management practices?

For instance, our work and that of Nick and co-authors both rely on a very specific way of teaching management. Surely that's not the only way to

14. Bloom co-leads the World Management Survey, which is a study of management practices worldwide that has been running since 2004. They find that there is a set of management practices that has a positive effect on firm's profitability and survival, and that there are large differences between the average set of good management practices in use between developed and developing countries. See: worldmanagementsurvey.org.

transmit that information. If you look at developed countries, a lot of learning comes from people moving from firm to firm and diffusing the knowledge that way. So I feel understanding better how those types of practices can spread through an economy is something very important that we need to understand.

TO: Given all the firms that you've worked with on testing products, but also more broadly, have you seen that randomized trials are more persuasive to firms?

AS: I've been finding that it's a bit of a double-edged sword for firms. I think the top managers who value statistics and the scientific method, they usually are more persuaded by randomized trials than people who either don't know much about science or haven't been exposed to RCTs. That's one dimension. What very often happens, though, is even when people are very convinced about the method, is they say, "why don't you do this with a different bank and then come back and show the results to me?" They understand that an RCT is very operationally intensive. I think that's still true, though it has become a bit easier over time to convince people. Because of all the work being done with different nonprofits and different academics, there is more knowledge out there that this is the gold standard, you might say.

TO: In terms of the behavior of firms, in the business literature there's a lot written about cultures of innovation.[15] Some firms have an incremental approach to change, lots of little tweaks, and some firms focus on big changes, brand new products, reinvention, and the like. Have you seen any patterns in terms of the culture of firms that are willing to engage in RCTs as a result of their approach to innovation?

AS: That's a very good question. To tell you the truth, it's difficult to say with certainty, given that I haven't talked to thousands of firms but maybe hundreds of firms. I think what's true is that usually the slightly better firms, in particular the firms that are better organized and operationally stronger, are the ones you can work with and are also more confident that they can work with an academic like me who wants to do an RCT. Sometimes you can do an RCT for something that's relatively incremental and that's something you can convince firms more easily to do. So, in that

15. A good example is George Day's book *Innovation Prowess* (2013), but a search for "innovation culture" will yield dozens of recent articles in business journals and magazines.

sense, the door is not immediately closed when you approach an organization that engages in somewhat small-step changes. Even with those small steps, if you want to make sure you're taking those steps, rather than haphazardly, in a more structured way then you also learn more because you have randomized. So I haven't found so much that whether firms like radical change versus incremental change matters but that the organizational capability and whether management has the bandwidth to engage in anything like an RCT is what matters.

Actually now that you say that, Sendhil Mullainathan has a paper that looks a little at the selection bias in the type of firms that engage in RCTs.[16][10]

TO: You're thinking of the OPower paper with Hunt? They look at the characteristics of MFIs that participate in RCTs versus the MIX data. Jonathan Morduch has done some work on the characteristics of the universe of MFIs versus who is in the MIX.[11] So there are two steps, there are the organizations that are willing to submit data to MIX and then among those, the ones willing to participate in an experiment. So it really illustrates that the firms in RCTs are likely systematically different.

AS: But that doesn't invalidate the experiment at all. It is an important thing to keep in mind when thinking about how the results might apply to a broader set of organizations, though.

TO: What is your theory of change? I don't presume you run these studies that can be quite frustrating and difficult just because you're curious. You have a goal of making the world a better place. How do you think about your research ultimately translating to that goal?

AS: I'm also curious hopefully! The way I think about this as a scientist is that change should come from better understanding of the underlying

16. Hunt Allcott and Sendhil Mullainathan review data from OPower, a firm that provides software to utility industry. OPower ran tests of a simple nudge on energy bills to encourage energy efficiency in 14 different markets in the US. The differences in effect size were economically and statistically significant. They also look at microfinance institutions that participate in randomized evaluations and find they are observably different from the average firm in the Microfinance Information Exchange (MIX), which aggregates operational information from MFIs around the world. (The current version of the paper drops the section on MIX data and Sendhil Mullainathan is no longer a co-author. The original version of the paper is still available online.)

concepts. And therefore it is very important to me that we run experiments and studies in a rigorous fashion and produce robust evidence. I wouldn't want to go around just offering my opinion. Once I've convinced myself that I've done or seen enough serious research to have a firm prior, it is important to make organizations aware of it. I used to think that good insights will spread by themselves. Sometimes that does happen. The rule of thumb training results have been widely cited, so lots of people that want to adopt a different training methodology have contacted us. But that is the exception. Usually I think that you have to put effort in to disseminate a result. That's part of why I've set up two organizations to help bring about this change. For the work on small business and entrepreneurship in emerging markets, I set up the SME Initiative[17] to bring together firms, banks, researchers, and others working in this area to facilitate collaboration among those different parties and help the spread of knowledge among them. On the domestic side, together with Sendhil and Eldar, I started Ideas42.[18] It is a nonprofit that aims to use insights from behavioral economics and psychology to help people make better decisions around retail financial choices, health care choices, and overall economic stability and mobility.

TO: What does it take to change your priors? Is there an example of something that you've really changed your mind on? How many studies would you have to see to decide that one of your own experiments was the outlier?

AS: First of all, I have changed my priors quite a bit. You should keep in mind that I studied at the University of Chicago, and I was in a context where one would obviously put more weight on rational behavior models. And I did initially find it very surprising to see the work on how much of a difference small channel factors can make such as what default is set or how a particular choice is framed. Those types of things have tremendous impact on how people behave. That to me is something where I really did change

---

17. The SME Initiative is a program at Innovations for Poverty Action that helps design and fund research on the impact of SME programs and to share knowledge from that work. See: http://www.poverty-action.org/sme.
18. Ideas42 (www.ideas42.org) was co-founded by Antoinette Schoar, Sendhil Mullainathan, Eldar Shafir, Simeon Djankov, Jerry Kling, and Michael Kremer in 2008. It has conducted projects on boosting savings, access to and use of reproductive health services, and increasing access to financial aid for higher education, as well as training NGOs on how to apply behavioral science findings to program design.

my prior. I used to believe that where it really mattered, people wouldn't make behavioral mistakes, but I realize that this is not true. People make big mistakes even in things like which mortgage they choose or the size of the house they can afford. That doesn't mean that I believe that people can't be trusted at all to make their own decisions. I certainly don't know that someone else could make a better decision for them. There's a lot we need to learn about what would it take to help people make better decision or to undo some of those channel factors.

What helps me change or confirm my prior? I do want to see work that I trust methodologically, but I also feel it is quite important to see that a particular idea holds across a large spectrum of replications and even in secondary data, and not just one experiment. To me, that gets back to the discussion we had at the beginning that external validity is key. For example, to come back to the idea of defaults, if we just saw that we could make people behave differently based on defaults in the lab, I would say OK but who cares? But the work of Dick Thaler,[12] Bridgette Madrian, and David Laibson[13] has shown that this effect holds across a large set of applications and can make a huge difference in the savings and 401(k) investments decisions of thousands of people. I find that very convincing.

17 Rachel Glennerster

Rachel is the Executive Director of the Jameel Poverty Action Lab at MIT. She helped found Deworm the World, a nonprofit which runs mass deworming programs in several countries. She is the co-author of *Running Randomized Evaluations: A Practical Guide* and, with Michael Kremer, of *Strong Medicine: Creating Incentives for Pharmaceutical Research on Neglected Diseases.*

TO: What are the factors that drive an organization toward more rigorous evaluation?

RG: It's a complicated question. The expansion in the use of rigorous evidence isn't just about more organizations doing them. It's also about more organizations using the results, consuming the results, consuming them more effectively and understanding the quality of different kinds of evidence. It's about funders providing funding more effectively, choosing the right projects to fund.

What motivates organizations who are working on different parts of this evidence chain isn't the same. One motivating factor is there's a lot better understanding of what kind of evidence is right for what kind of question. There is a greater understanding of what descriptive evidence is useful for, even if it is not going to tell me about causal impact, and what qualitative or administrative evidence is useful for. That understanding has come from a lot of discussion and international attention to rigorous impact evaluations in recent years. It's really been a global phenomenon. I go across the world and see organizations that have heard about randomized trials and want to do them and want to learn from those done by others.

Some of this interest is driven by donors. Some organizations feel there is pressure from donors to prove their impact. Sometimes it's coming from an internal recognition that they don't fully understand their own impact. It's part of a wider agenda on results in development and people asking, "are we really achieving what we set out to achieve in reducing poverty?" The wider agenda isn't just about impact but also about measuring progress and inputs and outputs more effectively. The impact story is only part of that.

If you are interested in what an organization needs to know before it can do its own rigorous evaluations it's important to recognize there are different kinds of training that need to be delivered to different kinds of people. Capacity building in developing countries is very important. I think a lot of the focus has been on, "can we get an organization to run an RCT?" But there are an awful lot of other things we need organizations to be doing better like collecting better descriptive data. So we need to view training and capacity building as a spectrum from thinking about questions clearly to collecting data better. Running an RCT is only part of that.

TO: Your framing is probably a better set of questions than I had formulated in advance, so I want to drill into what you were saying about being a better consumer of randomized evaluations. What does that mean and how does an organization get to be a better consumer of somebody's else's work?

RG: It's important to learn the broader lessons from a group of studies and not just ask, "can I replicate this one study in a new context?" When J-PAL was very young, a group of us went and talked to DfID about a range of studies that we'd done on education. We talked to a packed room full of people who worked on education and we talked about individual studies, and someone got up and said "It's all very well to hear about this study and that study, but what we want to know as an organization is if we have a pound to spend, where are we going to get the biggest bang for our buck?" And that made us think: "we're economists! We should have framed it like that to start with!" That's part of the motivation of these organizations, how can I spend my limited money most effectively? But I think what has also become evident over time is not just what we learn about this program or that program but that we're learning how education works, how you change health behavior. So we're gaining a more analytical/theoretical level of understanding and that information feeds into the design of new programs.

Let me just give you an example: not charging for preventative health products because of the behavioral biases, which means that people underinvest in preventative health. That's a general lesson that can be applied to all sorts of programs.[1]

I think pressure from the funders, donors, voters, politicians—depending on what type of organization, the pressure comes from different places—asking questions about why they weren't getting out of programs what they expected based on what they put in has been a big part of this drive. The next step, though, is not just responding to that pressure but thinking carefully through, "what do we know from these different kinds of evidence? What can we learn from different kinds of evidence to get to a greater level of effectiveness?"

TO: You talked there about "what do we put in?" There's some criticism of RCTs that they don't generally say much about what has been put in. Paul Niehaus of Give Directly makes the point that most impact evaluations have a single sentence about inputs. What do randomized evaluations tell us about what goes in?

RG: At J-PAL we're trying to put a lot of emphasis on getting our affiliates to document what goes in. We mean not just the cost of everything that goes in but also the details of the actual program so that someone can actually replicate the program if they wanted to. I think that's one of the benefits of having an organization that supports affiliated professors because it can help them do that. It's not really in the interests of many academics to put in the costs and to detail exactly what the intervention is at the level which someone who wanted to replicate it would need. And yet, if we're to learn from these evaluations, we do need that information. So now when J-PAL provides funding for a study, we require that you fill out a costing form for all the different elements of a project, and we do a lot of comparative cost-effectiveness analyses using those data. I think it's something that's extremely valued by the policy partners that we work with but would not necessarily make a big part of an academic study. But I think it's been quite influential in getting people to pay attention to different projects.

Knowing about costs is interesting even to academics because most academics are interested in testing something that is potentially scalable and not so interested in incredibly expensive interventions that no one

---

1. See interview with Michael Kremer (chapter 1) for more discussion of this point as generalizable lesson. See interview with Pascaline Dupas (chapter 14) for more discussion of some of the studies underlying this finding.

would implement outside of an experiment. And yet they don't have the incentives to document exactly what the costs are. So we try to help them with that, both when we fund the evaluation but also when our regional offices are running the evaluation on the ground, we make our staff collect the cost data.

TO: How much of what we are learning from evaluations now do you feel is about a program or specifically the skill of the people running the program and how much is about how human beings behave? In other words, how much is context and content versus universal human behavior? Where do you think the frontiers are in untangling that?

RG: I think there's a lot we're learning about how human beings behave, and I think that is one of *the* most valuable things that is coming out of the RCT literature, even if there is a set of original RCTs that are just testing a particular program. When you then do a literature review and look at all of those programs together, what often emerges, particularly if you approach this as a theoretically trained economist, is commonalities. What you see is some theoretical underpinnings of why some programs are working and some aren't. You see things about how humans are behaving in certain situations and that are more likely to generalize than any particular program. That's why I think it's so valuable. Now some RCTs are designed from the beginning to test an underlying theoretical or behavioral idea and some are designed to test a particular project, but both of them end up telling us about general behavior if you look at a whole set together.

That's not the only thing that RCTs are useful for. They can test specific programs and that's very helpful, and you can scale up those specific programs. But increasingly, because we have a wide set of projects, we are able to do more to pull out these general lessons. So, if you think about the example of teaching at the right level,[2] it's a policy idea that came out of a whole series of projects in education adjusting teaching to the level of a child in very different ways—with remedial education, with tutors or with computer learning, with splitting the classroom by ability—and yet they all home in on a problem in the current system that the teaching is above the level of the child. This finding is also supported by

2. See interview with Banerjee and Duflo (chapter 2) for more discussion of the issue of teaching to the level of the child rather than following a colonial-era curriculum.

descriptive statistical evidence about how children perform compared to the curricula.

These descriptive data give you a great diagnosis of the problem and now we've tested different ways to solve it. Then when you're thinking about the right context to scale up, you can think about, "does this context have that underlying problem? Is the teaching not at the average level of a child in the community?" So I think that's how we're learning a lot more useful things by drawing these common lessons.

TO: That's an example of a useful policy lesson, but it doesn't really rise to the level of an economic theory does it? That being said, I suppose it's not as if our theories of micro-behavior are well-defined and founded. So I suppose you could say that anything that teaches us about how people behave can ultimately feed better theory.

RG: A lot of the behavioral theory has been motivated by the results of randomized trials in developing countries, and then researchers have gone back and tested that theory with more randomized trials. You're right there is a difference between general lessons and theory. A good example is the work that's been done on preventative healthcare, loss aversion,[3] like Vivian Hoffman's work on bed nets,[4][1] work on the sunk cost fallacy,[5] the commitment savings work,[6] all of those are very good tests of specific behavioral biases. There are a whole range of studies that have been much more theory based. And as I said, there are other ones that are of specific programs but end up giving us either general lessons or more theory ideas.

3. A general phenomenon that people avoid losses more than they seek gains.
4. Hoffman's work on bed nets is focused on how pricing affects use, and in particular, whether bed nets received for free are sold (she finds that they are not) and whether free bed nets are used by different household members than purchased bed nets (she finds that children are more likely to be using free bed nets relative to the use of purchased bed nets, which skews toward adults).
5. A common phenomenon where people justify additional investment based on investments already made, not the expected return of the additional investment.
6. Commitment savings are accounts which require the account holder to make a commitment that limits their access to the funds. These commitments can be time based (the funds cannot be withdrawn for 3 or 6 months) or amount based (the funds cannot be withdrawn until a minimum threshold is reached). There are extended discussions of commitment savings in the interviews with Dean Karlan (chapter 6), Xavi Gine (chapter 8), and Dean Yang (chapter 12).

TO: One of the topics that has come up in many of the conversations I've had is the skills related to running randomized evaluations. [7] Do you think there is a unique skill set that is more attitudinal, perhaps in-born, or are these just learned skills that are different than what economics has traditionally taught PhD students?

RG: You certainly need to be willing to get your hands dirty, which is attitudinal. You have to be willing to get stuck in to the details of making a program work in a developing country, which is very different from a lot of work that economists do. You learn a huge amount about why developing countries are dysfunctional when you try to run something at a very big scale in one of them. You learn a lot about what the barriers are to making things run effectively, which leads on to other research ideas. There is an attitudinal part. You have to be willing to spend a lot of time working through very practical details and spend a lot of time on the ground. People in development have run big surveys in developing countries before and those people have had to combat a lot of the same issues, but an RCT goes a step further because you have to work with an organization to think through the design of a program. So there's even more work on practical issues.

Now those are skills that can be learned, but you have to come in with the right attitude. You have to be willing to spend a lot of time on the details. You have to have the attitude that you want to work with implementing partners. You have to be willing to do a lot of give and take, to listen to what the implementers want and have a willingness to compromise. But once you have that attitude, you can learn the skills about the different practical ways to respond to concerns, or to introduce elements of randomization. Of course, the heart of it all is still collecting very good data in very difficult situations. It's true that development economists have always done that, but I think we have even more people doing that now than we used to because of randomized evaluations.

It's pretty interesting how even people who should know how much work running a randomized evaluation is, when they do it themselves, universally say "boy, I had no idea it was this much work." There's certainly a lot of detailed practical learning and skills that people have to pick up to do this.

7. See discussions with Dean Yang (chapter 12), Antoinette Schoar (chapter 16), and Tyler Cowen (chapter 19) in particular.

TO: One way to look at your book,[2] and the training programs that J-PAL runs, is that it is equipping more people to move the economists out of the process. For an organization that wants to do a more rigorous evaluation, there is some pretty good information out there on how to do a randomized evaluation without bringing in a highly trained economist from a top 10 institution. Do you see a time where randomized evaluations are part of a pretty standard management toolkit, and if you're not trying to build new theories, there isn't really a need for economists anymore?

RG: The book is partly for people who weren't necessarily doing an economics PhD, but it is also for people doing PhDs who had the theory but not the practical experience. Part of the reason for writing the book is that there are a lot of people who want to do randomized evaluations but may not have a supervisor who has done them and don't know the practicalities. They don't know the details of how to collect good data in the field, or how to work with a partner, or in particular, how to think about power calculations. They know the equations, but they don't know how to think about the practical trade-offs. Being able to derive the power equation gets you very little of the way toward doing a good power calculation.

But it's also true that an increasing number of people, who may not be academic economists—or academic political scientists or other social scientists—are doing randomized evaluations. They may well be economists, political scientists, or have some other social science training, but they aren't academics. You see an increasing number of evaluations happening in organizations like the World Bank and DfID, though often run by economists within those organizations. So I don't want to say that I see a world where economists aren't involved. They may not be academics. I see a time when there are organizations doing randomized trials that are not academic organizations. Organizations like BRAC are already running randomized evaluations. For the most part though, NGOs want someone else to come in and help them, governments want someone to come in help them, not US or UK governments, or the like, which have lots of economists, of course. But those organizations that want to bring in someone from outside need to be good consumers, good partners in this process, because you get a lot more out of working with someone on an evaluation if you understand the process.

The old style of evaluation in the development world focused on independent evaluation. Because there wasn't independence of methodology, there was a big focus on the independence of who came in to do the evaluation. So what you had was the organization that was being evaluated and some person who didn't know anything about the organization would come in and do an evaluation. I think what's really changed with randomized trials is that because there is independence of the methodology—the result is what the result is—you can have these partnerships in evaluation. You may still often have an outsider who comes in, but the organization is integrally part of designing the evaluation without as much worry about bias in the evaluation because of that.

So in my work with Save the Children, one of the PIs on that project is someone with Save the Children who was intimately involved at every stage of designing the project: what arms we did, what the outcome variables were, writing up the results. So, yes, there are some organizations like the World Bank and BRAC and the very best NGOs that will be doing randomized evaluations on their own. There are also a lot of consulting organizations that are doing randomized evaluations, although they are mainly employing PhD economists and political scientists to do the work. So there will always be social scientists involved. But what you will also see is NGOs, governments, even private companies being much more intimately involved in the process of evaluation.

TO: Since doing randomized evaluations is difficult and requires experience in many cases, there is an argument that we need specialists who are going to be able to run trials effectively and reliably. But you also often hear that RCTs are "just one of the tools in the toolkit." That seems to argue for generalists. Where do you land on the benefits of specialization versus people being able to use the right methodology for a particular question or context?

RG: I don't see those as contradictory ideas at all, actually. You don't have to be able to use every tool in the toolkit as an individual. An organization may want to draw on all the tools. You'll probably still want to have people who are specialists in qualitative research, specialists in impact evaluations, and other people who are very good at doing process monitoring. I would say there's plenty of room to have people who do both randomized and other impact evaluations. I would make the distinction more between process monitoring, qualitative research, impact evaluations, and, I guess, other big descriptive pieces. Big longitudinal studies, like the Young Lives project,[8] can be very helpful, and there's a lot of expertise that goes into

8. The Young Lives project is a 15-year study of 12,000 children living below the poverty line in Ethiopia, India, Peru, and Vietnam. See www.younglives.org.uk.

doing those. So people may need to specialize in those areas, but organizations should be able to draw on different areas to answer the relevant questions.

TO: To pin you down on that, for the young, up-and-coming evaluator/ economist/political scientist/social scientist, which direction would you advise that person to go? To have experience with multiple methodologies or to have deep specialization in one of them?

RG: I think focusing on impact matters. You wouldn't want to try to do all of the categories. You could *try* to be very good at qualitative and long-term panels and process monitoring and impact evaluation, but I think that's too broad an area for one individual. I think it's fine to focus on causal impact but not only do randomized evaluations. I've done a regression discontinuity project. I have actually done big national panels too, though that was maybe a mistake of spreading myself too thinly. But I see a lot of crossover between different forms of causal identification. So I think focusing, yes, but I don't think you just have to focus on randomized evaluations. I don't think that makes sense.

TO: Returning to your example of lessons learned in education. What's the most important thing to be doing next? Is it documenting the differences from place to place to enable specific policies or is it to move on to the next big breakthrough in education beyond curriculum, say, to how do we help children learn?

RG: I think the next stage is to focus on quality. We don't know anything like as much as we would like to about how to improve the quality of education. Would a mapping of where people are learning more or less, would that kind of descriptive mapping be useful in generating hypotheses? Yes. That would be very useful. That's exactly the kind of thing descriptive work is useful at doing. It doesn't tell you causal effect, but it does generate important hypotheses that enable you to focus in on what might be driving the patterns you see. The problem with randomized evaluations is that they can only test very specific hypotheses. You can't take all the hypotheses in the world and test them one-by-one. You want to home in on the most likely ones using other methodologies. That's where I think there is a great complementarity with other methodologies. Mapping where we see descriptively there is lots of improvement and then coming up with some hypotheses based on that and testing those is a very good path forward. We can also generate hypotheses from observations in specific areas. We can generate hypotheses from theory. We can see what the world is excited about and pouring money into. But I agree that quality is a big frontier.

I just got off a call with people talking about secondary education. There has now been more work on quality in primary school but very little work on secondary. We've made a lot of progress in getting people into primary school, and as a result there are a lot more people going to secondary school. Secondary school is very expensive. If secondary education is not delivering what we want, there's a real challenge ahead of us to learn more about what works at the secondary level.

Jonathan is an Associate Professor of Economics at the University of California, Santa Cruz. Jon's interest in field experiments as a method for answering difficult real world questions was kindled as an undergraduate at MIT taking a class taught by Esther Duflo. After moving on to Princeton for his PhD work, he spent time as a research assistant in Kenya. Seeing how shocks—health, political violence, income, weather—affected families led him to focus his research on risk and risk management in poor households.

That focus has led him to places quite far from the typical economics field research—one of his studies examines how sex workers in Kenya dealt with a dramatic fall in their incomes during the political violence that erupted after the 2007 presidential elections. He has also collaborated extensively with Pascaline Dupas on studies of the impact of savings and interventions to help households save. In other research he's examined the returns to investment in fertilizer and intra-household income transfers.

TO: Why did you get into field experiments? How do you decide what you're going to be looking at? How do you decide what mechanisms or methods you're using to look at those questions?

JR: Well the way I got into field experiments is really because I took a class taught by Esther way back when she was just starting as an assistant professor. It was just amazing to me how simple and transparent the methods were—why not just randomize and eliminate concerns about omitted variables? The field was less developed at that time than it is now and was a bit more about straight impact evaluations rather than more elaborate experiments to test different theories of behavior, but it just seemed so obvious that this was a better way to do it. To see that you could cleanly identify causality in an experiment was exciting.

And I actually think some of those early experiments are hugely important, like "Do textbooks work in Western Kenya?"[1][1] It's nice to test bigger theories, but also just answering a simple and important question like that seemed so clean and nice.

Field experiments seemed to me to be the best way to answer basic questions. And the quality of evidence is extremely high. Not all of my work is with field experiments, like the sex worker study[2] and the post-election work.[2][3] But I think that the whole idea about being very serious about trying to identify causal effects is quite important.

Lab experiments, on the other hand, I think can be hugely useful for guiding field experiments, helping to form theories that you can test in the field.

But the questions that I'm most interested in answering, like, "why don't people save?"—seems fundamentally an impossible question to answer without doing something in the field.

TO: A lot of your research has been on that savings question. Based on what you have been doing for the last six years or so, what is your answer to the question of "why don't the poor save?"

JR: Pascaline and I have spent quite some time looking at this issue. We were both graduate students when we decided to do the first study where we gave out savings accounts to market vendors and bicycle taxi drivers.[4] We didn't have a very clear idea what exactly we'd find at that point. We had both lived in Kenya for a while, working on other projects as research assistants. Our perspective at that point was that it seemed like risk was a big issue for people, and we thought that providing savings accounts might allow people to save up to deal with that risk. We also thought that having a safe place to keep money might make it easier to save up than keeping money at home.

So the first project was just asking the question, "What is the effect of giving people savings accounts?" That project wasn't really so much about

1. This is one of the first field experiments run by Michael Kremer, discussed in his interview (chapter 1). In summary, a randomized group of schools were given new textbooks and other teaching aids. The evaluation found no impact on student learning.
2. These are studies examining the choices of sex workers and the impact on livelihoods of sex workers, retail shop owners, and small-scale artisans and vendors of post-election violence in Kenya in 2007. Data was gathered through interviews and surveys.

why people can't save as trying to see if savings accounts helped in the first place.

When we looked at the data to answer the question, we saw very big effects for female market vendors. As we looked at the data, we started thinking more about where the money is coming from, where it's going, and of course, why the account was better than saving on their own. The bank account that we gave out actually wasn't great—it offered no interest and had withdrawal fees. Inflation was also an issue for any cash savings. The question then became, "why would anyone ever use an account like this?" Based on that, we tried to design a study to get at that.

When you think about explanations for why people do or don't save, there are a number of possibilities. One that economists often talk about is behavioral issues. It's the same explanation for why people don't save enough for a 401(k) here in the US. Maybe people want to save and want to be good. But then, when the time comes to actually take money out of their pockets and put it into savings, people don't follow through on their plans and they end up spending more than they had planned. A second one that comes up a lot is that it's difficult to protect money from either a spouse or from the extended family.

In another study with Pascaline, we provided people with a number of different types of savings products, which differed in the characteristics they offered. One group got a simple lockbox and a key. Another got the same box but not the key—they had to call the program officers to get it opened. A third could set up a health savings account with their ROSCA [Rotating Savings and Credit Association]. And a fourth was encouraged to set up a side-ROSCA to save up for a health product. We looked at which groups saved the most, as well as who benefited and who didn't to see what types of characteristics mattered and which didn't.[5]

In the end, I think both of the common explanations have something to them. In a follow-up survey, we just asked people whether they would feel obligated to give money were a relative or a neighbor to come up and ask for money if they just had the money in cash at home. Most people said yes.

But when these people had access to a simple lockbox, and even though they have cash in the box, and the key to the box and can just open it, they feel much better about saying no. That's one big aspect of being able to save.

But in the same way, once the money is in the box, people also report being less likely to open the box up to spend on themselves. So there's evidence for both of those explanations. In each case it really seems that there's a mental accounting aspect going on—that once people put the money in the box, they have mentally put it toward savings and are less likely to spend it on something else.

TO: You looked at savings mechanisms that allow a saver to protect cash from others in the household or relatives. That study reminds me of Dean Yang and other's Malawi commitment savings project.[3][6] That work also suggests a key channel is protecting assets not just within the household but also from the broader social network. Then there is the "Pretending to be Poor"[4] work in Cameroon that also points in the same direction.[7]

Do you think that the ability, or lack thereof, to protect assets from the community is a significant barrier to building assets?

JR: That one is tricky. I'm sure this is an issue, and those papers make a compelling case for it. But then, on the other hand, we have done some work estimating returns to capital for very small retailers.[8] We found that the returns to increasing inventory a little bit are extremely high. So why don't people do that?

One argument people sometimes make for that is that shopkeepers don't want to have a really big shop because then people are going to come and ask you for money. I think that is potentially possible. But, when you ask people why they don't hold bigger inventories, they don't really say that it's about other people asking for money.

It's one of those situations where protecting money from a social network is clearly an issue, but how much it matters for actual decision making probably depends on the context. It seems plausible. We have done some detailed, structured interviews and protecting assets from others just doesn't really come up that much as being the ultimate constraint. It is there, for sure. I don't think the research really is definitive on that issue.

3. Farmers were randomly offered regular savings, commitment savings accounts, or no account. Farmers with commitment accounts were able to save more and invest more in the next agricultural season. The experiment is discussed in detail in the interviews with Giné (chapter 8) and Yang (chapter 12).
4. Based on interviews with borrowers at a credit cooperative who had sufficient savings to cover the entire loan amount, researchers found that borrowers reported borrowing to signal to relatives that they were too poor to provide resources to them.

Are you familiar with Suresh de Mel, David McKenzie, and Chris Woodruff's work with Sri Lankan firms?[5][9] In that study they give people cash grants and most recipients keep them in the business. David and Chris, along with Simon Quinn and Marcel Fafchamps, did another study in Ghana and found the same—that many people put the grants into the business.[10] It's not as if the average shop owners were optimally setting their inventories lower because they were worried about an implicit tax. Instead, they do put the money in the business and that makes it visible in some way. So, even if they are worried about an implicit tax, it isn't enough to discourage them from growing their business.

But there's another issue, which is the reverse of what we've been talking about. Do interventions actually allow people to exit the social network? As an example, in our most recent work we've been doing interventions at the ROSCA level. We essentially provide people with an outside option to be able to save—and over time people are less likely to participate in the ROSCA, and more likely to just save on their own in the box.

That's not saying that the entire social network has broken down or anything, but we do see effects. This is an important question but to look at those issues really definitively would require a different research program, which I think some people are trying to do. Basically, it's taking different social networks and giving a randomly varying number of them a savings account and seeing what happens to everybody else.

That's one of a whole host of issues that we are trying to look at in the future. But more work is needed to really say that people don't make investments because of having to either make loans to others in the community or hide their assets from others in the community.

TO: There is a critique about how the process of development advocated by the Washington Consensus, neoliberal economics, or however you want to describe it, is destroying the social structures of the poor.

Do you think about that? If it is really true that there is this implicit tax in these communities, part of that implicit tax is to sustain the community through shocks. As you introduce commitment savings devices and more people are able to protect their assets, do those existing structures start to break down? You do have some people benefit from protecting assets, but obviously not everyone is going to benefit if those implicit social insurance schemes start to crack.

5. Both the studies mentioned here are discussed in detail in the interview with David McKenzie (chapter 10).

JR: It's a fair point. I think the reason why we are interested in doing these types of projects is that it is a fact that people are quite vulnerable to risk generally. If you spend any time living in these communities, you see that when anything negative happens, people are in a lot of trouble. It seems pretty clear to me that these informal insurance networks are not fully insuring people from the negative shocks that they may face.

The effect on the rest of the network is not something that has been documented but people are working on it. The evidence isn't there yet as to what exactly happens to the rest of the insurance network when you introduce more formal insurance products like commitment savings or rainfall insurance.

But I think there is good reason to at least experiment with ways of managing risk because it's obvious that what is currently in place is not taking care of the risks that people face. It would be nice to see what the first-order impacts are of these interventions before abandoning the whole project because of some possibility that they will lead to the breakdown of society.

TO: I'll use that point to pivot to the happiness question. There is a lot of emphasis on economic outcomes in the research but relatively less attention on happiness outcomes. Charles Kenny makes the argument that we're just paying attention to the wrong things, that people are much happier than they ever have been. But that doesn't show up in economic growth or income measures necessarily.[11]

Do you think about how you measure people's preferences or happiness at the same level of income? How do you think that factors into what should be measured, what should be experimented on, and what we consider a success and failure?

JR: I think a lot of people are trying to measure things like happiness. To take one example I know, Florencio Devoto and co-authors did a project in Morocco[6] where they were providing water connections.[12] That study didn't find much impact on health, but it did find an effect on time usage and happiness. We do think very seriously about these things.

Our work is always guided by qualitative work and piloting, and so forth. I think there's a difficulty in how exactly you measure happiness writ large,

---

6. This is an experiment providing randomized subsidies for houses to connect to the municipal water system. The specifics are discussed in the interview with Pascaline Dupas (chapter 14).

but there are some things that are very specific to a particular study, more than just income alone. For example, in the lockbox and the safebox study, we ask people what their health goal was and one of the outcomes we measured is whether they got to that goal. That's an economic outcome, but it's also a question that is really specific to the project and is informed by what is measurable.

In that project the goal is something that people report on their own. I'm not coming in and telling them what they should be doing. It's not completely getting at everything that goes into people's preferences, but we put a lot of effort into trying to measure these things.

TO: In the original savings study, one of the more interesting findings was the difference between the returns for women and for men. As I understand it, the study wasn't really designed to examine gender differences. Where are you in your thinking about why the impact on men and women was so different?

JR: Well, in that study, exactly as you said, the issue is that we have a very big occupational difference between men and women in the sample. The women were almost all market vendors; most of the men were bicycle taxi drivers. And then in the follow-up work with lockboxes we actually find effects on the entire sample. But because we were working with ROSCAs, there are limitations too. A lot of people in Kenya are in ROSCAs, but not everybody, so it's not a completely representative sample. In that study we do find effects for men too. So really there's not a whole lot we can say at this point about gender differences. I wish we had more evidence about it.

TO: Did you find the gender difference surprising? What were your priors, going into this? When the differences were popping up, did you say, "Wow, I never expected that?" Or "OK, that makes some sense."

JR: Our prior was just that we had no idea whether the accounts would help. We were skeptical that people with the savings option would use it because the interest rate was negative. But it was just evident in the data that there was impact. I think that was what was surprising. The gender difference, I don't think we were overly surprised by that just because it's two totally separate, very different populations. Also the sample size is too small to really make strong gender conclusions.

We have a very small number of men who are also vendors, but it's not enough to really test gender differences statistically. The problem is that there are two explanations for any possible difference: one explanation is that men don't like to save, but the other is that they already have better savings opportunities and so don't need these accounts. Those are completely opposite explanations.

TO: Some of the apparent explanation from David McKenzie's findings in Sri Lanka is the returns to capital for the men's typical businesses were different from the women's typical businesses. That explanation makes some sense. In the Kenya study, similarly if the men are primarily bicycle taxi drivers, though there's an obvious question about how, at least until he gets ready to buy another bicycle or hire someone, marginally more savings would do him any good.

JR: That's fair enough. There are, however, some investments that bike taxi drivers could make. For instance, some people rent their bike where they could buy it. But you're right that definitely the production function is very different.

TO: You've also been looking at the gender differences in your intra-household transfers work.[13] I'm not quite sure I understood that part of the paper. At one point you suggest the men spend more on themselves, but in other places you seem to indicate the women also behave similarly. I'm not quite sure how those two findings were lining up.

JR: The experiment was one where people were given cash payments, essentially, with some probability. Over a few weeks we gave out these cash payments and then went back to check whether people spent the money that they were given or whether they shared it with each other.

Essentially, it was trying to compare the response to consumption when you get the positive shock versus when your spouse does. What came out of that was that men, when they got the money, were more likely to spend it on private consumption. Then looking at week-to-week labor fluctuations just from the income they get from their normal job, you observe actually that both of them seem to be spending a bit more on private consumption in weeks when they had higher income.

TO: The difference was whether it was an external shock versus a naturally occurring shock?

JR: Empirically, yes, that was what we found. It could be that people behave differently with respect to different shocks, or it could be that the experimental part of the study didn't have enough statistical power to pick up the effects for women.

TO: Why do intra-household transfers matter so much? What's the implication of all that work?

JR: It's related to how people cope with risk. A lot of evidence suggests
that informal insurance isn't fully insuring people against the risks they
are facing. The reason I wanted to look at this was to see how insurance
might be working, or not working, within the household. You can imagine
one of the reasons why it's difficult to have truly functioning informal
insurance schemes in which friends and neighbors help each other out is
because it's hard to monitor what other people in the network are doing.
It's also hard to know whether people in a broad network are good risks or
bad risks.

Within the household these types of information problems should be
much less of an issue. But even within households, insurance doesn't seem
to be complete. This was true in my work and in a number of other
studies.[14]

TO: This study seems to be pretty different from what happens normally.
These families are presumably not often subject to positive income shocks.
In this case, though, there was a 50 percent chance of getting an income
boost. How much do you think that tells us about what happens when
negative shocks happen, when the insurance piece of it really comes in?

JR: That's a good point. That's part of the reason why looking at fluctuations in labor income is important, even though it's not experimental. Of
course, the ideal thing would have been to identify some other real world
shock like rain and examine how that compares to the experiment. Nevertheless, that both the real world labor fluctuations and the experimental
shocks weren't fully shared suggest that the results were not really specific
to the way the shocks were constructed.

TO: Does the political violence work tell you anything about the intra-
household transfers or is it just about inter-household transfers?

JR: It doesn't tell us much. Basically that's a situation in which insurance
can't really work because everybody was affected at the same time. We
collected data on how people coped with the crisis, but for the most part
people couldn't cope very well. There was no one to ask for help because
everyone was affected, and people didn't have enough money saved up to
deal with it on their own.

TO: Did you see people rebalancing consumption in any significant way
against that, some sense that it was such a large and extended shock that

there would be some intra-household bargaining about, "here's some other things we're going to prioritize and we are going to shift resources around between what we are consuming."

JR: We don't have the data to test that. But even if we did, even though the shock was pretty big, it wasn't a devastating thing the way a serious drought would be, for example. If people had savings, they could have dealt with a pretty large portion of the shock without changing anything. Potentially bargaining issues could come up in response to shocks, but it would be unlikely with a shock of that size. The main result from that work is that we found that a population of sex workers we had been following in other projects had massive income declines. Then they seem to be compensating for that loss of income by switching to riskier behaviors. The striking thing there is that the shock actually wasn't that big, it was a relatively short duration, yet the response was quite large.

TO: What are the households like for these transactional sex workers? Are these single women? Do they have stable relationships?

JR: All the women are single. Collecting that data was interesting. In the first project with sex workers, we had them fill out "diaries"—actually pre-printed questionnaires with a bunch of questions that they could fill in—in which they filled out detail about their sexual behavior and many other outcomes.

But, of course, you can't just walk around asking people if they are a sex worker and what behaviors they engage in. Getting your sample is a bit of a challenge, and different people have used different approaches.

What we did was work with an organization called the Strengthening HIV/STD Control Project in Kenya that had formed peer groups of sex workers. Their criteria for inclusion sounds weird for people in the US—but their definition of a sex worker is any adult woman who is not married who has multiple partners. And so it sounds weird in the US to think of someone like that as a sex worker, but as it turned out all of the women we sampled who met this criteria were getting money for sex. It is just a fact that in that part of Kenya, and also in large parts of sub-Saharan Africa, there's much more of a transactional component to many sexual relationships.

So, by definition, the sample we have is single adult women. Some of them are co-habiting with a partner, but for the most part they're on their own. Many were married but are now widowed.

TO: But one of the things you found was that a lot of these women have long-term clients who would actually just transfer funds based on the relationship. So should we be thinking of these relationships more as polyandry rather than transactional sex? What's the component of long-term clients versus casual clients?

JR: They have a fair number of regular clients, and those clients help them out when something happens not tied directly to sex. But, on the other hand, we also find that they pay every time they have sex with a woman. So there's an aspect of it that's more like what we would think of as a boyfriend and aspects that are definitely transactional sex. It's a very different institution than what people think of as sex work in the US, for sure. Another big difference is that the sheer number of women in Busia who supply transactional sex is really high.

In terms of the mix of regular versus casual clients, it depends on which sample you're looking at, but only a small fraction of their clients are regulars. They typically have two or three regulars, not very many. But if you look at it terms of transactions, it's a larger percentage. It might be a quarter of the transactions. So they have a fair number of casual clients as well.

TO: I want to come back to the returns to capital in microenterprises in relation to how people are earning a living and coping with shocks. In your study on providing access to savings accounts, you found an implied return to capital of 5.9 percent a month. That sounds really great to me. How do I get into that business? If returns are so high, why would women like the sex workers go for riskier sex rather than opening a business? If returns to capital are so high, why isn't there a much more dynamic money-lending business? Why did it take the microcredit revolution to expand access to capital? Shouldn't a few people have started saving a little bit more and become informal moneylenders?

JR: I think it's a great question. There's an older study by Irfan Aleem in Pakistan that showed it's expensive to lend to people in developing countries.[15] The problem there was screening out the credit risks and the administrative costs—sometimes you would have to go visit a person time after time to get paid. The marginal cost of making a loan was huge. The interest rate had to be something like 50 percent per year just to cover costs.

So I think there are likely a lot of costs to moneylending that make it not that profitable necessarily to lend at even high rates. Especially when you're talking about very small loans.

TO: So, while you could be highly profitable in percentage terms, your absolute profit isn't much given the amount of work you have to put in.

JR: Yeah. And then if it costs money to screen out bad risks and you end up not giving out a loan to 50 percent of people who apply for a loan, you still have to pay the screening costs for everyone, not just the ones that get the loans.

TO: But as I read the *Portfolios of the Poor*, and this refers back to the inter-household transfers, there is a lot of small lending happening between households all the time.[16] It's not as if people are so worried about lending money that no one ever does it. In some sense everyone's a moneylender. Just very few people decided to actually take advantage of the possible returns.

So are these inter-household or extended family transfers truly different in some way? It's more a mutual insurance scheme, and so it's a huge leap to go from, "I'm helping out my family" to "I'm charging my family interest."

JR: [laughs] The transfers we see in our data are mostly for insurance. That's for sure. The data we have looks a lot like the *Portfolios of the Poor* data. The transfers we see are often for insurance purposes. Maybe it would be possible to start a really profitable moneylending business, I don't know. I would just think that as you start lending outside the families, enforcement and screening are going to become a big problem. I think there's also often a norm that people get some leeway to pay back if they have a really poor harvest or other shock, and that expectation of having to extend the loan for a longer time costs money too.

TO: Thinking about study design, replication, and external validity, what was the idea behind the design of the health information and subsidy study,[7] and the mini-replication of doing it four countries?[17]

JR: That project was done with Bruce Wydick who is a professor at USF. They have a master's program there where students at the end of their first year go to field sites and work in cooperation with professors. He had

7. This was an experiment to test the relative effects of various ways to encourage households to invest in health goods: information, subsidy, peer encouragement, or intra-household targeting. The core finding is that the binding constraint for households is liquidity. Providing information or other encouragement without subsidizing the products produces negligible increases in demand.

several groups of students. I became involved in the summer of 2008, and he had three teams that went to India, Guatemala, and Uganda. Those were pretty small scale. In the Kenya study there were a lot more hypotheses, but it was really about information versus nothing. So after we saw that the results showed the information didn't have much effect, we wanted to answer a deeper question about what other types of interventions we could have done and try to benchmark them against each other. That was the reason we did it that way. In the other three sites the students set up local partnerships. But in Kenya there's much greater infrastructure to do a larger project like that, so we were able to do something bigger with more hypotheses.

TO: So some of that is just opportunity. Do you think it increased what you learned by doing it in four sites or is it just confirmation of what you saw in Kenya?

JR: I think we learned something from the fact that the basic result held with totally different populations. I think we learn something when the results are similar from testing the same hypothesis across all four. If you really wanted to do something that was explicitly about external validity, you would want to do it in a hundred countries. At the end of the day we relied more on the Kenya results for writing up that work. All of the other ones became a small external validity section at the end of the paper. So I think it was useful because you often hear questions about the fact that a lot of these studies are taking place in one particular place in Kenya and how much can you generalize, so in this case we could answer that a little.

TO: One of the questions inherent in external validity is, "are we learning something about human behavior or are we learning something about local context?" Do you see that part of the question ever being resolved?

JR: Scientifically speaking, it's really hard to make that argument without having many sites. As you know IPA is devoting resources to doing replication studies. I believe that we learned something from the way people respond to these interventions. A lot of my work is in Kenya and sub-Saharan Africa, but technically speaking, it's not as if we did the exact same thing in other countries. So I think it's only by synthesizing results from various sites that you get anywhere. I guess that's why there needs to be more work. For us testing these hypotheses in the first place is the more interesting thing, but then in terms of validating them externally, I think it's hard to say that it's not something specific about one site or another without proof.

TO: If a lot of these replications show the same or similar results, do you think that gets us over the hump to say, "we have enough evidence from replications now to say that the presumption is for external validity, not against it?"

JR: Certainly I would say so. Ideally, though, we could say something about why we think external validity will or will not hold in other contexts. For example, if we knew that commitment savings worked because it helped to keep money from relatives, then we could form good hypotheses as to where the effect will be larger or smaller.

In some interventions it's much easier to make those guesses. For instance, the impact of deworming is going be closely related to just how bad the worm problem is, or whether people have running water. But most of the time we don't really know enough about what drives the underlying result to say where we think some intervention is going to work and where we think it won't.

In principle, it need not be the case that you have to do an experiment in literally every village in the world to say that there's external validity. If we did enough experiments that we could see that it works for certain people and in certain situations, and we could use that to predict where impacts would be largest based on people's characteristics, then we could try to make generalizations that way. That's something that really hasn't come very far in the evaluation world quite yet just because there aren't enough replication studies where we can see where effects are big and where they are small, and then use that to think about why they differ.

TO: Is that then an argument to be highly focused on specific populations so that you can fine-tune, experiment after experiment, and finally get down to the underlying factors?

JR: Exactly. I'm proud of the work we've done on savings, in particular. We never would have come this far in our understanding without working for many years in this one part of Kenya.

The questions we're asking, and the things we're testing, have evolved from a simple impact evaluation to a bigger research program over several years. We were only able to do this by working really closely with our field staff, some of whom have worked with us for many years, and the people in the community. I definitely don't think we could have gotten to where we are by doing some scattershot approach across a bunch of different countries all at once.

TO: Back to the study itself, one of the curious things is that people learn and they talk about what they learn, but the learning and peer interactions don't seem to have much impact. What do you see going on there? I would have guessed that dealing with lack of facts or false beliefs should have a large effect. If you can change false beliefs, shouldn't there be large effects?

JR: It's hard to completely answer that. We did some end-lines that had some qualitative information asking people those sorts of questions. And what it seems to have been is that even when the learning had an effect, relative to whatever discount they were getting for the products, the learning wasn't enough. Maybe we just couldn't pick up the small effects that the learning had. In the paper we tried to benchmark what the effects of targeting the wife versus the husband and giving them bigger payments versus smaller payments, and the effects were something like a 9 or 10 percent reduction in the price. So they were pretty small in relation to the subsidy. It could be that's what was happening with the learning as well. People would say that they talked to each other, and they learned and they wanted some of the health products more because other people had them, but that fundamentally wasn't enough to overcome the price barrier. We had thought that maybe there would be an effect of those interventions at intermediate prices because, of course, everyone is redeeming when the price is really low no matter what. So we don't have a tremendous amount of statistical power at any one price to look at the effects. In the overall results we didn't find much, but we did find results of information for one of the products in one of the sites—India—suggesting it's possible that there might be effects if you could, for example, couple liquidity with education. But at least according to the results we had, the second effect is so weak that it wasn't a fundamental reason why people weren't buying the products.

TO: I just want to clarify there between weakness and noisiness.

JR: In this case the dependent variable isn't noisy. We were looking at a specific thing like redeeming the coupon that we gave them. It's binary. So I think we can say pretty confidently that there would not have been an effect overall. We can look at the demand curves, and they lay right over the top of each other. Education doesn't have an effect at low prices because at low prices everyone wants it, and it can't have an effect at high prices because the liquidity constraint is too binding.

TO: I'm struggling to put together the findings on returns to working capital and liquidity constraints, on the one hand, and the microcredit findings, on the other. You've done work on Kenyan retail shops underinvesting in inventory and profit losses from not having change on hand. One of the reasons that people weren't buying health products was liquidity constraints. If those things are true, shouldn't it be easier to see an effect of relaxing liquidity constraints through microcredit? How do you square the evidence of large returns to working capital with limited returns to credit?

JR: I think the microcredit results are really about the finding that people don't take up the loans. The take-up in all of those studies is just really low. It could be that the product that is being offered is just not useful for people. For example, if they're famers, the way the product is structured is with very quick first repayment and then repayment at some regular interval. That wouldn't work very well for someone reliant on harvesting. The question is why is take-up so low? Are they loss averse? There's the literature on the returns to capital that pretty robustly shows large returns. So it does raise the puzzle of what is going on with microcredit, but the question that is not resolved is whether the products themselves are that useful or tailored well to the client's need.

TO: Back to health products, you've also done some work on how to effectively distribute subsidized health products.

JR: Yeah, that's work with Pascaline and Rebecca Dizon-Ross. What we're doing there is measuring leakage of subsidies to health clinics in Ghana, Kenya, and Uganda.[18] It's related to some other things that Pascaline has done, but it's trying to quantify the supposed problem that you can't give bed nets out for free in clinics because the clinics just don't do it properly or the nets are likely to be stolen. So we were trying to quantify how many nets were stolen or given to people who didn't need them or didn't qualify.

Fundamentally, what we find is that the leakage rates are a lot lower than people seem to believe. It's pretty encouraging. The performance of the programs is actually reasonably high.

TO: The performance of clinics seems to be the type of thing that would vary a lot from organization to organization or country to country. Were there significant observable differences between the three countries?

JR: The reason we did this in Uganda and Kenya as well as Ghana is because in the Transparency International rankings, Ghana is ranked much higher than the other two countries. It's still just three countries, though.

Performance was a bit worse in Uganda, consistent with what other people have found, but nowhere was it nearly as dire as you might think. You can imagine that it might be very different in other countries, in India, for example.

TO: I don't presume in this study you could possibly have done that, but where it is worse, there's the question of what drives the poorer performance. Is it specifics of governance, is it culture, is it pay schemes? Was there something observable that would help create hypotheses about where leakage is likely to be a problem? Are you close to forming some hypotheses to figure out what's inside that black box, figuring out why performance is different from place to place?

JR: We do some work trying to understand extrinsic and intrinsic motivation. What do people say about why they're doing their job? For instance, a lot of the health workers in the study do not report a lot of job security. They probably do have a good bit of job security but not so much that they can get away with anything, get away with large-scale diversion. They also say that they are nurses in part to be able to help other people. So one possibility is that health workers are differentially motivated than other professions or public service functions. You could design some tests to look at that. Of course, we couldn't do that because we can't at all control selection into the nurse pool. You can imagine a case where you could do this with more or less pro-social people and that could predict behavior. You could imagine varying the oversight or the extrinsic motivation that people have.

But what we found is that it wasn't just a simple matter that some clinics were poor. The strong indication was that the types of people that are nurses value people's health and doing a good job rather than their own private payoff. But I guess it's an open question of how that would look in India where so many studies show really bad performance of health officials. The absence levels we have are just way lower than what you see in some of the India papers.

TO: Are there ways in which your research has changed the way you make decisions? Or how you interpret the behavior of people around you?

JR: That's an interesting question. Yes, I'd say so. The one thing that's been driven home to me is all of the little ways in which we in developed countries have mechanisms to deal with pretty basic things. So, for instance, one of the hard things about running a small business in a developing country is having to deal with cash. In Kenya, a small business owner keeps his money on him, he has to bring it home at night to restock the next day, and so on. In a developed country much of that is done electronically these days. So it's amazing that a primitive technology like a lockbox makes such a difference. But when you give people one, they use it. They really do use it. Here it's unthinkable that your money would actually be that insecure. It's hard to even think about being in a society where all your money is in your pocket essentially. It's just a completely different mindset.

We have banking. We have direct deposit. It just highlights how incredibly complicated life would be if you have access to none of this stuff. A lot of these things are just taken out of our hands here. We just don't have the same sort of constraints that they do.

TO: So do you buy the cognitive load hypothesis that a whole lot of these puzzling, seemingly irrational behaviors can simply be explained by the fact that the poor have too many choices to make?[19]

JR: There is so much that people have to deal with on a day-to-day basis. For example, people who are running their small businesses are also managing their households, which are being hit with shocks. So yes I think this could be part of what holds people back. It's not something that's been really quantified, but I believe it could be important. We did the small change study because we noticed, for instance, that in Kenya oftentimes you try to buy something and market vendors run out of change.[20] Not just for big bills.

You might think it's just a white person issue. It's actually not, though. It turns out that this is really quite common that people don't have change, and they lose sales because of it. So we tried reminding people about having change, and it does change behavior. There are several explanations for this, but our preferred one is that there is a lot of stuff that people have to worry about, so they don't pay as much attention to having enough change. And yet it's not a small amount of sales that they lose, it's something like 5 percent of profits.

But they're trying to do a million things at once, so reminding them constantly makes it more salient to people and can actually change behavior.

The reason they're probably not doing it on their own is just because there's too much stuff going on.

TO: You mentioned earlier that part of the motivation for the study about distribution of health goods was that a lot of people assume that there is massive leakage and misdirection. It will take some convincing to get people to change their minds. Have you found that the evidence you've been able to generate from RCTs is more convincing to people and more effective at getting them to change their minds?

JR: In the academic world, at the end of the day even though there are academic debates about the style of work we do, it's still the case that when you present RCT results, it's a matter of interpreting the finding rather than not believing what the results are. I don't know that I have anything that is so controversial or surprising that you would expect to see people just not believe the result. And with a lot of the RCTs, you mentioned the microcredit papers, in general you see the results lining up when similar questions are studied, so even in other areas there's not that much controversy or disbelief on the academic side.

In terms of convincing policy makers, that's a good question. There are certain NGOs that work more closely with academics than others. The One Acre Fund, for example. The Gates Foundation has been very interested in the savings results because that's one of the core things that they're doing.[8] Maybe it was surprising that subsidizing savings accounts could have big effects for people. So I think that influenced what they're doing a little bit. In a wider policy world, my stuff hasn't had as much influence as Michael [Kremer]'s deworming or that kind of thing. But I think as far as the savings goes, it's had some effect on that.

TO: Thinking about how your work does change the world, what's your theory of change?

JR: I think of myself primarily as a scientist. That's what I'm trying to be. If you're in physics it's not like you're necessarily going to think about what the overall implications of the basic research you're doing are or how it's going to make it into consumer products. There's a role for basic research. A lot of the choices we make of how small scale it is and who we're working with is informed by trying to do the evaluation correctly.

8. Of note, in 2015 the Gates Foundation began moving away from savings promotion to focus on digital financial services.

There are academic questions and logical questions about things like the overall effect of interventions. For instance, if returns to capital are really high, does that mean that if you give out grants to everyone, the economy would increase by some large percentage, or is it that the people who are benefiting are actually harming the people in the control group or those outside the study? Those sorts of questions are really important. Those sorts of questions are hard to study but we should be studying them. For other questions the reason we do it is because it's what is feasible to do scientifically. I'm obviously very interested in development policy, but that's not what my role is. It's true that the work that we do may not dramatically change what's happening in the country of Kenya, but that's not really the point, I think.

19   Tyler Cowen

Tyler is a Professor of Economics at George Mason University, the Director of the Mercatus Center and the author or editor of more than a dozen books, including an Economics 101 textbook. He is best known, however, for his prolific blogging at his site Marginal Revolution where he covers topics from geopolitics to neurology to ethnic food and everything in between with an economic lens.

TO: What is your perspective on how the RCT movement in development economics fits into other broader patterns and its relative impact on the field as a whole?

TC: What I think is striking about economic science in the last few decades is the growth in diversity of methods. We're becoming much less of a unified science. There's experimental economics, there's model building, there's regression, there's simulation. More and more of what you do as an economist is defined by your method rather than your field. So RCTs are a big development and a quite new method—not new to humanity but new in their influence in the field. But like some of the other new methods, if you haven't done them and haven't specialized in using them, it's hard to know where to get started with them. It's part of this ongoing fragmentation of what economics is. But I would say in many ways that's for the better.

TO: The alternative view is that RCTs should be "just one of the tools in the economist's toolbox."[1] Your formulations says that we're getting more

1. This is an idea that appears in many of the interviews. See, in particular, the interview with Rachel Glennerster (chapter 17) for a discussion about specialization, and interviews with Jonathan Morduch (chapter 4), Dean Yang (chapter 12), and Chris Blattman (chapter 20) for a discussion of how various methodologies fit together.

specialization along the lines of methodology rather than equipping people with multiple tools to apply to the questions of interest.

TC: I think what we're lacking are incentives for a lot of academics to do what I would call synthesis—people who look at what's done with the different tools and put it together to try to figure out what is right. It's not what our profession rewards. You have some of that going on in the World Bank and other development agencies. You may get some of that in journalism or even in blogging. But I think that's what's missing is the actual tying of all of these things together

TO: Who, historically, is a good example of someone doing synthesis?

TC: Adam Smith was fantastic at synthesis. He wrote a book trying to tell people what made sense as a way of viewing the world and what should be done. He was writing at a time when in economics there was very little division of labor—there was only synthesis. Now we've gone too far in the other direction. We need some happy medium where people are rewarded not just for what we now call original research but also for synthesis. It should be seen as a form of original research in its own right.

TO: Aside from incentives, it's hard to imagine anyone making their mark in synthesis progressively.

TC: You're right. It's a very intangible skill and it's hard to tell how good someone is at it. Whereas with an RCT you do have some result and, if you did it the right way, you should believe in something as a result. So it's very easy to show you've done something useful with RCTs. That's one of their strengths. But at the same time when you have so many methods where it's easy to show that you've done something useful, you end up under-investing in areas where that's not so easy to show.

TO: You've tipped some combination of Banerjee, Duflo, and Kremer for a Nobel at some point.

TC: And soon. I think they should get it soon. I know they're pretty young, but I think it's already truly proved and it would be a nice statement, as it was with Bob Lucas,[2] to give them a prize fairly soon.

2. Robert Lucas was awarded the Nobel Prize in Economic Sciences in 1995. Central to the award is his work developing and applying the theory of rational expectations—the idea that economic actors incorporate rational beliefs about future economic conditions such as inflation and labor demand into their present

TO: How would you assess their level of impact on the field versus say Elinor Ostrom[3] or Jean Tirole[4] or some of the other recent winners?

TC: Well Elinor Ostrom has had a significant impact, but her impact is earlier. The impact of RCTs is just getting underway now. And I think it's revolutionized how we think about development economics. It's raised the bar for what we count as enough to persuade us in a lot of different areas. It's raised the status of microeconomics. It's made us realize just how hard it is to really know things.

A lot of RCTs are fairly circumscribed, which I don't intend as a criticism. But then you realize there are all of these other questions that you care about that aren't so circumscribed and you realize how much you are clutching at shadows in those areas.

TO: Is there an example of an RCT that really surprised you? Or one that shifted your priors in some significant way?

---

choices. The application of rational expectations suggests significant limits to the use of monetary and fiscal policy to affect the course of the economy.

   The Prize Announcement: http://www.nobelprize.org/nobel_prizes/economic -sciences/laureates/1995/press.html.

   Lucas's Nobel Lecture: http://www.nobelprize.org/nobel_prizes/economic-sciences/ laureates/1995/lucas-lecture.html.

3. Elinor Ostrom shared the prize in 2009 for her work on governance of the commons. The "tragedy of the commons"—the fact that goods that are jointly owned without clear property rights tend to be overused and degraded—is one of the first lessons in economics. Ostrom's work showed successful models of governing common goods and that the tragedy of the commons was not inevitable.

   The Prize Announcement: http://www.nobelprize.org/nobel_prizes/economic -sciences/laureates/2009/press.html.

   Ostrom's Nobel Lecture: http://www.nobelprize.org/nobel_prizes/economic-sciences/ laureates/2009/ostrom-lecture.html.

4. Jean Tirole was awarded the prize in 2014, particularly for his work on regulat-ing oligopolistic and monopolistic industries. His work showed the downsides of generally accepted principles of regulation in such industries, for instance, how collaboration between oligopolistic firms can yield benefits for consumers not just costs.

   The Prize Announcement: http://www.nobelprize.org/nobel_prizes/economic -sciences/laureates/2014/press.html.

   Tirole's Nobel Lecture: http://www.nobelprize.org/nobel_prizes/economic-sciences/ laureates/2014/tirole-lecture.html.

TC: Well those are two different questions. I would say that just about every reputable RCT has shifted my priors. Literally every one. That's what's wonderful about them, but it's also the trick. You might ask, "why do they shift your priors?" They shift your priors because on the questions that are chosen, and ones that ought to be chosen, theory doesn't tell us so much: "How good is microcredit?" or "What's the elasticity of demand for mosquito nets?" Because theory doesn't tell you much about questions like that, of course an RCT should shift your priors. But at the same time, because theory hasn't told you much, you don't know how generalizable the results of those studies are. So each one should shift your priors, and that's the great strength and weakness of the method.

Now, you asked if any of the results surprised me. I think the same reasoning applies. No, none of them have surprised me because I saw the main RCT topics to date as not resolvable by theory. So they've altered my priors but in a sense that can't shake you up that much. If you offer a mother a bag of lentils to bring her child in to be vaccinated, how much will that help? Turns out, at least in one part of India, that helps a lot.[1] I believe that result. But 10 years ago did I really think that if you offered a mother in some parts of India a bag of lentils to induce them to bring in their kids for vaccination that it wouldn't work so well? Of course not. So in that sense, I'm never really surprised.

TO: I've tried a bit to trace the intellectual history of the emergence of RCTs. I'm interested in your thoughts on why RCTs gained a lot of currency at the time that they did. It's not as if the early Kremer experiments were the first time field experiments had been done. One possible story is that there were a lot of critiques suggesting instrumental variable methods were not doing as much as we thought they were.

TC: I think it's much more practical than that. So let me just say that I'd also like to give a Nobel Prize to Joseph Newhouse who did the RAND Healthcare Study.[5] When you look at that study you realize how much was

---

5. The RAND Health Insurance experiment was one of the first large-scale social policy experiments in the US. The study randomized cost-sharing for medical insurance (what we now generally refer to as co-pays and co-insurance). The study found that paying some amount for health services reduced use of those services, but that the reduction was equal across highly effective and less effective services. While free healthcare improved some health measures among the poorest and sickest patients, overall there was negligible impact on health from consuming less healthcare. Cost sharing also did not change people's risky health behaviors such as smoking. See: http://www.rand.org/pubs/research_briefs/RB9174.html.

needed in terms of resources—to find those people, give some of them free healthcare, and follow up with all of them many years later. The budgetary costs must have been enormous.

When you look at the Poverty Action Lab at MIT, I think the key development is that you have a set of individuals who have the ability to put together the whole project in terms of raising money, having academic credibility, and developing the field network on the ground. That was and still is such a tall order. That's part of what's so impressive. Until someone could bring those things together, you simply couldn't do these field experiments credibly. I think it's a miracle and a credit to those people that their skills are so diverse that they could do this.[6]

But I think that also points to a problem: so few people can do all these things. So, to the extent that the few people with those skills gain in status, the result is a centralization of influence. That's not necessarily a bad thing. I'm not against centralization if you get more truth. But nonetheless there are very high barriers to entry when it comes to RCTs and that's worth thinking about.

TO: Do you think that remains true with all the effort put into teaching people to do RCTs, the investment that J-PAL and IPA have put into developing networks, Rachel Glennerster's book[7] and work training people around the world on how to run RCTs? One argument for RCTs is that they're not that intellectually complicated. They are easy to understand conceptually. Some would argue that there are more people with the skills to manage field projects than there are to really do econometrics correctly and responsibly.

TC: I'm not sure if that's true. Because you also need to get the money and not just manage people. I do think RCTs will spread and will come down in cost, but it will still be nothing like theory or econometrics on publically available data sets where there is so much competition that everything gets done. One reason those fields are exhausted is because they were so competitive. Try doing macro today on publically available data sets. What new tests can you find? Well you can wait for more years

6. See interview with Michael Kremer (chapter 1) where he credits the building of institutions like J-PAL as one of his proudest accomplishments.
7. Glennerster's book *Running Randomized Evaluations* is expressly about helping organizations run RCTs.

to pass or you may try some new countries, but it is very tough to be innovative in those areas.

In a sense that's a sign of how much we did how quickly. How soon will interesting RCTs exhaust themselves? Maybe the answer is never. Which in a way is nice but also shows how much we are just scratching the surface. But then again you have to wonder which balls are we drawing from the urn and how much should we generalize from them.

TO: That is one of the standard critiques. I can imagine some people saying there never has been an interesting RCT because they are so small, narrow, and localized.

TC: I wouldn't say that. I think there is a point to that criticism, but to me small, narrow, and localized criticism is interesting. Most of life is small, narrow, and localized. A lot of problems are small, narrow, and localized. We shouldn't be upset about that.

TO: Back to something you said a moment ago about the centralization of influence. A point you've made recently on your blog on anthropologists and economists is that the economics field is very hierarchical.[8] That's OK if the hierarchy is arranged the right way, but as you point out, hierarchies are difficult to change. When these new methodologies arrive, that seems to me to be a primary way that the hierarchy gets shaken. Is that true? How does the hierarchy change and centers of influence evolve over time?

TC: I think what used to be the case is you could climb to the top of the hierarchy by doing better or more interesting theory, or more elegant theory, or by applying better econometrics. I'm not saying those have gone away, but it's gotten tougher because the really good econometrics is already very good. Maybe you can refine it and make it better yet, but it's really hard to tell if you're actually getting more accurate or more useful estimates. There seem to be diminishing returns. More and more I see people want to eyeball the data and mix that with econometrics, rather than do more econometrics. If anything, there is a move back to what I would call commonsense approaches. And again with theory a lot of it is so arcane

8. See these posts on Marginal Revolution:
http://marginalrevolution.com/marginalrevolution/2014/12/the-superiority-of
-economists.html.
http://marginalrevolution.com/marginalrevolution/2014/12/are-anthropologists
-better-than-you-think.html.

that coming up with more mathematically refined theory has lost a lot of its status.

The source of status today is data sets that other people don't have and then doing something with them. The economist is a kind of collector who needs skills of management. And maybe the ultimate skill is knowing how to get the right connections to come across or produce new data sets. Then you apply what's often pretty simple theory and or relatively simple empirics to those new data sets and that's the new status game. I think it's a pretty good status game, and in part it has won out because the old status games were producing diminishing returns.

That's the margin we're at and if you ask if you are going to exhaust that margin soon, my guess is that we won't. We'll play at this margin of status for a long time because I don't think all possible producible or findable or accessible data sets are going to be dried up in the next few decades. That's hard to imagine.

But do I think we've run out of big ideas in theory? Absolutely.

TO: It's not just a great technological stagnation, it's a theoretical stagnation too?

TC: Sure. So, if you take an idea like signaling, it was in the 1970s. It's a big deal. It deserved a Nobel Prize. You could give it two Nobel Prizes, it was so good. There also was adverse selection. Herd behavior was one of the last big new ideas. Maybe that deserves a Nobel Prize. But that was in the early 90s. And if you ask what has really been done in theory that has trickled down into how economics is practiced and understood since the early 90s, I think there's actually very little.

So we are back to the skill of finding data sets—you see more and more papers co-authored, of course. And what qualities really correlate with being good at finding data, I don't know how well we really understand that. It's quite a new ball game.

TO: I was thinking back to the last few recipients of the Clark Medal[9] and the idea that who can generate a clever new data set correlates well with who has won the Clark Medal.

9. The Clark Medal is awarded to the "American [in practice, this has meant an economist working in the US] economist under the age of forty who is adjudged to have made a significant contribution to economic thought or knowledge." It was awarded in alternating years from 1947 until 2009 and has been awarded annually since. Recent winners:

TC: I would give Robert Townsend[10] a Nobel Prize. He's integrated economics and anthropology, and he's one of the first people to see that looking to anthropology is one of the best ways to produce new and useful data. Furthermore he's executed on that data and his papers are fantastic. They are deep and profound. I think they are still underestimated. He was really a leader behind all of this. But as far as I'm aware, he's never written a big ideological manifesto explaining the import in what he was doing. He has a foot in RCT innovations too, but I think he's done much more than that.

TO: Coming back to intellectual history, there is one story about trying to get better methods and answer questions more precisely. There's another story that's about novelty. People get excited about something new. What gains currency isn't necessarily going to be better, it's just going to be different. Do you feel that we're getting better at answering our questions or just finding different answers to different questions?

TC: Different questions. I'm not sure we're getting better, but "better" is a tricky word. I don't think you have to feel that we're getting better to be enthusiastic about these developments. One of my worries is RCTs that surprise some people. Take the RAND study from the 1970s that healthcare doesn't actually make people much healthier. You replicate that, more or less, in the recent Oregon Medicaid study.[11] When you have something that surprises people, they often don't want to listen to it. So it gets dismissed. It seems to me that's quite wrong. We ought to work much more carefully on the cases where RCTs are surprising many of us, but we don't want to do that. So we kind of go RCT-lite. We're willing to soak up whatever we learn

2016: Yuliy Sannikov for work in mathematical economics

2015: Roland Fryer for work on education, discrimination, and incentives

2014: Matthew Gentzkow for work on the economics of media

2013: Raj Chetty for work on economic mobility using novel data sources

2012: Amy Finkelstein for work on health economics

2011: Jonathan Levin for work in industrial organization

2010: Esther Duflo for work on field experiments

10. Robert Townsend is an economist at MIT. In addition to being an important voice in macroeconomic theory debates of the 1970s and 80s, he has a long-term project following a village in Thailand for decades.

11. The Oregon Health Insurance experiment is a randomized study on the expansion of Medicaid that looks at outcomes, including use of healthcare services, health and well-being, finance, and wages. The principal investigators are Amy Finkelstein (see note 9 in this chapter) and Katherine Baicker. The project has produced several papers, available at: http://www.nber.org/oregon/.

about mothers and lentils and vaccinations, but when it comes to our core being under attack, we get defensive. Maybe healthcare isn't that useful after all.

TO: I guess that has something to do with uncovering basic truths about the way people behave and make decisions versus uncovering lots of local contextual factors. For instance, I think about Asim Khwaja and Bailey Klinger's work on psychometric factors[12] accurately predicting creditworthiness with small adjustments for local culture. I wonder whether we aren't focusing enough on disentangling whether in RCTs we're learning about universal human behavior or just local contextual factors. It could be either that yields outcomes like healthcare doesn't make you healthier.

TC: I think the example you cite is closely related to my point. The results you cite are in some ways politically incorrect. I don't want to suggest that it shows that poverty is the fault of poor people themselves if they are not creditworthy. That's not the right way to describe it. But it is saying that there are certain internal qualities that make some people successful and others not. That's potentially a very big problem. And it's not really a comforting thing for most of development economics, especially aid-driven development economics, to hear. So I think findings like that can easily get ignored. People don't know quite what to do with it, and it suggests that a lot of what we're trying maybe isn't going to be very effective. Ideas that suggest we should do less tend not to be very popular. Ideas that imply "here's something we can do" tend to be more popular.

TO: Do you have a theory of change that builds off of that? If your aim was policy change, that view would presumably affect the way you went about trying to influence policy change. Since the more surprising results

12. Beginning with a project for the South African government, Khwaja and Klinger studied the use of psychometric tests—widely used in wealthy countries to assess employees on honesty, diligence, and conscientiousness—to assess the creditworthiness of small enterprise borrowers in Peru, Colombia, Kenya, as well as South Africa. They find that the psychometric tests, while not by any means perfectly predicting repayment, do add significant value at lower cost over traditional loan officer assessments. Their work evolved into an organization, the Entrepreneurial Finance Lab, which licenses its technology to banks. For more, see B. Klinger, A. Khwaja, and C. del Carpio (2013), *Enterprising Psychometrics and Poverty Reduction*, Springer, and www.eflglobal.com.

are unlikely to yield policy change, it suggests that you should pursue incremental nonthreatening policy change in order to get things done.

TC: I think as researchers, we should obsess over the unpopular, hard-to-process kinds of results at the margin. I think that's how we'll actually make subsequent big advances. But we're not well geared to do that, and that gets back to the point about synthesizers. We don't have many of them, but they ought to be well geared to do that—to take some of the counterintuitive or politically incorrect findings and, by reading more and thinking more, start figuring out what those findings really mean. Should we actually take some finding seriously and, if so, what do we do? And if that means don't do a bunch of things, those are going to be exactly the ideas that are underexplored, and we should look at more at the margin.

TO: Let me wrap up by asking about the influence of a variety of ideas in development economics. You have people working on quality of institutions, you have people working on micro-interventions on the idea that they'll compound over time like deworming and vaccination, and you've got people working on big-scale things like industrial policy. If you imagine looking back at the present moment from 2035, what idea in development economics now do you think will have changed the world most?

TC: That's a tough question. I think there will be more work done on the East Asian miracles, which we haven't quite figured out yet. And those results will end up being seen as some of the most important ideas, and it's not quite in any of your categories. I hesitate to use the word "culture" and sound like an anthropologist, but something along those lines.

It's interesting when you read the institutions people on RCTs, they are often very negative. But the institutions work is quite mushy. Jeff Sachs makes a good point.[13] If you go back to 1960, and this is retro-dicting, not even predicting, and try to come up with a good metric of the quality of institutions that will predict the growth winners over the next 50 years, you basically can't do it. And that's knowing who the winners were. So the

13. For an overview of this point, see Sachs' *Foreign Affairs* review of Acemoglu and Robinson's *Why Nations Fail* ("Government, Geography, and Growth: The True Drivers of Economic Development," *Foreign Affairs* Sep/Oct 2012): http://www .foreignaffairs.com/articles/138016/jeffrey-d-sachs/government-geography-and -growth.

people who want everything to be big scale, political economy, and institutions, that's not so easy either.

I think right now economists don't know that much about most of the important questions. Given that, there's a lot to be said for people who are producing real knowledge even if sometimes it's small. And that's a home run for RCTs even if it's a fairly circumscribed corner of the intellectual universe.

20 Chris Blattman

Chris is arguably the best example of a new path to research with impact in the economics profession, a "rock star" development economics blogger and tweeter (which, granted, is a small pond). His blog at chrisblattman. com is widely followed by academics, graduate students, practitioners—and others who aspire to those roles.

Blogging has given Chris the space to publish thoughts on everything from research methodology to the politics of academic publishing to development practice to advice for aspiring PhD students on where to focus their research. While a defender of rigorous research methods like RCTs, he also espouses the view that using RCTs to answer micro-questions is a bubble in academe—the next rounds of graduate students aspiring to top programs and appointments will need to look elsewhere.

Chris's research agenda has generally focused on conflict, political violence, post-conflict interventions, and how poverty interacts with all three. Currently he is Ramalee E. Pearson Professor of Global Conflict Studies at the University of Chicago's Harris School of Public Policy.

TO: What is your theory of change? How does your research change things?

CB: I have been fairly skeptical that this kind of academic research makes it very easily into actual policy change on the ground. Most people who do policy or aid jobs don't have time to read or access what we write. Most of us do a really rotten job of putting it in a format that works well. Even when we do, with my blog[1] that gets out to a lot of students and to some professionals, the policy messages that seem to resonate and succeed are boiled down with no nuance. And most academics are very uncomfortable

1. Blattman's blog is, as far as such things are measurable, one of the most popular and longest running blogs on development issues. See: www.chrisblattman.com.

in that sphere. The ones that stop being nuanced lose the esteem of their colleagues.

The theory of change relies on someone who doesn't have our impediments and discomfort in boiling what we have down to a talking point that resonates. And in selling it. I think that's one. The second, I would wholly attribute to Lant Pritchett who has a speech where he compares development to dance recitals.[2] All around the country and world there are all these dance recitals that are horrible and painful. But this whole system of really bad dancing is actually necessary to produce the one genius who after years of practice can give these sublime performances. The analogy to development is most of the stuff we do is crap and noise and it may make no difference at all, but every once in a while, because that system exists, one or two incredibility powerful ideas will come out and change the world.

The example he uses is 1992 in India when there was the financial crisis and the government, which happened to be filled with a lot of economist types who had been exposed to all this research and way of thinking in their undergraduate and graduate classes, had to do something. So that research filtered its way to a group of people who were in a position to do something. And those people made these decisions on where to take the country, to dismantle some of the economic bureaucracy, decisions that resulted in unprecedented growth. That one act probably created more value than any other set of ideas. It rivals anything else that's been done in history.

The only place I diverge from Pritchett is I think we have to take seriously the question of whether these economic ideologies that have come out of research have destroyed just as much wealth and well-being as they've created. I'm not sure where the ledger lies. So it may be positive or negative.

So I guess the short answer is, the theory of change is that hopefully the good ideas from research trickle out over time and drive good policy decisions down the road.

TO: It seems to me there is a bit of tension between that analogy and your writing on Impact Evaluation 2.0[1] or 3.0[2] and some things you've written on the importance of understanding where heterogeneity of results

2. You can hear an audio of a Pritchett talk using this analogy here: http://www .nyudri.org/aidwatcharchive/2010/03/how-is-the-aid-industry-like-a-piano-recita//. For more on Pritchett's view of how institutions change, see chapter 10 and his paper, "It's All about MeE"

comes from. There's the suggestion in Pritchett's analogy that this is all just a long game of trial and error and muddling through. So is the right answer working harder to get specific and finding the underlying causes of heterogeneity so we can fine-tune policies and interventions? Or is the best hope just getting to a bunch of smaller less-wrong answers?

CB: It's worth noting that I think people like Banerjee and Duflo deliberately want to bring people away from thinking about these dramatic changes in policy that can come from some of the right answers.[3] I think they see that as inherently unstable, difficult to predict and unscientific, and I think they're right. That doesn't mean I think we shouldn't be devoting any energy to figuring out better macro policy. I think that's where I differ with them. I do think the profession could do both, and if I had to choose, I might even say we should pour more energy into the big stuff than the small stuff.[4]

The fact is the profession has been neglecting these precise experimental answers for some time. We're readjusting the balance by bringing in some of this microeconomic experimentation. I'm optimistic about where the growth of experimentation is taking us.

I think there's this idea floating out there that the *randomistas* expect that we're going to produce these booklets of approved policies that work. So the minister of education in Tanzania can just pull the book off of his shelf and see what policy he should implement.[5] I don't think any of the *randomistas* actually think that way, but I think people outside the movement believe that they do. I do think that's part of how the randomized evaluation movement was sold to policy makers: "You're going to get answers."

I don't think that is what we're going to get. My sense is that we're going to see evaluations that are all over the map.[6] There may be a few things that

3. See the interview with Abhijit Banerjee and Esther Duflo (chapter 2), and of course, their book, *Poor Economics*.
4. See interviews with Lant Pritchett (chapter 9) and Nancy Birdsall (chapter 11) for more comments on the balance of effort being devoted to various questions in development economics.
5. See interview with Birdsall for a specific discussion of the process of educational policy change in Tanzania, and interview with Michael Kremer (chapter 1) for a discussion of what field experiments on education have shown.
6. Eva Vivalt, an economist currently at Stanford, has documented the dispersion of effect sizes in randomized evaluations. For more background, see her websites: evavivalt.com and aidgrade.org.

are just bombs, and we can say don't put any money into that. And a few things on the margin that we can say do or don't do. I expect what we're going to have after 5 or 10 or 15 years of experiments is going to be more subtle.

You read a book like *Poor Economics*[3] and it's not saying the right answer is to do this or that policy. What it's doing is building a different framework for our understanding of why people are poor and what constraints hold them back. What that means from a policy perspective is not an answer to which policy to implement. But it means you are hopefully making better judgments of what is happening in a particular context so that you can decide what constraints are important and how people act and change your perspective.

Poor Economics is a much better representation, I think, of what people in the randomization movement actually think. It's one of those rare books that both academics and policy makers can read and like. To what extent its message is an easy one for policy makers to internalize and use as a basis for decisions I just don't know. It could be pretty impactful. But the fundamental problem with our approach is that aid workers don't read policy books or academic papers—that's not a problem with aid workers, that's a problem with our approach. Writing a book is not a theory of change, and I think we all know that. We just like writing books and don't like the slog of running, basically, a political campaign.

TO: But you write a lot about what might be called the political side of things: the dispersion of knowledge, management technology, policy formation, and affecting how interventions are run. Economics has a rich literature in industrial organization and labor markets and principal–agent problems. So why has that not bled through into experimental development economics?

CB: I think it's a matter of where you focus your energies. Dean [Karlan] and Esther and Abhijit have actually done a lot of these things, a lot of outreach and engagement, by writing the books and starting organizations, and building serious outreach and communications efforts. So they're on that path, but I think their energies in their scholarship is on the narrower questions.

What is striking is there aren't other talented individuals that are focused on what you might call the political economy of policy reform. I actually had somebody from a search committee contact me to see if I knew of anybody who focused on these issues of policy reform[7] because they wanted to make it core to their curriculum. But they weren't finding anyone. They thought they were just missing something huge. Maybe we're all missing something, but it seems to be really rare. It hasn't caught on as a topic of academic interest.

TO: Do you think it's a factor of figuring out how to apply the tools to these questions? It's much harder to randomize the internal policy and politics of organizations. I don't see much in the field experiment literature that takes into account how the structure of an NGO affects what the product actually delivered is.

CB: A lot of the luminaries in this field are starting to dabble in governance.[8] They're starting to look at the incentives and constraints around behavior, and they're starting to look more at how we can get people in government, local or national, to be more accountable, to get governments working better. Some of that work is around issues of corruption; some is about better, more accountable systems. But it's all trying to figure out what the constraints are to better governance. In the same sense of having a theory of economic poverty, of understanding the market failures, we also need to have a way of understanding the human failures, the systemic failures, the governance failures. That's what a lot of the behavioral economists are working on.

We will learn some important things, but I'm much less confident we can learn generalizable lessons about organizations and institutions. I think there is a lot more in that realm that's context dependent. Less so maybe when you are in the political behavior realm. But frankly we just don't know. It may be that just as in behavioral economics we're finding systematic biases and human frailties that hold true for everyone, we might find some political elements that generalize. But I think, for the most part, the political elements are more culture specific. Right now people are thinking about randomizing incentives for politicians and local leaders, and doing audits and other interventions to study these things. It's just not clear to me when you move on to the next village, much less the next country, that

---

7. See interview with Lant Pritchett (chapter 9) for a discussion of his view that the RCT movement lacks a "positive theory of policy change."

8. See, for instance, Banerjee et al. (2014), "Improving Police Performance in Rajasthan, India"; Duflo et al. (2014) "The Value of Regulatory Discretion"; Duflo, Dupas, and Kremer (2012), "School Governance, Teacher Incentives, and Pupil–Teacher Ratios."

these aren't such complex systems that nothing replicates. We'll find out if and when these studies are replicated. But right now I see a lot of unbridled optimism and I'm more ... bridled.

TO: Let's switch to discuss some of your experimental work.

CB: I hope you'll find some place in your book to point out to readers that I've only actually published one experiment.[9] These things take forever, which is the first lesson that I've learned. I've now finished a few experiments and I couldn't say for most of the time I've been writing about experiments. I have this big bullhorn because of the blog, but I don't have the CV to match.

TO: What was the first experiment you were involved in?

CB: It was in 2001. I was a master's student at Harvard Kennedy School. A professor, Rob Jensen, ran an RCT in southern India to provide radio-based Internet to villages. This was the peak of the dot-com boom. Differential access to the Internet was a hot topic. Cellphones didn't exist for the most part. So radio-based Internet seemed like a hot idea, and I went to implement the project. It was a spectacular failure in implementation, mostly just random different reasons that go with neglect of all sorts by parties and participants in the whole thing. It was just a disaster, but it was an interesting exposure.

TO: A lot of your work has been looking at how poor people or poor households use cash. You've done two projects looking at what people do if you just hand them cash.

CB: I actually have four but only two have papers so far. You're likely thinking of the two Uganda ones, but I have one in Ethiopia that was a randomized trial of industrial jobs, basically sweatshop jobs. So people apply for these jobs, but they are awarded randomly. The control group who didn't get the job, half didn't get anything but half were offered a cash grant and some basic business training. So, if you wanted to get cute, you'd say it's sort of a sweatshop job versus Marxist noble self-labor versus whatever the alternatives are. The grant was intended to stimulate microenterprise. We also have a study of behavior change in Liberia where we are looking at high-risk young men, street criminals, that sort of thing. One of

9. This was true at the time of the initial interview. Since then, papers based on several of the experiments discussed in this interview have been published in peer-reviewed journals. See the end notes for citations.

our interventions was a cash grant. It's partly as a measuring tool, to see whether or not people spent cash differently after going through behavioral therapy that is designed to stimulate self-control and self-discipline. But it was also a way to stimulate microenterprises and incomes. So now I have these four studies.

TO: Let's start with the Uganda youth project.[4] What struck me was the percentage, 75 to 85 percent, of the money provided to the groups that seemed to have been invested in businesses. In many studies the percentage of loans or grants that actually go into business investment is much lower. How do you interpret your findings in the context of other work on microenterprises?

CB: The answer is probably the fact that a group made decisions about how this money was to be spent before they received it. It probably acted as a commitment device. We don't know that for sure—the nature of how we collected the data prevents us from really knowing. A lot of the data collection was retrospective. But it looks like what happened is the group sat down and decided, for instance, we're going to use half of it for training fees. So that half gets transferred to the vocational training institute. Then they decide to spend some of the money on tools, and they buy tools in bulk. Now, maybe that way of spending the money was effective and maybe it wasn't. It doesn't mean that the quality of the decisions were better. It means they were making investments, but maybe they were making wise investments they otherwise wouldn't have made or maybe they were making unwise investments they otherwise wouldn't have made. But it is remarkable given the context how much of the money went to investment.

TO: Is the youth population you studied in Liberia similar to the population you studied in Uganda?

CB: In Uganda we're really talking about fairly conventional populations of youth. They're not high risk. They're not necessarily even at-risk, if at-risk populations are youth who may be in bad neighborhoods but aren't yet engaged in crime or other antisocial behaviors but their peers are, and high-risk populations are the ones who are actively engaging in antisocial behaviors. We have very few people like that in Uganda period, let alone outside the capital. In Liberia we were specifically targeting the 1 or 2 percent riskiest, most difficult population when we went there. It's a much more extreme group.

TO: Using your analogy of "how tightly coiled the spring is,"[10] would you say that the Liberians were more tightly coiled than the Ugandans?

CB: In terms of how constrained they are? It's hard to say. On the one hand, you're a tightly coiled spring because there's something like a credit constraint that's holding you back. In one sense your intuition is right in that the Liberians are so poor that maybe they're really tightly coiled. On the other hand, there might be 10 things holding them back rather than just one. A big one is that they're in these really insecure environments. It's not clear that you can accumulate assets when you don't have secure property rights.

TO: Or all your friends are the kind of people who steal assets from others.

CB: Exactly. When half the people in your peer network are thieves, it's tough. Plus these guys might lead inherently riskier lives in the sense that they're more subject to things like theft or police confiscation or arrest. But farmers are also exposed to a lot of risks, and they seem to do OK with cash. So we didn't really know how to think about these youth and how they would react to the intervention, in particular to cash. It turns out in the end that they actually spend the money very wisely, if you will—they invest, they save—and while they do well in the short run they tend to fail. They are exposed to a lot of risks. Things get stolen or confiscated. They also have a lot of people in their lives who have bad things happen to them—a health shock, or the like—and so the money goes to something like that.

The second reason that they might not be a tightly coiled spring is that they might not have the ability to do much with money. We were trying to change those abilities. We were trying to make them more self-disciplined people, and that's a form of ability. So it was a bit of a mystery what they would do with cash, and we did it very cautiously but basically we thought, "if these guys didn't misuse cash, who would?"

TO: The other Uganda study is of a direct comparison between giving cash and the, let's say, more "normal" development program including training

10. See Blattman's use of the analogy in context in this post on his blog: http:// chrisblattman.com/2013/05/23/dear-governments-want-to-help-the-poor-and -transform-your-economy-give-people-cash/. The basic idea is that you are likely to see much larger impact when you release constraints on people who had been most constrained.

and other support, which exert some control over how recipients spend money. And you find that those control mechanisms are a waste.

CB: Well most of the current control mechanisms are wasteful because they are so expensive. In that program women were receiving cash and business training and extensive follow-up. But it's done in a very paternalistic way. If the cost of the program is something like $1,200 per participant, only about $150 of that is cash because there was no appetite for misplaced funds. So the program is spending an enormous amount of funds to check up and make sure the women use the funds the right way. It's just blatantly clear to me that this is unwise. It's not a cost-effective way to get accountability for results. The NGO was open to that but skeptical, so we experimentally test their paternalism. The results indicate that it doesn't have a lot of value, but it does have a lot of cost.

That's not to say that there aren't relatively costless things—whether it's framing, or putting it into bank accounts rather than handing out cash, or giving it to groups, things that are very cheap—that could lead to wiser decisions. There will soon be more and more evidence of what happens if you just give people cash or with minor controls, and I think the answer is in a lot of cases you're going to see higher returns. I don't think that is politically difficult because frankly that's the way it works in developed countries. Most poverty programs are basically cash. Whether it's unemployment insurance, or a welfare check, or food stamps—which isn't cash but it's very close to cash—that's what we're doing in developed countries. So why should we not have something similar in developing countries?

TO: What are you seeing in terms of the message that people, in general, don't misspend cash getting through and making an impact?

CB: I think the evidence that's coming out from all these cash transfer studies is creating some stubborn facts. And I think these stubborn facts are having a surprising degree of influence in the discussion. I think it's because they're pretty simple. They're consistent across studies. They're pretty simple facts. People are not misusing money. It's cheaper. People seem to be happier. They use the money well. It's that all of the front-line arguments against using cash are just running up against evidence. The people who argue against it are conceding the point. It's nice that it fits into a really simple narrative. It's nice that it's really counterintuitive to some people because that means that it gets talked about. It's very hard for me to tell how much real change there is. Just because the blogs and a few reporters have talked about it doesn't mean that it's sweeping policy circles. But I do get the sense that the dialogue is changing.

One of the interesting things is that if you look at the Syrian refugee crisis, the UN and the major donors are providing all the kinds of support they usually provide to refugees and internally displaced people, but they're providing it through ATM cards.[11] I think they're doing it partly because they're forced to. It's easier to distribute stuff when people congregate in camps and that's not happening as much as it has in some crises. They've been forced to use cash and not stuff by the nature of the way the refugees and IDPs have spread out. But the technology exists and the evidence can support them here, and I think that matters. Here's one of the most singular emergencies of the decade, and the principal means of aiding people is through cash. That's a big change.

TO: Let's turn back to your work in Liberia on youth rehabilitation.[5] One of the things you raise in one of the policy papers about Liberia is potential dangers of teaching people how to deal with conflict. If you teach ways of resolving conflict, you're going to surface a lot of conflicts that may not have come to the fore otherwise. Do you think that is somewhat unique to the conflict resolution space, or do you think there are a lot of areas where well-meaning programs to deal with a problem are actually surfacing more problems that may not be dealt with effectively and are therefore a net negative?

CB: Every project has the potential for unintended consequences. Let's say if we come to the conclusion that giving cash to the poor is an excellent thing. Well there are plenty of ways to distribute cash that will cause a riot. That doesn't mean giving cash to the poor is the wrong thing to do. But it does mean we have to be conscious of unintended consequences that may be fundamental to that intervention or may be idiosyncratic to the context or your design. That's true whether you are doing a rigorous evaluation or not.

The fact that we don't see unintended consequences unless we are doing something rigorous is one of the main arguments for doing evaluations. This is what medical controlled trials are all about—finding unintended side effects. There is a greater duty of care for physicians prescribing medicines with high probability of significant side effects. One of the incredible things about so-called peace-building aid and state-building aid is how cavalier the peace- and state-builders are with these interventions.

11. For details, see: http://www.unhcr.org/51127e696.html.

In that policy paper, I think the point we were trying to make is a general one about that cavalierness about unintended consequences. In the middle of the intervention we would find ourselves going into villages with these trainers who are saying that youth and elders are equal and all hell would break loose. People could accept the concept of different ethnic groups being equal. They might have some prejudice but they can conceptually accept it. People didn't like the concept of men and women being equal but that idea had been brought in before. Now to come in and say youth and elders are equal and young people don't have to listen to elders, well that was the last straw. No one knew that was what was going to drive communities crazy beforehand. But you find that out pretty quickly. I was disappointed in the cavalier approach of some of these peace-building groups. Whenever you're dealing with politically fragile situations, you have to be much more careful about what you do.

Very few academics have spent time or worked in a fragile state. In general, the places we've collected data from are places that are stable. If studies are done in Uganda, they're done in central Uganda. Or they're done in Kenya. But then violence breaks out around the Kenyan elections, and people are actually surprised.

TO: I'm really interested in your Ethiopia work where you're looking at the relative value of jobs versus cash.[6] You found a way to randomize getting a factory job, which seems to be the experimental coup of the decade. How did that come about?

CB: The idea occurred to me eight or ten years ago. It just seemed impossible that you could pull it off, and I didn't really have the networks to do anything. I didn't know any industrialists, and the idea that you could just cold call these people seemed a bit absurd. But it was always noodling around in the back of my mind.

So several years ago I was at a conference in London for the International Growth Center [IGC][12] and one of the guest speakers was an Ethiopian tycoon essentially. And he was speaking about how it's all about big firms and private sector development; all of this microentrepreneurship and NGO stuff or aid, none of it really matters. If you want growth you have to have big firms, or at least medium-size firms making big investments. He was speaking from the perspective of a very intelligent businessman with a personal experience of what the barriers to growth were. I think a lot of

12. Dercon is a development economist based at Oxford University currently serving as the chief economist of the UK Department for International Development.

economists would agree with what he was saying conceptually, but he was putting his own spin on it. He certainly didn't seem like your average tycoon, so I approached him right after his talk. We started chatting. And I mentioned this idea in an offhand way, and he said, "That's a great idea. Let's do it."

So we went over and found Stefan Dercon, who was managing the Ethiopia track for IGC.[13] And we grabbed him for twenty minutes, and he said, "Great. Let's do it."

I'd never been to Ethiopia. I could find it on the map but that was about it. But there I am flying to Ethiopia about a month later to get this set up, and within about two months we have about 20 firms lined up so that we can randomize it. After that, though, nothing happened. We had all these grand plans for manufacturing growth fall through for a number of reasons, some idiosyncratic to his business, some due to the investment climate in Ethiopia. Hermes [the Ethiopian businessman] keeps doing what he's doing, he's basically a real estate tycoon. That's where his money is, not in manufacturing. So for two years we just basically twiddled our thumbs. We ran our pilot and polished some things.

So it looked like the whole thing was going to die. I couldn't do a lot to get things going, my wife and I were about to have a baby. But two of my research assistants said they wanted to go down to the investment office and see if they could get things going. In Ethiopia, if you want to invest or start a new business, you have to go to the government and get a certificate. So the research assistants go down there, and they get a hold of the name and number of everyone who applied for a certificate in the last year and a half. There were about 300 names, and they just cold called these people. I would guess that for every 20 people they called three or four said it was interesting and they wanted to talk, and one or two of those signed up. So the idea that I thought was absurd for doing this is what turns out to have worked. At least in Ethiopia, these factory owners were genuinely interested in the questions we had. And they could see value for themselves in getting the answers. I think they figured they had the answer to our hypothesis, they know what a factory job does for a person, but they have some honest questions that we can help answer. Because we can

13. The International Growth Centre, founded in 2008 with funding from the UK Department for International Development, is a research center in London that focuses on development research and policy advice in collaboration with national governments.

follow up with people who leave and then give information back to the factory owner about who leaves and why and what other opportunities are out there and what market wages are. The factory owners are operating without much information. So the questions we're interested in, they're also interested in, and they think it will be useful for them in making business decisions.

TO: Thinking about that in the context of Nick Bloom's work[14] identifying levels of trust and information exchange as factors driving underperformance in mid-size manufacturers in India,[7] it seems remarkable the trust these factory owners have and their willingness to let you randomize who gets hired. I can't imagine an American firm ever doing that.

CB: I think American firms did a lot of experiments. In the whole scientific management movement there were an enormous number of industrial organization or management experiments done with lighting and work rules and that sort of thing. So I think firms are open to it. In Ethiopia it's certainly true that our limited experience was that any foreign-owned companies, Indian or Chinese, for example, were much more skeptical. Well, the Indian ones less so. But that might be that the people who are going and investing in Ethiopia might be a little wary of outsiders because they have more to be suspicious about. Maybe they're preyed on by government officials who want bribes. Who knows. Ethiopia is interesting because everyone's been trained as a good Marxist. I have actually had factory managers explain to me that they think the work I am doing is really important because the workers are exploited. This is the person who sets their wages. Socialism is in their bones to some extent, so me talking about empowering workers is great. But I think that might be true in a lot of places.

TO: What do you think are policy implications if you find that these formal sector factory jobs are really much better than microenterprise? Should we be shifting resources away from microcredit? Is it further reinforcement

14. Nick Bloom and co-authors including David McKenzie test an intervention providing operations consulting to textile firms in India. They find very large gains from simple improvements in operations, which raises the classic economics question: Why weren't the firms already taking these actions with large returns? Bloom et al. theorize that lack of trust in India prevents the use of professional managers in Indian firms, and therefore there is little opportunity for the spread of the technology of management. This result is discussed not only with David McKenzie (chapter 10), but also in the interviews with Dean Karlan (chapter 6) and Antoinette Schoar (chapter 16).

of the whole Doing Business report[15] concept of making it easier for small and medium enterprises to operate?

CB: Everyone seems to have different opinion on the policy implications. No one seems to agree on what people believe. Say the finding is that the factories are just hugely impactful on poverty, and they have a large effect for the individuals and not just a level effect. A lot of people, especially academic economists, will say, "of course, we're not surprised by this." I'm sure the referee reports will say it's obvious and wonder why it should be published because it just confirms intuitions. The paper will have something to say about the size and magnitude of the impact and that's useful but not that special.

Then there are going to be people who are blown away by the sign or the magnitude. I'm hoping that if the signs and magnitudes are as big as I think they might be, then we can shake some of the people who are focused on antipoverty through NGO interventions to think about helping medium and large firms. Take the Ethiopian government, for example. The Ethiopian government is very private sector oriented, but their main focus is on agri-business not urban manufacturing where the value added is higher. So this work might in general help to reorient people who are business-friendly but not focused on high-productivity sectors.

TO: That's a root problem of microenterprise in general. I think that most microenterprises aren't doing things where significant profits are even possible. They're going into low-return businesses. Those are some of David McKenzie's questions: Is it possible to do more than change a level and actually alter the slope of the curve?

CB: Well I think so long as you live in an economy that is only growing at 2, 3, 4 percent a year GDP per capita, and a bunch of that is really concentrated in a few extractive industries, which describes a lot of countries, I don't know that you're ever going to be able to create slope changes, to create accelerating growth. I think that comes from economies moving into a new equilibrium in a sustained way. In some sense that's the macro, big leap type of changes that, for instance, in the *Poor Economics* book we get steered away from. That's why I don't give up on those big changes and why I think it's worth devoting more energy into understanding them with as much rigor as we can muster. To change the slope, you have to be in one

15. The World Bank's annual Doing Business report ranks countries for the ease and cost of starting and running businesses. See: www.doingbusiness.org.

of these economies where the scope for you to improve and do better is just endless. You have to be in one of the economies that your children can do twice as well as you and their children even better. We're running a lot of these experiments in mostly stagnant, or at least not high-growth, economies. So I don't think we should be surprised that you're not seeing accelerating growth in the businesses no matter what you give them.

I think it also stimulates the conversation around industrial policy. There are a lot of people who just don't think you can have effective industrial policy and pick winners. They may be right. But I think governments' can create better climates and environments where you can get more competitive and larger firms. I think just directing more policy energy toward that would be a good thing. That conversation just isn't happening.

My classic example is that you take all of the Millennium Development Goal reports about how to eradicate poverty—whether it's their strategy documents or how-to documents or lessons learned—if you search for the words industry or firm, the only time that it comes up is when they are decrying the fact that not enough women are getting jobs in firms. Growing firms is just not on the agenda of these people.

Now African presidents and finance ministers talk about nothing else. And the average economist would say that firm growth is critical to incomes. But outside of those types of people, most of the people in development are not thinking or talking about growing firms.

TO: When you talk about African presidents and finance ministers, they're not really talking about small and medium-sized firms. They're talking about leaps into the modern economy and very large businesses.

CB: They're constantly strategizing about industrial policy. One of the things they're most puzzled about is how to run their industrial policy, and it's probably something they would say is the most important. Not just because of the jobs but also symbolically for them politically. And it generates tax revenue and all these other spillovers that benefit their economy. So they are constantly struggling with what to do. And they're constantly frustrated because they'll talk to academics or development agencies that are supposed to be focused on poverty alleviation, and yet none of us have anything to say to them. In fact the more accomplished that person is, the better their PhD, the more likely they are to say that there's nothing that you can do and you should just keep your nose out of it. And that's probably wrong.

TO: It's a little disheartening to me that Berk Ozler and David McKenzie[8] surveyed assistant professors and graduate students, and they responded that microfinance was overstudied. I feel like we've only begun to scratch the surface, we don't really understand what's happening and why in microfinance. How can it be overstudied when we really haven't answered any of the questions yet?

CB: If you're a PhD student at a top 10 university or an assistant professor, your job is not to fill in the gaps. Your job is to find where the frontier is and push it further. There are thousands of universities and thousands of researchers. There isn't going to be a shortage of microfinance experiments. So the barrier has been broken, the ideas are out there, and interest has been captured. Microfinance isn't that complicated. The theory people have outlined is pretty simple, and anyone can run a randomized control trial decently. A lot of people can write well. So the tools are there and the gaps are going to be filled in. It will take several years but it will happen.

If you're a PHD student doing a dissertation, though, your job is not to think what's important now. You have to think about what's important in five years. Your work is going to be published in five years because that's how long it is going to take you to do it, and then write it up and get it out there. So you have to look for what people haven't thought of yet. That's what you're rewarded for. There's a different system that rewards people for filling in the details. But your job as a young economist is to ask the questions and stimulate the ideas that no one's figured out yet.

TO: That's another disincentive to pre-specifying experiments isn't it? Because you want to maintain maximum flexibility in what you're doing for long enough in case there's a shift.

CB: You do deductive research after you do inductive research, right? The whole idea that everything ought to be pre-specified and we should only do deductive research, that's not how science works. Deduction is a necessary step, but often the frontier is being broken by people who are not doing that. Or they've gone through the inductive bit and are forced to do the deductive bit. So you can't look to those people to fill in the gaps, except every once in a while they might do some overarching thing that summarizes the literature and creates a new synthesis.

TO: You're saying though that there's a system for filling in the gaps, and a set of incentives. If the aid workers aren't reading the academic journals and the major news media is only looking at the sensational or counterintuitive stuff, then who is ever going to see or read the research that fills in gaps?

CB: I don't think that's true. I was talking about the people in the top 10 economics departments. But if you go to the top 100 departments, the people are incredibly smart in all of them. They might not have that special talent or aren't breaking through the ceiling, but they are very very smart. You go to the World Bank and it's full of very competent smart economists. We're at the point that BRAC[16] has its own internal research group. We have David Roodman writing a book[9] and doing a lot of the research at a think tank and doing really high-quality work filling in some of the gaps. There are dozens of World Bank projects that are probably evaluating microfinance right now that will be published in decent journals or policy reports or books like David Roodman's. That's where the gaps get filled in.

I don't know if philosophers of science still believe in Kuhnian scientific revolutions, but that's a little bit of what it's like. There are the Esther Duflos and the Dean Karlans who come up with a brilliant idea or have an influential article or a couple of really interesting experiments. And by the time the rest of us are figuring that out or arguing over the details or debating whether they are right or wrong, they're on to the next thing. They're not only on to the next thing but the next thing after that. That's their job.

If I'm going to get tenure at Columbia, that's my job as well. That's what I get evaluated on: do I change the way people think in my discipline. You don't change the way people think about your discipline by filling in the gaps.

TO: That points us to a question about bias within the research. A lot of field work is done in places where it's easy to work and have relatively good data sets or that have already been studied, so there is fieldwork infrastructure. In other words, places where PhD students from top 10 schools can easily work.

CB: And in places where there are relatively weak states, who can't prevent you from asking the kinds of questions they don't want you asking.

16. BRAC, started in Bangladesh in 1972 in reaction to the humanitarian crisis there, is now one of the world's largest development NGOs with programs in 11 countries.

TO: There is now a steady drumbeat recognizing the hidden biases in our "unbiased" research. For instance you see John Ioannidis's work[17] on medical research.

CB: There are different categories of bias. The bias that comes from working in a fragile state is where you can generalize the research to. In general, a lot of the work has been done in states that were poor but with at least a modicum of political stability. I think that's one of the reasons why development economics has under-appreciated the value of political stability.

TO: The way I think about this is that there are a lot of different categories of unobserved biases, whether it's who you study or how you study it, or very subtle things about research design, and on down to publication bias. How do you internalize that? Does it increase your skepticism about experiments? Does it increase your skepticism about nonexperimental approaches even more?

CB: Certainly seeing the ways in which even good experimental protocols followed by well-intentioned people still are resulting in biased research, it increases your skepticism in a healthy way. It increases it even further for research that is less transparent. Although a lot of the research where it's less transparent, the researchers are often less high and mighty about the quality of their methodology. People who are doing quasi-experiments or long-series historical stuff aren't calling their methodology the gold standard.

I still believe experimental stuff more than the long-term historical stuff where there's a nice headline result; hence it gets published in a top journal, hence it comes to our attention. There's a lot of selection going on there. There's less in the experimental area. I know this from personal experience, that if one of your experiments is a dog, you still have to finish it and write it up. That's partly because of the scientific imperative and partly because of the norms around experiments. But a big part of it is because you made a commitment to an organization or donor to finish the damn thing whether you like it or not. But if I'm just downloading some data set from the Internet and I'm not getting nice results, I would probably just put it on the back burner. So you end up not really believing much

---

17. John Ioannidis is a professor at the Stanford School of Medicine and is best known for his work challenging the reliability of published medical research. See "Why Most Published Research Findings Are False" (2005) *PLOS Medicine* 2(8), or for a layman's overview, D. Freedman (2010), "Lies, Damned Lies, and Medical Science," *The Atlantic*.

unless you know how careful and thoughtful the people behind the research are. You actually invest a lot of intellectual energy finding out who the people are that do the research and what their reputation is, then you go about reading the actual research.

TO: Are we at peak RCT? You've written that you advise students not to do an RCT because that's not the way you make your name any more.

CB: That's partly true. But the main reason I advise them against it is because it's long and expensive and they're not going to finish their dissertations on time. Plus you put all your eggs in one basket. So there are other reasons not to do experiments as a grad student. But certainly it's harder and harder to publish experiments in economics.

TO: If we trace a little bit of the recent intellectual history of development economics from instrumental variables (IV) to the local average treatment effect critique of IV approaches to RCTs, is this really just a question of novelty that's driving change or that people are taking on critiques of prior methods and trying to do better?

CB: I think both. The novelty maybe drove the overselling of RCTs, like these silly statements that everything ought to be evaluated randomly, or the people who say they don't believe any observational evidence. And those people are still out there. That was problematic and a lot of the backlash was pointed at that. I feel like it's hard for me to imagine that any serious economist thinks that RCTs shouldn't be a tool in the toolbox to answer a lot of questions.

To me what's more troubling is that there seems to be this prevailing idea that it's not clever enough to run an experiment, and so it's not clear that we should publish these things in the top five journals. There's an idea that they're too easy, and that if you want to get them published, you need to use the experiment to estimate a structural model. What a silly attitude. Why not regard these as a really important method for answering certain questions? And there are a lot of questions we have that are unanswered, so we're going to put a high value on people answering these questions. I think it will eventually go back to that. But there's this silly bar raising in economics that is a function of the fact that there's been a growing number of economists and a constant number of slots in the top journals.

TO: What does it take to change your priors? For example, if you had done an experiment …

CB: That's it. In reality, the thing that can change your priors is your experience. Certainly, when you read books or articles, you can have "a-ha" moments. But very often what changes your view of the world is your anecdotal experience.

TO: So how many papers or articles that found something fundamentally different from your experiment would it take to convince you that yours was the outlier and the others were right?

CB: Not many I suppose. One of my dissertation papers found some unintended positive political consequences of being exposed to violence.[10] It was not inconsistent with a rather silly methodological literature in American psychology—the idea that people can experience personal growth after tragedy and that's a good thing. That's not science though, and I didn't really believe my own paper.

Now I've been quite surprised to find in the past six years that I've seen eight or nine papers come out with similar findings. So that got me thinking that this might actually be true. At the same time I'm still suspicious because I imagine that for every paper published somebody has found a null result not published it. Though now after six years, the fact that I haven't seen a null result makes me think maybe there aren't any. So that changed my prior of suspicion about my own finding.

Now the thing to do, and this is the route I might take, is to do this deductively. Pick 10 places and let's test whether or not this is true. Does violence induce positive personal political action? And then you can write a book bringing all of this literature together.

But that's more political science then economics. Political science rewards writing books more than economics. Writing a political science book pushes you out to the frontier on a big question, but it also forces you to fill in the details. In economics, the mode is that you really have to have a silver bullet or a perfectly run trial. If you don't, then people won't be interested, and they won't read or cite your paper. In other social sciences, you try to build a really solid case in these areas where there are no silver bullets with lots of bits of very good and some circumstantial evidence. If you can find a silver bullet, great, but really that silver bullet only nails one important part in the bigger moving question.

Conclusion

In the summer of 2015 all the pathologies of the years of point and counterpoint about the RCT movement were on display in a raging online "conversation" about the research that many would credit as the origin of the RCT movement. Miguel and Kremer's work on deworming was suddenly controversial. The International Initiative for Impact Evaluation[1] (3ie) had sponsored an effort to replicate Miguel and Kremer's work (as well as other notable impact evaluation papers); the replicators rejected many of the original findings.[1]

In the media, the new conclusions were presented as definitively overturning the original work, despite not having been examined nearly as closely as the original research. Ben Goldacre, a prominent advocate for RCTs and research transparency in biomedical research, explicitly accepted the new results as conclusive, writing that Miguel and Kremer had "major flaws" but should not be "mocked" for having gotten things wrong (accepting the new results as conclusive) because they had made their data and code available to the replicators (and to others before them).[2] Goldacre didn't note that at the time he was writing the replicators had not yet released their data and code. In response to the replication, some within the RCT movement sharply questioned not only the skills but the *motives* of the replicators,[2] touching off a round of accusations of provincialism among economists. Of course, these accusations came mostly from epidemiologists and other medical researchers.

1. 3ie "funds impact evaluations and systematic reviews that generate evidence on what works in development programmes and why." The Initiative was founded in 2008 by the Gates Foundation, the UK Department for International Development and the Hewlett Foundation. For more on their replication papers series, see: http://www.3ieimpact.org/en/publications/3ie-replication-paper-series/.
2. See, for instance, Paul Gertler's post on the Berkeley Blog, "Good Science Gone Wrong? http://blogs.berkeley.edu/2015/08/03/good-science-gone-wrong/.

But many of the best aspects of the RCT movement were on display as well. Within a week there were several in-depth and transparent reviews of the arguments.[3] While the acrimony continued in some ways, for the most part detailed assessments of the evidence (within a Bayesian framework) reigned.

Still, as I wrote at the time, in my estimation the winner of Worm Wars (as it was called on Twitter) was Angus Deaton. At least insofar as he is associated with the argument that results of RCTs require the same skepticism, careful analysis and interpretation as results produced using other tools.

Pritchett's points also showed well. It's my impression that even after the more sober analyses gained prominence, no one's mind was changed. As discussed in the interview with Elie Hassenfeld, the Cochrane Collaboration had concluded the balance of evidence was against mass deworming much earlier, while others had concluded the opposite. As far as I can tell, none of the organizations or prominent individuals supporting mass deworming have retracted their support. The Schistosomiasis Control Institute was once again one of GiveWell's recommended charities at the end of 2015.[4]

Shortly after Worm Wars died down, new work questioning the impact of early childhood education[3] was released leading to the mildly ironic sight of James Heckman noting that the newly published work was suspect because it relied not only on randomization but on econometric techniques to make sure there was balance between treatment and control, and much smaller studies provided more reliable evidence.[4] A few months later Anne Case and Angus Deaton published a widely noted paper documenting a surprising rise in mortality among middle-aged white Americans in

3. See, for instance, a post by Macartan Humphreys of Columbia University, http://www.columbia.edu/~mh2245/w/worms.html; a post by Berk Ozler at the World Bank's Development Impact blog, http://blogs.worldbank.org/impactevaluations/worm-wars-review-reanalysis-miguel-and-kremer-s-deworming-study; two posts by Chris Blattman, http://chrisblattman.com/2015/07/23/dear-journalists-and-policymakers-what-you-need-to-know-about-the-worm-wars/ http://chrisblattman.com/2015/07/24/the-10-things-i-learned-in-the-trenches-of-the-worm-wars/; a post by Alexander Berger of GiveWell, http://blog.givewell.org/2015/07/24/new-deworming-reanalyses-and-cochrane-review/; and one from Michael Clemens and Justin Sandefur of CGD, http://www.cgdev.org/blog/mapping-worm-wars-what-public-should-take-away-scientific-debate-about-mass-deworming.
4. GiveWell's recommendation, and a full discussion of their perspective on deworming can be seen at:http://www.givewell.org/international/top-charities/schistosomiasis-control-initiative.

contrast to nearly every other population group around the world.[5] Almost immediately another version of Worm Wars (Mortality Wars?) erupted, with the sort of detailed examination of the data and analysis that Deaton advocates, questioning Case and Deaton's interpretation of the data.[5] A more fitting illustration of Deaton's point that all research must be closely examined and interpreted is hard to imagine.

As the Worm Wars, Pre-K Wars, and Mortality Wars revealed, the issues explored in the interviews—such as the relative value and place of RCTs for shaping policy, what qualifies as evidence, whether evidence (good or bad) truly shapes policy or changes minds—remain unresolved. It seems odd, therefore, titling this last note in the book a conclusion when conclusions have not been reached, nor will they ever be.

Still, I have reached some personal conclusions. Conducting these interviews, my aim was "to better understand, to think clearer, truer thoughts about the world, and how it might be changed for the better" as I wrote in the Introduction. I advanced in that aim, but not always in the ways I expected. Understanding and engaging with the debate on the use of RCTs in development economics has changed the way I think in both my professional and personal life. I spend more time thinking about theories of change, and am more skeptical about all research.

One of those conclusions is the need to reframe the debate in order to move forward. Both sides of the debate often point to the medical field to bolster their positions. Proponents of RCTs note that RCTs are required to test the efficacy and safety of new drugs before they are approved for use and social programs deserve the same scrutiny. Meanwhile critics say that medicine has a valid theory of external validity—that we understand how bodies work and so can be confident that what works for study subjects will work for others—which economics lacks, rendering the results of RCTs useless for guiding decisions in different contexts.[6] The appeals to medicine should stop, because the realities of the medical field don't support either point.

The quality of medical research and practice, it turns out, is shockingly bad. In recent years it has become apparent how little published medical research, despite the prominence given to RCTs, is reliable. One review by Bayer found that nearly two-thirds of a sample of 67 published papers couldn't be replicated by its scientists.[7] A 2003 review of 101 studies from

5. See blog posts by Jesse Singal, http://nymag.com/scienceofus/2015/11/gender -controversy-over-white-mortality.html, and Noah Smith for overviews, http:// noahpinionblog.blogspot.com/2015/11/gelman-vs-case-deaton-academics-vs.html.

highly influential journals that reported promising results found that only one yielded a treatment that was widely used 20 years later.[8] Another review of highly cited medical RCTs found that 25 percent of them were later contradicted or had their results materially reduced.[9] A 2015 study of 55 RCTs found that while 57 percent reported a statistically significant positive finding before pre-analysis plans were required, only 8 percent found statistically significant positive results after pre-analysis plans were required.[10]

Meanwhile, the existence of a movement advocating for "evidence-based medicine" highlights the fact that regardless of the reliability of the evidence from medical studies, it is difficult to get doctors to change practices. The US Centers for Disease Control has a long-standing campaign to remind doctors to wash their hands to prevent passing infections from one patient to the next; still today studies are finding no better than 50 percent compliance with hand-washing procedures.[11] A study of more than a million Medicare patients found that in a 12 month span at least 25 percent had received medical care that had been shown to be useless.[12] It's clear that medical research and practice should not be held up as an example to aspire to.

One of the (many) reasons that medical research is unreliable is that the presumed external validity cited by RCT critics isn't there. It was long assumed that because doctors had a good understanding of biological processes the race and gender of trial participants wasn't significant. In recent years, however, the presumption of external validity—a patient is a patient—has taken a lot of hits. There are substantial differences between how men and women, and people of different races and ethnicities respond to the same treatments, even to the same drugs.[13] That's not to mention the discoveries that epigenetics, changes in gene expression due to environmental factors, plays a large role in health and how individuals react to medical treatment.[14]

But the most remarkable thing is that despite the unreliability of medical research, the lack of evidence-based medical practice, and the significant issues with external validity in medical research, massive progress has been made in improving the health and longevity of people around the planet. While medical research and practice have many failings, they have saved hundreds of millions, perhaps billions of lives. The arguments from medical research and practice don't hold up for either side of the debate on RCTs among economists.

But that doesn't mean there is nothing to be learned from the medical field. Recognizing that the quality of evidence in general is not sufficient to support truly evidence-based medicine, some members of the medical research and practice community are shifting to talk about "evidence-generating medicine." In particular, evidence-generating medicine is about gathering more data about medical care in actual practice and patient outcomes outside of medical trials.[15] Perhaps I'm naive, but it seems to me that a move from focusing on "evidence-based policy" to "evidence-generating policy" could short-circuit many of the less productive arguments around the use of RCTs in economic development.

RCTs will continue to be one, among several, key tools for learning about the world. Whereas Greenberg and Shroder used to put together a digest in book form of social experiments using randomized designs and update it every few years, now I get an email curated by them with a list of 3 to 10 new papers every few weeks. As of the summer of 2016, there are more than 800 pre-analysis plans filed in the American Economic Association's RCT registry. Clever economists (and other social scientists) will find ways to put RCTs to use evaluating programs and policies that were presumed to be impossible to randomize (while other important questions will forever stay outside the domain of the *randomistas*). Indeed clever new ways to apply RCTs are quickly becoming a requirement—as Pritchett predicted the use of RCTs for simple program evaluation is quickly becoming the domain of private firms not academics (often with the explicit encouragement of academics).[6] A 3ie analysis in August 2016 found clear evidence that impact evaluations, the majority of which are RCTs, are continuing to rise, though at a slower rate, and David McKenzie found that RCTs are far from dominating development economics as less than 15 percent of papers published in development economics journals use RCTs.[16]

The growing use of RCTs inside of organizations for their own learning and evaluation, combined with better ongoing data on programs, policies and program participants in an "evidence-generating policy" framework would materially advance both internal and external validity and improve policies and programs in small and large ways. Such an approach would value both local knowledge and technocratic expertise. It would allow individuals and institutions to learn and take action. As I survey how the field has changed since I began paying attention in 2009, I'm hopeful that this is the direction of movement. I hope so, because as RCTs in economic development have proliferated so have the range of estimates of the impact

6. Ideas42 and ImpactMatters stand out as two examples of academics *creating* private firms to advance the use of impact evaluations outside of academe. Also see the interview with Rachel Glennerster where she talks about encouraging this trend.

of the programs evaluated.[17] It seems inevitable that there will be more examples of results that do not reproduce or effects that are the opposite of what earlier studies found.[7] A number of RCT proponents are also at the leading edge of advocating for research quality and reproducibility efforts.[8] Additional advocacy for data gathering outside of experiments would be a useful addition to the movement.

In the end, I remain an advocate for the use of RCTs in economic development, even for the increased use of RCTs. While my enthusiasm has been tempered by wrestling with the many valid points in the critiques of RCTs it hasn't been extinguished. Working on the book has helped me see that my personal theory of change puts high value on small, incremental changes; a high value on technocratic expertise; and ascribes a large role to individuals within institutions.

After all these interviews, and years of thinking about these issues, I stand by a defense of the use and spread of RCTs that I wrote several years ago.[18] Angus Deaton raised the concern that social experiments are disproportionately conducted on the poor and the weak. I take that concern seriously because I am not among the poor and the weak. But like a father in Ghana whose children are participants in an evaluation of contract teachers, I have a child whose future depends in part on RCTs.

I have a son affected by a rare syndrome that is disrupting many of the basic systems of his body, including causing the steady deterioration of his retinas. We are lucky that he was born in an age where the syndrome could be diagnosed, that the genetic and proteomic origins of the syndrome and its symptoms are at least partially understood. Those scientific breakthroughs were not the result of RCTs. But the various treatments being developed with that understanding thankfully are. I expect, even insist,

7. While not definitive, this likely outcome is hinted at in work by Allcott and Mullainathan on variance in impact of information about energy consumption discussed in several chapters, and by Rajeev Dehejia, Cristian Pop-Eleches and Cyrus Samii where they look at data on the likelihood that parents of two children of the same sex will have a third child (http://www.theigc.org/blog/from-local-to -global-extrapolating-experiments/), and work by Anett John (formerly Hofmann) following up on commitment savings evaluations (http://blogs.worldbank.org/ impactevaluations/when-commitment-fails-guest-post-anett-hofmann)

8. For instance, see Innovations for Poverty Action's Research Transparency Initiative, the Berkeley Initiative for Transparency in Social Science, co-founded by Ted Miguel and where Rachel Glennerster is on the executive committee, and J-PAL's Hypothesis Registry, a registry for pre-analysis plans for RCTs that pre-dated the American Economic Association's RCT Registry.

that any treatment be subjected to RCTs to prove their efficacy and safety. In fact I am an active participant, through both time and money, in setting up the infrastructure to enable experimentally testing possible treatments (an infrastructure that is in concordance not just with evidence-based medicine but evidence-generating medicine). I expect that were I in the shoes of that father in Ghana, I would feel the same way about an experiment that could help my children learn more in school. Indeed I wish there was much more experimentation in my children's schools despite the fact that our school district performs quite well according to statistics.

And as much as I long for a cure that permanently solves all of the complications of my son's syndrome, I don't believe that small efforts that are not aimed at a cure are diversions. Slowing down the rate at which his retinas are degenerating is a victory, just as figuring out how to help children in a local school in Ghana learn more is a victory even in the absence of "fixing" education as a whole or any of the other structural barriers to escaping poverty that Ghanaian children face. I enthusiastically support efforts to ameliorate the effects of the syndrome, not just cure them.

Still there are limitations. I don't want my child trapped in an algorithm irrevocably driven by an average treatment effect. My son and I will likely have to make decisions about participating in experiments with uncertain outcomes. I will want to control which experiments he participates in and who will have access to data about him. And an RCT cannot answer the most important question for me right now: what is the "right" way to tell a boy whose greatest joy in the world is reading that he will someday soon lose his sight?

And so, while I fall on the side of more RCTs in economic development, and better RCTs and evidence in medical research and practice, the debates about the use and value of RCTs will continue within my own family as well as in the wider world.

References

Introduction

1. Levitt, Steven D., and John List. "Field Experiments in Economics: the Past, the Present, and the Future." *European Economic Review* 53 (2009): 1–18. doi: 10.1016/j. euroeconrev.2008.12.001.

2. Jamison, Julian. "The Entry of Randomized Evaluation into the Social Sciences" (2016). dx.doi.org/10.2139/ssrn.2739005.

3. Gertler, Paul, James Heckman, Rodrigo Pinto, Arianna Zanolini, Christel Vermeersch, and Susan Walker, Susan M. Chang and Sally Grantham-McGregor. "Labor Market Returns to an Early Childhood Stimulation Intervention in Jamaica." *Science* 344 (6187) (2014): 998–1001. doi:10.1126/science.1251178.

4. Harrison, Glenn W. "Field Experiments and Methodological Intolerance." *Journal of Economic Methodology* 20(2) (2013): 103–17. doi:10.1080/1350178x.2013. 804678; Deaton, Angus. "Instruments, Randomization, and Learning about Development." *Journal of Economic Literature* 48 (June) (2010): 424–55. doi: 10.1257/ jel.48.2.424.

5. Kaplan, Robert, and Veronica Irvin. "Likelihood of Null Effects in Large NHLBI Clinical Trials Has Increased over Time." *PLoS One* 5 (August) (2015): 1–12. doi:10.1371/journal.pone.0132382.

6. Pritchett, Lant, and Justin Sandefur. "Learning from Experiments When Context Matters." *American Economic Review* 105 (5) (2015): 471–75. doi:10.1257/aer. p20151016.

7. Allcott, Hunt. "Site Selection Bias in Program Evaluation." *Quarterly Journal of Economics* 130 (3) (2015): 1117–65. doi:10.1093/qje/qjv015.

8. McKenzie, David. "A Rant on the External Validity Double Double-Standard." Development Impact Blog, World Bank, May 2, 2011, http://blogs.worldbank.org/ impactevaluations/a-rant-on-the-external-validity-double-double-standard.

9. Acemoglu, Daron, and James Robinson. *Why Nations Fail: The Origins of Power, Prosperity and Poverty*. New York: Crown, 2012; Banerjee, Abhijit V., and Esther Duflo. *Poor Economics: A Radical Rethinking of the Way to Fight Global Poverty*. New York: PublicAffairs, 2011; Deaton, Angus. *The Great Escape: Health, Wealth, and the Origins of Inequality*. Princeton: Princeton University Press, 2013; Easterly, William. *The White Man's Burden: Why the West's Efforts to Aid the Rest Have Done so Much Ill and So Little Good*. New York: Penguin, 2006; Sachs, Jeffrey D. *The End of Poverty: Economic Possibilities for Our Time*. New York: Penguin, 2005.

10. Banerjee, Abhijit, Esther Duflo, Nathanael Goldberg, Dean Karlan, Robert Osei, William Parienté, Jeremy Shapiro, Bram Thuysbaert, and Christopher Udry. "A Multifaceted Program Causes Lasting Progress for the Poor: Evidence from Six Countries." *Science* 348 (6236), May 15, 2015. doi: 10.1126/science.1260799.

Chapter 1

1. Glewwe, Paul, Michael Kremer, and Sylvie Moulin. "Many Children Left Behind? Textbooks and Test Scores in Kenya." *American Economic Journal: Applied Economics* 1 (1) (2009): 112–35. doi:10.1257/app.1.1.112.

2. Miguel, Edward, and Michael Kremer. "Worms: Identifying Impacts on Education and Health in the Presence of Treatment Externalities." *Econometrica* 72 (1) (2004): 159–217. doi:10.1111/j.1468-0262.2004.00481.x.

3. "The Price Is Wrong: Charging Small Fees Dramatically Reduces Access to Products for the Poor." *Jameel Poverty Action Lab Bulletin*, April 2011. http://www.povertyactionlab.org/publication/the-price-is-wrong.

4. See particularly chapter 8: "Health." In *World Development Report 2015: Mind, Society and Behavior*. Washington, DC: World Bank, 2015.

5. For an overview of the PROGRESA program and its impact, see: Skoufias, Emmanuel, and Bonnie McClafferty. "Is PROGRESA Working? Summary of the results of an evaluation by IFPRI." FCND Discussion Paper 118. Washington, DC, 2001. http://ebrary.ifpri.org/cdm/ref/collection/p15738coll2/id/77118.

6. Olken, Benjamin A., and Rohini Pande. "Corruption in Developing Countries." *Annual Review of Economics* 4 (2012): 479–509. doi: 10.1146/annurev-economics-080511-110917; Olken, Benjamin A., and Patrick Barron. "The Simple Economics of Extortion: Evidence from Trucking in Aceh." *Journal of Political Economy* 117 (3) (2009): 417–52. doi: 10.1086/599707; Olken, Benjamin A. "Monitoring Corruption: Evidence from a Field Experiment in Indonesia." *Journal of Political Economy* 115 (2) (2007): 200–49. doi: 10.1086/517935.

7. Kremer, Michael. "Patent Buyouts: A Mechanism for Encouraging Innovation." *Quarterly Journal of Economics* 113 (4) (1998): 1137–67. doi:10.1162/003355398555865.

8. Kremer, Michael, and Rachel Glennerster. *Strong Medicine: Creating Incentives for Pharmaceutical Research on Neglected Diseases*. Princeton: Princeton University Press, 2004.

9. Levine, Ruth, Michael Kremer, and Alice Albright. *Making Markets for Vaccines: Ideas to Action*. Washington, DC: Center for Global Development, 2005.

Chapter 2

1. Banerjee, Abhijit V., Shawn Cole, Esther Duflo, and Leigh Linden. "Remedying Education: Evidence from Two Randomized Experiments in India." *Quarterly Journal of Economics* 122 (3) (2007): 1235–64. doi:10.1162/qjec.122.3.1235.

2. Field, Erica, Rohini Pande, John Papp, and Natalia Rigol. "Does the Classic Microfinance Model Discourage Entrepreneurship among the Poor? Experimental Evidence from India." *American Economic Review* 103 (6) (2013): 2196–2226. doi:10.1257/aer.103.6.2196.

3. Banerjee, Abhijit V., and Esther Duflo. *Poor Economics: A Radical Rethinking of the Way to Fight Global Poverty*. New York: PublicAffairs, 2011.

4. Haushofer, Johannes, and Jeremy Shapiro. "The Short-Term Impact of Unconditional Cash Transfers to the Poor: Evidence from Kenya." *Quarterly Journal of Economics*, forthcoming (2016). https://www.princeton.edu/~joha/publications/ Haushofer_Shapiro_UCT_2016.04.25.pdf.

5. Banerjee, Abhijit, Esther Duflo, Rachel Glennerster, and Cynthia Kinnan. "The Miracle of Microfinance? Evidence from a Randomized Evaluation." *American Economic Journal: Applied Economics* 7 (1) (2015): 22–53. doi:10.1257/app.20130533.

6. Esther, Duflo, and Christopher R. Udry. "Intrahousehold Resource Allocation in Cote d'Ivoire: Social Norms, Separate Accounts and Consumption Choices." Working Paper 10498. NBER, Cambridge, MA, May 2004. doi: 10.3386/w10498. http:// www.nber.org/papers/w10498.

7. Banerjee, Abhijit, Dean Karlan, and Jonathan Zinman. "Six Randomized Evaluations of Microcredit: Introduction and Further Steps." *American Economic Journal: Applied Economics* 7 (1) (2015): 1–21. doi:10.1257/app.20140287.

8. Banerjee, Abhijit, Esther Duflo, Nathanael Goldberg, Dean Karlan, Robert Osei, William Parienté, Jeremy Shapiro, Bram Thuysbaert, and Christopher Udry. "A Multifaceted Program Causes Lasting Progress for the Poor: Evidence from Six Countries." *Science* 348 (6236), May 15, 2015. doi: 10.1126/science.1260799.

9. Benhassine, Najy, Florencia Devoto, Esther Duflo, Pascaline Dupas, and Victor Pouliquen. "Turning a Shove into a Nudge? A 'Labeled Cash Transfer' for Education." *American Economic Journal: Economic Policy* 7(3) (2015): 86–125. doi: 10.1257/ pol.20130225

10. Banerjee, Abhijit V., Shawn Cole, Esther Duflo, and Leigh Linden. "Remedying Education: Evidence from Two Randomized Experiments in India." *Quarterly Journal of Economics* 122 (3) (2007): 1235–64. doi:10.1162/qjec.122.3.1235.

11. Banerjee, Abhijit, Raghabendra Chattopadhyay, Esther Duflo, Daniel Keniston, and Nina Singh. "Improving Police Performance in Rajasthan, India: Experimental Evidence on Incentives, Managerial Autonomy and Training." Working Paper 17912, NBER, Cambridge, MA, March 2012. doi: 10.3386/w17912. http://www.nber.org/papers/w17912.

12. Duflo, Esther, Michael Greenstone, Rohini Pande, and Nicholas Ryan. "Truth-telling by Third-Party Auditors and the Response of Polluting Firms: Experimental Evidence from India." *Quarterly Journal of Economics* 128 (4) (2013): 1499–1545. doi: 10.1093/qje/qjt024.

13. Sen, Amartya. *Development as Freedom*. Oxford: Oxford University Press, 1999.

14. Microfinance CEO Working Group. "Measuring the Impact of Microcredit—Six New Studies." February 3, 2015. http://microfinanceceoworkinggroup.org/measuring-impact-microcredit-studies/.

15. Riccio, James, Nadine Dechausay, David Greenberg, Cynthia Miller, Zawadi Rucks, and Nandita Verma. "Toward Reduced Poverty across Generations: Early Findings from New York City's Conditional Cash Transfer Program." MDRC, New York, 2010. http://www.mdrc.org/publication/toward-reduced-poverty-across-generations http://www.mdrc.org/sites/default/files/full_588.pdf. For details on how the program was dramatically scaled back, see: Julie Bosman. "City Will Stop Paying the Poor for Good Behavior." *New York Times*, March 30, 2010. http://www.nytimes.com/2010/03/31/nyregion/31cash.html.

16. Banerjee, Abhijit Vinayak, Esther Duflo, and Rachel Glennerster. "Improving Immunisation Coverage in Rural India: Clustered Randomised Controlled Evaluations of Immunisation Campaigns with and without Incentives." *British Medical Journal* 340 (2010): c2220. doi: 10.1136/bmj.c2220.

17. Kaplan, Robert, and Veronica Irvin. "Likelihood of Null Effects in Large NHLBI Clinical Trials Has Increased over Time." *PLoS One* 5 (August) (2015): 1–12. doi:10.1371/journal.pone.0132382.

Chapter 3

1. For examples of Heckman's work on this topic, see: Heckman, James J., and V. Joseph Hotz. "Choosing among Alternative Nonexperimental Methods for Estimating the Impact of Social Programs: The Case of Manpower Training: Rejoinder." *Journal of the American Statistical Association* 84 (408) (1989): 878–80. doi: 10.1080/01621459.1989.10478848; Heckman, James J. "Randomization and Social

Policy Evaluation." In *Evaluating Welfare and Training Programs*, ed. Charles Manski and Irwin Garfinkel, 201–30. Cambridge: Harvard University Press, 1992; Heckman, James J. "Basic Knowledge—Not Black Box Evaluations." *Focus* 14 (1) (1992): 24–25. http://www.irp.wisc.edu/publications/focus/pdfs/foc141d.pdf; Heckman, James J., and Jeffery A. Smith. The Sensitivity of Experimental Impact Estimates (Evidence from the National JPTA Study). In *Youth Employment and Joblessness in Advanced Countries*, ed. David G. Blanchflower and Richard B. Freeman. 331–56. Chicago: University of Chicago Press, 2000.

2. Manski, Charles F. *Public Policy in an Uncertain World: Analysis and Decisions.* Cambridge: Harvard University Press, 2013.

3. Miguel, Edward, and Michael Kremer. "Worms: Identifying Impacts on Education and Health in the Presence of Treatment Externalities." *Econometrica* 72 (1) (2004): 159–217. doi:10.1111/j.1468-0262.2004.00481.x.

4. Bobonis, Gustavo J., Edward Miguel, and Charu Puri-Sharma. "Anemia and School Participation." *Journal of Human Resources* XLI (4) (2006): 692–721. doi:10.3368/jhr. XLI.4.692.

5. Taylor-Robinson, David C., Nicola Maayan, Karla Soares-Weiser, Sarah Donegan, and Paul Garner. "Deworming Drugs for Soil-Transmitted Intestinal Worms in Children: Effects on Nutritional Indicators, Haemoglobin, and School Performance." *Cochrane Database of Systematic Reviews* (7) (2015): CD000371. doi:10.1002/14651858. CD000371.pub6.

6. Greenberg, David, Mark Shroder, and Matthew Onstott. "The Social Experiment Market." *Journal of Economic Perspectives* 13 (3) (1999): 157–72. doi: 10.1257/ jep.13.3.157; Greenberg, David, and Mark Shroder. *The Digest of Social Experiments*, 3rd ed. Washington, DC: Urban Institute Press, 2004.

7. Gueron, Judith M., and Howard Rolston. *Fighting for Reliable Evidence.* New York: Russell Sage Foundation, 2013.

8. Acemoglu, Daron, and James A. Robinson. *Why Nations Fail: The Origins of Power, Prosperity and Poverty.* New York: Crown, 2012.

9. Deaton, Angus. *The Great Escape: Health, Wealth, and the Origins of Inequality.* Princeton: Princeton University Press, 2013.

Chapter 4

1. Bauchet, Jonathan, Jonathan Morduch, and Shamika Ravi. "Failure vs. Displacement: Why an Innovative Anti-poverty Program Showed No Net Impact in South India." *Journal of Development Economics* 116 (2015): 1–16. doi:10.1016/j. jdeveco.2015.03.005.

2. Banerjee, Abhijit, Esther Duflo, Nathanael Goldberg, Dean Karlan, Robert Osei, William Parienté, Jeremy Shapiro, Bram Thuysbaert, and Christopher Udry. "A Multifaceted Program Causes Lasting Progress for the Poor: Evidence from Six Countries." *Science* 348 (6236), May 15, 2015. doi: 10.1126/science.1260799.

3. Pitt, Mark M., and Shahidur R. Khandker. "The Impact of Group-Based Credit on Poor Households in Bangladesh: Does the Gender of Participants Matter?" *Journal of Political Economy* 106 (5) (1998): 958–96. doi:10.1086/250037.

4. Roodman, David, and Jonathan Morduch. "The Impact of Microcredit on the Poor in Bangladesh: Revisiting the Evidence." *Journal of Development Studies* 50 (4) (2014): 583–604. doi: 10.1080/00220388.2013.858122; Pitt, Mark. "Re-re-reply to 'The Impact of Microcredit on the Poor in Bangladesh: Revisiting the Evidence.'" Brown University Department of Economics Working Paper 2014-2, Brown University, Providence, RI, February 2014. http://www.brown.edu/academics/economics/sites/brown.edu.academics.economics/files/uploads/2014-2_paper.pdf; Roodman, David. "Bi-Modality in the Wild: Latest on Pitt & Khandker." David Roodman's Microfinance Open Book Blog, Center for Global Development, Washington, DC, December 16, 2011. http://www.cgdev.org/blog/bimodality-wild-latest-pitt-khandker.

5. Imbens, Guido W., and Joshua D. Angrist. "Identification and Estimation of Local Average Treatment Effects." *Econometrica* 62 (2) (1994): 467–75. doi: 10.2307/2951620; Angrist, Joshua D., Guido W. Imbens, and Donald B. Rubin. "Identification of Causal Effects Using Instrumental Variables." *Journal of the American Statistical Association* 91 (434) (1996): 444–55. doi: 10.1080/01621459.1996.10476902.

6. Banerjee, Abhijit, Dean Karlan, and Jonathan Zinman. "Six Randomized Evaluations of Microcredit: Introduction and Further Steps." *American Economic Journal: Applied Economics* 7 (1) (2015): 1–21. doi:10.1257/app.20140287.

7. The discussion of this paper is based on an earlier version (still available online as of this writing: http://scholar.harvard.edu/sendhil/publications/external-validity-and-partner-selection-bias). The current version does not include the section on MIX data and does not have Sendhil Mullainathan as a co-author; Allcott, Hunt. "Site Selection Bias in Program Evaluation." *Quarterly Journal of Economics* 130 (3) (2015): 1117–65. doi:10.1093/qje/qjv015.

8. Bauchet, Jonathan, and Jonathan Morduch. "Selective Knowledge: Reporting Biases in Microfinance Data." *Perspectives on Global Development and Technology* 9 (3/4) (2010): 240–69. doi:10.1163/156914910X499705.

9. Karlan, Dean, and Jonathan Zinman. "Microcredit in Theory and Practice: Using Randomized Credit Scoring for Impact Evaluation." *Science* 332 (6052) (2011): 1278–84. doi:10.1126/science.1200138.

10. de Mel, Suresh, David McKenzie, and Christopher Woodruff. "Returns to Capital in Microenterprises: Evidence from a Field Experiment." *Quarterly Journal of Economics* 123 (4) (2008): 1329–72. doi: 10.1162/qjec.2008.123.4.1329; de Mel, Suresh, David McKenzie, and Christopher Woodruff. "Are Women More Credit Constrained? Experimental Evidence on Gender and Microenterprise Returns." *American Economic Journal: Applied Economics* 1(3) (2009):1–32. doi: 10.1257/app.1.3.1.

11. Heckman, James, Neil Hohmann, Jeffrey Smith, and Michael Khoo. "Substitution and Dropout Bias in Social Experiments: A Study of an Influential Social Experiment." *Quarterly Journal of Economics* 115 (2) (2000): 651–94. doi: 10.1162/ 003355300554764.

12. McKenzie, David. "What Are the Under-researched Topics in Development According to Young Faculty?" Development Impact, World Bank, June 15, 2011. http://blogs.worldbank.org/impactevaluations/what-are-the-under-researched -topics-in-development-according-to-young-faculty.

13. Armendáriz, Beatriz, and Jonathan Morduch. *The Economics of Microfinance,* 2nd ed. Cambridge: MIT Press, 2010.

14. Coleman, Brett. "The Impact of Group Lending in Northeast Thailand." *Journal of Development Economics* 60 (1) (1999): 105–41. doi: 10.1016/S0304-3878(99)00038- 3; Coleman, Brett. "Microfinance in Northeast Thailand: Who Benefits and How Much?" World Development 34 (9) (2006): 1612–38. doi:10.1016/j.worlddev.2006 .01.006.

15. Collins, Daryl, Jonathan Morduch, Stuart Rutherford, and Orlanda Ruthven. *Portfolios of the Poor: How the World's Poor Live on $2 a Day*. Princeton: Princeton University Press, 2010.

16. Field, Erica, Rohini Pande, John Papp, and Natalia Rigol. "Does the Classic Microfinance Model Discourage Entrepreneurship among the Poor? Experimental Evidence from India." *American Economic Review* 103 (6) (2013): 2196–2226. doi: 10.1257/aer.103.6.2196.

17. Karlan, Dean, and Jonathan Morduch. "Access to Finance." In *Handbook of Development Economics*, vol. 5, ed. Dani Rodrik and Mark Rosenzweig, 4704–84. Amsterdam: Elsevier, 2009.

18. For an example, see: Johnston, Don Jr., and Jonathan Morduch. "The Unbanked: Evidence from Indonesia." *World Bank Economic Review* 22 (3) (2008): 517–37. doi: 10.1093/wber/lhn016.

19. Chaia, Alberto, Aparna Dalal, Tony Goland, Maria Jose Gonzalez, Jonathan Morduch, and Robert Schiff. "Half the World Is Unbanked." In *Banking the World*, ed. Robert Cull, Asli Demirguc-Kunt, and Jonathan Morduch. Cambridge: MIT Press, 2012.

20. Collins, Daryl, Jonathan Morduch, Stuart Rutherford, and Orlanda Ruthven. *Portfolios of the Poor: How the World's Poor Live on $2 a Day*. Princeton: Princeton University Press, 2010.

21. Banerjee, Abhijit V., and Esther Duflo. "The Economic Lives of the Poor." *Journal of Economic Perspectives* 21 (1) (2007): 141–68. doi: 10.1257/jep.21.1.141.

Chapter 5

1. Gueron, Judith M., and Howard Rolston. *Fighting for Reliable Evidence*. New York: Russell Sage Foundation, 2013.

2. Betsey, Charles, Robinson G. Hollister Jr., and Mary Papageorgiou. *Youth Employment and Training Programs: The YEPDA Years*. Washington, DC: National Academy Press, 1985. doi: 10.17226/613.

3. Kemple, James, with Cynthia J. Willner. "Career Academies: Long-Term Impacts on Labor Market Outcomes, Educational Attainment, and Transitions to Adulthood." MDRC, June 2008. http://www.mdrc.org/sites/default/files/full_50.pdf.

Chapter 6

1. Banerjee, Abhijit V., Shawn Cole, Esther Duflo, and Leigh Linden. "Remedying Education: Evidence from Two Randomized Experiments in India." *Quarterly Journal of Economics* 122 (3) (2007): 1235–64. doi: 10.1162/qjec.122.3.1235.

2. Karlan, Dean, and Martin Valdivia. 2011. "Teaching Entrepreneurship: Impact of Business Training on Microfinance Clients and Institutions." *Review of Economics and Statistics* 93 (2): 510–27. doi: 10.1162/REST_a_00074.

3. Ashraf, Nava, Dean Karlan, and Wesley Yin. "Tying Odysseus to the Mast: Evidence from a Commitment Savings Product in the Philippines." *Quarterly Journal of Economics* 121 (2) (2006): 635–72. doi: 10.1162/qjec.2006.121.2.635.

4. Banerjee, Abhijit V., and Esther Duflo. "The Economic Lives of the Poor." *Journal of Economic Perspectives* 21 (1) (2007): 141–68. doi: 10.1257/jep.21.1.141.

5. Mullainathan, Sendhil, and Eldar Shafir. 2013. *Scarcity: Why Having Too Little Means So Much*. New York: Times Books.

6. Karlan, Dean, and Jonathan Zinman. "Borrow Less Tomorrow: Behavioral Approaches to Debt Reduction." Working Paper. Financial Security Project at Boston College, FSP 2012-1. Center for Retirement Research at Boston College, May 2012. http://crr.bc.edu/wp-content/uploads/2012/05/FSP-WP-2012-1.pdf.

7. Karlan, Dean S., and Jacob Appel. 2011. More Than Good Intentions: How a New Economics Is Helping to Solve Global Poverty. New York: Dutton Press, 2011.

8. Karlan, Dean, and Daniel H. Wood. "The Effect of Effectiveness: Donor Response to Aid Effectiveness in a Direct Mail Fundraising Experiment." Economic Growth Center Discussion Paper 1038. Yale University, 2014. doi: 10.2139/ssrn.2421943.

9. Karlan, Dean. "Winners of the Heart + Mind Donations Contest." Freakonomics, June 2, 2011. http://freakonomics.com/2011/06/02/winners-of-heart-mind -donations-contest/.

10. de Mel, Suresh, David McKenzie, and Christopher Woodruff. "Returns to Capital in Microenterprises: Evidence from a Field Experiment." Quarterly Journal of Economics 123 (4) (2008): 1329–72. doi: 10.1162/qjec.2008.123.4.1329.

11. Karlan, Dean, and Martin Valdivia. "Teaching Entrepreneurship: Impact of Business Training on Microfinance Clients and Institutions." Review of Economics and Statistics 93 (2) (2011): 510–27. doi: 10.1162/REST_a_00074.

12. Bruhn, Miriam, Dean S. Karlan, and Antoinette Schoar. "The Impact of Consulting Services on Small and Medium Enterprises: Evidence from a Randomized Trial in Mexico." Economic Growth Center Discussion Paper 1010. Yale University, 2012. http://www.econ.yale.edu/growth_pdf/cdp1010.pdf, 10.2139/ssrn.2010710.

13. Drexler, Alejandro, Greg Fischer, and Antoinette Schoar. "Keeping It Simple: Financial Literacy and Rules of Thumb." American Economic Journal: Applied Economics 6 (2) (2014): 1–31. doi: 10.1257/app.6.2.1.

14. Karlan, Dean, Ryan Knight, and Christopher Udry. "Hoping to Win, Expected to Lose: Theory and Lessons on Micro Enterprise Development." Working Paper 18325. NBER, Cambridge, MA, August 2012. doi: 10.3386/w18325. http://www.nber.org/ papers/w18325.pdf.

15. Banerjee, Abhijit, Esther Duflo, Nathanael Goldberg, Dean Karlan, Robert Osei, William Parienté, Jeremy Shapiro, Bram Thuysbaert, and Christopher Udry. "A Multifaceted Program Causes Lasting Progress for the Poor: Evidence from Six Countries." Science 348 (6236), May 15, 2015. doi: 10.1126/science.1260799.

16. Bold, Tessa, Mwangi Kimenyi, Germano Mwabu, Alice Ng'ang'a, and Justin Sandefur. "Scaling-up What Works: Experimental Evidence on External Validity in Kenyan Education." Center for Global Development Working Paper 321. Washington, DC, March 2013. http://www.cgdev.org/publication/scaling-what-works -experimental-evidence-external-validity-kenyan-education-working. For papers on earlier tests of contract teachers, see: Banerjee, Abhijit V., Shawn Cole, Esther Duflo, and Leigh Linden. "Remedying Education: Evidence from Two Randomized Experiments in India." Quarterly Journal of Economics 122 (3) (2007): 1235–64. doi: 10.1162/ qjec.122.3.1235; Muralidharan, Karthik, and Venkatesh Sundararaman. "Contract Teachers: Experimental Evidence from India." Working Paper 19440. NBER, Cambridge, MA, September 2013. doi: 10.3386/w19440; Duflo, Esther, Pascaline Dupas, and Michael Kremer. "School Governance, Teacher Incentives and Pupil–Teacher

Ratios: Experimental Evidence from Kenyan Primary Schools." *Journal of Public Economics* 123 (2015): 92–110. doi: 10.1016/j.jpubeco.2014.11.008.

17. Banerjee, Abhijit, Dean Karlan, and Jonathan Zinman. "Six Randomized Evaluations of Microcredit: Introduction and Further Steps." *American Economic Journal: Applied Economics* 7 (1) (2015): 1–21. doi: 10.1257/app.20140287; Banerjee, Abhijit, Esther Duflo, Nathanael Goldberg, Dean Karlan, Robert Osei, William Parienté, Jeremy Shapiro, Bram Thuysbaert, and Christopher Udry. "A Multifaceted Program Causes Lasting Progress for the Poor: Evidence from Six Countries." *Science* 348 (6236), May 15, 2015. doi: 10.1126/science.1260799.

18. "The Price Is Wrong: Charging Small Fees Dramatically Reduces Access to Products for the Poor." *Jameel Poverty Action Lab Bulletin*, April 2011. http://www.povertyactionlab.org/publication/the-price-is-wrong.

Chapter 7

1. Goldberg, Nathanael. *Measuring the Impact of Microfinance: Taking Stock of What We Know*, Washington, DC: Grameen Foundation USA Publication Series, 2005. http://www.grameenfoundation.org/sites/grameenfoundation.org/files/resources/Measuring-Impact-of-Microfinance_Nathanael_Goldberg.pdf.

2. O'Dell, Kathleen. *Measuring the Impact of Microfinance*, Washington, DC: Grameen Foundation USA Publication Series, 2010. http://www.grameenfoundation.org/resource/measuring-impact-microfinance.

3. Microfinance CEO Working Group. "Measuring the Impact of Microfinance: Our Perspective." April 2010. http://www.grameenfoundation.org/sites/grameenfoundation.org/files/archive-dev09/Measuring-the-Impact-of-Microfinance-Our-Perspective.pdf.

4. Microfinance CEO Working Group. "Measuring the Impact of Microcredit— Six New Studies." February 3, 2015. http://microfinanceceoworkinggroup.org/measuring-impact-microcredit-studies/.

5. Banerjee, Abhijit, Dean Karlan, and Jonathan Zinman. "Six Randomized Evaluations of Microcredit: Introduction and Further Steps." *American Economic Journal: Applied Economics* 7 (1) (2015): 1–21. doi:10.1257/app.20140287.

6. Pitt, Mark M., and Shahidur R. Khandker. "The Impact of Group-Based Credit on Poor Households in Bangladesh: Does the Gender of Participants Matter?" *Journal of Political Economy* 106 (5) (1998): 958–96. doi:10.1086/250037.

7. Roodman, David. "Microfinance Groups, Feeling Misunderstood, Misunderstand Research." *David Roodman's Open Book Blog*, Center for Global Development, April 9, 2010. http://www.cgdev.org/blog/microfinance-groups-feeling-misunderstood-misunderstand-research.

Chapter 8

1. Ashraf, Nava, Xavier Giné, and Dean Karlan. "Finding Missing Markets (and a Disturbing Epilogue): Evidence from an Export Crop Adoption and Marketing Intervention in Kenya." *American Journal of Agricultural Economics* 91 (4) (2009): 973–90. doi:10.1111/j.1467-8276.2009.01319.x.

2. Giné, Xavier, Cristina Martínez Cuellar, and Rafael Mazer. "Financial (dis-)information: Evidence from an Audit Study in Mexico." Policy Research Working Paper 6902, World Bank, Washington DC, June 2014. http://www-wds.worldbank.org/servlet/WDSContentServer/WDSP/IB/2014/06/03/000158349_20140603154236/Rendered/PDF/WPS6902.pdf.

3. Cole, Shawn, Xavier Giné, Jeremy Tobacman, Petia Topalova, Robert Townsend, and James Vickery. "Barriers to Household Risk Management: Evidence from India." *American Economic Journal: Applied Economics* 5 (1) (2013): 104–35. doi:10.1257/app.5.1.104.

4. Drexler, Alejandro, Greg Fischer, and Antoinette Schoar. "Keeping It Simple: Financial Literacy and Rules of Thumb." *American Economic Journal: Applied Economics* 6 (2) (2014): 1–31. doi: 10.1257/app.6.2.1.

5. Giné, Xavier, Karuna Krishnaswamy, and Alejandro Ponce. "Strategic Default in Joint Liability Groups: Evidence from a Natural Experiment in India." Working Paper. World Bank, November 2011. http://siteresources.worldbank.org/DEC/Resources/StrategicDefaultInJointLiabilityGroups.pdf .

6. For an example of research that came out of this work, see: Giné, Xavier, and Martin Kanz. "The Economic Effects of a Borrower Bailout: Evidence from an Emerging Market." Policy Research Working Paper 7109. World Bank, Washington, DC, November 2014. http://documents.worldbank.org/curated/en/2014/11/20378033/economic-effects-borrower-bailout-evidence-emerging-market.

7. Giné, Xavier, Jessica Goldberg, and Dean Yang. "Credit Market Consequences of Improved Personal Identification: Field Experimental Evidence from Malawi." *American Economic Review* 102 (6) (2012): 2923–54. doi: 10.1257/aer.102.6.2923.

8. Stiglitz, Joseph E. "Peer Monitoring and Credit Markets." *World Bank Economic Review* 4 (3) (1990): 351–66. doi:10.1093/wber/4.3.351.

9. Muralidharan, Karthik, Paul Niehaus, and Sandip Sukhtankar. "Building State Capacity: Evidence from Biometric Smartcards in India." Working Paper 19999. National Bureau of Economic Research, Cambridge, MA, March 2014. http:www.nber.org/papers/w19999, doi: 10.3386/w19999.

10. Giné, Xavier, and Dean Karlan. "Group versus Individual Liability: Long Term Evidence from Philippine Microcredit Lending Groups." *Journal of Development Economics* 107 (March) (2014): 65–83. doi: 10.1016/j.jdeveco.2013.11.003.

11. Brune, Lasse, Xavier Giné, Jessica Goldberg, and Dean Yang. "Facilitating Savings for Agriculture: Field Experimental Evidence from Malawi." *Economic Development and Cultural Change* 64 (2) (2016): 187–220. doi: 10.1086/684014.

12. Dupas, Pascaline, and Jonathan Robinson. "Why Don't the Poor Save More? Evidence from Health Savings Experiments." *American Economic Review* 103 (4) (2011): 1138–71. doi:10.1257/aer.103.4.1138.

13. Rosenzweig, Mark. "Thinking Small: *Poor Economics: A Radical Rethinking of the Way to Fight Global Poverty.*" Review essay. *Journal of Economic Literature* 50 (1) (2012): 115–27. doi: 10.1257/jel.50.1.115.

14. Banerjee, Abhijit V., and Esther Duflo. *Poor Economics: A Radical Rethinking of the Way to Fight Global Poverty.* New York: PublicAffairs, 2011.

15. Todd, Petra E., and Kenneth I. Wolpin. "Assessing the Impact of a School Subsidy Program in Mexico: Using a Social Experiment to Validate a Dynamic Behavioral Model of Child Schooling and Fertility." *American Economic Review* 96 (5) (2006): 1384–1417. doi: 10.1257/aer.96.5.1384.

16. Giné, Xavier, and Hanan G. Jacoby. "Markets, Contracts and Uncertainty: A Structural Model of a Groundwater Economy." Working Paper. World Bank, January 2015. http://siteresources.worldbank.org/EXTABCDE/Resources/7455676 -1401388901525/9576629-1401388974813/Hanan_Jacoby.pdf.

Chapter 9

1. For a specific Pritchett, Lant. "The Policy Irrelevance of the Economics of Education: Is 'Normative as Positive' Just Useless, or Worse?" In *What Works in Development? Thinking Big and Thinking Small,* ed. Jessica Cohen and William Easterly, 130–73. Washington, DC: Brookings Institution Press, 2009.

2. Pritchett, Lant, and Deon Filmer. "What Education Production Functions *Really* Show: A Positive Theory of Education Expenditures." *Economics of Education Review* 18 (2) (1999): 223–39. doi:10.1016/S0272-7757(98)00034-X.

3. Pritchett, Lant, and Justin Sandefur. "Learning from Experiments When Context Matters." *American Economic Review: Papers and Proceedings* 105 (5) (2015): 471–75. doi: 10.1257/aer.p20151016; Pritchett, Lant, and Justin Sandefur. "Context Matters for Size: Why External Validity Claims and Development Practice Don't Mix." Journal *of Globalization and Development* 4 (2) (2014): 161–97. doi: 10.1515/ jgd-2014-0004.

4. The best overview is Kahneman's own book, Kahneman, Daniel. *Thinking, Fast and Slow.* New York: Farrar, Straus and Giroux, 2011.

5. Gueron, Judith M., and Howard Rolston. *Fighting for Reliable Evidence*. New York: Russell Sage Foundation, 2013.

6. Pritchett, Lant. "Can Rich Countries Be Reliable Partners for National Development?" Center for Global Development, February 3, 2015. http://www.cgdev.org/publication/ft/can-rich-countries-be-reliable-partners-national-development.

7. Andrews, Matt, Lant Pritchett, and Michael Woolcock. "Escaping Capability Traps through Problem Driven Iterative Adaptation (PDIA)." *World Development* 51 (November) (2013): 234–44. doi: 10.1016/j.worlddev.2013.05.011.

8. Pritchett, Lant. "It Pays to be Ignorant: A Simple Political Economy of Rigorous Program Evaluation." *Journal of Economic Policy Reform* 5 (4) (2002): 251–69. doi:10.1080/1384128032000096832.

9. Pritchett, Lant, Salimah Samji, and Jeffrey Hammer. "It's All about MeE: Using Structured Experiential Learning ("e") to Crawl the Design Space." Working Paper 322. Center for Global Development, Washington, DC, April 2013. http://www.cgdev.org/sites/default/files/its-all-about-mee_1.pdf. doi: 10.2139/ssrn.2248785.

10. Kremer, Michael. "The O-Ring Theory of Economic Development." *Quarterly Journal of Economics* 108 (3) (1993): 551–75. doi: 10.2307/2118400.

11. Glewwe, Paul, Michael Kremer, and Sylvie Moulin. "Many Children Left Behind? Textbooks and Test Scores in Kenya." *American Economic Journal: Applied Economics* 1 (1) (2009): 112–35. doi: 10.1257/app.1.1.112.

12. Blattman, Christopher, and Paul Niehaus. "Show Them the Money: Why Giving Cash Helps Alleviate Poverty." *Foreign Affairs* 2014 (May/June) (2014): 117–26. https://www.foreignaffairs.com/articles/show-them-money.; Baird, Sarah, Craig McIntosh, and Berk Ozler. "Cash or Condition? Evidence from a Cash Transfer Experiment." *Quarterly Journal of Economics* 126 (4) (2011): 1709–53. doi: 10.1093/qje/qjr032; Haushofer, Johannes, and Jeremy Shapiro. "The Short-Term Impact of Unconditional Cash Transfers to the Poor: Evidence from Kenya." *Quarterly Journal of Economics*, forthcoming (2016). https://www.princeton.edu/~joha/publications/Haushofer_Shapiro_UCT_2016.04.25.pdf.

Chapter 10

1. de Mel, Suresh, David McKenzie, and Christopher Woodruff. "Returns to Capital in Microenterprises: Evidence from a Field Experiment." *Quarterly Journal of Economics* 123 (4) (2008): 1329–72. doi:10.1162/qjec.2008.123.4.1329.

2. McKenzie, David, and Christopher Woodruff. "Experimental Evidence on Returns to Capital and Access to Finance in Mexico." *World Bank Economic Review* 22 (3) (2008): 457–82. doi:10.1093/wber/lhn017.

3. McKenzie, David, and Christopher Woodruff. "Do Entry Costs Provide an Empirical Basis for Poverty Traps? Evidence from Mexican Microenterprises." *Economic Development and Cultural Change* 55 (1) (2006): 3–42. doi:10.1086/505725.

4. Haushofer, Johannes, and Jeremy Shapiro. "The Short-Term Impact of Unconditional Cash Transfers to the Poor: Evidence from Kenya." *Quarterly Journal of Economics*, forthcoming (2016). https://www.princeton.edu/~joha/publications/Haushofer_Shapiro_UCT_2016.04.25.pdf.

5. Fafchamps, Marcel, David McKenzie, Simon Quinn, and Christopher Woodruff. "Microenterprise Growth and the Flypaper Effect: Evidence from a Randomized Experiment in Ghana." *Journal of Development Economics* 106 (2014): 211–26. doi:10.1016/j.jdeveco.2013.09.010.

6. de Mel, Suresh, David McKenzie, and Christopher Woodruff. "Business Training and Female Enterprise Start-up, Growth, and Dynamics; Experimental Evidence from Sri Lanka." *Journal of Development Economics* 106 (2014): 199–210. doi:10.1016/j.jdeveco.2013.09.005.

7. de Mel, Suresh, David McKenzie, and Christopher Woodruff. "What Generates Growth in Microenterprises? Experimental Evidence on Capital, Labor and Training." Working Paper. MIT, February 2013. http://economics.mit.edu/files/8666.

8. David McKenzie and Christopher Woodruff . "What Are We Learning from Business Training and Entrepreneurship Evaluations around the Developing World?" World Bank Research Observer. 29 (1) (2014): 48–82. doi: 10.1093/wbro/lkt007.

9. Blattman, Christopher, Eric P. Green, Julian Jamison, M. Christian Lehmann, and Jeannie Annan. "The Returns to Microenterprise Support among the Ultra-Poor: A Field Experiment in Post-war Uganda." *American Economic Review: Applied Economics* 8 (2) (2016): 35–.64. doi: 10.1257/app.20150023.

10. McKenzie, David, and Christopher Woodruff, 2015. "Business Practices in Small Firms in Developing Countries." Working Paper 21505. NBER, Cambridge, MA. doi: 10.3386/w21505. http://www.nber.org/papers/w21505.

11. Hirshleifer, Saronjini, David McKenzie, Rita Almeida, and Cristobal Ridao-Cano. "The Impact of Vocational Training for the Unemployed: Experimental Evidence from Turkey." *Economic Journal* (2015). http://onlinelibrary.wiley.com/doi/10.1111/ecoj.12211/abstract. doi: 10.1111/ecoj.12211.

12. de Mel, Suresh, David McKenzie, and Christopher Woodruff. "Measuring Microenterprise Profits: Must We Ask How the Sausage Is Made?" *Journal of Development Economics* 88 (1) (2009): 19–31. doi: 10.1016/j.jdeveco.2008.01.007.

13. Samphantharak, Krislet, and Robert M. Townsend. Households as Corporate Firms: An Analysis of Household Finance Using Integrated Household Surveys and Corporate Financial Accounting. New York: Cambridge University Press, 2009.

14. Emran, M.Shahe, A. K. M. Mahbub Morshed, and Joseph E. Stiglitz. "Microfinance and Missing Markets." MPRA Paper 41451. University Library of Munich (2011). https://mpra.ub.uni-muenchen.de/41451/1/MPRA_paper_41451.pdf.

15. Drexler, Alejandro, Greg Fischer, and Antoinette Schoar. "Keeping It Simple: Financial Literacy and Rules of Thumb." *American Economic Journal: Applied Economics* 6 (2) (2014): 1–31. doi: 10.1257/app.6.2.1.

16. Banerjee, Abhijit, Esther Duflo, Rachel Glennerster, and Cynthia Kinnan. "The Miracle of Microfinance? Evidence from a Randomized Evaluation." *American Economic Journal: Applied Economics* 7 (1) (2015): 22–53. doi:10.1257/app.20130533.

17. McKenzie, David. "Beyond Baseline and Follow-Up: The Case for More T in Experiments." *Journal of Development Economics* 99 (2) (2012): 210–21.

18. Klinger, Bailey, Asim Khwaja, and Carlos del Carpio. *Enterprising Psychometrics and Poverty Reduction*. New York: Springer-Verlag, 2013. doi: 10.1007/978-1-4614-7227-8. http://www.springer.com/us/book/9781461472261.

19. Bloom, Nicholas, Benn Eifert, Aprijit Mahajan, David McKenzie, and John Roberts. "Does Management Matter? Evidence from India." *Quarterly Journal of Economics* 128 (1) (2013): 1–51. doi:10.1093/qje/qjs044.

20. Iacovone, Leonardo, William Maloney, and David McKenzie. "Upgrading Management Technology in Colombia." AEA RCT Registry. October 17, 2014. https://www.socialscienceregistry.org/trials/528/history/2924.

21. Allcott, Hunt, and Sendhil Mullainthan. "Behavior and Energy Policy." *Science* 327 (5970), 2010: 1204–1205. doi: 10.1126/science.1180775.

22. Gibson, John, and David McKenzie. "How Cost Elastic Are Remittances? Estimates from Tongan Migrants in New Zealand." University of Waikato, Hamilton, New Zealand. Working Paper in Economics, 06/02. March 2006. ftp://wms-webprod1.mngt.waikato.ac.nz/RePEc/wai/econwp/0602.pdf.

Chapter 11

1. Birdsall, Nancy, Ruth Levine, and William Savedoff. "When Will We Ever Learn?: Improving Lives through Impact Evaluation." Center for Global Development, Evaluation Gap Working Group, Washington, DC, 2006.

2. Pritchett, Lant. *The Rebirth of Education: Schooling Ain't Learning*. Washington, DC: Center for Global Development, 2013.

3. Birdsall, Nancy, and William D. Savedoff. *Cash on Delivery Aid: A New Approach to Foreign Aid*. Washington, DC: Center for Global Development, 2010.

4. Clemens, Michael. "A Labor Mobility Agenda for Development." Center for Global Development Working Paper 201, Washington DC, January 2010; Clemens, Michael, Claudio E. Montenegro, and Lant Pritchett. "The Place Premium: Wage Differences for Identical Workers across the U.S. Border." Center for Global Development, Working Paper 148, Washington, DC, July, 2008; Clemens, Michael. "Economics and Emigration: Trillion-Dollar Bills on the Sidewalk?" *Journal of Economic Perspectives* 25 (3) (2011): 83–106. doi: 10.1257/jep.25.3.83.

5 Moss, Todd, Caroline Lambert, and Stephanie Majerowicz. "Oil to Cash: Fighting the Resource Curse with Cash Transfers." Center for Global Development, CGD Brief. Washington, DC, May 2015.

6. Scott, James C. *Seeing Like a State: How Certain Schemes to Improve the Human Condition Have Failed.* New Haven: Yale University Press, 1999.

7. Mullainathan, Sendhil, and Eldar Shafir. *Scarcity: Why Having Too Little Means So Much.* New York: Times Books, 2013.

8. Andrews, Matt, Lant Pritchett, and Michael Woolcock. "Escaping Capability Traps Through Problem Driven Iterative Adaptation (PDIA)." *World Development* 51 (2013): 234–44. doi:10.1016/j.worlddev.2013.05.011.

Chapter 12

1. Maccini, Sharon, and Dean Yang. "Under the Weather: Health, Schooling, and Economic Consequences of Early-Life Rainfall." *American Economic Review* 99 (3) (2009): 1006–26. doi:10.1257/aer.99.3.1006.

2. See, for example: Fogel, Robert. "New Findings on Secular Trends in Nutrition and Mortality: Some Implications for Population Theory. In *Handbook of Population and Family Economics,* vol. 1A, ed. Mark Rosenzweig and Oded Stark. 433–81. Amsterdam: Elsevier Science, 1997.

3. Brune, Lasse, Xavier Giné, Jessica Goldberg, and Dean Yang. "Facilitating Savings for Agriculture: Field Experimental Evidence from Malawi." *Economic Development and Cultural Change* 64 (2) (2016): 187–220. doi: 10.1086/684014.

4. Banerjee, Abhijit, Esther Duflo, Rachel Glennerster, and Cynthia Kinnan. "The Miracle of Microfinance? Evidence from a Randomized Evaluation." *American Economic Journal: Applied Economics* 7 (1) (2015): 22–53. doi:10.1257/app.20130533.

5. Karlan, Dean, and Jonathan Zinman. "Expanding Credit Access: Using Randomized Supply Decisions to Estimate the Impacts." *Review of Financial Studies* 23 (1) (2010): 433–64. doi:10.1093/rfs/hhp092.

6. Dupas, Pascaline, and Jonathan Robinson. "Why Don't the Poor Save More? Evidence from Health Savings Experiments." *American Economic Review* 103 (4) (2013): 1138–71. doi:10.1257/aer.103.4.1138.

7. Ashraf, Nava, Dean Karlan, and Weley Yin. "Female Empowerment: Impact of a Commitment Savings Product in the Philippines." *World Development* 38 (3) (2010): 333–44. doi:10.1016/j.worlddev.2009.05.010.

8. Brune, Lasse, Xavier Giné, Jessica Goldberg, and Dean Yang. "Facilitating Savings for Agriculture: Field Experimental Evidence from Malawi." *Economic Development and Cultural Change* 64 (2) (2016): 187–220. doi: 10.1086/684014.

9. Ashraf, Nava, Diego Aycinena, Claudia Martinez, and Dean Yang. "Savings in Transnational Households: A Field Experiment among Migrants from El Salvador." *Review of Economics and Statistics* 97 (2) (2015): 332–51; Ambler, Kate, Diego Aycinena, and Dean Yang. "Channeling Remittances to Education: A Field Experiment among Migrants from El Salvador." *American Economic Journal: Applied* Economics 7 (2)(2015): 207–32. doi: 10.1257/app.20140010.

10. Giné, Xavier, Jessica Goldberg and Dean Yang. "Credit Market Consequences of Improved Personal Identification: Field Experimental Evidence from Malawi." *American Economic Review* 102 (6) (2012): 2923–54. doi: 10.1257/aer.102.6.2923.

11. Ashraf, Nava, Diego Aycinena, Claudia Martinez A., and Dean Yang.. "Savings in Transnational Households: A Field Experiment among Migrants from El Salvador." *Review of Economics and Statistics* 97 (2) (2015): 332–51.

Chapter 14

1. Dupas, Pascaline, and Jonathan Robinson. "Savings Constraints and Microenterprise Development: Evidence from a Field Experiment in Kenya." *American Economic Journal: Applied Economics* 5 (1) (2013): 163–92. doi:10.1257/app.5.1.163.

2. Dupas, Pascaline, Sarah Green, Anthony Keats, and Jonathan Robinson. "Challenges in Banking the Rural Poor: Evidence from Kenya's Western Province." Working Paper 17851. NBER, Cambridge, MA, February 2012. doi: 10.3386/w17851.

3. Dupas, Pascaline, and Jonathan Robinson. "Why Don't the Poor Save More? Evidence from Health Savings Experiments." *American Economic Review* 103 (4) (2011): 1138–71. doi:10.1257/aer.103.4.1138.

4. Bloom, Nicholas, Benn Eifert, Aprajit Mahajan, David McKenzie, and John Roberts. "Does Management Matter? Evidence from India." *Quarterly Journal of Economics* 128 (1) (2013): 1–51. doi:10.1093/qje/qjs044.

5. Banerjee, Abhijit V., and Esther Duflo. *Poor Economics: A Radical Rethinking of the Way to Fight Global Poverty.* New York: PublicAffairs, 2011.

6. Fryer, Ronald G., Jr. "Financial Incentives and Student Achievement: Evidence from Randomized Trials." *Quarterly Journal of Economics* 126 (4) (2011): 1755–98. doi:10.1093/qje/qjr045.

7. Devoto, Florencia, Esther Duflo, Pascaline Dupas, William Parienté, and Vincent Pons. "Happiness on Tap: Piped Water Adoption in Urban Morocco." *American Economic Journal: Economic Policy* 4 (4) (2012): 68–99. doi:10.1257/pol.4.4.68.

8. Kenny, Charles. *Getting Better: Why Global Development Is Succeeding—And How We Can Improve the World Even More.* New York: Basic Books, 2011.

9. Meredith, Jennifer, Jonathan Robinson, Sarah Walker, and Bruce Wydick. "Keeping the Doctor Away: Experimental Evidenceon Investment in Preventative Health Products." *Journal of Development Economics* 105(C) (2013): 196–210. doi: 10.3386/w19312.

10. Benhassine, Najy, Florencia Devoto, Esther Duflo, Pascaline Dupas, and Victor Pouliquen. "Turning a Shove into a Nudge? A 'Labeled Cash Transfer' for Education." *American Economic Journal: Economic Policy* 7 (3) (2015): 86–125. doi: 10.1257/pol.20130225.

11. Baird, Sarah, Craig McIntosh, and Berk Ozler. "Cash or Condition? Evidence from a Cash Transfer Experiment." *Quarterly Journal of Economics* 126 (4) (2011): 1709–1753. doi: 10.1093/qje/qjr032; Baird, Sarah J., Ephraim Chirwa, Jacobus de Hoop, and Berk Özler. "Girl Power: Cash Transfers and Adolescent Welfare: Evidence from a Cluster-Randomized Experiment in Malawi." Working Paper 19479. NBER, Cambridge, MA, September 2013.

12. de Mel, Suresh, David McKenzie, and Christopher Woodruff. "Returns to Capital in Microenterprises: Evidence from a Field Experiment." *Quarterly Journal of Economics* 123 (4) (2008): 1329–72. doi: 10.1162/qjec.2008.123.4.1329; McKenzie, David and Christopher Woodruff. "Experimental Evidence on Returns to Capital and Access to Finance in Mexico." *World Bank Economic Review* 22 (3) (2008): 457–82. doi: 10.1093/wber/lhn017; Fafchamps, Marcel, David McKenzie, Simon Quinn, and Christopher Woodruff. "Microenterprise Growth and the Flypaper Effect: Evidence from a Randomized Experiment in Ghana." *Journal of Development Economics* 106(C) (2014): 211–26. doi: 10.1016/j.jdeveco.2013.09.010.

13. Mullainathan, Sendhil, and Eldar Shafir. *Scarcity: Why Having Too Little Means So Much.* New York: Times Books, 2013.

14. Collins, Daryl, Jonathan Morduch, Stuart Rutherford, and Orlanda Ruthven. *Portfolios of the Poor: How the World's Poor Live on $2 a Day.* Princeton: Princeton University Press, 2010.

15. Baland, Jean-Marie, Catherine Guirkhaner, and Charlotte Mali. "Pretending to be Poor: Borrowing to Escape Forced Solidarity in Cameroon." *Economic Development and Cultural Change* 60 (1) (2011): 1–16. doi: 10.1086/661220; Brune, Lasse, Xavier Giné, Jessica Goldberg, and Dean Yang. "Facilitating Savings for Agriculture: Field Experimental Evidence from Malawi." *Economic Development and Cultural Change* 64 (2) (2016): 187–220. doi: 10.1086/684014.

16. Cohen, Jessica, and Pascaline Dupas. "Free Distribution or Cost Sharing? Evidence from a Randomized Malaria Prevention Experiment." *Quarterly Journal of Economics* 125 (1) (2010): 1–45. doi: 10.1162/qjec.2010.125.1.1.

17. Dupas, Pascaline. "Short-Run Subsidies and Long-Run Adoption of New Health Products: Evidence from a Field Experiment." *Econometrica* 82 (1) (2014): 197–228. doi: 10.3982/ECTA9508.

18. Duflo, Esther, Michael Kremer, and Jonathan Robinson. "Nudging Farmers to Use Fertilizer: Theory and Experimental Evidence from Kenya." *American Economic Review* 106 (6) (2011): 2350–90. doi: 10.1257/aer.101.6.2350; Duflo, Esther, Michael Kremer, and Jonathan Robinson. "How High Are Rates of Return to Fertilizer? Evidence from Field Experiments in Kenya." *American Economic Review* 98 (2) (2008): 482–88. doi: 10.1257/aer.98.2.482.

Chapter 15

1. Taylor-Robinson, D. C., N. Maayan, K. Soares-Weiser, S. Donegan, and P. Garner. "Deworming Drugs for Treating Soil-Transmitted Intestinal Worms in Children: Effects on Nutrition and School Performance." *Cochrane Database of Systematic Reviews* (7) (2015): CD000371. doi:10.1002/14651858.CD000371.pub6.

2. Miguel, Edward, and Michael Kremer. "Worms: Identifying Impacts on Education and Health in the Presence of Treatment Externalities." *Econometrica* 72 (1) (2004): 159–217. doi:10.1111/j.1468-0262.2004.00481.x.

3. Bleakley, Hoyt. "Disease and Development: Evidence from Hookworm Eradication in the American South." *Quarterly Journal of Economics* 122 (1) (2007): 73–117. doi:10.1162/qjec.121.1.73.

4. Croke, Kevin. "The Long Run Effects of Early Childhood Deworming on Literacy and Numeracy: Evidence from Uganda." Working Paper. Harvard University, Cambridge, MA, July 2014. http://scholar.harvard.edu/files/kcroke/files/ug_lr_deworming_071714.pdf.

5. Bryan, Gharad, Shyamal Chowdhury, and Ahmed Mushfiq Mobarak. "Underinvestment in a Profitable Technology: The Case of Seasonal Migration in Bangladesh." *Econometrica* 82 (5) (2014): 1671–1748. doi:10.3982/ECTA10489.

6. Banerjee, Abhijit V., Esther Duflo, Rachel Glennerster, and Dhruva Kothari. "Improving Immunisation Coverage in Rural India: Clustered Randomised Controlled Evaluation of Immunisation Campaigns with and without Incentives." *British Medical Journal* 340 (c2220) (2010). doi:10.1136/bmj.c2220.

7. Haushofer, Johannes, and Jeremy Shapiro. "The Short-Term Impact of Unconditional Cash Transfers to the Poor: Evidence from Kenya." *Quarterly Journal of*

Economics, forthcoming (2016). https://www.princeton.edu/~joha/publications/ Haushofer_Shapiro_UCT_2016.04.25.pdf.

Chapter 16

1. Drexler, Alejandro, Greg Fischer, and Antoinette Schoar. "Keeping It Simple: Financial Literacy and Rules of Thumb." *American Economic Journal: Applied Economics* 6 (2) (2014): 1–31. doi: 10.1257/app.6.2.1.

2. Bloom, Nicholas, Benn Eifert, Aprajit Mahajan, David McKenzie, and John Roberts. "Does Management Matter? Evidence from India." *Quarterly Journal of Economics* 128 (1) (2013): 1–51. doi:10.1093/qje/qjs044.

3. Bruhn, Miriam, Dean S. Karlan, and Antoinette Schoar. "The Impact of Consulting Services on Small and Medium Enterprises: Evidence from a Randomized Trial in Mexico." Economic Growth Center Discussion Paper 1010. Yale University, 2012. http://www.econ.yale.edu/growth_pdf/cdp1010.pdf, 10.2139/ssrn.2010710.

4. Bruhn, Miriam, Dean Karlan, and Antoinette Schoar. "What Capital Is Missing in Developing Countries?" *American Economic Review* 100 (2) (2010): 629–33. doi:10.1257/aer.100.2.629.

5. Hsieh, Chang-Tai, and Benjamin A. Olken. "The Missing 'Missing Middle.'" *Journal of Economic Perspectives* 28 (3) (2014): 89–108. doi:10.1257/jep.28.3.89.

6. Schoar, Antoinette. "The Divide between Subsistence and Transformational Entrepreneurship." In *Innovation Policy and the Economy*, ed. Josh Lerner and Scott Stern, 57–81. Chicago: University of Chicago Press, 2010.

7. Haltiwanger, John, Ron S. Jarmin, and Javier Miranda. "Who Creates Jobs? Small vs. Large vs. Young." *Review of Economics and Statistics* 95 (2) (2013): 347–61. doi:10.1162/REST_a_00288.

8. Hombert, Johan, Antoinette Schoar, David Alexandre Sraer, and David Thesmar. "Can Unemployment Insurance Spur Entrepreneurial Activity? Evidence from France." Research Paper FIN-2013-1020. HEC Paris, October 2014. doi: 10.2139/ssrn.2329357.

9. Karlan, Dean, Ryan Knight, and Christopher Udry. "Hoping to Win, Expected to Lose: Theory and Lessons on Micro Enterprise Development." Working Paper 18325. NBER, Cambridge, MA, August 2012. http://www.nber.org/papers/w18325.pdf.

10. Allcott, Hunt. "Site Selection Bias in Program Evaluation." *Quarterly Journal of Economics* 130 (3) (2015): 1117–65. doi:10.1093/qje/qjv015.

11. Bauchet, Jonathan, and Jonathan Morduch. "Selective Knowledge: Reporting Biases in Microfinance Data." *Perspectives on Global Development and Technology* 9 (3) (2010): 240–69. doi: 10.1163/156914910X499705.

12. Thaler, Richard H., and Shlomo Benartzi. "Save More Tomorrow: Using Behavioral Economics to Increase Employee Saving." *Journal of Political Economy* 112 (1) (2004): 164–87.

13. Carroll, Gabriel D., James J. Choi, David Laibson, Brigitte C. Madrian, and Andrew Metrick. "Optimal Defaults and Active Decisions." *Quarterly Journal of Economics* 124 (4) (2009): 1639–74. doi: 10.1162/qjec.2009.124.4.1639.

Chapter 17

1. Hoffman, Vivian, Christopher B. Barrett, and David R. Just. "Do Free Goods Stick to Poor Households? Experimental Evidence on Insecticide Treated Bednets." *World Development* 37 (3) (2009): 607–17. doi:10.1016/j.worlddev.2008.08.003; Hoffman, Vivian. "Intrahousehold Allocation of Free and Purchased Mosquito Nets." *American Economic Review* 99 (2) (2009): 236–41. doi:10.1257/aer.99.2.236.

2. Glennerster, Rachel and Kudzai Takavarasha. *Running Randomized Evaluations: A Practical Guide.* Princeton: Princeton University Press, 2013.

Chapter 18

1. Glewwe, Paul, Michael Kremer, and Sylvie Moulin. "Many Children Left Behind? Textbooks and Test Scores in Kenya." *American Economic Journal: Applied Economics* 1 (1) (2009): 112–35. doi:10.1257/app.1.1.112.

2. Robinson, Jonathan, and Ethan Yeh. "Risk-Coping through Sexual Networks: Evidence from Client Transfers in Kenya." *Journal of Human Resources* 47 (1) (2012): 107–45. doi: 10.3368/jhr.47.1.107; Robinson, Jonathan, and Ethan Yeh. "Transactional Sex as a Response to Risk in Western Kenya." *American Economic Journal: Applied Economics* 3 (1) (2011): 35–64. doi: 10.1257/app.3.1.35.

3. Dupas, Pascaline, and Jonathan Robinson. "Coping with Political Instability: Micro Evidence from Kenya's 2007 Election Crisis." *American Economic Review* 100 (2) (2010): 120–24. doi: 10.1257/aer.100.2.120 Dupas, Pascaline, and Jonathan Robinson. "The (Hidden) Costs of Political Instability: Evidence from Kenya's 2007 Election Crisis." *Journal of Development Economics* 99 (2) (2012): 314–29. doi: 10.1016/j.jdeveco.2012.03.003.

4. Dupas, Pascaline, and Jonathan Robinson. "Savings Constraints and Microenterprise Development: Evidence from a Field Experiment in Kenya." *American Economic Journal: Applied Economics* 5 (1) (2013): 163–92. doi:10.1257/app.5.1.163.

5. Dupas, Pascaline, and Jonathan Robinson. "Why Don't the Poor Save More? Evidence from Health Savings Experiments." *American Economic Review* 103 (4) (2012): 1138–71. doi:10.1257/aer.103.4.1138.

6. Brune, Lasse, Xavier Giné, Jessica Goldberg, and Dean Yang. "Facilitating Savings for Agriculture: Field Experimental Evidence from Malawi." *Economic Development and Cultural Change* 64 (2) (2016): 187–220. doi: 10.1086/684014.

7. Baland, Jean-Marie, Catherine Guirkinger, and Charlotte Mali. "Pretending to Be Poor: Borrowing to Escape Forced Solidarity in Cameroon." *Economic Development and Cultural Change* 60 (1) (2011): 1–16. doi:10.1086/661220.

8. Kremer, Michael, Jean Lee, Jonathan Robinson, and Olga Rostapshova. "Behavioral Biases and Firm Behavior: Evidence from Kenyan Retail Shops." *American Economic Review: Papers and Proceedings* 103 (3) (2013): 362–68. doi: 10.1257/aer.103.3.362.

9. de Mel, Suresh, David McKenzie, and Christopher Woodruff. "Returns to Capital in Microenterprises: Evidence from a Field Experiment." *Quarterly Journal of Economics* 123 (4) (2008): 1329–72. doi:10.1162/qjec.2008.123.4.1329.

10. Fafchamps, Marcel, David McKenzie, Simon R. Quinn, and Christopher Woodruff. "Microenterprise Growth and the Flypaper Effect: Evidence from a Randomized Experiment in Ghana." *Journal of Development Economics* 106(C) (2011): 211–26. doi: 10.1016/j.jdeveco.2013.09.010.

11. Kenny, Charles. Getting Better: Why Global Development Is Succeeding—And How We Can Improve the World Even More. New York: Basic Books, 2011.

12. Devoto, Florencia, Esther Duflo, Pascaline Dupas, William Parienté, and Vincent Pons. "Happiness on Tap: Piped Water Adoption in Urban Morocco." *American Economic Journal: Economic Policy* 4 (4) (2012): 68–99. doi: 10.1257/pol.4.4.68.

13. Robinson, Jonathan. "Limited Insurance within the Household: Evidence from a Field Experiment in Kenya." *American Economic Journal: Applied Economics* 4 (4) (2012): 140–64. doi: 10.1257/app.4.4.140.

14. Morduch, Jonathan. "Between the Market and State: Can Informal Insurance Patch the Safety Net?" *World Bank Research Observer* 14 (2) (1999): 187–207.

15. Aleem, Irfan. "Imperfect Information, Screening, and the Costs of Informal Lending: A Study of a Rural Credit Market in Pakistan." *World Bank Economic Review* 4 (3) (1990): 329–49. doi: 10.1093/wber/4.3.329.

16. Collins, Daryl, Jonathan Morduch, Stuart Rutherford, and Orlanda Ruthven. *Portfolios of the Poor: How the World's Poor Live on $2 a Day*. Princeton: Princeton University Press, 2010.

17. Meredith, Jennifer, Jonathan Robinson, Sarah Walker, and Bruce Wydick. "Keeping the Doctor Away: Experimental Evidence on Investment in Preventative Health Products." *Journal of Development Economics* 105 (2013): 196–210. doi: 10.1016/j.jdeveco.2013.08.003 doi: 10.3386/w19312.

18. Dizon-Ross, Rebecca, Pascaline Dupas, and Jonathan Robinson. "Governance and the Effectiveness of Public Health Subsidies." Working Paper 21324. NBER, Cambridge, MA, July 2015. http://www.nber.org/papers/w21324 doi: 10.3386/w21324.

19. For an overview of these issues, see: Mullainathan, Sendhil, and Eldar Shafir. *Scarcity: Why Having Too Little Means So Much.* New York: Times Books, 2013.

20. Beaman, Lori, Jeremy Magruder, and Jonathan Robinson. "Making Small Change among Small Firms in Kenya." *Journal of Development Economics* 108 (2014): 69–86. doi: 10.1016/j.jdeveco.2013.12.010.

Chapter 19

1. Banerjee, Abhijit, Esther Duflo, Rachel Glennerster, and Dhruva Kothari. "Improving Immunization Coverage in Rural India: Clustered Randomized Controlled Evaluation of Immunization Campaigns with and without Incenitves." *British Medical Journal* 340 (2010): c2220. doi:10.1136/bmj.c2220.

Chapter 20

1. Blattman, Chris. "Impact Evaluation 2.0." Presentation to the Department for International Development (DFID), London, February 14, 2008. http://chrisblattman.com/documents/policy/2008.ImpactEvaluation2.DFID_talk.pdf.

2. Blattman, Chris. "Impact Evaluation 3.0?" Presentation to the Department for International Development (DFID), London, September 1, 2011. http://www.chrisblattman.com/documents/policy/2011.ImpactEvaluation3.DFID_talk.pdf.

3. Banerjee, Abhijit V., and Esther Duflo. *Poor Economics: A Radical Rethinking of the Way to Fight Global Poverty.* New York: PublicAffairs, 2011.

4. Blattman, Christopher, Nathan Fiala, and Sebastian Martinez. "Generating Skilled Self-Employment in Developing Countries: Experimental Evidence from Uganda." *Quarterly Journal of Economics* 129 (2) (2014): 697–752. doi:10.1093/qje/qjt057.

5. Blattman, Christopher, Alexandra Hartman, and Robert Blair. "How to Promote Order and Property Rights under Weak Rule of Law? An Experiment in Changing Dispute Resolution Behavior through Community Education." *American Political Science Review* 108(4) (2014): 100–20. doi: 10.1017/S0003055413000543.

6. Blattman, Christopher, and Stefan Dercon. "More Sweatshops in Africa? Pilot Results from an Experimental Study of Industrial Labor in Ethiopia." International Growth Centre Working Paper. London, March 2012. http://www.theigc.org/wp-content/uploads/2014/10/Blattman-Dercon-2012-Working-Paper.pdf.

7. Bloom, Nicholas, Benn Eifert, Aprajit Mahajan, David McKenzie, and John Roberts. "Does Management Matter: Evidence from India." Quarterly Journal of Economics. 128 (1) (2013): 1–51. doi:10.1093/qje/qjs044.

8. McKenzie, David. "What Are the Under-researched Topics in Development according to Young Faculty?" Development Impact, World Bank, June 15, 2011. http://blogs.worldbank.org/impactevaluations/what-are-the-under-researched -topics-in-development-according-to-young-faculty.

9. Roodman, David. *Due Diligence: An Impertinent Inquiry into Microfinance.* Washington, DC: Center for Global Development, 2011.

10. Blattman, Christopher. "From Violence to Voting: War and Political Participation in Uganda." *American Political Science Review* 103 (2) (2009): 231–47. doi: 10.1017/S0003055409090212.

Conclusion

1. Aiken, Alexander M., Calum Davey, James R. Hargreaves, and Richard J. Hayes. "Re-analysis of Health and Educational Impacts of a School-Based Deworming Program in Western Kenya: A Pure Replication." *International Journal of Epidemiology* 44 (5) (2015): 1572–80. doi: 10.1093/ije/dyv127; Davey, Calum, Alexander M. Aiken, Richard J. Hayes, and James R. Hargreaves. "Reanalysis of Health and Educational Impacts of a School-Based Deworming Program in Western Kenya: A Statistical Replication of a Cluster Quasi-randomized Stepped-Wedge Trial." International Journal of Epidemiology. 44 (5) (2015): 1581–92. doi: 10.1093/ije/dyv128.

2. Goldacre, Ben. "Scientists Are Hoarding Data and It's Ruining Medical Research," *BuzzFeed,* July 22, 2015. http://www.buzzfeed.com/bengoldacre/deworming-trials.

3. Lipsey, Mark W., Dale C. Ferran, and Kerry G. Hofer. "A Randomized Control Trial of a Statewide Voluntary Prekindergarten Program on Children's Skills and Behaviors through Third Grade." Peabody Research Institute, September 2015. http://peabody.vanderbilt.edu/research/pri/VPKthrough3rd_final_withcover.pdf.

4. Heckman, James. "Vanderbilt Pre-K Study: You Get What You Pay For," The Heckman Equation, October 5, 2015. http://heckmanequation.org/content/vanderbilt -pre-k-study-you-get-what-you-pay.

5. Case, Anne, and Angus Deaton. "Rising Morbidity and Mortality in Midlife among White Non-Hispanic Americans in the 21st Century." *Proceedings of the National Academy of Sciences of the United States of America* 2 (November) (2015): 15078–83. doi:10.1073/pnas.1518393112.

6. For example, see: Dehejia, Vivek. "The Experimental Turn in Economics." *Mint on Sunday,* January 31, 2016. http://mintonsunday.livemint.com/news/the -experimental-turn-in-economics/2.4.3926705564.html.

7. Naik, Gautam. "Scientists Elusive Goal: Reproducing Study Results." *Wall Street Journal*, December 2, 2011. http://www.wsj.com/articles/SB10001424052970203764 804577059841672541590.

8. Contopoulos-Ioannidis, D. G., E. Ntzani, and J. P. Ioannidis. "Translation of Highly Promising Basic Science Research into Clinical Applications." *American Journal of Medicine* 114 (6) (2003): 477–84.

9. Ioannidis, John P. "Contradicted and Initially Stronger Effects in Highly Cited Clinical Research." *Journal of the American Medical Association* 294 (2) (2005): 218–28. doi:10.1001/jama.294.2.218.

10. Kaplan, Robert, and Veronica Irvin. "Likelihood of Null Effects in Large NHLBI Clinical Trials Has Increased over Time." *PLoS One* 5 (August) (2015): 1–12. doi:10.1371/journal.pone.0132382.

11. Chassin, Mark R., and Carrie Mayer. "Improving Hand Hygiene at Eight Hospitals in the United States by Targeting Specific Causes of Noncompliance." *Joint Commission Journal on Quality and Patient Safety* 41 (1) (2015): 4–12.

12. Gawande, Atul. "Overkill." *The New Yorker*, May 11, 2015: 42–51. http://www .newyorker.com/magazine/2015/05/11/overkill-atul-gawande.

13. Regitz-Zagrosek, Vera. "Sex and Gender Differences in Healt." *EMBO Reports* 13(7) (2012): 596–603. doi: 10.1038/embor.2012.87; Burroughs, Valentine J., Randall W. Maxey, and Richard A. Levy. "Racial and Ethnic Differences in Response to Medicines: Towards Individualized Pharmaceutical Treatment." *Journal of the National Medical Association* 94(10 suppl) (2002): 1–26.

14. Weinhold, Bob. "Epigenetics: The Science of Change." *Environmental Health Perspectives* 114 (3) (2006): A160–67.

15. Embi, Peter J., and Philip R. Payne. "Evidence Generating Medicine: Redefining the Research-Practice Relationship to Complete the Evidence Cycle." *Medical Care* 51 (July) (2013): S87-S91 doi: 10.1097/MLR.0b013e31829b1d66.

16. Brown, Annette, Jorge Miranda, and Shayda Sabet. "Are Impact Evaluations Still on the Rise?" Evidence Matters. International Initiative for Impact Evaluation, August 11, 2016. http://blogs.3ieimpact.org/is-impact-evaluation-still-on-the-rise/. McKenzie, David."Have RCTs Taken over Development Economics?" Development Impact. World Bank, June 13, 2016. http://blogs.worldbank.org/impactevaluations/ have-rcts-taken-over-development-economics.

17. Vivalt, Eva. "Heterogenous Treatment Effects in Impact Evaluation." *American Economic Review: Papers and Proceedings* 105 (5) (2015): 467–70. Doi: 10.1257/aer. p20151015.

18. Ogden, Timothy. "Transcendental Significance Critique." Financial Access Initiative Blog. September 29, 2011. http://www.financialaccess.org/blog/2015/7/29/ transcendental-significance-critique.

Index

Printed in the United States
by Baker & Taylor Publisher Services